D1518255

Explaining Criminal Conduct

Theories and Systems in Criminology

Paul Knepper

PROFESSOR,
EAST CAROLINA UNIVERSITY

CAROLINA ACADEMIC PRESS
Durham, North Carolina

ISBN 0-89089-607-0
LCCN 2001091154

Cover Art:
Paul Hartley
"Detectives Don't Rest" (c. 1980)
Collage, Pencil, Acrylic, and Oil on Paper
30" × 40"

North Carolina artist Paul Hartley, a native of Charlotte, has taught painting and drawing at East Carolina University for twenty-five years. *Carolina Arts* (May 2000) describes him as "a skilled draftsman who combines intensely detailed natural images with an experimental and labor-intensive process." "My own interest," says Hartley, "is in creating something, not just in representing nature or the 'real' world. I do, however, want to create something with enough of nature's attributes, its visual complexity, to engage the viewer in really looking."

CAROLINA ACADEMIC PRESS

700 Kent Street
Durham, North Carolina 27701
Telephone (919) 489-7486
Fax (919) 493-5668
www.cap-press.com

Printed in the United States of America

To Lynn E. Knepper

Contents

Preface

"A novel," Camus once wrote, "is never anything but a philosophy expressed in images."[1] Criminology is like that. A theory of crime represents a moral philosophy expressed as an explanation.

This book is about theories of crime. It is not so much about explaining crime as about describing how criminologists have thought about crime. Within the history of explaining crime, there are seven original ideas: human nature, the human body, the mind, society, language, race, and the heart. All explanations in criminology, from eighteenth century political theory and nineteenth century science to contemporary social science, derive from one of these. They represent what might be called modalities. To the philosopher, a modality marks the line at which differences of judgment are considered differences in kind rather than degree. Each represents a way of looking at the world through a set of concepts particular to itself.[2] Criminal conduct has been understood, then, politically, biologically, psychologically, sociologically, linguistically, racially, and spiritually.

Since the nineteenth century, the modality of society has furnished the paradigmatic outlook. Most texts in criminology theory seek to evaluate theories of crime in terms of the findings of social science research. Social science gives to quantifiable ideas the status of observable reality and attempts to rule out those ideas not falsifiable within this framework. Social science represents, however, only one modality—one historically identifiable means of explaining criminal conduct. This book reviews the social science outlook alongside others. The task is to identify the consistent elements within each mode so that they can be considered from the standpoint of logical coherence and as invitations to public activity. Or, in other words, to extract what is philosophical from different ways of looking at crime. The goal, as Oakeshott says somewhere, is to enlighten rather than instruct.

My interest in criminology began with W. Byron Groves—or Casey, he told us to call him. He taught at the University of Wisconsin Green Bay where, during the early 1980s, I pursued an undergraduate degree. I had no idea what to make of the tallish, lanky frame that stood in front of the class each day. He wore slacks with a t-shirt and sneakers. He walked as he talked, stopping occasionally to scratch a few words on the board or sip from a can of soda. There was always a smile on his face that the eyeglasses never seemed to fit, below a head of thick, black curls. He guided us through a picture-less text that had to do with theories of crime. Never did he fail to challenge, evoke, and entertain, and most of this in the first fifteen minutes. He found meaning beneath the surface, a pattern pieced together by zeroing in on a few telling words, philosophical expressions, and comments in footnotes. Before the end of that first semester, I too wanted to be a criminologist. I wanted to see what Casey could see.

Somewhere in my office I still have the letter he sent me while I was in graduate school working on the PhD. I remember the day it arrived. I stopped from my assigned task of keyboarding data to examine the note Casey had written on university letterhead. It was an academic family tree. There was Casey, along side his brother, his father above, and his grandfather at the top of the page. My name appeared under Casey's. I had arrived. If Casey thought I was a criminologist, then it must really be true. I also remember the day, not long after taking my first job as a professor, that a mutual friend called to say Casey had been killed in a car accident. He was just thirty-seven.

After thinking for fifteen years or so about what Casey said I came to conclusion that he was looking in the wrong direction.[3] This book pursues an understanding of criminology free from the sort of criminology he pursued as well as from the conventional, social-scientific brand he critiqued so well. I do not think that serious study in criminology requires, or even allows for, checking moral values at the door. On the contrary, I believe that moral judgment is indispensable for those engaged in the study of crime as well as those involved in the administration of justice. My ambition, which I started but did not finish here, is to describe the moral life in such a way that both criminal conduct and ethical conduct can be understood.

It would be a very long list, and very incomplete, if I tried to acknowledge all those who have shaped my thinking about what I have written here. And so I must settle for naming only a few. Eric Reyes and David Turnage read and commented on chapters. Yolanda Burwell, Mary Jackson, and Rabbi Michael Cain gave me ideas at key places that I have freely borrowed and most likely distorted. Keith Sipe believed in the project from the beginning; Glenn Perkins saw it through publication. And most of all, I want to thank Cathryn Ann Knepper, who was always willing to listen.

Finally, I would like to note that I concern myself in these pages with ideas first and last. I offer details about the lives of individuals to make the narrative more interesting, not in any effort to supply insight into their ideas. In the same way, when I offer my own critique, I am taking issue with the ideas, not the people. I have a great deal of respect for the individuals whose ideas I attempt to refute. Some I know personally and happen to like very much. Others I know only through their writings and admire from a distance. If it appears that I have singled anyone out for special criticism, it is because their ideas have consumed a large portion of my thinking, and only means that I would relish an evening with them discussing criminology, as I did with Casey.

Explaining Criminal Conduct

Chapter 1

Science and Tradition in Criminology

It is the question crime victims ask. Crime victims experience a range of wounds long after their physical injuries have healed and their property has been replaced. Persistent feelings of fear, isolation, helplessness, and listlessness accompany persistent memories of the crime. The crime scene replays, interrupting sleep and work, intimate moments and solitary thoughts. The question persists for months, years. And each time the episode repeats, the mind adds new details to make the ending change. The victim seeks a way to undo what has been done, to right the wrong, to bring the world back to the way it was. And the question victims ask—whether parents of murdered children, those victimized by robbery and rape, even those victims of household break-ins, is always the same: *why did this happen to me?*

The question of why crime occurs, especially from the victim's perspective, cannot be satisfied with simple answers. Victims' understanding of the way the world works, about what to expect from people, and what happens in various places, changes. When crime victims ask why, they are asking many questions: Will they catch him? What will happen when they do? Am I still at risk? If only I had…this would not have happened. Why do things like this happen? Did I do something to deserve this? Why God?[1]

Criminology tries to answer such questions. Criminologists search for the origins of crime. They try to uncover the meaning of crime and also things related to crime, including law, society, government, and justice. Finding the origins of crime represents the most significant part of the effort to devise a better response to crime. Criminologists hope to prevent crime and the hurt and pain that criminals cause their victims.

The first criminologists, that is, the first of these searchers to call themselves criminologists, insisted that science provided the most reliable route to the source of crime. They pursued a scientific explanation for criminal behavior; an outlook that has cast a long and significant shadow over criminology. The scientific tradition in criminology made criminology a social science and has enabled criminologists to take their place at universities, institutes and government agencies throughout the world. Criminology, as an academic pursuit, would not exist today without its adherence to the scientific method. But unfortunately, criminology suffers from its own success. The number of theories continues to multiply, and criminologists cannot find the true theory because the scientific technique on which they rely does not allow them to prove anybody wrong. And the question arises about whether in investing so heavily in science criminologists did not make some rash concession.

This book covers the entire spectrum of criminology, including socio-biological, psychiatric, and social-scientific approaches found in other criminology books. It also covers approaches from political and moral philosophy not found in other criminology books. This chapter explains the book's perspective. Part One explores how social-scientific criminology began with a brief history of criminology. Part Two explains the dilemma of contemporary criminology with reference to the fact/value distinction within social science. Part Three outlines the method of a traditional criminology, of using reason and history to sort out explanations of crime.

The Criminologists

"Now what I want is, Facts," says Mr. Thomas Gradgrind in Dickens's *Hard Times*, "Facts alone are wanted in life."[2] Criminologists agree. The first criminologists desired to study the facts of crime, and criminologists have pursued a scientific understanding of crime ever since. Contemporary criminology has been defined as the "use of scientific methods to study the nature, extent, cause, and control of criminal behavior."[3] The search for the facts of crime began about a hundred years ago, at a time when no one knew what kind of science criminology would become.

THE FIRST CRIMINOLOGISTS. Criminology originated in Europe, in the late nineteenth century, with a group of doctors and professors interested in criminality. Inspired by the autopsy research of an Italian army doctor, Cesare Lombroso, this group wanted to understand the behavior of the "criminal man," those individuals with a penchant for crime and violence. They hoped to create a new science of criminality, a scientific understanding of criminal conduct as opposed to moralistic and philosophical speculation. Lombroso preferred to describe their field of study as "criminal anthropology," a term the group adopted at the First International Congress of Criminal Anthropology held in 1885 in Rome and the Second Congress of Criminal Anthropology held four years later in Paris.[4] But others within the group disputed the importance of biological factors in criminal behavior, and it was out of this debate that modern, social-scientific criminology began.

Exactly who coined the term "criminology" cannot be identified with certainty. Paul Topinard, who directed the *Ecole anthropologie* in Paris, claimed to have created it in 1889. He disagreed with Lombroso's concept of the criminal man so he preferred to describe his study of crime as criminology rather than criminal anthropology. Topinard himself, however, noted in 1885 the title of a book by an Italian, the Baron Raffaele Garofalo, called *Criminologica*. Baron Garofalo never explained how he decided upon this title. But in the preface to his book, he did hint at a possible source. He referred to another work, published the year before, entitled *Socialismo Sociologia criminale.* Written by an Italian socialist, the book described social, economic, biological and meteorological influences on crime rates.[5] But whoever ought to receive credit for the term criminology, it was the criminal anthropologists that founded the profession of criminologist. The understanding of criminality they pursued found a wide audience. It was, until the First World War, the subject of an international conference for lawyers, judges and government officials, every four years.[6]

American criminology began as a legal science rather than medical science. John Henry Wigmore, dean of the law school at Northwestern University in Chicago, helped found it. Although he never actually taught a course in criminology, he maintained a lifelong interest in the study of crime. Wigmore tried to encourage "the study of modern criminal science, as a pressing duty for the legal profession and for the thoughtful community at large."[7] In 1909, he organized the National Conference on Criminal Law and Criminology. The conference, with President William H. Taft as keynote speaker, drew delegates from law, sociology, medicine, psychology, police and philanthropy. The following year, the law school created the American Institute of Criminal Law and Criminology and named Wigmore its president. The Institute began publication of the *Journal of Criminal Law and Criminology*, the first English language publication on the topic. The Institute also published the Modern Criminal Science Series featuring English translations of works by European criminologists. Garofalo's *Criminology*, which appeared third in the series, was Wigmore's favorite.[8]

Wigmore advocated studying the works of European criminologists because he thought it was important "to recognize that criminal science is larger than criminal law. The legal profession in particular has a duty to familiarize itself with the principles of that science, as the sole means for the intelligent and systematic improvement of the criminal law."[9] The legal profession, however, expressed virtually no interest in the study of crime along the lines suggested by Wigmore. Criminology never became a specialty area for academic lawyers in the United States as it did in Europe. Wigmore did provide encouragement for non-lawyers to take up the topic, and in 1952, the journal he founded became the official journal of the American Society of Criminology.

What became the American Society of Criminology began with August M. Vollmer, the chief of police in Berkeley, California. For Vollmer, criminology comprised part of police science. He founded the first crime laboratory in the United States and the first police school for training recruits. Vollmer's school drew upon the expertise of police inspectors at the Berkeley Police Department as well as professors at the University of California. The original police school offered instruction in police procedure, fingerprinting, first aid, criminal law, anthropometry, photography, public health, sanitation, and occasional lectures on psychiatry, criminology, and anthropology. During the 1930s, he headed the institute for criminology and criminalistics at the University of California at Berkeley.[10] In 1941, Vollmer, along with several of his students, founded an organization of "college police training officials" that later took the name of the American Society of Criminology (ASC).

The Society Vollmer founded developed an interdisciplinary outlook. The members defined criminology as "the study of the causes, treatment and prevention of crime," a study that included the fields of scientific crime detection, crime prevention, law enforcement administration, traffic administration, probation, juvenile delinquency control and penology. In 1963, the Society introduced a newsletter that later became *Criminology*, an "an interdisciplinary journal of criminology." By 1968, the Society dropped "scientific crime detection" from its definition, and later definitions of criminology shifted the scientific emphasis from crime detection to all professional knowledge concerning these fields.[11] Vollmer himself came to share this broader, interdisciplinary outlook. By 1931, when Vollmer became professor of police administration at the University of California, the first in the United States, he had reached a conclusion about criminology: "the mechanics of law enforcement are of less importance than a knowledge of human beings." The college-level curriculum he developed featured course work in psychology, English, chemistry, physics, sociology, psychiatry, political science, public health and foreign language.[12]

Developments in Europe paralleled the United States. Criminology became less of a specialty for medical doctors and law professors and more of an interdisciplinary field of study for academics and government researchers of various academic backgrounds. In 1935, the London School of Economics made Hermann Mannheim Britain's first lecturer in criminology. He had studied political science in Germany and had been on the law faculty at the University of Berlin.[13] In 1959, the Institute of Criminology opened within the faculty of law at Cambridge University. Sir Leon Radzinowicz, known for his *History of the English Criminal Law*, became the institute's first director. Despite its location within the university, the institute was founded to apply a combination of various academic perspectives to the study of crime. Lord Butler, Secretary of the Home Office, insisted that the nation needed an academic program of criminology research. He believed that changes in crime policy should be based on "reliable information about the phenomenon of crime, its social and personal roots..." and that "these inquiries would have to be undertaken by teams of research workers with varying backgrounds—sociologists, statisticians, psychologists, and psychiatrists...."[14]

In the Federal Republic of Germany (West Germany), criminology began as a minor area of interest for academic lawyers referred to as "criminal law theory." During the 1960s, academic chairs in criminology were established at the universities of Heidelberg, Tübingen, and Cologne, helping make criminology an interdisciplinary study. The Max Planck Institute for Foreign and International Criminal Law at Freiburg University, organized before the war, established in 1970 a criminological research unit. By 1980, German criminology included forensic medicine, psychiatry, psychology, sociology and criminal law.[15] In the Scandinavian countries, Norway became the first to establish criminology as an academic field of inquiry. The Institute of Criminology and Criminal Law of the University of Olso opened in 1954; in the late 1960s, this institute became the first in Scandinavia to offer criminology degrees.[16] Australia's first criminology department opened at Melbourne University in 1951. The Institute of Criminology opened at the University of Sydney in 1959 within the University's faculty of law; the initial appointments at Sydney included a criminologist, a psychiatrist, and a statistician.[17]

SOCIAL-SCIENTIFIC CRIMINOLOGY. By the time Cambridge opened its Institute of Criminology it had become clear what kind of science criminology would be; it would not be a medical science, legal science, or police science but a social science. It became a social science due to the influence of American sociology in general and to one American sociologist in particular, Edwin Sutherland.

Sociology's claim to criminology began in 1921, when Edwin Sutherland joined the sociology department at the University of Illinois. Sutherland began systematizing criminological research for his *Criminology* (1924), the first important American criminology textbook. Sutherland reviewed the work of the criminal anthropologists on criminal behavior, and he preferred Garofalo's multiple-factor approach, explaining crime as the product of geographic, economic, political and social factors. Sutherland took the position that criminologists ought not assume the correctness of cultural and legal definitions of crime, criminality, and crime rates; sociology should be the primary perspective for understanding crime and criminal law.[18] "Criminology," Sutherland wrote, "includes the scientific study of making laws, breaking laws, and reacting toward the breaking of laws."[19] So important was Sutherland's contribution in this regard that Britain's notable criminologist Hermann Mannheim declared that if the Nobel committee ever awarded a prize for criminology, it should go to Edwin Sutherland.[20]

Sutherland had a tremendous influence on the American Society of Criminology. Criminology listened to what Sutherland had to say and the American Society of Criminology became more sociological. A 1994 study of ASC members found that about three-fourths had received the PhD in sociology and somewhat more than half were employed as faculty in an academic department that offered degree programs in sociology.[21] Following his death, the Society recognized Sutherland by creating an award in his name (although Sutherland had actually never been a member).

European criminology heard what Sutherland had to say as well and the sociological view crossed the Atlantic. British criminology abandoned the medico-psychological-legal model in the 1970s. The National Conference on Teaching and Research in Criminology held at Cambridge in 1968, led to the National Deviancy Conference in York, and the return of sociological criminology in Britain. This led to the appearance of studies in the "sociology of law" emphasizing social, economic and political issues and featuring statistical methods. Research articles in the *British Journal of Criminology* have, since then, avoided legal and biological orientations in favor of social science treatments.[22] In Germany, sociologists wrestled criminology away from the grasp of doctors and lawyers during the post-war years, and by 1983 the number of social scientists working as criminologists outnumbered the number of doctors and lawyers.[23] In the Scandinavian countries, the scientific tradition based on law and medicine became the social-scientific tradition based on sociology. Institutes devoted to the sociology of law opened in Finland, Norway and Sweden, and the orientation of American sociology became the major orientation of Nordic criminology. Even the research conducted by psychologists and psychiatrists accepted the sociological outlook on crime.[24]

Sutherland's outlook exerted such an influence because sociology, as a system of thought, denies all others. Sutherland had explained what crime was (a social phenomenon), and told criminologists how to investigate it (by following the methods of sociology). Medicine, law, and policing did not provide a means of acquiring knowledge about crime in society; they represented aspects of society to be explained by sociology. Sociological criminology not only aims to explain why crime exists in society, but also what law and police are doing there as well. In addition to the power of the sociological imagination, sociologists perfected research techniques for the study of crime. Sociology had never been prominent at American universities prior to the Second World War, but during the postwar years, use of scientific technique became the prevailing model of sociological inquiry. By scientific technique, sociologists meant survey research and statistical analysis, methods needed to distinguish sociology from its social work and journalistic aspects.[25]

From the 1930s on sociologists became increasingly preoccupied with refinement of statistical technique. At first, they offered simple counting, cross-tabulations and percentage distributions. Following the war, sociologists adapted techniques developed by army statisticians, and extended the basic technique of cross-tabulation to multivariate statistical analysis. Linear regression replaced cross-tabulation as the preferred technique during the 1960s as the development of computers and software packages allowed sociologists to conduct more sophisticated analyses. During the 1970s, path analysis and log-linear analysis grew out of linear regression, and in the 1980s, the LISREL method of structural equation modeling. By 1985, nearly three-fourths of the articles appearing in prominent sociology journals, *American Sociological Review* and the *Journal of American Sociology*, presented data analysis featuring multivariate statistical techniques.[26] The more statistics that can be thrown at an issue, practically speaking, the more scientific the research.

And by 1987, multivariate statistical analysis became *the* method of inquiry for sociological criminology. In that year, Michael Gottfredson and Travis Hirschi, two prominent criminologists, carefully explained who criminologists were, what they studied, and how they went about studying it. Criminology advanced explanations on crime based on "respect for data" (the data sets being obtained from government agencies and social surveys), "renewed emphasis on basic correlates" (the sociological staples of community and class), a multidisciplinary approach (implying a unity of method across psychology, biology, and economics), and an indifference to policy studies (social scientific statements remain free of the taint of political ideology).[27] The debate that launched the profession of criminology, in case anyone still wondered, was over. Lombroso's medical science had lost; Garofalo's social science had won. Wigmore and Vollmer became citations in historical accounts of criminology; Sutherland supplied the working hypothesis for generations of criminological research.

Criminology has claimed its place as a social science at universities throughout the world. But what do criminologists know about crime, a hundred years later, that was not known before the profession began? That is the dilemma of contemporary criminology.

The Dilemma of Contemporary Criminology

Criminologists applaud themselves for avoiding arm-chair philosophizing and groundless speculations about crime.[28] Unlike politicians, philosophers, and theologians, they study what is, not what ought to be. As social scientists, criminologists venture into the real world of people's everyday lives to learn how people really behave. They seek to uncover the laws for how society operates and avoid making claims about what society should be like. Trouble is, pursuit of the facts of crime throughout the twentieth century has left criminology with a profound dilemma: *too many theories and no means of distinguishing true from false.*

THE CRIMINOLOGIST'S DILEMMA. Pennsylvania State University criminologist Thomas Bernard confronted the dilemma in revising *Theoretical Criminology*, one of the finest distillations of criminological thought ever published. Originally written by George Vold, the book has been revised three times. In the preface to the fourth edition, Bernard explained the eleven year gap between the third and fourth editions had been due the difficulty of fitting new materials into original chapter divisions. Bernard explained that scientific knowledge proceeds by theory falsification. Scientific methods do not prove for all time that a theory is true, rather, they allow scientists to rule out those theories found to be untrue. "In the process of working on successive editions of this book," Bernard reflected, "I became convinced that criminology was failing to make scientific progress...in each successive edition, I threw out quite a bit of material because, in my opinion, no one would be interested in it any more. But I had not thrown out any material because I thought it had been falsified. This suggests an astounding lack of scientific progress over a forty-year period of increasingly vigorous and sophisticated empirical research."[29]

The dilemma is at the heart of criminology. All of the social sciences that contribute to criminology—political science, social psychology, economics, and sociology of course, approach crime as the result of multiple causes. All of the social sciences that contribute to criminology also share their reliance on the research method; they propose theoretical explanations, collect data, and analyze the data using statistical techniques. They make conclusions about their explanations from the findings of the statistical analyses. What has kept criminology from ruling out particular theories is the priority each discipline assigns to the causes. Criminology cannot find a unified theory of crime because the primary vehicle for conducting social science, statistical methodology, cannot work out the differences.[30] Sociology has achieved a prominent place, not because sociologists have demonstrated a more reliable route to knowledge than other social scientists, but because sociology as a system of thought asserts a conceptual scheme that denies all others.[31]

Some, including Thomas Bernard, have become philosophical about it (but have resisted abandoning social science for philosophy). He has decided that it is time to scuttle theory-testing in favor of *theoretical integration*. Competitive testing of theories has failed because all the theories contain an element of truth.[32] So rather than subject theories to competitive testing in an attempt to rule out those without empirical support, the integration strategy seeks to reduce the number of theories by combining them. Integration proceeds by "concept integration," meaning one theory absorbs another because concepts overlap, and by "prepositional integration," that is, showing that although the theories begin with different concepts they make the same predictions about crime.[33] In other words, rather than trying to find out which theories are true, criminologists ought to combine theories according to the idea of parsimony, that a simpler explanation is better than a convoluted one.

Trimming the conceptual fat and stirring theories together is the integrationist view of progress. It does not satisfy all criminologists. Some insist that attempts to create unified theories of crime will necessarily distort concepts. Travis Hirschi, a former president of the American Society of Criminology, points out that although a criminologist may attempt concept absorption as an exercise in open-mindedness, it ultimately results in taking sides in the disputes that have divided criminologists for decades. It allows criminologists to dismiss one or more disciplinary perspectives in the name of doing everybody a favor.[34] Others—the dedicated researchers—complain that integration will only make the "unified" theories that result more difficult to test. The integration project has meant a retreat from testing and will make progress only in the sense that criminologists will turn their backs on the prospect of finding scientifically-valid explanations.[35]

Integration represents an agnostic approach to the dilemma. It does not move criminology any closer to separating those theories that are false from those that are true. Integration answers the question about true and false in criminology by not asking the question.

THE FACT/VALUE DISTINCTION. Understanding the way out of the dilemma requires an understanding of the nature of the problem. The problem is not professional criminologists commitment to research or even their reliance on statistical methods. The problem has to do with the attempt to separate social science from political philosophy by means of the fact/value distinction. The commitment to research and the conduct of statistical methodology follow from this stance.

Bernard and the authors of *Theoretical Criminology* take their view of science from Karl Popper. Sir Karl Popper, who for many years taught at the London School of Economics, specialized in the philosophy of science. He explained that a scientific explanation makes a prediction about the way the world works and is in principle falsifiable. *Falsifiability* is the mark of an authentic scientific theory; a scientific theory about the world is a theory that can be disproven, unlike philosophy or religion, using empirical research methods. Popper used the term "metaphysics" to refer to all theories not empirically testable, a catch-all term including all religious, ethical and aesthetical conjectures about the world. In making this distinction, Popper alluded to the basic assumption of social science, the distinction between facts and values. Values cannot be studied scientifically, so they cannot be part of a scientific explanation.[36]

This difference between what science can and cannot study is known as the *fact/value distinction*, and it is the basic working assumption of social scientists.[37] Max Weber, one of founders of social-scientific thinking, taught that "statements of fact are one thing, statements of value another, and any confusing of the two is impermissible."[38] Social-scientific criminologists, following Weber, claim to study *what is*, not *what ought to be*. The fact/value distinction allows the social scientist to say, "I study the facts of crime. I cannot help it if the facts do not agree with your views. You are entitled to your views, but please do not assert them over reality." The fact/value distinction allows social-scientific criminologists to assert empirical validity as the primary standard for judging any theory of crime; whether the ideas have been substantiated by social-scientific research.[39]

But what works for scientists does not work for social scientists. The fact/value distinction simply does not exist the same way in the world of human activity as it does in the natural world.[40] For the scientist, the distinction between facts and values is relatively simple. Objectivity in science means that the scientist uncovers facts independent of what the scientist thinks about them. A scientist can study rocks, plants and animals apart from what he or she thinks about them — whether the scientist likes the color of a particular rock, believes that families should garden together, or surmises that a particular laboratory animal would make a good household pet. The rocks, plants and animals exist on their own; the scientist's feelings, or any other person's feelings about them, do not determine their existence. In social science, people's subjective feelings color the existence of the objects of study. As Friedrich Hayek, a Nobel-prize winning economist (who also taught at the London School of Economics) puts it, the objects of study are "opinions." Not the opinions of the social scientist, but the opinions of those whose actions produce the topic of interest.[41]

"Crime" and "punishment," Hayek points out, do not exist as objective facts because neither can be defined without inferring people's conscious intentions with regard to them. Crime and punishment cannot be recognized directly in a person's mind but can be recognized only from what a person does and because the social scientist has a mind similar to that person. This is the basic idea of intent, which can only be inferred from a person's actions. Although the criminal law distinguishes between levels of intent ("negligently," "recklessly," "knowingly," "purposively," "with malice"), it cannot be done precisely. The law of criminal procedure recognizes that judging intent is a matter of probability and requires that the conviction be reached according to a standard of certainty.

Auguste Comte and Emile Durkheim, two more founding members of social science, tried to get around this problem with the idea of *social facts*. The founders of social science acknowledged that individual actions remain subjective (although Comte would eventually deny the possibility of introspection altogether), and as scientists of society they avoided legal judgment as a means of inquiry into crime and punishment. They defined crime as a violation of social convention; crime represents those acts for which a person is punished. When people act collectively, laws or law-like regularities emerge that operate the same way that physical laws, like gravitation and magnetism, operate in the natural world. When social scientists limit themselves to these social facts, and avoid speculating on individual motivation, they can produce objective knowledge about the social world. This represented the positive method, as Comte called it. "The superiority of positive politics," he wrote, "consists in the fact that it *discovers* what is made necessary by these natural laws while other systems [of political philosophy] *invent*."[42]

The idea of objective social facts is, in Hayek's words, "sheer illusion." Social scientists create the facts of crime by defining crime as those acts for which a person is punished. This pushes the subjective element a step back but does not remove it. "If...," to use Hayek's example, "we see that every time a person commits a certain act he is made to wear a chain around his neck, this does not tell us whether it is a reward or a punishment."[43] The records of government agencies, reports of crime to the police, and national victims' surveys that supply grist for the statistical mill, may have the appearance of objective data, but they are not. They represent the aggregated judgments of persons in individual situations. They are not the product of the social scientist's imagination, but the product of individual decisions nevertheless. What Cambridge historian Edward Hallett Carr said about historical facts found in documents applies to social facts found in data: "No document can tell us more than what the author of the document thought—what he thought happened, what he though ought to happen or would happen, or perhaps only what he wanted others to think he thought, or even only what he himself thought he thought."[44]

SCIENTISM IN CRIMINOLOGY. The fact/value distinction commits social-scientific criminology to scientism. *Scientism* is the view that everything can be explained as a matter of science and that the scientific method is the only route to knowledge. Hayek described scientism as "an attitude which is decidedly unscientific in the true sense of the word, since it involves a mechanical and uncritical application of habits of thought from fields different from those in which they have been formed."[45] There is no scientific fact to demonstrate that all human experience conforms to the type that can be understood by science; no scientific finding that proves the place of scientific findings in the world. To maintain that everything that can be known can only be known by means of the scientific method, is scientism, a kind of secular fundamentalism.[46]

When Weber, Comte and Durkheim said that social scientists stick to the facts and leave out the values, they did so for the purpose of using their science to attack their rivals' values. They wanted to establish a science of society in the same way natural scientists had created astronomy, physics, and so on. To do so, they needed to distance themselves from the pronouncements of philosophers and political and religious leaders. They attempted to bring ethics, moral judgment, spiritual matters and aesthetic sensibility within the realm of social science. They did not deny that values exist; values may be helpful in identifying problems for study. But they insisted that values exist within the realm of science, that is, as part of a belief system with its source in one or more (depending on the disciplinary background of the social scientist) aspects of society: economy, politics, culture. The practitioners of scientism unselfconsciously draw grand conclusions from their research. Convinced as they are about possessing the most reliable strategy for uncovering truth, they make sweeping pronouncements about human nature, morality, justice, and political values based on a survey of college students or observation of children at play.[47]

The scientistic strategy in criminology reduces every debate to an argument about research technique. When students express skepticism about the existence of one or more social facts, they are admonished that they must set their values aside if they ever want to become credible criminologists. When a criminologist challenges social science orthodoxy, the challenge is dismissed as ideological cant. When critics outside criminology object to the suggestions of social science research on political or moral grounds, they are told that their objections are out of line. Because the social-scientific method provides the only route to learning about crime, legitimate disagreements can only be about whether this or that variable should have been included and whether the dependent variable was better suited for one statistical procedure or another.[48]

But avoiding reference to their own suggestions for how to respond to crime as a political or moral agenda does not mean that social scientists have no agenda. The very idea that criminologists need to conduct research to find out about the causes of crime presumes that the causes of crime are not already known. When the Institute of Criminology at Cambridge was established, one editor at London's *Daily Telegraph* expressed some skepticism about exactly what could be accomplished. The "department may well make illuminating contributions to the philosophy of law. It may also provide agreeable summer schools, in which magistrates, youth workers and the police can exchange experiences. But the causes of crime are always so much what they always have been that they are unlikely to be removed by giving them a different name."[49] Great progress in devising a better solution to crime is possible only on the assumption that the conventional wisdom behind the government's current response is wrong. However indifferent social-scientific criminologists may be to the moral and political values at stake in public policy concerning crime, they have shown by the very act of arguing for the need for a better understanding of crime that there are some political and moral values about which they are not indifferent at all. Professional criminologists' skepticism about the place of morality and politics is on the surface; it is for use on other people's morality and politics.[50]

The fact/value distinction will simply not bear the weight social- scientific criminologists have put on it. George Vold, Thomas Bernard, and Jeffrey Snipes demonstrate this in their *Theoretical Criminology*. In the first chapter, they counter-pose science and religion with their claim that in the grand sweep of history, two major explanations for crime can be found: "one relies on spiritual, or other-world, explanations while the other relies on natural, or this world, explanations."[51] After citing examples of mortal combat in medieval times ("let the gods decide") and the witch-hunts in eighteenth-century Massachusetts, they explain why they are not going to devote any more space to the spiritual version. "Spiritual explanations provide a way of understanding crime that is satisfactory to some people," they begin, "The problem is that, because spiritual influences cannot be observed, these theories cannot be falsified. Thus these theories cannot be considered scientific, even if some thoughtful and intelligent people believe that they represent the best explanation of crime."[52]

This explanation, although well-intentioned, is incredulous. A few pages earlier, Thomas Bernard explained how forty years of "vigorous and sophisticated empirical research" had failed to falsify a single "scientific" theory. So how is it that spiritual explanations are to be rejected because they cannot be falsified, and scientific explanations are preferred, even though they cannot be falsified either? Now the authors are thoughtful and intelligent people themselves who go on to conduct a thorough and useful discussion of theory in criminology. But by drawing a line as they do between what belongs in a discussion of crime at a university and what ought to be left to a starry-night chat around a campfire, they have left two distinct impressions. First, that all appeals to morality and politics reflect personal preferences or emotions, and two, that because moral values cannot be observed and studied scientifically, they are unimportant.

The social-scientific version begins by asserting that the observable (or measurable in social science terms) world is the real world, or at least is all that exists for purposes of doing social science and that the scientific method provides the most reliable route to understanding the real world. Whether moral values ultimately prove true or false cannot be determined because they cannot be studied using the methods of social science. Social science deals with observable reality while values are a matter for philosophy and the realm of unobservable metaphysics. But the power to define reality in society is the power to banish values to the realm of idiosyncrasy and personal taste. Social-scientific criminologists, when they talk about crime scientifically, are talking about reality, but when others talk about crime in political or moral terms, this is not reality. People who recognize God as the source of moral values might take exception that their belief has nothing to do with reality. Imagine this statement the other way around: "I respect your theory as an artifact of your scientistic thinking—you are entitled to your views. In no way do I want to disparage it when I point out that it has nothing to do with real life."[53]

The trouble with "separate but equal" when it comes to scientific facts and moral values is that it means about as much as it did during the era of Jim Crow. Saying that everybody is entitled to their values as a matter of personal choice denies any basis for criticism of value-based decisions. This is not what Popper had in mind by separating science from metaphysics. True, metaphysical statements are not subject to systematic observation as are scientific statements. But, as Popper pointed out, neither is every scientific statement. Universal statements about the natural world, such as physical laws, are not verifiable by means of empirical research either. (Isaac Newton developed calculus to convince himself of the law of gravitation.) While metaphysical ideas cannot be tested in the same way, they can nevertheless be criticized. The problem with social scientific criminology is not the application of the scientific method. Making probabilistic statements about the world is a good idea. The mistake of social science lies in the certainty it attributes to technique and its doctrine of the superiority of that technique. Its contemporary dilemma lies not in seeking scientific knowledge but in its failure to recognize any other.

The Return of Political Philosophy

"Man of the worldly mind!" Marley's ghost demands of Ebenezer Scrooge, "do you believe in me or not?" Criminologists, it seems, need a visit from that famous other-wordly visitor. Like Scrooge, criminologists trust only in what they can perceive through their senses. And, in an age of technological marvels in so many fields, it is hard to imagine an alternative to the scientific method as means of finding truth. But in the bigger scheme of things, the scientific tradition reflects only one path to knowledge. As it turns out, a rabbi explained the way out of the criminologist's dilemma centuries ago.

EPISTEMOLOGY AND CRIMINOLOGY. Maimonides, a leader of the Jewish community at Cairo, became the greatest rabbi of the medieval era. He produced several volumes of Jewish thought, including his *Mishneh Torah*, a code of Jewish law, and the *Guide for the Perplexed*, a discussion of theological concepts.[54] The Torah says that people are created in the image of God. Unlike animals, people have the ability to think, reason, and understand. The intellect allows people to perceive things without using the physical senses, an ability that makes people like God, who perceives things without physical senses. Maimonides explained the fact/value distinction in the *Guide*. He distinguished between "true and false," which are known through rational inquiry, and "good and bad," which are learned from tradition (originating in revelation).[55] Maimonides expressed the spiritual view of the universe, that there is order in the world. This belief in order led to the scientific revolution of the sixteenth century. Neither Copernicus, Kepler, Galileo nor Newton perceived their religious views to conflict with their science. The idea that science and religion are fundamentally incompatible came later.[56]

Those who founded the scientific method recognized reason as a valid route to knowledge about the real world, in addition to, or as part of, the kind of systematic observation carried out by science. The usefulness of reason as a means of separating true from false can be expressed by understanding the difference between "scientific proof" and "mathematical proof."[57] Scientists pursue proof by perception and observation. They propose a hypothesis to explain some phenomenon and then make systematic observations. If the observations compare favorably with the hypothesis, then the evidence supports the hypothesis. And if, by using the hypothesis, scientists can make accurate predictions, the hypothesis may become a scientific theory. But even the most widely accepted proofs in science involve some amount of doubt. They remain provisional, until something better, with greater predictive validity comes along. "Mathematical proof" follows a different road to knowledge. The classic mathematical proof begins with a series of axioms, statements that are self-evidently true. Then, by arguing logically step-by-step, the mathematician can arrive at a conclusion. If the axioms are correct and the logic flawless, then the conclusion is undeniable. Mathematical proof is not provisional. Mathematical theorems rely on this logic and once proven remain until the end of time.[58]

Contrary to the claim of social science, it is possible to obtain knowledge about the real world while sitting in an arm-chair and thinking about the real world. Consider the "Seven Bridges of Königsberg," a question solved by Swiss mathematician Leonhard Euler.[59] In the Prussian city of Königsberg, now known as the Russian city of Kalingrad, there are seven bridges. The city is built on the River Pregel; there is an island, with two branches of the river, flowing around, creating four landmasses connected by the seven bridges. Some of the more curious residents of the city wondered whether it was possible to make a complete journey throughout the city by crossing all seven bridges without having to cross any bridge more than once. The residents had pursued the scientific approach. They had tried various routes, leading to failure, and leading to the reasonable conclusion that it could not be done. They could be reasonably secure such a journey was impossible, but relying on experience meant that they could never know for sure. Euler too failed to find a way. But he proved it could not be done and he did so without taking a single step.[60]

Euler looked at a plan of the city. He constructed a simplified representation using letters and numbers, replacing the sections of land with points and the bridges with lines. He then reasoned that to make a successful journey (crossing all bridges only once) would require that each point should be connected to an even number of lines. This is because when the traveler enters any land area he or she must enter by one bridge and leave by another. There are only two exceptions: when the traveler begins and ends the journey. A journey that begins and ends at two different points would involve an odd number of lines, but a journey that begins and ends at the same point must have an even number of lines. So, Euler concluded, for any network of bridges it would be possible to make a complete trip throughout a city crossing each bridge only once if all the land areas had an even number of bridges, or if two landmasses had an odd number of bridges. In the case of Königsberg, there are four land areas and all of them are connected to an odd number of bridges. Euler had learned by means of reason what observation had failed to reveal. (He was less successful at using algebra to prove that God exists.)[61]

The distinction between scientific thought and non-scientific thought, as Euler's demonstration shows, ought to be discarded. The distinction should be made between logical and illogical thought. This distinction would make inference a prominent intellectual tool in criminology. To evaluate the conclusions of theories as logical or illogical would also provide for rational argument about moral, political and ethical ideas. The "ought to" statements submerged in the attempt to be social scientific could come to the surface and be subject to the same criticism as claims of fact. The same general strategy, of rational argument, can be used to evaluate both explanations of criminal behavior and the policy proposals based on those explanations. The idea that criminologists can "study crime for its own sake" without regard to public policy distracts from the real issues. This is not to elevate reason as the ultimate means of divining true from false in criminology. Maimonides wrote that an understanding of good and bad was to be had not by reason, but by an understanding of tradition, that is, history.

The study of history has a vital place in criminology. History, properly studied, can provide a means of evaluating the moral claims of criminological theories. Michael Oakeshott, a British philosopher of the twentieth century, explains what it means to "properly study" the past.[62] It does not amount to an effort to hold up contemporary moral claims to some yardstick of moral truth recovered from the past; there are no more inexorable laws of history than there are social laws. He suggests that history, as a form of intellectual inquiry, contains no direct lessons, messages or advice for practical life. The search for the inner meaning of the past is an exercise in historicism, not history.[63] Nor can history be understood as historiography, a survey of what historians have said about it. The work of different historians reflects, in part, individual impressions about the past and cannot be made to tell a coherent story.

Oakeshott says that what can be known from history derives from understanding the historical past: it does not exist. What has happened cannot be observed. Historical inquiry is about the present, and specifically, about what can be concluded about the past based on what can be observed in the present. Unlike the scientist who makes predictions about what will happen, and sets about disconfirming these expectations, the historian looks at the present to see what has happened. The historian deals in what has survived from the past. The historian makes inferences, by assessing and authenticating documents, monuments and other relics of the past, about what has happened in the historical past. The conception of the historical past that emerges is not static, but constantly changing. The historical past is always open to revision, owing that its formulation depends on hypothetical reasoning, the discovery of additional or other relics, and different historians. What emerges is real, and not the product of historians' imaginations, but the continuity of what has survived. In this way, history reveals the permanent.[64]

Reliance on reason and history mean that criminology represents more political philosophy than social science. The fact/value distinction, so important to social-scientific criminology, does not need to exist in a political philosophy of crime. Oakeshott compared the moral life to writing poetry, a comparison based on "the poetic character of all human activity." A poem represents in words what the poet had in mind. It is not the case that the "writing" follows the "thinking," because what the poet wants to say and what the poet says are the same thing. The poet does not know what to write until it is written. In the same sense, Oakeshott says: "Moral ideals are not, in the first place, the products of reflective thought, the verbal expressions of unrealized ideas, which are then translated (with varying degrees of accuracy) into human behavior; they are the products of human behavior, of human practical activity, to which reflective thought gives subsequent, partial and abstract expression in words."[65] A balanced moral tradition, Oakeshott contends, is one in which the intellect acts as a critic of moral conduct, but one in which morality originates in the conduct. Moral behavior cannot be derived from ideology or a set or moral rules; rather, moral behavior represents a habit of conduct within moral tradition.

THE CRIMINOLOGIST'S METHOD. This understanding of morality suggests two aspects of the criminological method. Every theory in criminology implies a better response to crime.[66] "Response to crime" means every suggestion for how to control, reduce, eliminate, and discourage crime. Crime prevention, the prospect of protecting people from the loss, hurt and pain caused by those who commit crimes, is the *raison d'être* of criminology. Some theories are more practical in the sense that they prescribe changes in the criminal justice system or policies that can be implemented by government. Others are less so because they view crime in the context of broader social, economic, and cultural happenings, and some doubt the ability of the criminal justice system, of government itself, to respond appropriately to crime. But the purpose of every theory is to make a point about what should be done about crime. There is a moral to every criminological story, and the task of the professional criminologist is to uncover that moral so that it can be evaluated.

Rather than attempting to split the empirical claims from the moral claims (and claim to deal only with the empirical), criminologists need to consider both together. The "policy implications" represent the prime means for evaluating the theory. In many cases, and maybe all cases, historical examples can be found for particular ideas. Many criminological ideas have been tried in one sense or another and it is possible, by examining their historical legacy, to consider their effect. It is fair to ask of historical application the extent to which the policy or practice as experienced embodied the theory. This does not, however, send the theory into the eternal orbit of personal opinion or insulate the theory from the refining fire of criticism. Even those theories for which no suitable historical application has been found the method still works. It can be asked of every theory, in a hypothetical sense, what the theory would imply if applied. The primary question to ask of every theory, then, is not

"What does the research show?" but "If this theory is true, what would it mean?"

Once the crime prevention aspect has been made clear, either by historical example or hypothetical terms, the goal is to find out whether the prevention aspect is good or bad. Evaluation of the crime prevention aspect of each theory is not an empirical question. It is not enough to say that a particular prevention project decreases crime. There are numerous examples, drawn from history and the present political map, of nations with despotic regimes and low crime rates. Despotic leaders have shown that government-sponsored terrorism leads people to behave themselves in public places. The question is not whether this can be confirmed by statistical analysis of survey data. To construct some measure of "despotism" or "fear," then attempt to correlate this with crime rates in various countries while statistically controlling for such things as "culture" and "poverty," is pointless. Even if it could be confirmed in this way, why bother? Who would want safe streets at that price? Some methods, even if they are effective at reducing crime, ought not be used because they are immoral.

Having explored the establishment of criminology as a profession, the problem of relying on the social scientific method, and the outline for a traditional criminology, it is now possible to explain the plan of this book. This book divides criminology theory based on seven modalities or organizing ideas. Although there are hundreds of criminological theories, they really attribute crime to one or more of seven sources: human nature, body, mind, society, language, race, and heart. The theories of the past few decades derive, either implicitly or explicitly, from these ideas. Each of these ideas corresponds, roughly, to the major disciplinary perspectives within criminology: political science/economics, biology, psychiatry/psychology, sociology, philosophy/literary criticism, and theology. Two ideas, race and social construction, fit less neatly into disciplinary categories, and operate across disciplinary boundaries. Race has been understood in political, social, economic, cultural, and biological terms. Social construction expresses a philosophical idea, and has been expressed by literary fields (as postmodernism or deconstruction), economics (Marxism), sociology (social constructionism, critical theory) as well as criminology (radical, critical criminology).

Each chapter, from chapter two through chapter eight, explores one of these theoretical perspectives. Generally, the chapter begins with an elaboration of the basic idea through the work of a major thinker. These include Cesare Beccaria, Cesare Lombroso, Sigmund Freud, Emile Durkeim, Karl Marx, W.E.B. Du Bois, and C.S. Lewis. Each chapter also contains an assessment of the theory with reference to the historical legacy of the ideas. The last chapter contains an argument about the place of law and government in criminology and sketches a moral philosophy of crime.

Conclusion

Criminology has already claimed its place within the social sciences as the scientific study of crime. If it is to make any meaningful contribution to an understanding about what is to be done about crime, it must take its place as political philosophy. Nobody expressed this better than Martin Luther King, Jr., who said, in his speech accepting the 1964 Nobel Peace Prize: "I refuse to accept the idea that the 'isness' of man's present nature makes him morally incapable of reaching up for the 'oughtness' that forever confronts him." Finding a better response to crime is about reaching for the oughtness, traditionally, the province of moral philosophers. This search for the origins of crime begins with a look at a time before professional criminologists offered a social-scientific criminology, when criminology was a matter of political philosophy.

Chapter 2

Crime and Human Nature

Until the professional criminologists began their search, crime was no mystery. Why people rape, rob and steal did not require extensive analysis of society. The origins of crime could be found within each person, or to be more specific, within human nature. To find the origins of crime, criminologists need look no further than the freewill of individuals, the ability of persons to choose.

It is called classical criminology, although those who wrote it did not think of themselves in those terms. The label "classical criminology" came later. What Cesare Beccaria, Jeremy Bentham and the founders of classical criminology wrote was more political philosophy than social science. They reasoned that not only do people choose for themselves, they ought to be able to choose for themselves as much as possible. This idea of personal liberty led to thinking about what sort of limits ought to be placed on that liberty and about what sort of government people ought to create for themselves. Since people could choose good or evil, the challenge for classical thinkers was to design a political system that would encourage people to do the right thing. When they wrote about the administration of justice, the shadow of a theory of crime appeared. People will choose right unless it is in their own self-interest to choose wrong; they weigh the costs and benefits of alternative courses of action and will choose crime whenever the benefit to themselves outweighs the cost.

The governmental tools classical criminologists devised for encouraging people to choose the law-abiding rather than the law-violating course of action are familiar. They formed the basis of legal systems in Europe, North America and elsewhere. Exploring the classical approach to crime is to explore the conceptual foundations of the American legal system, those ideas important to understanding why the system is designed the way it is. For many years, professional criminologists closeted the classical school as a well-intentioned but misguided ancestor of authentic criminology. In the first edition of *Theoretical Criminology* in 1958, George Vold dismissed it as "administrative and legal criminology" and as "pre-scientific in any modern sense of the human behavior sciences." About the only reason Vold could find for including it at all in his criminology textbook was that it had at least given up the "supernatural as a principle of explanation and as a guide to criminal procedure."[1] Later generations of classical criminologists have, however, extended the classical view of human nature beyond the legal system. The most recent versions of classical criminology do not concern themselves soley with the administration of justice.[2]

This chapter begins with the work of Cesare Beccaria, founder of classical criminology, and the relevant ideas of other Enlightenment thinkers. Part Two explains their thoughts about the administration of justice with reference to the ubiquitous symbol of justice: a blindfolded woman holding a sword and scales. Each aspect of the symbol—the blind-fold, the sword, the scales, the fact that justice is a woman—reveals central aspects of classical criminology. Part Three describes the legal legacy of classical thought; the principles it provided for organizing criminal justice. Part Four explores twentieth-century versions of classical thought including the economic approach, rational choice theory, routine activities theory, and the general theory of crime. Part Five offers a critique of the classical perspective particularly the idea that justice can be deduced from a set of abstract principles.

Beccaria and the Enlightenment

Cesare Beccaria, an Italian mathematician, produced the finest example of classical thought in his *Dei Delitti e delle Pene* or *Of Crimes and Punishment*. First published in 1764, Beccaria's little book enjoyed tremendous popularity throughout Europe. By the time the first English translation appeared in London in 1767, it had gone through six Italian editions and several in French. Voltaire provided a preface for the French translation. It was a book that influenced the administration of justice throughout the world, read by Gustavas III of Sweden, Catherine the Great of Russia, and Empress Maria Theresa of Austria.[3] So popular was the book in North

America that it was printed three times before 1800. Thomas Jefferson, who acquired a copy in December 1769 while serving in the Virginia legislature, enjoyed the book so much that he copied into his commonplace book various passages in Italian which cover eighteen printed pages. He summarized Beccaria's views in the preamble to his crime-and-punishment bill reported to the Virginia legislature in 1779.[4]

Beccaria's book influenced legal systems across Europe and as far east as Russia. Catherine the Great, who reigned from 1762 to 1796, introduced Beccaria's principles to the national assembly of delegates she convened in Moscow in 1767. The code they formulated emphasized that punishment ought not proceed from arbitrary rule, prohibited torture, and outlawed punishments that maimed the individual. The code discouraged violent methods of crime control in favor of crime prevention. The law followed Beccaria's prescription that the certainty of punishment served as a better means of prevention that severity. "People should fear the Laws, and nothing but the Laws. Would you prevent crimes? Order it so, that the Light of Knowledge may be diffused among the People."[5]

How a mathematician came to write one of the most influential books in criminology is a curious story. Beccaria himself did not, by himself, write the book that has made him the founder of classical criminology. He was born the oldest son of an influential family in Milan, Italy. As a young man, he married against his parents wishes and joined a circle of reformers calling themselves *Accademià dei pugni*, "the academy of fisticuffs." Beccaria's circle included the Verri brothers, Pietro and Alessandro; two individuals with extensive knowledge of political philosophy and the administration of justice. The brothers introduced Beccaria to French and British political philosophers including Montesquieu, Diderot, Hobbes, and Hume. Pietro was writing a history of torture and Alessandro held the official title of "protector of prisoners" at the prison in Milan. Pietro Verri urged Beccaria to write something on the topic of crime and punishment. Beccaria, who had little knowledge of the legal system, had long conversations with the brothers. Beccaria took notes while they talked, and Pietro organized them into a manuscript and sent it to a publisher.[6]

Perhaps the brothers decided to ghost-write the book to avoid reprisal from officials in Milan and the State of Lombardy whose practices the book criticized. The book was published anonymously. As it became famous, Beccaria took credit for it, which led to a falling out with the Verris. French intellectuals welcomed Beccaria to Paris, but his visit did not go well, and he ended his trip early. In 1770, he returned to Milan, took a post in the Austrian administration, and kept that position for the next twenty-four years. Without his circle of friends, he never produced anything worthy of publication about the administration of justice or any other topic. After his death in 1794, Beccaria's reputation as a great reformer silenced by a repressive government grew, although the silence was more likely self-imposed. And, in a larger sense, few of the ideas in the book were original. Whether Beccaria or the Verris produced it, the ideas in the book represented a synthesis of Enlightenment writers protesting political repression the kingdoms of Europe.[7]

Nowhere in Europe did the abuses of power lead to greater bloodshed than in France, and nowhere were the abuses of the French kings greater than in the administration of justice. Or, rather, the administration of injustice. The monarchs of the *ancien régime* did not merely exercise undue authority over the government, they claimed to be the government. Louis XVI and his wife, Marie Antoinette, lived in opulence while the people scratched for food. It was Marie Antoinette who when told that the people had no bread to eat, replied, according to popular legend: "Let them eat cake instead." Their abuse of power culminated in the French Revolution. Both the king and his wife died, along with thousands of others, by means of a killing machine invented by a doctor: Joseph Ignace Guillotine.

Victor Hugo's epic novel *Les Misérables* tells the story of French injustice on the eve of the revolution. Although it is a work of fiction, Hugo's narrative contained many parallels to the actual history of the period. The story opens just as Jean Valjean escapes from nineteen years of imprisonment for trying to steal bread for his sister and her starving children. As an ex-convict, he cannot find employment and resorts to a life of crime until he meets a kindly priest while attempting to steal candlesticks from the church. He resolves to begin again, chooses a new identity, and using knowledge gained while imprisoned, opens a successful glass-making factory. He is elected mayor, but cannot escape the grasp of a vindictive police inspector who had been responsible for security at the prison, and threatens to reveal his former identity. He leaves public office to prevent the conviction of a man for a crime he himself had committed. He flees to Paris, where he pledges to raise a little girl, Cosette, because of a promise he made to her dying mother. Hounded by the police inspector, Valjean moves from house to house. Meanwhile, Cosette grows into a young woman and falls in love with a young revolutionary, Marius. To save the one person he loves, he leaves the safety of the barricade to save the injured Marius, and insures the two will be married. On his deathbed, Valjean receives the love to release him from bitterness.

French judges and magistrates did retain the power to impose capricious penalties. Trials occurred in secret or not at all. Persons could be tried for imaginary crimes such as magic and heresy. The social standing of the accused was taken as a fact in evidence, in deciding the charge and fixing the punishment. Law books and law practice enshrined social rank as essential to legal judgment. Trials occurred in different courts arranged according to the social standing of the accused.[8] There was no court for appeal of criminal or civil cases. French courts sent convicts to prison colonies; many never returned. And there was certainly room for private vendettas to be carried out by public officials under the cover of discretionary authority. Louis XVI, who reigned on the eve of the revolution, introduced the infamous *lettre de cachet* as a means of a terror. The letter, a royal warrant, meant imprisonment for an uncertain length of time without formal accusation, or worse.

French procedure also invoked the *amende honorable*, a public means of torture intended to bring shame on those who threatened public order. The execution of Damiens the regicide provides one of the more hideous episodes of this practice. In 1757, the court ordered Damiens to "make *amende honorable* before the main door of the Church of Paris," for his crime. The court order specified that he be "taken and conveyed in a cart, wearing nothing but a shirt, holding a torch of burning wax weighing two pounds" and then, "in the said cart, to the Place de Grève, where on a scaffold that will be erected there, the flesh will be torn from his breasts, arms, thighs and calves with red-hot pincers, his right hand, holding the knife with which he committed the said parricide, burnt with sulfur, and, on those places where the flesh will be torn away, poured molten lead, boiling oil, burning resin, wax and sulfur melted together and then his body drawn and quartered by four horses and limbs and body consumed by fire, reduced to ashes and his ashes thrown to the winds." As the court officials carried out each aspect of the sentence; Damiens himself shouted. "My God, have pity on me! Jesus help me!" he cried in between loud and horrible cries of anguish.[9]

The French police also operated a shadowy network of spies. They collected information about anyone who might threaten the power of the kingdom. In Paris, there was a police inspector assigned to the book trade. The inspector collected information about "dangerous" and highly suspicious persons living in the city. The police made frequent trips to the Bastille, the main prison of Paris, threatening those condemned there into giving them the names of others. The police and their informants also frequented the café's, waiting to overhear words that could trigger official intervention. They created dossiers for hundreds of poets, writers, and essayists including Montesquieu and Rousseau.[10] What were these dangerous ideas that frightened the monarchies of Europe?

The *Enlightenment* represents the "dawn of the age of light" after the Dark Ages in Europe, a period beginning in last half of the seventeenth century and continuing into the first half of the eighteenth. The Enlightenment did not produce a coherent system of thought. Enlightenment thinkers contradicted each other and most contradicted themselves. They came from diverse backgrounds and pursued diverse objectives; they championed diverse themes of reason, nature, happiness, progress and liberty. But they all agreed on one thing: people were free to choose. They could choose their own vocation, choose their own rulers, and choose their own society. They could, by exercising their will, free themselves from the corruption and excesses of existing political, social, and economic institutions.

John Locke, "the philosopher of freedom," supplied the most powerful image of the Enlightenment view of human nature. Locke originally studied medicine. He did not earn a degree, but he did perform surgical operations. In 1666, Dr. Locke removed an abscess from the chest of a grateful man and the patient launched Locke's political career. The patient, Anthony Cooper, was the Earl of Shaftesbury, a lord of the realm, who introduced Locke's theories of government to lawmakers Locke described human nature at birth as *tabula rasa*, a blank sheet of paper. Whether human beings became good or evil depended on their experience; if they experienced evil, they would choose evil. If they experienced good, they would choose good. If governments treated their citizens with fairness and respect, instead of terror and treachery, people would respond.

People did not naturally steal, loot and riot—all this they learned from corrupt government. Locke envisioned an original state of nature characterized by happiness and tolerance. People, in their natural state, pursued freely life, health, and possessions; it was a state of perfect liberty.

The Enlightenment philosophers wrote about nature. None took the space to define it; they all seemed to know what it meant. Nature was the proper standard for measuring human activity; if something was "according to the law of nature," it was reasonable and therefore, it was good. Thomas Hobbes, an Oxford graduate who tutored for a wealthy family, described the state of nature as anarchy in which only the strong survived. Human nature consisted of emotions, particularly a desire for wealth, a desire for glory, and fear of violent death. People in the state of nature fought with one another; conflict ensued as they pursued gain by theft, sought glory through accumulation of power, and tried to secure their gain, and their lives, from others. Rousseau, on the other hand, thought of people in their natural state as basically good. Jean-Jacques Rousseau, a French-speaking Swiss from Geneva, advanced a view of the "noble savage," that of primitive society as superior to civilization. Prior to civilization, people lived in a state of innocence. "If man is good by nature, as I believe I have shown him to be," Rousseau wrote, "it follows that he stays like that as long as nothing foreign to him corrupts him."

The Enlightenment philosophers wrote about reason. Generally, they set for themselves the task of making the kinds of changes in political life that seventeen-century scientists had done for the natural world, particularly those in astronomy and physics. They elevated reason as the primary means of inquiry about the world and disdained ideas from tradition and superstition. Some of the French idealists favored destruction of the cathedrals. In Paris, men carried the goddess of reason, personified by actress Demoiselle Candeille, shoulder-high into the cathedral.[11] While they disagreed about exactly what reason meant, they believed it could unlock the rational plan behind the universe and make society more sensible. As Voltaire remarked, "The only way to have good laws is to burn all existing laws and start afresh."[12] Once these laws had been uncovered, and written into new laws, progress would follow. Both human and nature itself were perfectible, and with reason as a guide, humankind was on the road to perfection.

And, the philosophers of the Enlightenment wrote about—the part that the monarchists feared most—liberty. Liberty, in a sense, meant freedom from social conventions, from the restraint of social institutions. Rousseau wrote that social conventions corrupted the soul and inhibited the process of self-fulfillment. Rousseau's concept of human nature expressed the Bohemian ideal, in which the hero fights against all of society's standards, values, and restraints. Rousseau himself suggested that self-discovery could be accomplished through education. In his *Confessions*, Rousseau insisted that a proper education really amounted to a lack of education. A century later, Puccini gave Rousseau's view of human nature artistic expression in his popular opera *La Bohème* (1896).[13]

In an economic sense, liberty meant a minimum of government regulation. Adam Smith, the leading figure of the Scottish Enlightenment, described human nature as freedom to engage in commercial activity. Smith, who had met Voltaire while traveling in France, held the chair of moral philosophy at the University of Glasgow for a number of years. "The propensity to truck, barter and exchange one thing for another is common to all men..." he wrote in his master work, *The Wealth of Nations*. Individuals worked to find means of generating the greatest income for themselves, but in their self-interested pursuits, they end up creating the most beneficial division of labor for society. The best government could do to encourage this process was to stay out of it; to adopt a policy of *lassiez-faire*, that is "allow to do." If government allowed the market to operate, "the invisible hand" of competition would regulate the extremes of laziness and greed and "the simple system of natural liberty" would establish itself. Each person ought to be free to pursue individual economic interest, short of violating principles of fair competition, in "the system of perfect liberty" otherwise known as commercial capitalism.[14]

But it was liberty in the political sense that created the most revolutionary stir in the eighteenth century. Locke did not believe in the divine right of kings to ascend to the throne. The authority of government rested on the consent of the people and not on "myth, mysticism and mystery." His ideas brought William and Mary to the throne following the Battle of the Boyne and sent his patron, Lord Shaftesbury to the Tower on more than one occasion. People, as John Locke put it, had natural rights. "Man being born...," as Locke put it in *Of Civil Government* (1690), "with a title to perfect freedom, an uncontrolled enjoyment of the rights and privileges of the law of nature." Locke specified three natural rights: to life (self-preservation), to liberty, and to estate (to own property). These rights, and the concept of natural rights, became the basis for the French Declaration of the Rights of Man (1789) and the American Bill of Rights (1791).

Beccaria's book referenced all these ideas and more. He condensed all the Enlightenment thought the Verri brothers had taught him into a one-hundred page book focused on the administration of justice. In England, as in the United States, the most recognized symbol of these ideas would be expressed in the figure of woman.

The Figure of Justice

On one side of the steps leading to the main entrance of the Supreme Court Building, across from the United States Capitol in Washington, there is a marble statute of a woman, holding a sword and scales. A similar figure stands atop the Central Criminal Court at Warwick Square, in London, a building popularly known as the Old Bailey. The woman stands with outstretched arms holding a sword and scales; rays of light emanate from her head. A similar figure appears in artwork on courthouses throughout the United States and Europe.

The figure of justice has ancient roots. In Greek mythology, the goddess Themis advised Zeus. Themis remained with Zeus after he purged the old pantheon; she kept her seat next to him as he reigned from Mount Olympus. Themis carried the scales of justice in one hand and a sword in another, and in most depictions, her eyes are covered. Justicia, in Roman myth, resembles Themis. Justicia settled disputes wearing a blindfold; she also carried a sword and scales. The Egyptians looked to Maat, daughter of the Sun god Ra. She carried a sword but without a scales.[15] What each aspect of the figure represents — the scales, the sword, the blindfold, the woman — provides a useful means of outlining the major themes of classical criminology.

THE SCALES OF JUSTICE. The scales of justice symbolize judgment. They can be understood as an expression of the process of fact-finding, of weighing the evidence leading to a determination of guilt or innocence. They can symbolize the trial as a search for the truth; the prosecution and defense each presents its case. But the scales acquire their greatest significance as a symbol of the classical formulation of *proportionality*.

The classicists taught that crime and punishment should be proportional. The court should measure the amount of punishment in proportion to the harm caused by the criminal act. Beccaria wrote that the harm done to society, and not the intention of the lawbreaker, should be the true measure of the severity of the crime. Punishment should be measured in proportion to the amount of harm caused by the act; to impose more severe punishment than the act justified was superfluous and tyrannical. Bloody, stern punishments only encouraged assassination and revolt. By measuring carefully the amount of punishment, the government could encourage lawful behavior. "It is better to prevent crimes than to punish them," Beccaria wrote, "That is the ultimate end of every good legislation."[16]

Crime prevention could be accomplished by deterrence. Beccaria taught that deterrence is the chief aim of punishment. Two kinds of deterrence can be put to work preventing crime. *Specific deterrence* has to do discouraging repeat lawbreakers. If judges apply just the right amount of punishment, and apply it in the right way, then lawbreakers will "learn their lesson" and refrain from further illegal behavior. *General deterrence* has to do with discouraging potential lawbreakers by punishing actual lawbreakers. When lawbreakers are punished, and the public knows of it, the punishment "sends a message" that the law must be obeyed. Beccaria offered general deterrence as a rational alternative to torture. Secret torture of suspects, to say nothing of the injustice of it, was bad public policy. How could the punishment deter further unlawful behavior if no one knew about it? Beccaria urged the sovereigns to publish the laws and punish infractions publicly so that people could understand their purpose and anticipate the consequences of their acts.

In order to optimize the deterrent value of sanctions, Beccaria offered his well-known formula: punishment should be swift and certain. Justice delayed amounted to justice denied from the standpoint of society. If lawbreakers received punishment immediately following their crimes, they would associate the offense with its consequence, and learn a valuable lesson in citizenship. Certainty, Beccaria reasoned, was more important than severity. If citizens knew that punishment was sure to follow an unlawful act, they would be more likely to avoid illegal behavior than if the punishment was severe and the chances of detection slim. Arbitrary, inconsistent punishment sent the wrong message.

Deterrence theory in classical criminology draws on the doctrine of *utilitarianism.* Jeremy Bentham, one of the utilitarian philosophers, turned his attention to law and government. An attorney's son, Bentham studied law at Oxford, was admitted to the bar in 1772, but he never practiced. Living on his family fortune, he abandoned the practice of law for the work of a reformer of the legal system. He crusaded for an end to ignorance and tradition. He wanted to create a coherent foundation for the irrational structure of laws that had emerged over the centuries. He aimed to create jurisprudence, a science of law built from a proper understanding of human nature.

Bentham disagreed with the natural rights theory of Locke; people comprised no sense of community other than the aggregate of individuals. "Nature hath placed mankind under the governance of two sovereign masters: *pain* and *pleasure,*" he wrote.[17] When he looked at society, he saw individuals in possession of basic personal liberty, and because of it, self-seeking and intolerant behavior. His solution was for government, not to restrict individual liberty, but to make intolerance unprofitable by relying on a basic understanding of human nature. Government should restrain individual liberty that results in the destruction of a greater portion of the happiness of others. Rather than attempt to impose some sense of the "common good" or "public interest," government should aim to bring about "the greatest good for the greatest number." Bentham wrote that the pursuit of the common good embodied moral decision-making because the pleasure of one person coincided with the pleasure of another.[18] Consequently, he advocated the democratic ideal that "everybody count for one and nobody count for more than one."

The utilitarian foundation of classical criminology insists that government represents a mechanism for shaping human behavior through careful application of benefits and burdens, rights and responsibilities, privileges and sanctions. Prevention is the chief aim of the administration of justice. Technically speaking, pleasure and pain do not guide behavior; it is the *anticipation* of pleasure or pain. Pain ought not be inflicted to avenge the crime because vengeance served no purpose. The crime cannot be undone. Punishment itself, because it added to the overall amount of pain, was evil in itself. Punishment should be measured out as frugally as possible, Bentham taught. He said, "Punishment, which, if it goes beyond the limit of necessity is a pure evil."[19] Bentham shifted the emphasis in criminal law from punishing wrong to creating incentives for doing right.

THE SWORD OF JUSTICE. The sword represents the authority to punish, and in the case of capital crimes, the power of life and death. The classical criminologists believed that the government's authority to enforce its laws derived from the *social contract*. The social contract finds expression in the writings of Hobbes, Rousseau, Locke, Beccaria and other Enlightenment thinkers. The basic idea is that citizens subject themselves to governmental authority in exchange for the rule of law. Citizens surrender their right to complete personal liberty, and in return, the government protects each person from the intrusions of others. Hobbes wrote that civilization began when people, "weary of the war of every man against every man," established government. Without government, there was anarchy and chaos. Only the strongest enjoyed their liberty; they enslaved the weak. To end this situation, there had to be government and government had to be the absolute authority. Government came about by consent of the people, Hobbes explained, but once established government had to embody unrivalled power. The justice of the social contract meant that once citizens agreed to surrender their liberty, government preserved personal liberty by enforcing the rule of law. "For covenants without the sword are but words and of no strength to secure a man at all," Hobbes preached. Hobbes envisioned government as *leviathan*, an image he borrowed from the book of Job. Leviathan appears as a sea monster, the most fierce and powerful master of the sea.[20]

Locke's version of the social contract followed from his view the law of nature. The law of nature ordained that each person had personal liberty, that is, no person had authority over another, and each person had a duty to respect others and not interfere with their pursuit of personal liberty. Personal liberty included the opportunity to make whatever impact they could upon the world, and by working to appropriate some portions of the earth's resources for themselves, accrue property. Government was necessary to preserve the individual's right to life, liberty and property by umpiring disputes between individuals over the exercise of these rights. Government protected the good all individuals had in common, and derived its authority to do this solely on the consent of its subjects. Government never usurped the individual's right to self-determination.[21]

Hobbes and Locke disagreed about the authority of government. Both began with self-preservation as the foremost right and insisted that preservation of life represented the primary aim of government. Hobbes contended that citizens surrender their rights to government and insisted on the government's right to exist so long as it could maintain order. Locke, on the other hand, wrote that people never surrender completely their rights. Government had the right to exist so long as it reflected the consent of the governed and respected the natural rights of citizens. If government abused these rights, the people were justified in replacing it altogether. The people defer power to government based on the democratic principle of government by consent, but they never surrender their sovereignty.

In 1971, Harvard philosopher John Rawls provided a restatement of contractarian thought. Rawls thought about his theory for twenty years before his book appeared and he has refined it in a series of articles since then.[22] He agreed with the classicists that the most distinctive feature of human nature is the ability to choose; the most fundamental duty to others is to allow people to choose for themselves. But rather than ground his theory in a state of nature that existed prior to civilization, Rawls relied on a theoretical strategy known as foundationalism, that is, of starting with a self-evident point and deducing the contents of a theory. Rawls asks: What sort of government would people voluntarily agree to? He imagines a situation he calls "the original position" in which the founders of a society choose rules for their society, and to avoid the complication of narrow self-interest, he further imagines that they operate behind a "veil of ignorance;" they must choose their society without knowing their personal qualities or what place they will occupy in the society they create.

Rawls decides that they would found government on *two principles of justice*: (1) Each person is to have an equal right to the most extensive basic liberty compatible with similar liberty for others (the "principle of equal liberty"), and (2) social and economic inequalities are to be arranged so that they operate to the greatest benefit of the least advantaged member of society (the "difference principle") and attached to offices and positions open to all under conditions of fair equality of opportunity (the "principle of fair equality of opportunity"). Government established on this just basic structure would preserve the right to acquire property, to political liberty and the kind of rights afforded by due process of law.[23]

JUSTICE IS BLIND. The blindfold symbolizes fairness and impartiality. Laws are to be enforced, verdicts to be rendered, and punishment to be administered without regard to the personal characteristics or social standing of individual citizens.

The legal doctrine of "equal justice under law," chiseled in the marble above the entrance to the United States Supreme Court, reflets the classical emphasis on individual liberty. In a society of free, independent and self-determined individuals, interests are bound to collide. Locke observed that it would be convenient if all the people living in proximity to one another recognized a single umpire rather than trying to solve disputes for themselves. Government, he said, existed to serve as an impartial referee. Each individual possessed a natural duty of recognize every other person as an equal and to give due respect to each person's rights under the law. Government too had to recognize the equal standing of each person. So while each person recognized the authority of government to make a final decision, government recognized that each person had equal standing.[24]

Beccaria emphasized that the court direct its response to the criminal *act*, not the criminal *actor*. The legislature wrote the laws and judges should not have authority to interpret them, but only to apply them. He advocated a strict adherence to the letter of the law. He acknowledged that mechanical application of criminal penalties had its drawbacks but maintained that whatever problems this created would be preferable to judicial discretion. Tidy application of the laws as written, Beccaria wrote, is preferable to the disorder created by allowing judges to seek the spirit of the laws.[25] From the standpoint of classical criminology, the blindfold illustrates the focus on the lawbreaking, not the lawbreaker. The individual stands accused, not for who they are, but for what they have done.

JUSTICE IS A WOMAN. The figure of a woman can represent many aspects of classical criminology. Perhaps she embodies liberty as depicted in Eugene Delacroix' "Liberty Guiding the People" (1830), or the statue in New York Harbor by French sculptor Frederic-August Bartholdi. Perhaps she embodies the goddess of reason, an advisor to the gods. She can also represent *mercy*, a basic aspect of the neo-classical view of justice.

In a rational system of justice, Beccaria pointed out, there would be no need for mercy. "Clemency..." he wrote, "should be excluded from perfect legislation, where the punishments are mild and the method of judgment regular and expeditious."[26] Rawls made the same argument. Mercy is superfluous when decisions flow from a government with a just basic structure; they are fair as a matter of *pure procedural justice*. That is, so long as government is founded on the two basic principles of justice, the administration of justice is automatically just. The rule of law represents a system of order to regulate the conduct of citizens and provide a framework for social cooperation. The purpose of the criminal law, Rawls explains, is to uphold the duties that accrue under the rule the law; duties that prohibit citizens from injuring one another and depriving them of their liberty or property. "For this reason, a coercive government is always necessary, even though in a well-ordered society sanctions need not be severe and may never need to be imposed," Rawls observes.[27] Effective machinery for the detection, capture and conviction of lawbreakers serves a surety, a guarantee that compliance with the rule of law will be supported by punishment of those who do not comply. This loss of liberty to government constitutes a rational decision because of the greater loss of liberty without government.[28]

In France, Beccaria's principles found expression in Article VIII of the "Declaration of the Rights of Man and of the Citizen," passed by the revolutionary National Assembly in 1789, and in the French Code of 1791, in which the legislature wrote them into criminal law. The attempt to apply Beccaria's ideas directly, however, ran aground. The effort to obtain exact proportionality between the criminal act and the punishment led to equivalent penalties across very different circumstances. Mechanical application of proportionality between the act and punishment meant equivalent sentences for first-time as well as repeat lawbreakers, for young and old, for the sane and the insane. The system of recognizing proportionality with adjustments is known as *neo-classicism*. Neo-classical criminology applies classical principles but allows for the defendant's criminal history, youthfulness or mental condition in making legal judgments.[29]

The systems of criminal justice said to apply classical criminology actually reflect neo-classical provisions. The French legislature after 1791 moved progressively over the years to return discretion to judges the experiment with pure classicism had taken away. The practice of parole, prominent in the American system, had been invented by the French. The English word parole comes from the French phrase *parole d'honneur*, which means "word of honor." It originated with the practice of releasing convicts early, based on their word of honor, that they would obey the law upon release.[30] The origins of parole likely explain the English phrase, "French leave," which refers to leaving a party without saying goodnight to the hostess. (A practice known in France as taking "English leave.") Over the years, it has come to mean "absent without leave;" to abscond.[31]

In England, where Jeremy Bentham urged governmental and legal reforms, the practice never faded. "The prerogative of mercy," one historian has written about eighteenth-century English justice, "ran throughout the administration of the criminal law, from the lowest to the highest level."[32] Much has been written about England's bloody code with more than two hundred capital offenses on the statutes by 1820. Most of those condemned to death in eighteenth century English courts did not go to the gallows, however, but to prison or the colonies.

English courts extended mercy to the accused by various means including benefit of clergy. The origins of "benefit of clergy" are obscure but the practice may have started with exemption of clergymen from the jurisdiction of secular courts (to be tried in ecclesiastical courts). From the sixteenth century on, the courts extended the practice to all those connected with the church. To receive a sentence of transportation to the colonies rather than a trip to the gallows, the court allowed the defendant "to pray his clergy," which meant reciting a Psalm.[33] In the eighteenth century, Parliament began to enact legislation specifying that some crime remain felonies "without benefit of clergy," yet the practice of mercy continued. Judges acquitted on the slightest technicalities of procedure such as when the defendant was described on the warrant as a "farmer" rather than a "yeoman."[34]

Application of Classical Principles

In the age of liberty, deprivation of liberty became the primary sanction. The ancient world had prisons, but imprisonment became the chief means of punishment during the Enlightenment.

Jeremy Bentham and Thomas Jefferson both offered prison designs. Bentham drafted plans for his panopticon, the central event in his life between 1789 and 1812. The panopticon, or "all-seeing eye," was Bentham's design for a two-story, circular prison. The cells followed a radial pattern surrounding an interior tower, which would serve as the center of security. From this point, the guards could view into each cell. The guards looked through a system of Venetian blinds arranged so that the prisoner never knew when the guards were watching. Prisoners ate, slept, and worked under virtual surveillance provided by efficiency of architectural design. Bentham envisioned panopiticon hill villages as institutions for paupers and orphans as well, to be located across England, about a day's walking distance apart. He lobbied King George III to finance construction, but the king never authorized the funds. Bentham believed the king denied his funding because the first would have been built on land belonging to Lord Spencer, who feared that such an institution would devalue his property.[35] While Bentham styled himself as a legal reformer, he never considered constitutional change until after rejection of his model prison in 1811.[36]

Thomas Jefferson designed a prison to be built at Richmond, Virginia. Jefferson, who favored labor and solitary confinement as a means of punishment rather than labor at public works, encouraged the Virginia legislature to build a prison. When the directors of Virginia's capitol-building committee wrote to him in France in 1785 to ask about plans for that building, he sent along his plans for a prison. He had acquired a copy of P.G. Bugniet's drawings for a prison at Lyons and produced a scaled-down version for construction at Richmond. The Virginia legislature eventually authorized public expenditure for a prison, but selected the design of Benjamin Henry LaTrobe. When finished in 1800, the prison at Richmond represented the fourth in the United States, following prisons built in Philadelphia; Trenton, New Jersey; and Frankfort, Kentucky. Robert Mills, who designed South Carolina's penitentiary, sought Jefferson's advice as well.[37]

It was John Haviland that became the architect of the classical school. He came to America in 1816 and designed a prison built in a cherry orchard near Philadelphia. His design featured a radial plan, with a central tower and rectangular cell blocks radiating outward, like the spokes from the hub of a wheel. The interior featured cast iron bars and concrete pillars. The exterior, dressed stone and

turrets; styled after the castles Haviland had seen in England and
Ireland as a boy. The exterior exuded permanence, austerity, inevitability; a secular cathedral for making amends with the government. Haviland's design for Pennsylvania's Cherry Hill prison became the model for prisons throughout the world. Britain, France,
Prussia, and Belgium sent officials to Cherry Hill and built domestic
prisons like it. Britain's facsimile at Pentonville became the model
for prisons in the colonies from Burma to Hong Kong. Spain built a
prison on the Haviland model, as did Portugal, Sweden, Denmark,
Finland, Austria, Hungary and Japan.[38]

The idea of a regular police force also flowed from classical ideas.
The English nobility remembered the abuses of monarchial powers
during the reign of the Stuart kings, and they despised the French
sovereigns use of spies and informers. They choose to secure their
own property rather than consent to a standing domestic army. A
gentleman had dogs, firearms, lights and bells at his country estate,
and took a brace of double-barreled pistols to bed with him every
night.[39] In England, as the colonies in America, law enforcement
resided with the sheriff. The colonial sheriffs carried out many duties for which they collected fees: they executed writs, maintained
public accounts, arrested suspects, subpoened witnesses, kept prisoners, broke up fights, suppressed riots, and carried out sentences.[40]
Not until Bentham did Parliament authorize a police force.

Between 1795 and 1800, Bentham corresponded with Patrick
Colquhoun, a Glasgow merchant, and together they formulated
plans for a police force. In his *Treatise on the Police of the Metropolis*, Colquhoun stated that the police represented not merely the
arm of the court in carrying out its orders, but had a role in the prevention of crime. Bentham and Colquhoun wrote the Thames River
Police Act of 1800, which mobilized a force to police London's
riverside docks. Parliament revised the act six times before 1829
and eventually extended police throughout the city of London. In
1811, Sir Richard Ford served as magistrate of Bow Street; he com-
manded a mounted force of sixty, known as the Bow Street Run-
ners. In 1822, the Unmounted Horse Patrol became the first uniformed police in England. To deter daylight robberies, the division
wore the distinctive dress of the Napoleonic era: blue coats and
trousers, black hats and Wellington boots. By 1828 there were
about four-hundred-fifty paid police patrolling the streets of London.[41]

CRIME AND HUMAN NATURE · 45

Between 1822 and 1830, Bentham wrote his book *The Constitutional Code* in which he emphasized the need for a preventive police force under government control. The Select Committee on the Police of the Metropolis, convened by British Home Secretary Sir Robert Peel, heard testimony about Bentham's proposal, and urged Parliament to pass in 1829 the Metropolitan Police Act. The Act established a police force within a seven-mile area of London to be headquartered at an old fort named Scotland Yard. Charles Rowan, a military colonel, became the first superintendent. He administrated a force of some 165 officers, nicknamed "Bobbies" after Sir Robert. Bentham emphasized that suspects be identified with first and last names, and to assist in identifying repeat lawbreakers, he advocated tattooing the complete name on the suspect's wrist, following the custom of the British Navy's practice of marking recalcitrant conscripts.[42]

New York became the first American city to install a regular police force. In 1845, the city consolidated watches to provide around the clock patrol. In 1852, New Orleans and Cincinnati followed New York's model, Philadelphia and Boston in 1854, Chicago in 1855, and Baltimore in 1857. New York's police force also became the first American force to wear uniforms. After a heated debate, the commissioner stated in 1853 that officers who refused to wear the uniform would not be hired. Carrying firearms, a matter of personal choice, became part of the standard uniform in the United States, unlike in England.[43]

Before his death, Jeremy Bentham bequeathed his original manuscripts to the University College of London and he made an unusual request: he stipulated that the curators of his manuscripts embalm his body and put it on permanent display. The administrators have complied. The University has commissioned a complete edition of Bentham's writings projected to fill 36 volumes. His body has been preserved as well. To this day, Bentham peers out from a wooden-framed glass box in the library, where he sits entombed like a pharaoh of ancient Egypt.[44] If Bentham was worried that he would be forgotten, he need not have been; his ideas have been preserved. In fact, the idea of people as rational calculators has found contemporary expression in the work of political scientists and economists. *Choice theory* takes as its starting point that view of human nature emphasized by Enlightenment thought: people have volition. People exercise their freedom to choose and human behavior can be analyzed as a matter of choice.

Choice Theory

No criminologist did more to reinvigorate classical criminology than James Q. Wilson. Wilson taught political science at Harvard University for nearly thirty years before relocating to California. Wilson has written the most widely-used text in American government along with books on urban problems, government regulation, Black politicians, bureaucracy, moral theory, and crime. He began his career in criminology in the 1960s after chairing the White House Task Force on Crime in 1966. In a series of articles written for *The Public Interest*, Wilson critiqued the "social science view" of crime prominent during the Johnson presidency. Wilson's *Thinking About Crime* (1975)[45] challenged sociology's claim to criminology expressed in *Principles of Criminology* by Edwin Sutherland and Donald Cressey, and the basis for government intervention Richard Cloward and Lloyd Ohlin had made in *Delinquency and Opportunity*. In the process, he "almost single-handedly rehabilitated the deterrence literature."[46]

"To assert that 'deterrence doesn't work'," Wilson wrote, "is tantamount to either denying the plainest facts of everyday life or claiming that would-be criminals are utterly different than the rest of us."[47] He culled evidence from evaluation of police response to domestic violence, gun laws, and driving-while-drunk showing that the probability of being punished can lead to change in behavior. He pointed out that punishment represented only half of the cost-benefit equation. Punishment emphasized the cost side of the equation when understanding humans as rational calculators implied that people would respond to inducements as well. Job creation did not represent an alternative strategy but rather the inducement side of the same strategy. Wilson encouraged criminologists to abandon their search for the "root causes" of crime in society and accept, along with St. Francis of Assisi, that there are some things that cannot be changed. Criminologists ought to concentrate on the criminal justice system and find ways to alter the "perverse incentives" it presently offered. "We trifle with the wicked, make sport of the innocent, and encourage the calculators."[48]

THE ECONOMIC APPROACH. About the same time, Gary S. Becker proposed an *economic approach* to crime. Becker, while a professor of economics the University of Chicago, received the 1992 Nobel Prize in Economic Science for his application of economic theory to every-day problems, including his analysis of crime. In his early work, Becker formulated a cost-benefit model of crime using the linear equations common to econometrics.[49] But, as Becker told his audience in a 1995 lecture sponsored by the Federal Reserve Bank of Richmond, "The essence of the economic approach to crime is amazingly simple. It says that people decide whether to commit crime by comparing the benefits and costs of engaging in crime."[50] He recognized that the motivation to commit crime likely varies across individuals, but insisted the same general principles guide the decision of criminals, whether in the United States, Europe, Latin America or Africa. People will make rational decisions based on the extent to which they expect their choice to maximize their benefit (profits) and minimize their cost (losses.)

The benefits of crime, Becker explained, included the monetary gain, the objective in property crime, as well as the "psychic" or "sick thrills," to be had for some people, in crimes of assault, rape and other violent crimes. The costs include the punishment, from probation to fines to imprisonment, and more importantly, the like- lihood of being caught. For risk-takers involved in crime, the cer- tainty of being caught is more important than the magnitude of punishment following conviction. Changes in the benefits and costs are the major tools for understanding why crime rates change over time. Becker attributed the decrease in property crime during the 1980s and 1990s, as shown by information from the National Crime Victimization survey, to an increase in courts' willingness to convict and imprison criminals. The prison and jail population grew to about 1.7 million by 1999, about one percent of the Ameri- can population. It is a "sad commentary on modern morality... that so many people must be jailed to bring crime down to more tolerable levels," Becker concluded, but insisted never-the-less, that crime reduction does not depend on improvement in morality. Crime rates decreased beginning in the 1980s despite widening in- come inequality, further breakdown of families, and with "no obvi- ous recovery of morality."[51] Crime decreased because the probabil- ity of conviction and imprisonment had increased.

Changes in the benefits and costs also explains, Becker suggested, why certain individuals or groups are more likely to commit crimes than others. In every society, the poor and less-educated are more likely to commit violent crimes and the affluent and more-educated more likely to commit embezzlement, fraud and white-collar crimes. This is so, he reasoned, because the poor have more to gain from crime because they have less to gain from working at a legal job. Teenagers commit more crime than adults for the same reason — legal work affords lower earnings and fewer opportunities for them than it does for adults. Teenage crime is also high because the first crime is "free," there is essentially no punishment for juveniles who commit their first offense. In addition to the law-and-order approach then, more resources should be devoted to improving the legal opportunities for teenagers, the poor, and other groups likely to turn to crime otherwise. Sensible fiscal policies, which help keep unemployment down, will also help reduce crime among unemployed groups.[52]

Rational Choice Theory. Becker's economic analyses contributed to additional work by economists and rational choice theorists. *Rational choice* theory zeroes in on the reasoning aspect of cost-benefit calculation. If all people made decisions with the careful logic of economics professors, predicting their choices could be done with a great deal of certainty. Up to a point, that is, because even pure rationality cannot find the optimal solution to every situation. Jean Buridan, a French philosopher, pointed this out early on. Buridan told a story about a donkey standing between two equal stacks of hay. The donkey starved to death because it could not decide which was the better of the two. Buridan invented the table to illustrate that action implies choice and that choice implies responsibility. But Buridan's donkey also illustrates that even the most careful cost-benefit analysis has its breaking point. People are quite capable of not making the optimal choice which makes prediction difficult. It also makes altering the cost-benefit ratio by means of public policy less certain because people, whether individuals or groups, make bad choices because they have been habituated to make bad choices.[53]

Ronald Clarke and Derek Cornish developed rational choice theory beginning in the 1970s. At the time, Clarke worked as a researcher within the Research and Planning Unit of Britain's Home Office. When Clarke joined the Research and Planning Unit in 1973, it was located at Romney House on Marsham Street, not far from Scotland Yard. Cornish and Clarke replaced Becker's view of rationality with *partial rationality;* that there are limits or constraints on rationality. While people engage cost-benefit calculation, they do not always arrive at the optimal solution because they lack information, adhere to moral values, follow cultural habits, and cling to other irrationalities. Unlike Buridan's donkey, people make irrational choices rather than starve. The premise of rational choice theory is that "offenders seek to benefit themselves by their criminal behavior; that this involves the making of decisions and of choices, however rudimentary on occasion these processes might be; and that these processes exhibit a measure of rationality, albeit constrained by limits of time and the availability of relevant information."[54]

While rational choice theorists begin with choice they focus on the factors that constrain that choice. Becker's analysis viewed criminals as rational decision-makers whose behavior is best-understood as an optimal response to the incentives set by government via expenditures on law enforcement and corrections. In his equation, he specified that crime was a function of the probability of conviction, punishment if convicted, potential income gain, and the willingness to break the law. From the rational choice point of view, the calculation is more complicated. The benefits of crime are both monetary and non-monetary. The costs are formal—arrest, conviction, and so on—and informal—including parental disapproval, guilt, and other elements. Cornish and Clarke referred to the aggregate of opportunities, costs, and benefits as *choice-structuring properties,* that is "the characteristics of offenses which render them differentially attractive to particular individuals or subgroups (or to the same individuals and groups at different times)."[55]

Cornish and Clarke advised criminologists to explain particular types of crime rather than attempt a grand theory for all crimes together. They distinguished between "criminal involvement" and "criminal events." Becker's economic analyses made criminal choice analogous to work, a job that a person chooses to do. Cornish and Clarke pointed out that the choice to pursue crime as a vocation is a different matter than whether to commit a specific criminal act. Most theories, they point out, deal with the choice to become involved in crime. They emphasize rational calculation at the point of thinking about committing a particular crime. Choice at this level has to do with the individual's immediate situation.

After Clarke became head of the Research and Planning Unit, researchers carried out a series of studies that have become known as situational crime prevention. Generally, they collected basic information about very specific crime problems, such as vandalism against public telephones and fights at pubs after closing. Rather than attempt to change behavior through public policy, they focused on the immediate situation. They introduced simple, practical means of altering the balance of effort, risks and rewards such as architectural design, locks, and improving visibility. This led to sixteen strategies for situational crime prevention.[56]

Situational crime prevention focuses on reducing the opportunity to commit crime. Situational crime prevention holds that people are likely to choose crime when the balance of effort, risks and rewards amount to a positive inducement. Criminal acts are less likely to occur when the act generates less reward, produces guilt, requires significant effort, or creates on-the-spot risk. Reward can be reduced by removing the target altogether, such as replacing cash-box operations with a credit-card reader, pay-in-advance policy, or other scheme. Guilt can be increased by setting rules and making it easy to follow them, such as by adequately staffing checkout lanes, and by training store employees to greet each customer with a polite "May I help you?" while making eye contact. Effort can be increased by target hardening, that is, by adding locks and other physical security devices that require extra time and effort to tackle. The risk of detection can be increased by exposing the area to surveillance by passers-by, other customers, and store employees.[57]

ROUTINE ACTIVITIES THEORY. While Clarke and the British Home office pursued a rational choice theory approach to crime prevention, American criminologists worked on *routine activities* theory, a complementary approach. Routine activities theory converges with rational choice theory at the point of opportunity, that is, by looking at whether a criminal event occurs as a function of opportunity. In 1978, Michael Hindelang, Michael Gottfredson, and James Garofalo, published *Victims of Personal Crime*. Their ideas made use of the National Crime Survey, or National Crime Victimization Survey as it is now known. Beginning in 1973, the Bureau of Justice Statistics has sponsored an annual survey of 50,000 households. The survey provides a national victimization rate for a number of household and personal crimes by asking people whether they have been victimized during the previous six months. The authors looked at the survey information for insight into multiple victimization, at that portion of society victimized more than once.

Hindelang, Gottfredson and Garofalo proposed that the chance of being victimized more than once was a function of *lifestyle*, the patterned ways in which people distribute their time and energies across a range of activities. Two researchers, using data from the British Crime Survey, found that multiple victims had two lifestyle indicators in common that made victimization more likely: the number of weekend nights out and the frequency of alcohol use.[58] Another researcher, using information from the American General Social Survey, found that smokers had higher risk of being assaulted. About 32 percent of smokers reported that they had been assaulted compared to 17 percent of non-smokers.[59]

Lifestyle theory does not view bar-hopping or smoking as causes of crime in any simple cause-and-effect sense. Rather, the lifestyle approach shows how the lifestyle of potential victims structures criminal opportunity. Essentially, the more time people spend with non-family members in public places, particularly at night, the greater their exposure to criminal activity. Following certain lifestyles makes people more likely to frequent public places. The interactions people maintain tend to be with those who share the same lifestyle and the probability of being victimized increases according to the extent to which victims and offenders share the same lifestyle. Or, as Marcus Felson, a criminologist at Rutgers University, put it: "Although the fox finds each hare one by one, the fox population varies with the hare population on which it feeds."[60]

Felson, along with Lawrence Cohen, identified three elements for a crime to occur. First, there had to be a *motivated offender*, someone willing to break the law to attain peer approval, get excitement, attain sexual gratification or domination of others. Second, there had to be a *target*, cash or something worth taking; some person to assault, rape, rob, or murder. Third, there had to be opportunity. The absence of anything or anyone that would otherwise prevent the crime from occurring they called *capable guardianship*. They set out to understand how illegal activities feed off various aspects of everyday life. Cohen and Felson analyzed crime rates in the United States during the second half of the twentieth century. They were particularly interested in why crime rates had increased since the

Second World War. Many explanations for crime did not seem to fit the American experience during this period. If poverty, unemployment, and urban development explain crime rates, then crime should have decreased. But just the opposite had occurred: crime increased during a time of plenty. They conceptualized that changes in the lifestyles of many Americans had changed and these changes made them more vulnerable to household crimes.

The end of the war and America's economic boom led to an increase in the number of targets. Homes included electronic and other consumer items that had not existed prior to the war, including small television sets, radios, and other items. Technological improvements made these items easier to steal—carrying off a television in the 1950s, with its vacuum tubes encased in an oak cabinet, required two people and a truck. At the same time, the level of capable guardianship decreased. The war years took women out of the home during the days for war-related work in the factories and they have stayed in the workplace ever since. The economic boom of the post-war years, coupled with two-wage earners, allowed families to take longer vacations. Whole neighborhoods emptied during the day; some houses sat empty for weeks at a time as families journeyed in their station wagons for vacation destinations farther and farther away. Crime increased as a function of shifts in the *routine activities* of people, the lifestyle patterns that influence the risk of exposure at times, places, and contact with those likely to commit crimes.[61]

THE GENERAL THEORY OF CRIME. Another extension of classical theory appeared in 1990; *A General Theory of Crime*, by Michael Gottfredson and Travis Hirschi. Hirschi, a sociologist at the University of Arizona, published his first book in the 1960s, *Causes of Delinquency*, and it became the most popular sociological theory of crime.[62] It took Hirschi to the top of the American Society of Criminology and helped earn for him in 1986 the Edwin H. Sutherland award.

Gottfredson and Hirschi took the same starting point as Bentham, then fused the economic approach, rational choice, and lifestyle theories into their "general theory" of criminal conduct. Crime is a matter of choice, or rather, it reflects *low self-control*. "Nearly all crimes are mundane, simple, trivial, easy acts aimed at satisfying the desires of the moment, as are many other acts of little concern to criminal law." Low self-control is the common element in crime and social problems. Since crime involves pursuit of immediate pleasure, persons with low self-control pursue other immediate pleasures that are not criminal. The same persons likely to break the law are those likely to engage in acts leading to social problems—out-of-marriage pregnancies, alcohol abuse, car crashes, unstable marriages, unemployment. Persons with low self-control engage in a variety of irresponsible or reckless acts, such as illicit sex, smoking, drinking, gambling, aggressive driving, as well as crime. Criminals do not enjoy healthy lifestyles, they do not exercise regularly and eat low-fat foods. Rather, they live fast and die young.

Gottfredson's and Hirschi's view of self-control has to do with "the thinking of ordinary people." While psychologists have researched the concept of the willingness to delay gratification as a personality construct, Gottfredson and Hirschi insist that there is no personality trait predisposing people toward crime.[63] Specifically, Gottfredson and Hirschi describe six aspects of crime. (1) Criminal acts provide immediate gratification of desires; persons with self-control delay gratification. (2) Criminal acts provide easy or simple gratification of desires—money without work, sex without courtship, revenge without court delay. (3) Criminal acts are exciting, risky, or thrilling. They involve stealth, danger, deception and power. (4) Crimes provide few or meager long-term benefits. In fact, the pursuit of crime interferes with commitments to job, marriages, family and friends; those with low self-control have irregular employment and unstable relationships. (5) Crime requires little skill or planning. The cognitive and manual skills required are minimal. (6) Crimes result in pain or discomfort for the victim. Persons with low self-control tend to be indifferent, self-centered and insensitive to the needs of others although not necessarily antisocial.

Unlike Beccaria and Becker, however, they did not look to government as the primary means of structuring choice. Some persons seem to be born with more self-control than others, but the major difference between criminals and non-criminals has to do with the amount of self-discipline that comes about by means of proper parenting. Self-control must be taught; it requires careful, deliberate efforts to monitor children's behavior, recognize wrongful behavior, and punish that wrongful behavior. Two-parent households with one or two children have more success instilling self-control than households with three or more children and single-parent households who simply have less time for supervision. The law cannot make people behave. Children who grow up in households where self-discipline is not taught, or where parents demonstrate their own lack of self-control by engaging in crime, are unlikely to be changed by the criminal justice system. The legal response falls into the category of too little, too late. Short of responsible parenting, schools have the best chance of teaching self-control.

The Limits of Abstract Reason

The dream of criminologists, from the eighteenth century founders to the present, has been to devise a better theory, and from that theory, to make reforms. Some would make a few adjustments, some overhaul the system, and some would overhaul society and the system along with it. The Enlightenment relied on *rationalism*, which began in the sixteenth century in the attempt to formulate a new method of inquiry derived from reason. Reason represented to the rationalists a hidden spring from which they could drink knowledge. They proposed to derive principles for the proper organization of society from reason alone. The superiority of rationalism over tradition and superstition came from the appearance of being self-contained, of containing a set of principles independent of any historical occurrence.[64] Beccaria's book represented a crib to the administration of justice, a how-to manual of jurisprudence for rulers who had decided to abandon tradition. T.S. Eliot had rationalists, or somebody like them, in mind when he wrote: "They constantly try to escape, from the darkness outside and within, by dreaming of systems so perfect that no one will need to be good."[65]

Classical thinking has accomplished a great deal in criminology. It is hard to imagine criminal justice without the ideas of due process, equal justice, and the rule of law. But the question is whether it is possible to generate a fool-proof system of justice derived from reason alone; whether, in jettisoning all reference to history, the classicists did not make a mistake. The Enlightenment philosophers so important to Beccaria's work, and their ideas of "natural rights" and "social contract," presuppose the very ideas that are said to generate them. Rather than draw on history, they based their claims on abstract ideals of nature and agreements made at the genesis of civilization. As soon as the attempt is made to see these ideas as historic events, rather than abstract ideals, the rationalist project begins to unravel. In its historical context, Beccaria's system of justice certainly represents an improvement over the system that carried out the execution of Damiens in 1757. But the progress made by the French Declaration of the Rights of Man must be measured against the terror of the Revolution that produced it. Before it was over, more than 40,000 people lost their lives, most of them peasants.

Consider the early history of the United States. The founders came to "dissolve the political bands" which had connected them with the British, and start over with laws "written in the whole volume of human nature." John Jay claimed in 1777: "The Americans are the first people whom Heaven has favored with an opportunity of deliberating upon, and choosing the form of government under which they could live. All other constitutions have derived their existence from violence or accidental circumstances, and are therefore probably more distant from their perfection...."[66] The founding documents of the United States government, the Declaration of Independence and the United States Constitution, represent the sacred documents of rationalism. At the constitutional convention of 1787, the delegates sent to Independence Hall in Philadelphia drafted the organic law for the Republic, and more. They crafted the social contract for a new nation, the agreement between individual and society authorizing the government to enforce its laws.

What the founders said they were doing, and what they actually did, are two different things, however. They said they were after a national government founded on inalienable rights and dedicated to the principles of due process and equal justice under law. The citizens of the new nation, they said, were entitled to no less by virtue of being human. But they actually produced a different sort of government with a very limited view of citizenship. The founding fathers were, after all, fathers—all men of property. No women signed the documents, nor did any Indian or Black person. Nor did any member of these groups cast a vote for ratification in any state legislature, or for that matter, neither did any cast a vote for any legislator who did cast a vote. The founders' guarantee of rights extended only to citizens, and they did not consider Americans Indians, Black people, women and others to be citizens. The constitution they drew up preserved slavery. This difference between the airy ideals of equality and the reality of slavery within the American founding has been expressed as that of a *Herrenvolk* democracy, a society in which citizens have equal standing and "citizen" is understood to mean White men of property, and others are understood to be permanent aliens or outsiders.[67]

If the Constitution represents a social contract, this omission represents more than a technicality. Locke had described the lack of a common judge in the state of nature as the need for government. People, guided by reason, freely came together to form a government. Because they freely consented to join with others, the government that resulted derived from the consent of the people. By consenting to join with others in the formation of civil society, each citizen is obligated to obey the laws of the government. Neither of these groups had a say in the formulation of the rights and responsibilities provided for by the contract. None of these groups voluntarily agreed to anything. Not only were they not invited, they were deliberately and forcefully denied the equal protection of the laws in courts of the United States. The fact that only some Americans were represented at the founding raises an inescapable question about what obligation accrues to those who were not a party to the original agreement. In what sense are African Americans, for example, obligated to abide by laws derived from a social contract to which they were not a party?[68]

Answering this question provides a useful means of understanding the limits of deriving a concept of justice from abstract reason. One answer, expressed by Harvard philosopher John Rawls, attempts to answer the historical predicament of *Herrenvolk* democracy with reference to abstract reason. It makes no difference that no African American participated in America's original position because African Americans would have agreed to the principles in the document had they been invited. The social contract represents for Rawls the rational choice of rational actors in the original position. The veil of ignorance would exclude knowledge of one's class position and social status, so that the principles found in the social contract would appeal to all, regardless of race. Rawls believes that the principles African Americans would adopt would have been the same principles as any other of the rational actors, because no one would want to risk being placed in a disadvantaged position when the veil is removed. Rawls also believes that as rational actors, no one behind the veil of ignorance would choose a set of principles that would provide for their own oppression.[69]

But the question cannot be disposed of so easily. If the government that resulted from the original position without African-American participants had resulted in equal justice for African Americans, then it might be reasonable to conclude that African Americans would have agreed to it had they been there. The fact that the government that resulted in their absence meant the extension of slavery for another hundred years makes it harder to accept that the exclusion of African Americans made no difference.[70] Given the historic exclusion of Black people and the lack of pure procedural justice, Rawls suggests that civil disobedience is justified. Civil disobedience, Rawls explains, "addresses the sense of justice of the majority of the community and declares that in one's considered opinion the principles of social cooperation among free and equal men are not being respected."[71] The civil disobedience argument, in acknowledging that the government formed by means of social contract might not express justice, acknowledges that historical reality may prove different from the organization envisioned in the abstract principles. It provides a better argument for why African Americans ought to seek to replace the government that does not respect the principles of justice rather than seek to repair it. It seems hard to justify why the grievances outlined in the Declaration of Independence provide better grounds for revolution than the gross abuse of justice that occurred during the slavery period.

Rawls's discussion of civil disobedience moves in the direction of American history and a second answer. This response recognizes that while that while African Americans were excluded from the original agreement, they have since been grafted in by the process of amendment and subsequent legislation. The Fourteenth Amendment, ratified in 1868 in the wake of the Civil War, extended citizenship to African Americans. The United States Supreme Court's decision in *Brown v. Board of Education* (1954) ended legal segregation. The Voting Rights Act of 1964 extended the right to vote. No one expressed this answer better than Texas Congresswoman Barbara Jordan, who spoke in July, 1974, during the House Judiciary Committee's proceedings to impeach Richard M. Nixon:

'We the people' is a very eloquent beginning. When the Constitution of the United States was completed on the seventh of September 1786, I was not included in that 'We the People.' I felt for many years that somehow George Washington and Alexander Hamilton just left me out by mistake. But through the process of amendment, interpretation, and court decision, I have finally been included in "We the people."

Today, I am an inquisitor. I believe hyperbole would not be fictional and would not overstate the solemnness that I feel right now. My faith in the Constitution is whole, it is complete, it is total. I am not going to sit here and be an idle spectator to the diminution, the subversion, the destruction of the Constitution."[72]

She then went on to explain the rule of law and a president who had put himself above the rule of law.

Essentially, Jordan's perspective relies on positive law, and the idea that people can make institutions for themselves that ensure liberty and justice for all. Jordan makes an eloquent statement about the expansion of citizenship within the American experience, but she invests too heavily in the rule of law. True, the process of amendment, legislation and court decision has meant wider recognition of citizens. But the same institution that began to dismantle segregation in the 1950s and 1960s had authorized legal segregation in the 1890s. The United States Supreme Court also approved of sterilization of the "feeble-minded," (mostly young African-American women) in the 1920s, and the internment of Japanese Americans based on ancestry during the 1940s. Jordan wanted to believe that the political current of the post-war years will continue to flow in the same direction. Yet the same history reveals that what the law gives, the law takes away.

A third answer can be found in the work of Alan Keyes. Keyes, a candidate in past two presidential elections, served as a representative to the United Nations during the Reagan Administration. Like Jordan, Keyes maintains that resolving the problem of founders' limited sense of rights at the founding requires an appreciation for history. But Keyes's answer takes a deeper view of history than Jordan's allows. Unlike Jordan, Keyes does not see how the question can ever be resolved with positive law alone, because making the question of rights subject to the consensus of opinion fails to provide a sure foundation. The only way to resolve the dilemma is to read the United States Constitution with the Declaration of Independence in mind. The Constitution expresses a compromise necessary for sealing the contract, a compromise recognizing "free persons" as persons and all others as "three-fifths" of a person. The

Declaration of Independence expresses a truth, "We hold these truths to be self-evident, that all men are created equal."

In order to ratify the constitution in 1787, with its recognition of slavery, the founders had to overlook what they said a few years earlier. And if the documents they created became the only recourse, it is difficult to see why later generations agreed to amend the original contract. The Declaration of Independence referenced a tradition of recognizing "transcendent justice;" a tradition present at the founding that existed through the Civil War and civil rights era. If there had been no respect for that tradition, there would have been no crisis of conscience, no war to end slavery. Justice cannot be held hostage to majority opinion. The justice on which the institutions of government derive their authority must reflect the sense that there is a higher law than an agreement between individuals expressed in a document; a higher law that informs the structure of government and the administration of justice by government.[73]

The question of obligation for persons not a party to the social contract only arises if the Constitution represents a contract. Oakeshott avoids referring the "founding" at all, refusing to acknowledge the existence of any abrupt historical changes. What appears to be constructed from abstract principles actually represents a reworking of some historical practice somewhere. Jefferson, Oakeshott contends, took his "inalienable rights" from Locke who had simply abridged the historic rights of the British in his *Second Treatise*.[74] Locke had taken rights accorded to British citizens as a matter of long tradition and made them the products of abstract reason. Oakeshott contends that no political philosophy can stand alone, completely removed from historical practice. The idea of the social contract can serve as a guide political action only if given some content to the aspects of social and political order that were eliminated in the first place.

Oakeshott counters Rawls's original position with an allegory of his own. In "The Tower of Babel," he tells his own version of the account from Genesis. Nimrod, following the death of his grandfather Noah, proposed to build a tower, a tower so high as to seal the gates of Heaven from releasing flood water ever again. Nimrod convinced the people of Babel to go along with him. They were an "underprivileged" people, "resentful on account of what was withheld than grateful for what was given," and began their work with enthusiasm. Slogans, including "Up with the Tower" and "Take the

Wait out of Wanting," began appearing on bumpers and refrigerator doors. Everyone either worked on the tower or for those who did. A new lifestyle emerged as did new political philosophies, oriented toward tower-building, in which words like "justice" acquired the pre-fix "social." Researchers reported statistics for every aspect of the work, the University of Babel initiated a "Tower Studies" major, and secondary schools recognized the faithful with the Tower Medal. Nimrod himself spent his days at the top of tower, and not long after the summit disappeared in the clouds, catastrophe struck. A rumor spread among the people of Babel that Nimrod—who by this time had become a shadowy figure anyway—intended to cut a deal personally with God and leave everyone else out. In their panic, they rushed the tower, filling it from top to bottom, and just as the last person set foot inside, the weight of humanity at the top forced the whole structure down. It entombed what had been the city of Babel.[75]

Oakeshott's allegory suggests an outcome very different than Rawls's. If the people of Babel had retained a sense of past history (particularly the part about what happened to Noah's generation), they would not have conceived such an ambition for themselves. They would not have imagined a life for themselves only in reference to their wants, but a life of reflection on past survivals. They would not have been so willing to believe a wild rumor. Historical understanding leads to skepticism about schemes promising unknown comforts. And, if they had revered their history, they would not have invested so much of their destiny in a sole leader and a government by his design.[76] Oakeshott avoids the temptation of imposing some new, yet-to-be-experienced design in favor of a social order that would permit endless adjustments. Oakeshott opts for a future without any plan or scheme, without any prescription for government other than it allow individuals to pursue their own ends and purposes.[77]

Conclusion

It is a mistake to see justice as accruing from some rational principles that can be written in a book. If that is the case, the principles of justice can be destroyed as easily as they are created. This is especially true when it comes to a better response to crime; the "human-itarian with the guillotine," as Edmund Burke, speaking of the Jacobins in Revolutionary France, put it. "Men who today snatch the worst criminals from the hands of justice tomorrow may approve the slaughter of whole classes."[78] This became clear particularly during the twentieth century, when some criminologists decided that they were not moralists, but scientists.

Chapter 3

The Anatomy of Crime

It is a common enough idea that evil things are ugly and good things beautiful. In his novel *Dracula*, Bram Stoker retold a tale from medieval folklore about a mysterious count from Transylvania. As the story unfolds, the true nature of the count, a corpse by day and an engaging personality after dark, is revealed. Others are fooled, but Mina Harker can see the evil, written into the count's skin and bones.[1] In the nineteenth century, the idea that the body might reveal something about the heart acquired a scientific basis. The rise of science led criminologists to apply the positive method to the understanding of crime, and they developed a branch of criminology known as biological positivism. As a system of thought, biological positivism asserts that human behavior can be understood using the methods of natural science and that the origins of human behavior are found within the human body itself.

The search for the anatomy of crime began with Cesare Lombroso, an Italian army surgeon who emphasized the importance of the skull, bone structure and other physical attributes. During the course of the twentieth century, as new technology provided more intrusive means of analysis, the search focused on the brain. At first, brain size and weight, then brain waves, and most recently, brain biochemistry. The first biological positivists did not concern themselves with the idea of a criminal type of person. Rather, they worried about the breeding of criminal types and the production of a criminal race. During the early twentieth century, criminal anthropology led to a number of social policies including identification, sterilization, and confinement of criminal types.

Although the current generation of biologistic criminologists rejects some of the scientific theories out of which the biologistic tradition grew, the significance of biological positivism is not the explanations of criminality, but the attempt to explain crime using science applied to the body. Part One describes Lombroso's criminal anthropology and the beginnings of biological positivism. Parts Two through Four explore the biologistic criminologists search for the origins of crime in the body, in the brain, and in heredity. Part Five discusses the legacy of criminal anthropology in the form of the eugenics campaigns in the United States and Germany. Part Six discusses biological positivism as a system of thought; it focuses on current interest a moral sense.

The Science of Criminology

It was the criminologists working from the perspective of biological positivism who invented the word "criminology." The term, introduced at a criminal anthropology conference in 1889, was meant to carve out of portion of the emerging human sciences specializing in the criminal type, or subspecies, of human being.[2] Criminology would be the scientific study of the human animal, to be distinguished from the speculative ideas of theology, philosophy, and law. Scientific discoveries in geology, biology, and anatomy offered criminologists the opportunity to understand human behavior. In France, Auguste Comte wrote about the new science of social physics in 1824, and established sociology as a branch of physiology devoted to the collective development of the human race. In Germany, Wilhelm Wundt set up the first laboratory for the study of physiological psychology at Leipzig in 1879, and established psychology as a laboratory science. And in Italy, Cesare Lombroso became a professor of legal medicine and public hygiene in 1876; he established criminology as the study of criminal behavior.

Cesare Lombroso, who had been trained in medicine, received his first appointment at the University of Turin in 1876, and in 1906, became the first professor of criminal anthropology. His primary work, *The Criminal Man*, first published in Italy in 1876, expressed the search for a criminal type of person. He achieved fame in the United States due to the efforts of his daughter, Gina Lombroso-Ferrero, who edited an English version of his book for publication in 1911. Lombroso founded a school of criminological theory on the idea that the worst criminals are of a different biological type or subspecies of human resembling an early stage in human evolution; the various theories of "born," "congenital," "incorrigible," and "instinctive" criminality are known as *criminal anthropology*.[3] John Wigmore offered Lombroso a position of visiting professor at the American Institute of Criminal Law and Criminology at Northwestern University for 1909–1910, but Lombroso declined due to illness.[4]

Lombroso's interest in crime began while working as a doctor for the Italian army. He noticed that those soldiers with tattoos seemed to violate military law more often. Later, while stationed with the army at Pavia, he received permission to examine mental patients in the hospital of St. Euphemia. He began trying to discover anatomical differences between criminals, lunatics, and normal people. His research did not proceed very well, until 1870 when he obtained the body of Vilella, an infamous serial murderer who had terrorized the province of Lombardy. While conducting the autopsy, Lombroso noticed an irregularly shaped skull, but a shape not unknown to him. When he realized where he had seen a skull shaped like Vilella's, he believed he had solved the mystery of habitual criminality.[5]

"At the sight of that skull," Lombroso later wrote, "I seemed to see all of the sudden ... the problem of the nature of the criminal — an atavistic being who reproduces in his person the ferocious instincts of the primitive humanity and the inferior animals."[6] Criminals were reversions to primitive, subhuman types of humans; they became that way through a process of *degeneration*, a pathological condition that reproduces the physical, psychological, and behavioral qualities of remote ancestors, including apes, snakes, and birds. While humankind's prehistoric past remained dormant in most people, it arises in some, leading to violence and vice. Degeneration produced a condition of *atavism*. Atavistic criminals had not fully-evolved but remained in an arrested state of evolutionary development.

The production of atavistic criminals represented an instance of *recapitulation*, an idea popular among nineteenth century scientists. The growth of a single individual within a species, they thought, mirrors the evolutionary development of the entire species. Ernst Haeckel, a German zoologist, had summarized the concept as "ontogeny recapitulates phylogeny." The dominant idea of nineteenth century science, it allowed scientists to reconstruct biological process from a single specimen.[7] Actually, the idea of atavism had been suggested by Darwin himself. In the *Descent of Man* (1871),

Darwin brought together information from medicine, linguistics, and anthropology to support his argument that all biological life ascended from a common origin. Morals became part of human societies because they had some sort of survival value. The tendency of humans to care for the sick and weak through social institutions resulted in perpetuation of less fit human types. Darwin speculated that the "black sheep" of families, those members who demonstrated antisocial behavior without apparent cause, were reversions to early, primitive human beings.

Lombroso hoped he had discovered the criminal species of human. Eventually, he came up with a four-fold typology: born criminal, passionate criminal, insane criminal, and occasional criminal. He subdivided the occasional criminal into four groups: pseudocriminal, criminaloid, habitual criminal and epileptoid. Gina Lombroso-Ferrero reported that born criminals—the atavistic degenerates—represented about one third of lawbreakers and committed the most serious crime. The other two-thirds committed less serious crimes and did not display the characteristics of atavists.[8] Lombroso's discovery pointed to physiology as the means to understand criminality, and established biological positivism as a major perspective. *Biological positivism* asserts that (1) the same methods used by scientists to study the natural world of rocks and plants and animals ought to be used to study people and that (2) the explanation for human behavior can be found in the body itself. Humans, their bodies and their behavior, should be subject to careful observation, to measuring, counting, and weighing. While it would be difficult to find a criminologist presently pursuing Lombroso's atavistic criminal concept, many agree with his borrowing from science to understand crime. Lombroso did not find the biological origins of criminal behavior, but the way he went about looking—using the methods of science—would generate the right answer.

While the technology has changed since Lombroso, biological positivism as a system of thought remains. Contemporary biologistic criminologists insist on the importance of both biological and social causes of criminal behavior. Biology is not all there is to the etiology of crime, but constitutional factors ranging from the organic level (genetics), to the cellular level (neurons), to the biochemical level (hormones), all shape human behavior. In this sense, the biologistic perspective remains "fundamentally at odds" with the "religio-legal perspective of the classical school."[9] "It is important not to generalize too quickly from one species to another," explains Kenneth Moyer, a psychologist at Carnegie-Mellon, "However, we now have good evidence that man, for all of his encephalization, has not escaped from the neural determinants of his aggressive behavior." For biologistic criminologists, the body represents a lodestar; a point on which to focus the understanding of social and psychological factors that lead to behavior.[10]

Lombroso, together with law professors Enrico Ferri and Raffaele Garofalo, formed the Italian positivist school of criminology. They established a research journal of criminal anthropology and took on all challengers at the quadrennial international conference on criminal anthropology. Ferri insisted that criminality was the product of social milieu as well as inherited characteristics, not a matter of volition or individual choice. As criminology advanced, the accumulation of knowledge about human behavior would enable the formulation of natural laws of human society, and culminate historically in the social phase in which the ancient ideal of legal justice would be replaced by physical, biological and social sanctions.[11]

Enrico Ferri followed Lombroso's four-fold scheme in his study of homicide, and later, proposed another two: habitual criminal and involuntary criminal. Ferri's habitual criminal engaged in crime because of a criminogenic social environment. The involuntary criminal represented a class of pseudo-criminals who did not possess the heredity, mental, or social milieu of the other types.[12] Garofalo created four categories of criminals: murderers, violent criminals, criminals without probity (respect for property rights), and lascivious criminals. Garofalo rejected the legal formulation of crime, arguing that if crime is to be studied scientifically, it could not be limited to the definition supplied by legislatures. In his *Criminology* (1885), he tried to formulate a universal definition of crime, "the natural crime," based on the moral sentiments of society. Moral sentiments appear in all civilized societies, which represent the average moral sense of the community. Murderers and violent criminals, the true criminals, lack basic moral or altruistic sensibilities due to the arrested state of development.[13]

Garofalo and Ferri advocated that traditional legal notions of responsibility, such as intention, be abolished in favor of strict liability. Garofalo advocated a "rational system of punishment" whereby the penalty would be inflicted in proportion to the risk of future danger rather than the intentionality. In his 1877 tract *The Denial of Free Will and the Theory of Imputability*, Ferri viewed moral culpability as an "impossible basis for defense of society" and argued that it must be replaced by a concept of social accountability. As a school, the Italian positivists aimed to distinguish their scientific approach from the philosophical approach of Becarria and the classicists. "The illusion of free human will leads to the assumption that one can choose freely between vice and virtue," Ferri argued, "This is what constitutes the different and opposite principles of the positive and classical schools of criminology."[14] Benito Mussolini, fascist dictator of Italy, enjoyed Ferri's work so much that he asked him to draft a new criminal code. But the Italian Chamber of Deputies adhered to classicist principles and rejected the Ferri draft of 1921.[15]

Contemporary biological positivism has retreated from Ferri's determinism. The current versions of biological determinism are framed around an understanding of criminogenic factors and biological predispositions. While there is no biological cause for criminal violence within particular specimens of the human animal per se, irregular functioning of biological processes endow individuals with personality characteristics and behavioral tendencies that increase their risk for antisocial behavior, some of which may be against the law. Diana Fishbein, a professor at the University of Maryland, describes a softer version of determinism she calls *conditional freewill*. Conditional freewill allows for human choice within sets of "decision limiting factors" including current circumstances, learning experiences, physiological abilities and genetic predispositions. These factors interact internally (physically) and externally (environmentally) to determine a final action which can be predicted as a matter of probability, but not specifically.[16]

Because contemporary biologistic criminologists want to study criminal behavior as something apart from the law, they are reluctant to explain what a concept such as conditional freewill means in a courtroom. Fishbein's formulation is, however, analogous to the legal doctrine of diminished responsibility or partial capacity. *Diminished responsibility* refers to a legal standard invented by the California Supreme Court that can be thought of as a psychological state halfway between insanity and rationality. The court applied the doctrine in a series of cases beginning in 1949. Although it has since been abolished by the California legislature, the doctrine persists in other states.[17]

The Criminal Body

Lombroso brought the prestige of science to the age-old art of judging by appearances. His work offered a scientific approach to a problem familiar to non-scientists, a provocative combination. Sir Arthur Conan Doyle incorporated criminal anthropology in his 1902 Sherlock Holmes mystery *The Hound of the Baskervilles*. Dr. Mortimer, "the man of science, the specialist in crime," appears in the first chapter. Mortimer's credentials include scientific papers on atavism and reversion. He is so confident that he refers to Mr. Holmes as "the second highest expert in Europe," then adds, after seeing Holmes's reaction, "But as a man of practical affairs it is acknowledged that you stand alone."

Lombroso taught that the criminal type of human displayed physical signs of atavism he called *stigmata*. The stigmata included long arms, thin beard, fewer lines in the palm of the hand, and a gap between the big toe and the other four (the "prehensile foot"). The criminal type had a thin nose with flared nostrils, heavy eyebrows that met above the bridge of the nose, and thin ears that came to a point at the top. In addition to these primitive bodily characteristics, atavists distinguished themselves through sensory peculiarities (exceptional strength, acute agility, insensitivity to pain), the lack of a moral sense (absence of remorse, cruelty, penchant for gambling), and a preference for tattoos and slang expression.[18] (When Holmes finally captures the villain, he appears as "a throwback...both physical and spiritual.")

Later researchers followed-up the criminal-body theme. In 1913, Charles Goring published his book *The English Convict*. Goring explored the physical resemblance among fathers and sons, between brothers, and across prisoner populations. Although Goring meant to refute Lombroso, who he regarded as a "traitor to science" that had produced nothing but "self-evident confusion," he himself attributed criminality to inherited "defective intelligence."[19] Goring teamed up with Karl Pearson, the Francis Galton Professor of Eugenics at the University of London, to carry out statistical tests of Lombroso. Goring and Pearson measured the features of 3,000 criminals and compared the results with measurements of college students and soldiers. They found no differences in the physiognomies of criminals and non-criminals. Pearson created the statistics to measure Goring's hypothesis about similarities among fathers and sons. He created the correlation coefficient, or Pearson's product-moment correlation coefficient, and the chi-square or goodness of fit test that have been employed by statisticians ever since.

In the 1930s, Earnest A. Hooton, a Harvard anthropologist, carried out a massive study in criminal anthropology. Hooton measured 14,000 prisoners and compared them to 3,000 non-criminals to provide statistical evidence of Lombroso's stigmata. Hooton insisted that differences in physical type, of racial, family, or individual origin, influence the choice of offense. These constitutional factors, along with social influences, shaped the weaker physical types or as Hooton put it: "Crime is the resultant of the impact of the environment upon low grade human organisms." His three volumes are filled with statistical tables and cartoon-like drawings to show how one group of criminals is of a different physical type than another. Murderers and robbers, Hooton found, were tall and thin, and likely to commit financial crimes of forgery and fraud, while burglars were short, heavy and more likely to commit assault, rape and other sexual crimes. Neither Hooton's statistical tables, nor the "nasty little human figures" he drew to illustrate his work, received scholarly attention from other criminologists, who noted that Hooton offered suspect data to support a dubious political philosophy.[20]

Perhaps the most well-known study of the criminal body in the United States was conducted by William H. Sheldon. Sheldon, a University of Wisconsin psychologist, came up with *somatotyping* in 1940. Sheldon believed that the body was the source of consciousness and behavior. Religion, for example, was made possible by the evolution of the large frontal lobes of the human brain which allowed for conceptions of past and future. Sheldon viewed body physique as determinant of personality and behavior. Using photographs of nude men, collected by arrangement with the student health departments at five universities, Sheldon identified three primary body structures: endomorph (fat, weak), mesomorph (strong, muscular), ectomorph (thin, frail). He developed an inventory of personality traits to distinguish three basic personality types: viscerotonia (relaxed, outgoing, sensual), somatotonia (vigorous, athletic, active), and cerebrotonia (restrained, inhibited, secretive). Matching body types with personality types, Sheldon felt he had shown that endomorphs were viscerotonic, mesomorphs somatonic and ectomorphs cerebrotonic. Somatotyping 200 youth in a reformatory, Sheldon claimed to find that delinquent types tended to be mesomorphic and somatotonic. Biology, according to Sheldon, was destiny.[21]

Skin has also been the subject of biocriminological research. Lombroso could only guess about the meaning to tattoos. He reasoned that any man who would subject himself to the pain of such a procedure had to possess less sensitivity to pain in general, and greater resemblance to primitive humans in particular. Along with one of his students, Lombroso adapted the plethysmograph, a device for measuring changes in the volume of a limb, to test his theory. The device produced a continuous record of pulse and blood pressure changes.[22] But not until the invention of the galvanometer could Lombroso's idea be tested. The galvanometer measured the amount of electric activity passing between electrodes placed at two points on the skin. The machine's inventor found that the amount of current varied with mental activity due to the influence of sweat glands. The Galvanic Skin Response or electrodermal response provides the basic technology used by the polygraph machine, which appeared in 1921.[23]

The galvanometer allowed researchers to look for the link between *skin conductance* and criminality. Skin conductance researchers attach electrodes to the fingertips to measure skin resistance to electricity; resistance is associated with sweating, which is associated with stress and emotional arousal. Emotional underarousal is thought by some criminologists to be an underlying cause of criminal behavior. The idea is that this underarousal translates into a lack of fear, which leads to taking greater risks and more dangerous activities, which include acts of crime and aggression. Several researchers since 1978 have looked for differences in skin conductance among populations of psychopathic gamblers, criminals, psychopaths, and conduct-disordered adolescents, but the differences have been slight.[24] Most biologistic criminologists have left the search for the origins of criminality in bones, bodies, and skin and moved on to the brain.

The Criminal Brain

In searching Vilella's head for the origins of criminal behavior, Lombroso followed clues of the natural science known to him, including phrenology and craniometry. As techniques for brain research developed in the twentieth century, biological positivists have looked past the head to the functioning of the most specialized neurological organ within the head. Technology for brain imaging has made it possible to study living human brains, something Lombroso could never have done relying on autopsy and dissection as he did.

Phrenology has been remembered as an effort to determine character from bumps on the head, but it really had to do with the brain. Franz Joseph Gall, a German medical doctor, was convinced that the brain was the center of thought. Gall measured brains for evidence of the "destructiveness organ," which a number of researchers believed to be associated with violence, particularly murder. He measured the cranium because it was easier to measure than the cortex, and because he recognized that the skull precisely covered the cortex, he surmised that the shape of the skull provided a roadmap to brain activity. Gall identified thirty-seven organs or brain faculties; his colleague, Johann Gaspar Spurzheim, found eleven more.[25]

Together they founded *phrenology*, the belief that the contours of the head indicated a person's character. Phrenology spread to the United States after Spurzheim's visit in 1832. Phrenology parlors opened from coast to coast and phrenologists crisscrossed the country on lecture tours. Phrenological societies organized in major cities and claimed many distinguished members. John Q. Adams and John C. Calhoun joined the Phrenological Association of Washington, DC; other friends of phrenologists included Martin Van Buren, Nicholas Biddle, and Noah Webster.[26] In myth, Doyle's Dr. Mortimer could see Sherlock Holmes's genius immediately; he compliments Holmes for his "dolichocephalic skull" and "well-marked supra-orbital development." In reality, phrenological criminologists carried out extensive investigations. An investigation at Eastern State Penitentiary in Philadelphia concluded that 17.3 percent of prisoners between 1856 and 1865 possessed highly-developed destructiveness faculties.[27]

While the phrenologists measured heads, several French anatomists carried out experiments on the brain itself. They found a connection between particular portions of brain tissues and bodily functions. Using pigeons as guinea pigs, one researcher demonstrated that removing various portions of the brain interfered with basic senses and coordination.[28] Paul Broca, a French surgeon, became the first to demonstrate this connection within the human brain. Broca had a patient that functioned normally except that he could not talk. When the man died in 1861, Broca examined the man's brain and found a lesion in a portion of it. Broca determined that the center for speech was located in the left side of the cerebral hemisphere of the brain, later known as "Broca's area." Broca, who founded the Anthropological Society of Paris in 1859, had provided the first anatomical proof of localized brain function. While Gall did not offer a determinist argument, but rather said that a person's will or spirit determined behavior, Broca confidently pursued a straightforward biological determinism.[29]

Broca advanced *craniometry*, the practice of judging various mental capacities by the size of localized brain areas. Generally, the larger the brain, the greater the intelligence. Broca and his students made careful measurements of brain capacity to confirm the craniometrists' belief that the brain is larger in men than in women, in men of eminence than mediocre men, and in superior than inferior races.[30] Craniometrists dissected the brains of famous people, including Walt Whitman, Rudolf Wagner, Georges Cuvier, and Ivan Turgenev. When Lombroso died in 1909, his body was taken to the University of Turin where, as he requested, an autopsy was done and his brain preserved in the Institute of Anatomy.[31] Craniometrists also measured the brains of criminals. When Broca found that, contrary to expectation, criminal brains averaged larger than normal brains, he attributed this to disease. He also speculated that death by hanging tended to engorge the brain, leading to faulty measurement. One of his students published a study of the brains of 119 assassins, murderers and thieves. Again, the findings confounded Broca's general theory: the average weight exceeded honest men, and several criminals had large enough brains to meet the craniometrists criterion for genius. Broca's student, who had learned to reason like a craniometrist, decided that too much of a good thing is bad for some people—it produces criminal genius.[32]

Craniometry has persisted in one form or another. When Albert Einstein died at Princeton Hospital in 1955, his body was cremated, the ashes scattered. The hospital's pathologist kept the brain, however, in the interest of science. When he put it on a scale, he found that genius had been contained in a physical organ no weightier than the average person's. A mediocre two pounds, twelve ounces. But he placed the famous brain in a jar of formaldehyde, and for the next three decades, it yielded microscopic sections and photographic slides for each new research technique. Loyal craniometrists have measured the density surrounding blood vessels, the percentage of glial cells, and the branching of neuron fibers. By the 1980s, when only a few shreds remained, all the analyses proved inconclusive (although one researcher claims to have conclusive proof of excessive branching in the parietal sector of Broadmann area 39).[33]

Most brain scientists have moved on from external features to the inner workings. In 1929, a German neurologist reported finding "brain waves" in human beings after attaching two electrodes to the surface of the skull. The clearest of these, which measured about ten oscillations per second, he called "alpha waves." A few years later, a Swiss neurologist perfected the technique by inserting tiny electrodes into brain tissue and producing a weak electric current. In 1952, a team of researchers at Yale University carried out more extensive experiments using electric stimulation of the brain. They inserted tiny electrodes throughout the brain, sent current into the tissue, and generated emotions. Subjects reported feeling fear, anger, sadness, and so on, depending on the location of the electrode. This work led to development of the electroencephalogram or EEG.[34]

As early as the 1940s, reports began to appear of EEG abnormality within criminals. There are a number of studies showing diffuse or slow brain wave activity in populations of psychiatric prisoners, military prisoners, convicted murderers, psychopathic criminals, and aggressive epileptics. Other studies have found no significant differences between these populations and normal populations. The confusion has been explained by methodological problems including inconsistent duration of the recording, small numbers of electrodes, failure to control for conditions such as sleep, and the selection of research subjects. The larger issue surrounding this research, however, has to do with defining what is meant by "EEG abnormality." Do a certain percentage of convicted criminals display abnormal brain wave activity, or is slow, diffuse brain wave activity "abnormal" because it is associated with the brains of convicted criminals?[35]

About 1900, physiologists had started to report findings about the endocrine glands. These glands made secretions within the body, unlike tear, salivary, and sweat glands that secreted fluids near the body's surface. In 1915, a Harvard physiologist found that the adrenal glands, located near the kidneys, secreted a substance into the blood. The substance—hormone—influenced blood pressure.

Later researchers traced hormone secretion to adrenal glands near the thyroid, pituitary, and pancreas that had to do with growth, blood sugar, sexual characteristics, and other bodily processes. One kind of hormone, androgens, had to do with sexual characteristics, and the most abundant androgen in the body, testosterone, appeared to influence behavior.[36]

Biologistic criminologists have speculated that testosterone sparks aggressive behavior in men. Sexual arousal and aggression results in elevations of male androgen blood levels. They have hypothesized that use of synthetic androgens (steroids) contributes to violence, particularly sexual aggression.[37] The speculation that testosterone influences aggressive behavior in men is also related to use of a synthetic chemical compound used to treat sex offenders that results in "chemical castration." Depo-Provera is the trade name for medoyxprogesterone acetate, a synthetic chemical that suppresses the production of testosterone. The drug has been approved by several courts as a treatment for sex offenders. The goal of the treatment is to lower the level of testosterone in men to that found in women, with the aim of diminished sexual desire. A study of 21 individuals receiving weekly doses reported positive results at controlling sexual behavior. Sexual behavior, and even impregnation, are possible during treatment never-the-less, and the drug appears to be most effective when the patient volunteers for treatment and a "sexually consenting pair-bonded partner is available."[38]

Other biologistic criminologists interested in brain biochemistry have investigated links between premenstrual syndrome (PMS) and criminality among women. Lombroso and Lombroso-Ferraro reported in 1894 that among eighty women arrested for resistance to public officials, 71 were menstruating at the time of the offense. In 1971, two researchers surveyed 45 women at the North Carolina Correctional Center for Women about their menstrual cycles. When they reviewed prison officers' behavioral reports, they found that 41 percent of aggressive acts occurred during the premenstrual and menstrual phases of the cycle.[39]

Other brain research centers on brain neurochemistry. Brain neurochemistry has to do with the nervous system, and particularly the electrical impulses within the brain that trigger nerves and muscles. Nerves carry messages from the brain to muscles through neurons, the cells of the central nervous system. The electrical impulse jumps gaps between neurons, called synapses, via chemicals stored in neurons, called *neurotransmitters*. Neurologists have identified several neurotransmitters, such as dopamine, norepinephrine, and serotonin. Biological positivists have searched for links between these neurotransmitters and aggression. There have been several reports about a correlation between serotonin and aggressive behavior.[40]

The Criminal Race

The most volatile part of the born criminal idea was not that there were biological throw-backs walking the streets, or even that some of these could not be readily recognized but were criminals beneath the skin. The most alarming part had to do with the prospect of a whole generation of criminals. The idea that innate criminality was not randomly distributed within the human population, but could be inherited, raised the very real possibility that criminality could breed on its own. Charles R. Henderson, who introduced Lombroso to prison administrators at the St. Paul conference of the National Prison Association in 1894, defined a philanthropist as a person working to improve the welfare "not of dependent persons," but "of community and of the future race."[41] Biologistic criminologists have explored heredity, genetics, and intelligence as mechanisms for producing a criminal race.

HEREDITARY TRANSMISSION OF CRIME. Lamarckism offered one of the first scientific theories for the inter-generational transmission of crime. Jean-Baptiste Lamarck, a French naturalist and the first to refer to what he studied as "biology" in 1802, was the major thinker of evolutionary biology. He theorized that changing environmental conditions led to new needs, and animals developed new behaviors in response, which led to a permanent change in cell structure. In his *Philosophie Zoologique* (1809) Lamarck proposed two laws of evolutionary development. He proposed that in every animal, more frequent use of an organ developed it while disuse diminished its capacity until it disappeared (the first law). He also postulated that nature preserved within the species, by means of reproduction in the new individuals, all acquisitions and losses brought about by nature in individuals (the second law.) Lamarck's view had appeal because he suggested that racial character could be enhanced by improving the social milieu; his formula offered a kind of biological alchemy that guided criminal anthropologists until the middle of the twentieth century.

Jean de Lanessan, a professor of medicine at the University of Paris in 1879 was among the first to apply Lamarckism to criminality. A member of the French Anthropological Society Broca founded, Lanessan turned Lombroso's idea of the atavististic criminal upside-down. Lombroso's determinism insisted that heredity determined behavior; Lanessan's determinism insisted that behavior determined heredity. Lanessan theorized that degenerates had been formed in a criminal social milieu, absorbed its values, and passed them on through heredity to their children. A penchant toward crime began as a conscious action, but repeated enough times became part of the cell structure. Lanessan feared that the parents at work in factories abandoned their children to *vauriens* (good-for-nothings) in the streets who taught them their evil ways. *Criminal children* learned criminal behavior through social milieu that became physically implanted over time and passed on to future generations through a biological catastrophe. He suggested that lawmakers fund studies to discover what organic traits had been passed on to children in this way to prevent this class of criminals from becoming a permanent part of the French race. As Lanessan's view became popular, adherents warned that if these degenerates were not dealt with, the pathologies of insanity and crime doomed the French people through a national degenerational syndrome.[42]

In the United States, the Lamarckian view of heredity and crime was advanced by Josephine S. Lowell, a prominent social reformer. Lowell's brother, Colonel Robert Gould Shaw, led the Massachusetts 54th Colored Regiment in its charge on Fort Wagner during the Civil War. (The regiment depicted in the film *Glory*.) Lowell became the first woman commissioner of the New York State Board of Charities in 1876 and lobbied the legislature to open the first eugenics institution in the United States. She believed that immorality led to damaged germ plasm and degeneration to a less civilized state. As commissioner, she encouraged the board to see feebleminded women as a biological threat to society. Isaac Kerlin, director of the Pennsylvania Training School at Elwyn, also advocated a Lamarckian approach.[43]

Concepts such as degeneration and germ plasm supplied the science for studies of the inter-generational transmission of crime.

Generally, the authors of *family studies* did not worry about the mechanism of inheritance. If a behavior appeared in more than one generation of a family, it was an inherited characteristic. The genealogical approach of tracing crime within generations of family members had popular appeal because it could be readily understood by non-scientists and because it seemed to confirm the folklore of bad blood, bad families, and white trash. The Eugenics Record Office at Cold Spring Harbor, New York, became a major source for cacogenic research. Funded by Mrs. E.H. Harriman, the wife of the railroad magnate, the office was established to investigate heredity and social problems. Between 1877 and 1926, fifteen family studies appeared in print.[44]

The first family study to appear was produced by Richard Dugdale, a New York City linen merchant. In 1874, while Dugdale served as a member of the Prison Association of New York, he sat on a jail inspection subcommittee. Dugdale's committee conducted a survey that turned up some interesting facts; for example, six of the inmates in the Ulster County jail were blood relatives. He wrote a report entitled *The Jukes*, which appeared in the annual report for the prison association for 1875, and three years later, appeared as a book by Putnam's. The book became a bestseller and transformed Dugdale into a towering figure among social reformers in the United States and Europe. In the book, he described how over seven generations, the Juke family had produced 1,200 bastards, beggars, murderers, prostitutes, thieves, and syphilitics. Dugdale offered complex charts and statistics to show how the immorality of the Juke clan was due to degeneration.[45]

Dugdale's study received only sightly less attention than that of Henry H. Goddard. Goddard directed research at the Vineland Training School for Feeble-minded Girls and Boys in New Jersey. He studied the Kallikaks, a family in the pine barrens of northern New Jersey. He traced two lines of descendents from Martin Kallikak who seduced a simple-minded tavern girl before marrying a solid Quaker woman.[46] Martin and his wife produced 496 descendents of superior intelligence and productive social life; Martin and the tavern girl produced 480 illegitimate, alcoholic, epileptic, criminal, sexually-immoral and feeble-minded descendents right down to Deborah, a young woman confined in Goddard's institution. Goddard generated family trees using symbols of "N" for normal intelligence and "F" for feeble-mindedness. The research was done by his assistant, Elizabeth S. Kite, who published her version in 1912, the same year Goddard's book appeared. Kite conducted the field work and Goddard supplied the theory using language borrowed from genetics.[47]

If the criminologists who produced family studies had followed recognizable scientific methodology, they would not have been able to produce their findings. They began by identifying living representatives of degeneracy and then worked backwards using interviews, observations, and public records to construct the degenerate line. They presumed the existence of the very theory the genealogical research supposedly proved. Along the way, they altered definitions of family, the supposed cause (blood relatives, related by marriage, adopted children) and definitions of the presumed effect (feeble-mindedness, prostitution, alcoholism, etc.) to guarantee the flow of bad blood. Goddard, who made much of low IQ as a sign of inherited feeble-mindedness, did not bother to conduct IQ tests, but instead sent a researcher to determine the family's lineage. Kite inferred IQ from the appearance of those she visited, and assigned IQs to those she never met using the descriptions of family members.[48] And if the genealogical criminologists had studied the families trees of wealthy families along with those of impoverished families, they might have uncovered a few additional facts about inherited characteristics and individual behavior. When the descendents of Cornelius Vanderbilt gathered in 1973 there was not a millionaire among them.[49]

During the first few decades of the twentieth century, evolutionary biologists came to reject Lamarckism.[50] In 1886, August Weismann, a German biologist, theorized that all living things contained a special hereditary substance that preserved the species by passing on information from one generation to the next. Weismann spoke of "germ plasm" as a bearer of hereditary unit characters, but germ plasm remained a mysterious substance until after 1900, when the scientific world discovered earlier work by an Austrian monk, Gregor Mendel. Nearly forty years earlier, Mendel had conducted a study of pea plants in his monastery garden. He cross-bred white-flowered and red-flowered pea plants, and noticed that rather than blending to produce pink flowers, the result produced a consistent ratio of red-flowered and white-flowered plants. The mathematical rules for predicting outcomes, Mendel's laws of inheritance, have become the mathematical guide to current genetic research.[51]

Recent heredity-and-crime research has abandoned the genealogical approach in favor of a comparative approach. The most popular methods have been twin studies and adoption studies.[52] Generally, the idea is to find people who share the same genetic material but occupy different social environments, or different genetic material and the same social environment, and compare them.

Twin research took off in the 1920s after geneticists recognized a difference between identical (MZ for monozygotic) and fraternal (DZ or dizygotic) twins. Identical twins share the same genetic constitution; their hair color, eye color, head shape and so on resemble one another. Fraternal twins, although they were born at the same time, share no more genetic materials than siblings born at different times. The difference suggests a "natural experiment." Find twins of each type that grew up in the same family environment, then compare them. Since both kinds of twins share a common family environment, but not the same genetic material, comparing the concordance (the percentage of twins displaying the same trait) across twin pairs would theoretically provide evidence of genetic contribution to behavior.[53]

Johannes Lang, a German physician, produced one of the first concordance twin studies, in 1929. He located thirty pairs of same-sex twins, at least one of which was a known criminal. He separated the pairs into fraternal and identical twins, then noted that in ten of thirteen MZ twins, both were criminal, while only two of the seventeen DZ twins were both criminal. The difference, he concluded, pointed to a genetic contribution to heredity. Many later studies have been conducted in Scandinavian countries, where records are kept of twins. The Danish Twin Register, for example, contains a full listing of twins born between 1870 and 1920.[54]

Adoption studies examine persons raised from infancy by non-related adoptive parents rather than biological relatives. The extent to which the behavior of the adopted children matches the behavior of the birth parents, rather than the adoptive parents, is taken as evidence of genetic contribution to criminality. Due to the difficulty of finding numbers, many of these studies are conducted in Scandinavian countries. The largest adoption study was conducted in Denmark using 14,427 adopted children, all non-family adoptions between 1924 and 1947. It appeared in the journal *Science* in 1984. The researchers looked through criminal records to determine the portion of criminal parents with criminal children. The researchers found that adoptive-parent criminality had little effect on adoptees' tendency to break the law, while biological-parent criminality did appear to have a significant effect.[55]

These studies reflect methodological problems specific to twin and adoptive populations. Exactly which twins are fraternal and which are identical is not as easy to determine as it seems. Current methods of blood typing and chromosomal assessment provide for 95 percent accuracy in determining twin status; these methods were not available to Lange and other twin studies. Adoption studies also suffer from a statistical weakness in that the persons Danish adoption agencies selected to be adoptive parents are less likely to generate criminal records than the parents of children placed into adoption, which means that the statistical difference may be an artifact of the size of the populations. Both methods suffer from the same problem inherent in the cacogenic family studies—defining who is criminal and who is not. Official records are not evidence of criminal behavior because they do not account for those who have committed criminal acts but have not been caught.

The conclusions of these studies are held hostage to the research methods.[56] Exactly what these studies prove, or fail to prove, depends on one's view of the shortcomings. Those who debate the findings agree that behavior results from a combination of genetics and environment. Those who believe in biological causes estimate the genetic contribution to behavior higher, those who favor social environment estimate the social environment higher than genetics. Biologistic criminologists agree that behavior is polygenetic, meaning there is no single gene responsible for criminal behavior.[57] Or, nearly all biologistic criminologists.

GENETIC CRIMINALITY. The search for the crime gene followed advances in genetic theory during the early twentieth century. In 1909, Thomas H. Morgan, a University of Kentucky zoologist studying fruit flies, found the substance Weismann had guessed about. He received the Nobel prize in Physiology and Medicine for his theory dealing with the role of chromosomes and genes in heredity. Morgan, and others, found submicroscopic protein molecules in germ cells, and theorized that complicated patterns of genes aligned on chromosomes, unique for each person, provided the genetic code for heredity. James Watson and Francis Crick formulated the celebrated double-helix model of gene replication in 1953, and three years later, the normal human chromosome complement was counted. The chromosome pair that determines sex is called "XX" for women and "XY" for men, named after the way chromosomes appear in a microscope.

In 1963, several medical researchers announced in the *New England Journal of Medicine*, the discovery of a twelve-year old boy with "one of the rarest viable sex-chromosome combinations" — an extra Y. The boy displayed no unusual effects, an amazing result given that less dramatic chromosomal anomalies had been found to produce visible birth effects.[58] In 1959, French scientists found that "the trisonomy of chromosome 21," for example, produced Down's syndrome.[59] The XYY configuration, or Klinefelter's syndrome, became subject of research by geneticists and gene-oriented criminologists.

In 1965, Patricia A. Jacobs and two colleagues karotyped 197 prisoners at a hospital in Scotland. They found 12 or 3.5 percent with the XYY chromosome. Popular reports of the research emphasized the XYY as a genetic cause for violence; the extra male chromosome suggested the possibility of supermales with exaggerated masculinity, aggressiveness and violence. After testimony regarding the XYY Syndrome resulted in acquittal at a murder trial in Australia four years later, researchers rushed to replicate the Jacobs study.[60] Researchers did genetic research on inmates in prisons and mental hospitals, and turned up slight proportions of XYY men. Popular interest in the topic, and the inconclusiveness of the research, led to a study comparing the frequency of XYY among men not in prison. As it turned out, there was no significant difference in convictions for violent crime among men with the XYY genotype than those with the more common XY genotype.[61] The absence of statistical support has not, however, ended the search for the chromosomally-challenged criminal.

There are those who still believe that the extra-chromosome theory has some value. Richard Herrnstein, a Harvard psychologist, offered the case study of a serial murder with XYY syndrome, as evidence of the currency of this concept. Herrnstein surmised that the man's low IQ, abnormal personality and estrangement from his family may all be attributable to this "chromosomal anomaly that may have a broad range of physical and psychological consequences."[62]

On the other hand, many biology-minded criminologists acknowledge that genetic research will never discover anything like a crime gene. The heritable traits that result in antisocial behavior are too complex to be found on a specific location on a chromosome.[63] The genes biologists study are DNA segments that "code for" or build proteins. While research has led to mapping of these segments, geneticists have yet to identify genes for the most elementary features of the body, such as height and skin color. The genes of biologistic criminology are hypothetical constructs, tiny levers presumed to operate within the human machine.[64] Locating a gene for criminal behavior is about as futile as long-term weather forecasting, and for the same reason. In weather forecasting, the butterfly effect means that dynamical systems of the earth are profoundly sensitive to slight variation—a butterfly stirring the air in Peking today transforms a storm over New York City tomorrow. So much more so for human conduct, the myriad actions and reactions within a single moment of lived experience.[65]

INTELLIGENCE AND CRIMINALITY. Sir Francis Galton first proposed the idea of intelligence as an inherited characteristic. "Whenever you can, count," advised Galton. In his laboratory, he measured heads, noses, arms, hair, breath, and reaction times. He compiled statistics on weather, the ratio of identical twins, the frequency of yawns, and the number of fidgets-per-minute while listening to a lecture. He made his own "beauty map" of the British Isles (by secretly pricking holes in a piece of paper kept in his pocket); he classified girls he passed on the street as "attractive, indifferent, or repellent." (For the record: London had the highest number of attractive girls, Aberdeen the lowest.)[66] He also agreed with his cousin Charles Darwin about intelligence: there must have been some variation in the mental ability of families and these differences accrued to offspring through adaptation.

Galton viewed intelligence not as something learned, but as a kind of behavior that survival of the fittest concentrated in nationalities and races. He theorized that persons inherited their appearance, and also mental aptitude for art, law, and military strategy. In *Hereditary Genius* (1869), Galton attributed the success of about one thousand members of eminent families-jurists, military leaders, writers—to superior intelligence handed down from one generation to the next. He calculated that one thousand average people should produce genealogies with about four eminent persons, while the families he selected had produced more than five hundred.[67] Galton designed a test for measuring mental imagery, but it did not catch on the way Binet's did.

The IQ, or intelligence quotient, was developed by Alfred Binet, director of the psychology laboratory at the Sorbonne. In 1904, the minister of public education commissioned Binet to develop a technique for identifying which children in French schools needed remedial education. Originally, Binet had viewed intelligence along the lines of Broca and hypothesized that intelligence had to do with the volume of the head. But Binet's own measurements failed to confirm Broca's assertion; Binet did not find larger differences in the anterior of the skull where Broca had located the seat of intelligence. Binet abandoned Broca's theory, invented a practical method, and created the concept of IQ.[68]

Binet collected a large number of common tasks, such as counting coins or judging facial symmetry. Rather than attempt to find the most telling activities, he hoped to bring together a large number of diverse activities to create a statistically significant measure. He ranked the tasks from the least difficult to the most difficult and assigned an age level to each task, the youngest level at which a child could be expected to perform the task. A child began the test for the youngest age then proceeded until he or she could no longer perform the task. The age associated with the last task performed Binet called the "mental age," and calculated this age by subtracting it from the child's chronological age. In 1912 a German psychologist argued that the mental age should be divided by chronological age, and the intelligence quotient was born.[69]

Binet himself carefully avoided speculating on the meaning of the IQ. He explained that IQ was not a measure of inborn intelligence, nor did it provide a way to rank intelligence among normal children. Unfortunately, Goddard introduced the Binet test to the United States. Goddard's reworking of Binet's 1908 scale became the principal method of IQ testing until Lewis Terman's Stanford Revision in 1916. Goddard used the Binet test to define several levels of moral degeneracy: "idiots" had a mental age of two years or under, "imbeciles" had mental ages between three and seven, and "feeble-minded," ages eight to twelve. Goddard invented the word "moron," from the Greek word for foolish, to label high-grade moral defectives.[70] Goddard reviewed sixteen studies of institutionalized delinquents. Generalizing to adults he insisted that between 25 to 50 percent of prisoners are mentally defective. "It is hereditary feeble-mindedness," Goddard explained, "not hereditary criminality that accounts for the conditions."[71]

Travis Hirschi and Michael J. Hindelang conducted a meta-analysis of IQ and crime in 1977. Hirschi and Hindelang found that more than a hundred studies have found a link between intelligence-test scores and criminal behavior. They interpreted this differently than Goddard and the hereditarians, however. Hirschi explained this relationship in terms of "academic competence," not inherited intelligence. The school experience encourages youngsters to avoid crime. Young people who experience frustration and failure at school are less likely to master the social skills needed for competence in society, and more likely to engage in antisocial behavior, including breaking the law.[72] Hirschi and Hindelang recognized a liability with the whole enterprise of testing that Binet himself worried about. Binet recognized that those with low IQs would struggle, but worried that this would result from self-fulfilling prophecy and low teacher expectations rather than in-born ability.[73]

IQ returned to academics with the publication of *The Bell Curve* in 1994 by psychologist Herrnstein and Charles Murray, a political scientist. Using a national data set, Herrnstein and Murray statistically plotted a checklist of social problems-crime, unemployment, births outside of marriage and so on against IQ and parental status. Lower IQ, they reported, contributes to greater crime, poverty, illegitimacy, unemployment, welfare dependency, and other things that middle-class Americans worry about. They insisted on the importance of a "cognitive elite" to run the country and expressed concern about "dysgensis" due to higher fertility rates among the "cognitive underclass." They noted that Jewish people scored higher on IQ tests, and that those of African and Latin origin scored lower. Because Blacks and Latinos reproduce faster than Whites and Asians, this dysgenic pressure will worsen social problems and crime among them. Those in the nation's prisons had an average IQ of 92, eight points below the national average, and they suggested that since lower cognitive aptitude led to greater criminal activity, there would be less crime if the IQ could be raised.[74]

The Bell Curve revived academic debate about intelligence as old as Binet's first IQ test. The fact that IQ scores can be plotted on a graph and correlated with academic performance, or anything else, does not mean that intelligence is genetic, or even that intelligence is inherited. IQ does not even mean that there is something like "intelligence" in the sense that Herrnstein and Murray use the term. The fact that people have attached a name to something, and have created a measure, does not mean that a thing exists independent of its measure. Intelligence is a complex construct; there may be several dimensions, such as verbal, mathematical, aesthetic, and spatial. A single person may possess "multiple intelligences" in various measure—the ability to remember things, to calculate numbers, to respond in social situations. What does IQ represent? What does the test actually measure? What the IQ captures may represent one aspect of mental ability—specifically, the ability to take tests. Test-taking ability may correlate nicely with social information, but it says nothing at all about individual differences in mental capacity or the way society should be organized.[75] Herrnstein and Murray served microwaved eugenics, left-over from the American and German campaigns before the Second World War.

Eugenicist Legal Reforms

The criminal anthropology of the nineteenth century fueled the campaign for eugenics during the first part of the twentieth century. *Eugenics* refers to the idea of improving racial stock through selective breeding of superior stock and elimination of inferior stock. Galton, who advocated regulation of marriage and family size according to the genetic stock of the parents, coined the term in 1883. Eugenicists viewed delinquency, along with dependency and defectiveness, as biological conditions that could be altered by social policies. Between 1915 and 1925, eugenicists initiated a campaign for the identification, institutionalization, and sterilization of people they considered to be social defectives.[76] Their efforts impacted the treatment of criminals in several ways.

To identify criminals in need of special treatment, eugenicists used anthropometry. Alphonse Bertillion, a French police inspector, created *anthropometry* as means of identifying repeat suspects. The Bertillion system, which was the chief means of criminal identification from about 1883 until the development of fingerprints in the early 1900s, involved a procedure for taking body measurements (width of the head, length of right ear, slope of forehead, and so on). While Bertillionage never provided an accurate means of identification, it persisted after fingerprints because of its usefulness as a tool for identifying those who, owing to their atavistic characteristics, required special attention.[77] Hamilton D. Wey, the physician at the Elmira Reformatory in New York, measured the bodies of Elmira inmates in order to map out the causes of crime. In his annual medical reports, he presented numerical data, graphs of the criminal nose, and photographs of deformed criminals. The information provided the institution's warden, Zebulon Brockway, with a rationale for the increasing number of unreformable criminals.[78]

The IQ test, in the hands of eugenicists, also became a tool for identification. Prevention of crime was a matter of preventing native morons—a quasi-scientific term in 1900—from breeding, and from keeping foreign morons out of the country. In 1913, Goddard dispatched two women to screen the population of immigrants through Ellis Island. He believed that the women, who had a keener sense of observation than men to begin with, could spot a feeble-minded individual by sight alone. After fingering likely candidates, Goddard's researchers administered the IQ test. They tested thirty-five Jews, twenty-two Hungarians, fifty Italians and forty-five Russians. They concluded that 83 percent of the Jews, 80 percent of the Hungarians, 79 percent of the Italians, and 87 percent of the Russians were feeble-minded.[79] Such ideas led to immigration restriction. The Immigration Restriction Act of 1924 was based on explicitly eugenicist proposals. The law introduced quotas for immigration into the United States based on the proportion of each nationality within the population in 1890. Leading eugenicists testified to Congress that the racial stock of Americans had deteriorated due to the influx of peoples from southern and eastern Europe.[80]

Those identified by the eugenicists went to special institutions. The first eugenic institution in the United States, the Asylum for Feeble-minded Women at Newark, New York, opened in 1878. Other institutions for defective delinquents in New York included the Eastern New York Reformatory at Napanoch in 1900, the Albion State Training School in 1920 and Woodburne Institution for Defective Delinquents in 1932. New Jersey, Pennsylvania, Maryland, and Vermont also established such institutions: New Jersey's Reformatory for Women at Clinton Farms, Maryland's Patuxent Institution for Defective Delinquents, Pennsylvania's Training School at Elwyn, and Vermont's Brandon School for the Feeble-minded.[81]

Isaac Kerlin, director of Pennsylvania's Training School at Elwyn, advocated the colony plan for congenital moral imbeciles. The colony or asylum village model called for gathering all eugenic populations into a single location, to conduct farming and inmate labor, rather than at separate institutions across the state. The "Pennsylvania Plan," called for separate housing of feeble-minded populations into dormitories for epileptics, hospital cases, and able bodied women.[82] While the colony model never materialized on the scale Kerlin envisioned, farm colonies did open at Pennsylvania and in Virginia. The Virginia State Farm for defective delinquents, which opened in 1926, confined drug addicts, feebleminded, and psychopaths, along with those with tuberculosis and venereal disease.[83]

The creation of institutions for defective delinquents coincided with legislation authorizing discretionary commitment. Fixed sentences gave way to flexible, indeterminate sentences, the length of stay decided by institution administrators and scientific experts. As Henry M. Boies, a member of the Lunacy Committee and Prison Discipline Society, explained in 1901, the eugenic model required such discretion. For a judge to pronounce a specific sentence proportional to a specific crime was absurd; it was a matter of science, not law. To remedy a defect of character required an unspecified amount of time, depending on the condition of the individual.[84] Pennsylvania initiated a highly discretionary system in 1909, Massachusetts in 1911, and New York passed a defective delinquent law in 1920.[85]

After defective populations had been institutionalized, the eugenicists carried out a final step: sterilization. Vermont's Henry M. Perkins, who presided over the American Eugenics Society during the early 1930s, encouraged legislation directing voluntary sterilization.[86] Others, like Boies, advocated the "negative eugenics" of sterilization. The Pennsylvania Prison Discipline Society initiated statistical reports showing prisoners to have inherited physical diseases (consumption, syphilis) as well as mental conditions (imbecility, insanity, idiocy). By 1900, the reports identified prisoners as a criminal race, and by 1907, the prison inspectors wrote of the need for "restricting the liberty and power of degenerates to transmit their criminal propensities to unfortunate progeny."[87] Indiana passed the first sterilization bill in 1907, where the physician at Indiana State Reformatory had, beginning in 1899, performed vasectomies on 236 men.[88]

Nationwide, eugenicist policies resulted in some 60,000 sterilizations. Thirty-three states passed laws between 1911 and 1930 requiring sterilization for a variety of behavioral traits thought to be genetically determined: criminality, alcoholism, feeble-mindedness and other conditions, depending on the state. Many of these sterilizations occurred on institutionalized populations, men as well as women. The directors of New Jersey's Vineland institution arranged for sterilizations for those who had low intelligence, or who had illegitimate or biracial children. The total number of sterilizations is likely higher than 60,000 because a significant number were never added to official records. At Vineland, for example, the physician who delivered the baby of a resident reported afterward that he ligated her fellopian tubes due to a history of insanity in the family and her moron status.[89] The Eugenics Board of North Carolina sterilized 1,620 persons, mostly young, African-American women, between 1960 and 1968.[90]

The issue of involuntary sterilization reached the United States Supreme Court in *Buck v. Bell* (1927). Carrie Buck became pregnant at age eighteen, the victim of rape. The family where she lived took her to the State Colony for Epileptics and Feeble-Minded at Lynchburg. She was found to have a mental age of nine on the Binet-Simon scale, along with her mother Emma, who was said to have a mental age of less than eight. After the birth of Carrie's daughter Vivian, the superintendent of the Colony, Albert Priddy, recommended that Carrie be sterilized because she was a "moral delinquent." He concluded that Vivian had inherited the condition from her mother, who had inherited the condition from her mother, and recommended that she be sterilized despite the fact that Virginia law did not clearly authorize sterilization. At trial, attorneys for the Colony described Buck as a member of the "shiftless, ignorant and worthless class" of Southern whites. In an appeal to the Supreme Court, Carrie's attorney pointed out that if the practice were allowed, whole classes of persons could be singled-out for a form of tyranny practiced in the name of science. The Court rejected the arguments for denial of due process and equal protection. Oliver Wendell Holmes, who wrote the opinion for the majority, reasoned that if the nation could require its best and brightest to defend itself during time of war, it could require the lesser sacrifice of those who drained the strength of society. Carrie Buck ought to be kept from procreating because, Holmes concluded, "three generations of imbeciles are enough."[91]

The American eugenics project ended in the 1930s with the rise of Nazism and the nation's entry into the war. The theory of eugenics had become increasingly influential in Germany throughout the 1920s and 1930s resulting in a series of laws, including registration, sterilization, and extermination. Nazi ideology attributed social ills, including habitual criminality, alcoholism, prostitution and pauperism to heredity. Those considered "alien to the community" were defined in biological terms. As Nazi legal theorist Hans Frank explained in a 1938 speech: "This state of being degenerate, this difficult or alien quality tends to be rooted in miscegenation between a decent representative of his race and an individual of inferior racial stock. To us National Socialists criminal biology, or the theory of congenital criminality, connotes a link between racial decadence and criminal manifestations."[92]

The Nazi concept of "congenital criminality," that is, a condition existing at birth, coincided with the legal doctrine of *a priori culpability*. Proposed by Carl Schmidtt, Nazi Germany's leading constitutional lawyer, this doctrine made persons accountable for their status, not their behavior. Schmidtt insisted that a criminal was not one guilty of breaking the law, but one who possessed the character of a criminal. From this perspective, capital punishment ought to be inflicted not only on those who committed murder, but on any person whose personality rendered them the "murderer type."[93]

Nazi criminology did not say anything that the criminal anthropologists had not said. Lombroso indulged himself in racist and anti-Semitic remarks. "There exist whole tribes and races more or less given to crime," he wrote. "In all regions of Italy, whole villages constitute hotbeds of crime, owing no doubt, to ethnical causes." The frequency of crime in southern Italy, Lombroso stated, "is fundamentally due to African and Oriental elements," and to gypsies, which he classified as "an entire race of criminals." He noted that murder occurred frequently among Jews, and discussed other "hereditary" crimes of fraud, forgery, libel, and "chief of all, traffic in prostitution."[94]

Criminal anthropology, and the eugenicists that adopted it, unloosed a virulent strain of scientific racism. In the United States, at the beginning of the twentieth century, physicians suggested that personal restraints on self-indulgence did not exist within the Black population because the smaller brain of the Negro had failed to develop a center for inhibiting sexual behavior.[95] Frank Blackmar, who produced a cacogenic family study, attributed the hereditary downfall of his "Smoky pilgrims" to the "negro blood in [their] veins." Arthur Estabrook and Ivan McDougle explicitly warned of the consequences of race mixture among Indians, Blacks and Whites in their 1926 account of *Mongrel Virginians*.[96] Henry M. Boies feared the impact of generations of immigrants diluting the "Teutonic" foundations of the American population; each new wave of immigrants brought its own curse—Jewish corruption, Black criminality.[97] Earnest Hooton wrote that "criminals as a group represent an aggregate of sociologically and biologically inferior individuals" along with fewer "pure racial types and more of the mixed types that occur among civilians."[98] And whatever *Der Führer* thought about Jesse Owens's triumph at the Berlin Olympics in 1936, Owens himself had to contend with Americans back home who thought like Dean Cromwell, his coach. Cromwell explained Owens's success by saying: "The Negro excels in the [track and field] events he does because he is closer to the primitive man than the white man. It was not that long ago that his ability to spring and jump was a life and death matter to him."[99]

Contemporary biologistic criminologists reject the criminal anthropologists' attempt to link race with behavior and the biological determinism of nineteenth-century criminal anthropology.[100] They advance education and public health solutions to crime and poverty; many specifically denounce the racist policies of the past. The effort continues, however, to explain moral behavior as a matter of biology.[101] Current attempts to apply biologistic thinking include sociobiology and evolutionary psychology. Biologistic criminology, it seems, resembles the life of an insect that appears to die, but then metamorphoses into a new and different shape.

The Problem with the Moral Sense

Few of those investigating the anatomy of crime today think that Lombroso and the criminal anthropologists offer a credible theory of crime.[102] Contemporary researchers possess dramatically-improved technology for their research, pursue more conscientious scientific methods, and have the advantage of twentieth-century advances in genetics and evolutionary biology. Lombroso could only study brain tissue within cadavers. Using current technology of positron emission topography and functional magnetic resonance imaging, neuro-psychologists can study brain functioning within live research subjects. Measurements taken by means of autopsy and filling skulls with sand have been replaced by the precision of computer-aided analysis. No longer must the research rely on mystical references to germ plasm and heredity. The discovery of DNA and mapping of gene sequences allows for a better understanding of inheritance. Contemporary biologistic criminologists have replaced the crude biological determinism of a century ago with concepts of conditional freewill and the legally-responsible biological deviant.[103] The question remains, however, whether Lombroso would have found the origins of crime if he had had the advantages of modern science. Has modern science found the origins of crime within the human body?

James Q. Wilson thinks it has. In 1985, Wilson and his colleague Richard Herrnstein published *Crime and Human Nature*, and argued that biology, along with other factors, explained criminality. Since then, Wilson has come to the conclusion that "the real question was not why some people are criminals but why most people are not."[104] In his presidential address to the American Political Science Association in 1993, he claimed to have found "a natural moral sense" within human beings consisting of "a directly felt impression of some standards by which we ought to judge voluntary action."[105] Wilson reviewed research culled from the social and biological sciences, including child psychology, cultural anthropology and evolutionary biology, to explore the universality of moral judgment.[106] "Modern science..." Wilson told the political scientists, "has destroyed that view [of human nature as tabula rasa]. It is now clear that nature has prepared the child to be an...intuitive moralist."[107]

Wilson made a claim for what Darwin had surmised more than a hundred years ago: a moral sense evolved within humans because it has adaptive value.[108] Darwin recognized that the process of natural selection would generate a selfish world. Things existed because they survived the struggle. Darwin's problem was to explain altruism and the moral sentiments such as sympathy, generosity, and kindness. He worried about the problem, particularly the elaborate cooperation of "social insects" — ants who seemed to be devoting themselves to society rather than pursuit of individual interests. About a hundred years later, William Hamilton solved Darwin's problem with his idea of kin selection. Hamilton said that genes exist not just in one person but in those related. Drawing on genes, rather than instincts as Darwin had, Hamilton reasoned that siblings share half of their genes, first cousins share one-eighth, and so on. Consequently, action that endangered one individual, but benefited two or more siblings or first cousins, would have adaptive value in this broader sense. Wilson extended Hamilton's argument to include not only kin but non-kin as well.[109] Human behavior does not flow directly from genes, Wilson explains, but via a psychological mechanism. The moral sense exists as a matter of evolutionary psychology.[110]

What *The Moral Sense* offers—contrary to what Wilson told his political-science colleagues—is not really science. Despite his careful description of research findings, he is not really making an empirical argument. He is not making a claim for the moral sense based on discovery of a "morality gene" or some other biological condition, but rather, is attempting to infer its existence from the behavior it is said to determine.[111] Wilson's argument becomes hopelessly tautological. There is a biological basis for the moral sense because people behave morally. Moral behavior—what the theory purports to explain—becomes the evidence that the theory is correct. Evolutionary psychology is not a legitimate specialty in biology; it is a kind of popular psychology whose practitioners are not scientists. There is no scientific method at work in evolutionary psychology, no confirmation from genetics or paleontology. There is only the academic community's sense of plausibility.[112]

Evolutionary psychology is not science because it cannot be falsified. Explanations of this sort amount to "just so" stories. Why do some men pursue marriage and families? Well, procreation is a natural biological process, programmed into human genes because it has adaptive value. A long time ago, one primitive man mated for life with a primitive woman, and for some unknown reason, both of them decided to look after their offspring. This, as it turned out, tended to give the man a better chance of preserving his genetic material, and so over millions of years, nature "has selected for" these genes. It is natural to pair-bond for life and feelings of fidelity, loyalty and so on probably came about because of this biological process. Why do some men rape women? Well, procreation is a natural biological process, programmed into human genes. Long-term monogamous relationships are a relatively new thing in biological time. Nature prepared men to live in a pre-historic world, not modern civilization. Over millions of years, nature "has selected for" these genes, and so it is natural to want to impregnate as many females as possible. Some males, particularly young men who do not have regular access to a female, coerce women to engage in sex because it had adaptive value. Next question. No contrary evidence can be found because of the post hoc aspect of the theorizing: pick a behavior, think about why it has adaptive value, then conclude that nature must have selected for the genes leading to this behavior.[113]

To say that moral ideas reflect biological processes at work in the natural world is to say that there is a certain inevitability about human behavior. If moral judgments are inborn within the human species, they simply are. There is no need to convince a person programmed genetically with a moral sense to pursue moral judgment. So why does Wilson need to write a book to do just that? It seems that although nature endowed all people with a moral sense, she also endowed them with just enough common sense to question whether it is really there. Wilson explains that the moral sense is not "a strong beacon light" but rather "a small candle flame" in danger of being extinguished by "strong winds of power and passion, greed and ideology."[114] His conclusion is important for his argument because if nature endowed each person with a moral sense that operated automatically, there would be no reason to convince people it was there. But as "a small candle flame," the moral sense needs its defenders among the skeptics in a skeptical world.

"Thinking seriously about the kind of animals we are will help us understand our persistent but fragile disposition to make moral judgments and the aspects of human relations that must be cultivated if that disposition is to be protected and nurtured."[115] In this way, Wilson tries to endow his moral sense with just the right balance of nature and nurture. It is a delicate balance because on the one hand, if Wilson is saying that there is a moral sense but it can be overrun with the immoral passions of greed and selfishness, then he has no point to make. The idea that people have the capacity to choose good or evil, that is what Locke meant by tabula rasa, the view of human nature Wilson claims science has destroyed. If, on the other hand, Wilson means to say that what a person thinks is a moral decision is actually only what nature conditioned (by the process of selection) that person to think (because it has adaptive value), the moral sense becomes nonsense. Because if thought is nothing more than an artifact of one's genetic make-up, what evidence is there for the existence of a moral sense? Here is Darwin himself on the problem: "The horrid doubt always arises whether the convictions of a man's mind, which has developed from the mind of lower animals, are of any value or trustworthy. Would anyone trust the conviction of a monkey's mind, if there are any convictions in such a mind?"[116]

By insisting that nature provided a mediating psychological mechanism, not simply the genetic material leading to moral behavior, Wilson hopes to avoid the dilemma of sociobiology. Although sociobiology does not appear in the index to *The Moral Sense*, it has everything to do with his work. Sociobiology came from another Wilson. Edward O. Wilson defined *sociobiology* in 1975 as "the systematic study of the biological basis of all social behavior." For two decades or so, Edward O. Wilson's toughest criticism came from a colleague who had an office in the same building at Harvard's Museum of Anthropology, Richard C. Lewontin. Wilson and Lewontin debated publicly, while privately, they avoided speaking to one another. Wilson, who described himself as a naturalist, tended to advance genes as the source of behavior. His ideas led to explanations for a wide range of human activities, from dancing and cooking to religion and warfare. Lewontin, a geneticist, emphasized that genes did not determine behavior. After all, the segments of DNA called genes contain codes for proteins, not for external body parts. "How the cells of the nose know that they are the nose, nobody knows" he would say. Lewontin saw a role for culture as an explanation for human behavior. Both did share a basic faith in biology as an explanation for human behavior.[117]

What they disagreed about so bitterly was the politics of biological inheritance. A genetic basis for behavior implied a biological determinism; if behavior is fixed in the genes then there is nothing that can be done about it. Existing political arrangements are all there can be because they have been selected by nature herself via the evolutionary process. If human nature is universal, there is no point in trying to bring about other political systems because they would be unsuited for people. Critics denounced Edward O. Wilson as an apologist for the status quo, an ideologue for The Establishment. Lewontin wanted room for a better world, for the possibility that political revolution could lead to a better society.[118] And this is where James Q. Wilson comes in. A conservative, Wilson sees danger in viewing human nature as "infinitely malleable." In the preface, he reveals that he worries about the reluctance in American culture to recognize absolute human values. His book is an attempt to shore up the foundations of democratic government, threatened by the dilution of character, virtue and values in modern American culture. So, he has turned to science for the substance of his theory—it is only the conclusion that is political.

But in pursuing science as the source of morality, Wilson reveals his belief in *naturalism*. Scientists who advance naturalist explanations believe, or at least for the purpose of doing science believe, that nature is a closed system. Matter in motion is all that exists; mind, consciousness, conscience are really special configurations of matter. God, along with other religious ideals, exist within this system; there is a natural explanation for why people believe. In pursuing a biological basis for moral judgment, Wilson has taken the naturalist road. He attempts to reduce qualities of human judgment to aspects of the human nature, that is, the human animal. Which raises the question about why Wilson, or anyone, should be concerned if the candle flame of the moral sense dies out or not.

What would happen if the candle died out? If worse came to worse, the American democracy might collapse. Loss of the moral flame might lead to revolution, maybe even threaten civilization itself. Unbridled greed, selfishness, and the lust for power might plunge civilization into anarchy and put the lights out permanently. That certainly sounds like reason for concern. But what would happen if the flame continued to flicker? Civilization would continue, for some longer length of time, another millennium or so, who knows. And then the lights would go out anyway. Civilization is still destined to end either way, whether it goes out with a bang or whimper.

H.G. Wells contemplated the end of the world—the peaceful death from natural causes that Wilson would prefer happens later rather than sooner. In 1895, when the implications of Darwin's theory reached beyond academic science, Wells wrote *The Time Machine*. Wells's time traveler journeyed to the "remote and awful twilight" of a dying earth, when evolutionary processes had exhausted the earth's resources. There the traveler found a crude, and soon to be extinct, tentacled object about the size of a soccer ball. The last appearance of that species formerly known as *homo sapiens*, the final adaptation of the human animal wresting existence from an exhausted earth. Wells's traveler nearly fainted at the sight of how it would all end.[119] Why should Wells's ending appear so tragic, or comic, if all humanity comes to an end, just as it began, a cosmic accident?

The only way to see tragedy in the loss of the moral sense is to refer to some standard outside of nature. Wilson holds up his sense of right and wrong against the injustice he sees in a world without it. That is, he speaks of the death of *humanity's* moral judgment as if he had another source for *his* moral judgment; a vantage point from somewhere beyond nature to judge nature's actions. He writes as if there is someone out there who will know, or care, what happens to mother nature. If nature is all there is, then there can be no external moral judgment, no one out there to see the last light go out. The moral sense must be, like everything else, the unintended and meaningless outcome of blind forces. If nature is all that exists, if there is no God and no prospect of life of a different sort outside of nature, then all civilizations will end the same way: in nothing.[120]

Conclusion

Contemporary criminologists regard many of the concepts offered by biological positivism as myths that do not contribute to the body of scientific knowledge of criminality. Yet, as Thomas Kuhn, a philosopher of science, observes: "If these out-of-date beliefs are to be called myths, then myths can be produced by the same sorts of methods and held for the same sorts of reasons that now lead to scientific knowledge."[121] The question of science in criminology is not about grasping the findings of research based on the latest scientific technology, but about whether a science directed at the human body can make any valid claims about criminal conduct. That the brain itself could not explain human behavior was a conclusion reached more than a hundred years ago by a neurologist who specialized in brain anatomy. This scientist was no army surgeon who experimented with cadavers to relieve boredom. He studied at Ernst Brücke's Institute of Physiology, and later, spent three years at Theodor Meynert's Institute of Cerebral Anatomy. His name was Sigmund Freud.

Chapter 4

Inside the Criminal Mind

The classical criminologists founded their views on a straightforward view of human nature, that of human beings as volitional. They made no distinction between the thinking of law-abiders and lawbreakers; the same reasoning process was behind the decision to obey the law or to break it. The biological positivists founded their view on the human body. Human behavior could be reduced to a physiological process within the body, and probably within the brain itself. Psychiatric criminology insists that human beings are more complex than either of the classical or biologistic criminologists can imagine. For psychiatric criminologists, people have a mind that exists separate from the brain, and the mind itself can be broken or abnormal.

Since the time of ancient Greek philosophy, this distinction between mind and body has been known as *dualism*. Dualists try to distinguish physiology from psychology, bodily processes from mental processes. Dualists contend that the mind has an irreducible role in explaining human behavior. Of all the dualists, none has been more influential than Sigmund Freud. Although Freud wrote very little about criminality, no other theory of psychiatry has influenced criminology as much as psychoanalysis. The importance Freud assigned to the mind, and especially the mental sphere of unconsciousness, led to a formal separation between psychiatry and neurology.

Psychopathology has to do with understanding the broken mind. Psychiatrists have traditionally distinguished between forms of psychopathology: psychosis and neurosis. Those persons suffering from a *psychotic disorder* appear incoherent, delusional, irrational; they seem unable to maintain contact with reality. Psychotic persons seldom make dangerous criminals. Psychotic mental illness seldom leads to crime because the more severe the mental disorder, the less likely the person is capable of any purposeful activity, including criminal activity. For this reason, psychiatric criminologists have limited their search to persons with *neurotic disorders,* who are not incoherent or delusional, but act strangely never-the-less. Neurotic persons are aware of reality but seem to operate according to rules different than normal people.

This chapter traces the idea of the criminal mind in psychiatric criminology. It opens with an overview of Freud's theory of the mind along with his views of crime, law and society. Part Two reviews psychopathology as an explanation for criminal behavior, specifically, the concepts of psychopathy, sociopathy and personality disorders, and developmental pathways. Part Three examines mind-altering drugs and the psychology of addiction. Part Four considers the influence psychiatric criminology has had on the criminal justice system: insanity and the courts, sex psychopath laws, and investigative techniques. Part Five provides a critique of psychiatric ideas, beginning with reification, tautology, and concluding with the mind-body problem.

Freud's Theory of the Mind

Psychiatry began in France, shortly after the first phase of the French Revolution, when the great Philippe Pinel loosed the chains of the beleaguered souls confined in the asylums of Paris. In 1794, Pinel became director of the Salpêtrière Hospital, a sixteenth-century arsenal converted into an asylum for women. The Revolutionary Commune reluctantly agreed to his experiment there, as they did two years earlier, when Pinel held the post of chief physician at La Bicêtre, the asylum for men. Pinel believed that the capacity for rational thought persisted in some patients, despite their unusual behavior, a mental disease he called *manie sans delire.* There was no cranial damage or brain lesion in most patients. For Pinel, insanity was a mental condition resulting from social and psychological stresses, and that which occurs psychologically is most effectively treated psychologically. He abandoned medical therapy (purging and blood-letting) on most of his patients, and implemented moral therapy, a program featuring personal contact, purposeful activities, clean rooms and fresh air.[1] But it was another physician who studied at the Salpêtrière who had the greatest influence on psychiatry, even greater than the great Pinel: an Austrian neurologist named Sigmund Freud.

Originally, Freud began a theory of the mind based on biology. Darwinism was at its zenith when Freud enrolled in the University of Vienna to study medicine, and during his years of medical study, Freud learned from prominent brain anatomists. He studied brain physiology at the microscopic level.[2] While working at the Vienna General Hospital in 1882, Freud demonstrated impressive skills in brain anatomy. But Freud concluded that such a mechanistic view of human behavior could not explain abnormal behavior. He abandoned the effort to find a physiological base of mental processes and described mental processes without reference to neurological development. Freud's discovery of the unconscious convinced him that the mind should be the main focus for understanding why people do what they do.[3]

Freud's theory of the mind began with his interest in *hysteria*, what he called "the most enigmatic of all nervous diseases."[4] During the nineteenth century, "nervous diseases" encompassed a variety of conditions, including anxiety, insomnia, and depression. In 1882, Freud learned of the case of Anna O. from another physician, Josef Breuer, who had been treating the young woman for severe hysteria (her real name was Bertha Pappenheim, a woman who became a pioneer feminist and social worker in Germany).[5] Hysteria had been considered a woman's disease, brought on by some complication in her sexual organization, and was thought to reveal itself through several symptoms, such as paralysis. By Freud's time, neurologists had documented hysteria in men and had discounted the wandering-uterus explanation. And as a student of brain physiology, Freud knew that muscle paralysis could be brought about by anatomical lesion but he had observed that the paralysis exhibited by hysterics did not always correspond with anatomy.

To solve the puzzle of hysteria, Freud traveled to Paris in 1885 to study at Salpêtrière Hospital. There he met the eminent neurologist Jean-Martin Charcot who conducted demonstrations featuring women with hysteria. Charcot induced hysteria-like symptoms in his patients using hypnosis, which he used as treatment. He also performed autopsies on those who had suffered from the mental disease, and following Lamarck, Charcot believed that the contortions associated with hysteria had been inherited, the product of a weakened brain transferred across generations. Freud knew too much about brain anatomy to buy Charcot's determinism, but he did believe that in using hypnosis Charcot was on to something.[6]

He concluded that hysteria was a matter of psychology, not physiology. Back in Vienna, he plunged into hypnosis while he translated two of Charcot's works on the subject. When he returned to France in 1889 to perfect his hypnotic technique, he made his famous discovery. While examining patients at a mental hospital in Nancy, he had "the profoundest impression of the possibility that there could be powerful mental processes which nevertheless remained hidden from the consciousness of men."[7]

Freud began treating a woman, Frau Emmy von N., when he returned to Vienna that year. She had a severe facial tic and stammered when she spoke. "Be quiet. Don't talk. Don't touch me," she cried. She said that she saw gruesome animals. Freud decided to pursue Breuer's talking cure, and when he did, he found the source of her mental condition: hidden memories of childhood abuse. At age five, her brothers had thrown dead animals at her; several relatives had tried to choke her on three occasions. "Hysterics suffer mainly from reminiscences," Freud concluded. Since the memory of life events was too painful, hysterics could not face them. They pushed them down or repressed them as a defense mechanism.[8] Freud later concluded that physical examinations proved useless without an understanding of the psychological side of human behavior. Within the next few years, Freud published his two monumental works, *The Interpretation of Dreams* (1900) and *The Psychopathology of Everyday Life* (1904).[9]

Initially, Freud divided the sphere of the mind into three regions: consciousness, unconsciousness, and preconsciousness. Through the *conscious* realm of the mind the individual is aware of the world (seeing as well as thinking about things seen) and experiences pleasure and painful experiences. The origins of personality are found in the unconsciousness. The *unconscious* region contains all thoughts, ideas and images that may become conscious at any moment, as well as instincts and repressed memories. The conscious and unconscious mind never communicated directly but only through the preconscious. The *preconscious* region contains elements of the other two and can be revealed only though dreams, jokes and slips of the tongue.[10]

Freud later discussed the structure of personality in terms of id, ego and superego. The *id* lies at the very depths of the mind. It contains the animalistic, hedonistic urges that never leave the unconscious realm—greed, envy, selfishness. The mental contents of the id are unorganized and often contradictory. The *ego* is an organized region, organized by reason. The ego performs a realistic evaluation of the external environment. It interacts with the id, and with the *superego*, which imposes external constraints on behavior. The superego represents the conscience, the inner voice within that produces guilt about plans to do something wrong even though no one else knows about them. The superego is just as rigid and inflexible as the id, and like the id, receives an inheritance from the past in the sense of moral principles.[11]

Freud described psychic energy within the mind as a real force comparable to electricity in the natural world. Psychic energy allowed the mind to perform psychological work, such as problem-solving, perceiving and remembering. All psychic energy originated within the id. The ego came into being through a process of *psychosexual development* by harnessing energy from the id through the process of identification. The superego developed out of the ego through the process of socialization. Before the superego came into being, the child learned rewards and punishments from parents; as the superego developed, it took on those punishments for itself. In later years, Freud described the balance of energy as affected by instincts. The most important instincts were "eros" and "thanatos"—life and death. The life instinct operated for self-preservation—hunger, thirst, and sex. The energy of the life instinct Freud called "libido." The death instinct operated as a force for destruction, the self and others.[12]

Libidinal energy is the basis for psychosexual development. Freud conceived of human sexuality broadly. Sexuality begins at birth in the sense that an infant derives pleasure from sucking, a pleasure Freud placed at the beginning of personality formation. Individuals progress through the stages of oral, anal, phallic, and latency to the genital, unless they become fixated at a particular stage along the way. A person with a oral fixation might replace thumb-sucking with cigarette smoking (although Freud denied that his cigar-smoking amounted to a fixation). The stages of psychosexual development provided an explanation for various forms of sexual dysfunction, but more importantly for criminology, they emphasize the place of unconscious motives within Freud's overall explanation of human behavior.[13]

Eventually, Freud turned to the writings of anthropologists, archaeologists and sociologists. Freud believed that the development of the superego had to do with civilization itself. Freud viewed pre-civilized society as given over to aggression and chaos and the development of civilization as a means of placing restrictions on individuals. He borrowed Darwin's notion of the primal horde to explain the origins of civilization, in which a single male controlled a harem of females and who kept rivals at a distance though totems and taboos. The disenfranchised sons, however, realized that they could overpower their father and conspired to commit patricide. Faced with the probability of new coalitions and endless challenges, they extended the patriarchal system of totems and taboos. From these social beliefs developed a social contract of a sort, as law replaced these informal social rules of castes, tribes, and classes.[14]

Acceptable social behavior could only be purchased through *sublimation*, or channeling of libidinal energy into approved social ends. Freud made a distinction between early primitive cultures, which regulated antisocial acts through shaming rituals, and modern civilizations or guilt cultures, which regulated members through internal controls. The superego punished the ego for allowing antisocial behavior through guilt, civilization's ally. Freud believed that each culture developed its own communal social ego, the residual teachings of great moral figures. Unlike Hobbes, however, Freud believed the social contract and government was bound to collapse unless conformity was purchased. "What is to be done to increase the ego's capacity to extract pleasure from the environment, while still maintaining society's need to control aggressive, individualistic behavior?" Freud asked. He favored the ego and rationality as the proper basis for ethics. Moral teachings could not curb the power of the id, and the superego's guilt could backfire when it became too repressive.

Freud never offered a theory of crime; most psychoanalytic approaches to crime extend his other concepts, such as superego development. The superego operated according to the "morality principle:" it punished the ego for bad thoughts or bad actions. Its means of punishment were to give feelings of guilt and anxiety in the mental sense, and in the physical sense, to cause "an accident." If one never learned right from wrong through parents and socialization, the superego could not develop. Highly-moral people possessed a well-developed superego, and criminals a weak superego or lacked a morality principle altogether.[15] Freud suggested that criminal acts resulted from an *overdeveloped superego*, which led to feelings of guilt and anxiety. The person with a heightened sense of guilt might commit crimes hoping unconsciously to be caught and punished.[16]

Freud discovered the unconscious mind in 1889 and American psychiatrists discovered Freud about 1917. Freud's popularity increased during the Great War as a generation of soldiers returned home, some of whom slipped into episodes of inexplicable behavior. A condition commonly referred to as "shell shock." The men relived horrific experiences in their minds, triggered, perhaps, by scents and sounds reminiscent of warfare. The United States Army turned to the psychiatrists that had been mobilized to help screen recruits, and the psychiatrists turned to Freud to come up with a therapy. That there is an unconscious mind, and that it influences human behavior, has shaped the understanding of mental illness ever since.

The Psychopathology of Crime

Freud's theory of the mind made it possible to talk about criminality as a disorder of the mind, a matter of psychopathology. The "concept of psychopathy [is] one of the most durable, resilient and influential of all criminological ideas."[17] The word itself is derived from the Greek for "soul" or "mind" (*psyche*) and "suffering" or "ill" (*pathos*). As the term is used by psychiatric criminologists, the concept of psychopathy explains criminal behavior as the product of mental abnormality. Psychopathy results in maladaptive behavior, some of which may be dangerous or against the law.[18] Generally speaking, *psychopath* refers to person who commits crimes without remorse or evidence of a conscience. It is associated with the "criminal mind" or "criminal personality."

THE AMERICAN PSYCHOPATH. American psychiatrists imported the term "psychopath" from Germany. German psychiatric concepts found their way into American psychiatry with the translations of German works into English, and as German neurologists immigrated to the United States. Emil Kraepelin, a German psychiatrist who in 1909 published a comprehensive text on mental disorders as an aid to clinical diagnosis, described abnormal personalities under the heading "psychopathic personalities." He identified several types including eccentric, hedonist, quarrelsome and unrepentant, which comes closest to the current understanding of the term. Kraepelin believed that psychopathology was inborn and usually, but not necessarily, hereditary. Later editions of his work distinguished between "constitutional psychopathic states" and those without psychological symptoms, the "psychopathic personalities."[19]

Bernard Glueck, a graduate of Georgetown University Medical School, popularized psychiatric criminology in the United States. In 1915, he directed the first psychiatric unit in a prison for men at Sing Sing (New York State Prison at Ossining). "Criminology is an integral part of psychopathology," Glueck insisted, "crime is a type of abnormal conduct which expresses a failure of proper adjustment at the psychological level."[20] He wrote a series of articles clinically defining a psychopath as impulsive, irritable, emotional, and promiscuous; a pathological personality type common to drinkers, drug addicts, gamblers and sex perverts. Glueck diagnosed about 20 percent of the inmates at Sing Sing as "constitutionally inferior, psychopathic," and expressed his frustration at the inability to convince non-psychiatrists of the existence of a pathological personality.

Other psychiatrists bolstered Gleuck's formulation. William Healy, director of the Chicago Juvenile Psychopathic Institute in 1909, constructed a research sample of 1,000 juvenile delinquents. His book *The Individual Delinquent* (1915) devoted an entire chapter to "psychic constitutional inferiority" or psychopathology, a borderline condition between feeble-mindedness and insanity.[21] In 1935, Healey and Franz Alexander pursued an authentic Freudian theory of crime. In the *Roots of Crime*, they argued that crime is a substitute for some other activity the criminal would like to do, such as sexual intercourse. In the case study of one thief, Alexander and Healey discuss four unconscious motives for stealing: overcompensation for a sense of inferiority, an attempt to relieve a sense of guilt, spite toward one's mother, and immediate gratification in the form of a carefree existence in prison.[22]

Benjamin Karpman, chief psychotherapist at St. Elizabeth's Hospital in Washington, DC, pursued Freud's psychoanalytic perspective as well. Karpman organized a symposium on the psychopath at St. Elizabeth's in 1923 and published a series of case studies to show how arrested sexual development led to habitual criminality. Psychopaths were "all instinct and impulse," individuals unable sublimate their libidinal energy. Later psychoanalytic discussions attributed psychopaths to an underdeveloped, rather than an overdeveloped libido, but Karpman maintained that sexual psychopaths persisted in insatiable and uncontrollable desires.[23]

The psychiatrist Hervey Cleckley produced the most influential work on the concept of psychopath. In *The Mask of Sanity* (1941) Cleckley described the psychopathic personality from case studies of his patients, along with illustrative characters from fiction (Shakespeare's Richard III best epitomizes the psychopath). Psychopaths grew up in good families, they were intelligent and rational, but also lied, cheated, and stole without restraint. They did not display evil, but could be quite charming socially. Cleckley outlined sixteen attributes of the psychopathic personality: superficial charm and good intelligence, absence of delusions or other signs or irrationality, absence or neuroses, unreliability, untruthfulness, lack of remorse, inadequately motivated sexual behavior, failure to learn by experience, egocentricity and incapacity for love, poverty of affective (emotional reactions), fantastic behavior, suicidal ideation, impersonal sex life, and failure to follow a life plan.[24]

Cleckley's list was reworked by researchers during the next two decades. Robert Hare produced a twenty-item list, the "psychopathy checklist": glibness/superficial charm, grandiose sense of self-worth, proneness to boredom, pathological lying, conning/manipulative, lack of remorse or guilt, shallow affect, callous/lack of empathy, parasitic lifestyle, poor behavioral controls, promiscuous sexual behavior, early behavior problems, lack of realistic long-term goals, impulsivity, irresponsibility, failure to accept responsibility for own actions, many short-term marital relationships, juvenile delinquency, revocation of conditional release (from prison), and criminal versatility.[25] Other psychiatric diagnosticians have added egocentricity to grandiose self-worth and a twenty-first criterion: imperviousness to shame.[26]

Later researchers also distinguished between primary and secondary psychopathy. Hare defined the *primary psychopath* as lacking emotion (callous, guiltless, unemphatic psychopaths). The primary psychopath is the true psychopath, lacking anxiety, affect; they are aggressive, impulsive and undersocialized. The *secondary psychopath* or neurotic psychopath, exhibits an abnormal excess of emotion; antisocial behavior is secondary to anxiety and emotional problems. They are introverted, withdrawn and guilt-ridden.[27]

Current models of psychopathy flow from a neurophysiological model. Many studies of psychopathy and electrophysiology have been conducted.[28] Psychopaths have also been subjected to polygraphy, to see whether a person without a conscience can beat a lie detection machine. The University of Minnesota's David T. Lykken offers a theory of psychopath based on *evolutionary psychology*. He compares the primary psychopathic version of human to the bull terrier breed of dog, a class of persons who seem to lack a conscience, moral values and habits of good conduct. They lack a biological endowment of ordinary fearfulness that the rest of the human species acquired though the ordinary process of evolutionary adaptation. Despite being well-socialized into traditional families, they do not respond to training because the threat of punishment and pull of conscience are weak. Lykken's psychopaths are individuals who are psychologically daring and adventurous and who begin early to play by their own rules in life. Lykken finds the psychopathic personality in a number of individuals, including Oscar Schindler (the central character in the film *Schindler's List*) who saved hundreds of Jews from the Nazis. Other historical figures who "had the 'talent' for psychopathy but who did not develop the full syndrome" include Lyndon Johnson, Winston Churchill, and Chuck Yeager.[29]

FROM SOCIOPATH TO APD. Psychiatric criminologists have stretched the concept of psychopathy to include social influences on the one hand and profound mental disorder on the other. In 1930 an American psychiatrist introduced the term *sociopath* to refer to persons with a disposition to violate social conventions of behavior.[30] Rather than a defect of reason, they have certain mental conditions that make them less socialized than others. Generally, psychopath has been used to describe the remorseless criminal, particularly those who commit atrocities or bizarre crimes. Sociopath has been described as "a less serious, less criminally-inclined form of deviance than is currently implied by 'psychopath.' "[31]

Sociopath found its way into the American Psychiatric Association's *Diagnostic and Statistical Manual* when it first appeared in 1952. The DSM III (1980) introduced the concept of antisocial personality disorder, and the concept survived intact in the DSM IV, published in 1994. The concept of *antisocial personality disorder* (APD) takes the place of psychopathy, sociopathy and dyssocial personality. There are four criteria for APD: (1) pervasive pattern of disregard for the rights of others occurring since age 15, (2) the individual is at least 18 years of age, (3) there is evidence of conduct disorder with onset before age 15, and (4) occurrence of antisocial behavior is not exclusively during the course of schizophrenia or manic episode. The evidence of the first criteria includes deceitfulness, impulsivity, irritability, irresponsibility, and lack of remorse.[32]

The concept of APD fuses sociopathy and psychopathy into a single disorder, a distinction some psychiatric criminologists find important. Psychopath is a term reserved for individuals in whom the normal process of socialization failed to produce a conscience and habits of conventional social behavior. This referred not to ordinary criminals, but a subset of criminals with inherent peculiarities of temperament; individuals who came from good homes, with conventional middle class backgrounds, but who inexplicably turned to antisocial behavior. Sociopath, on the other hand, refers to persons whose criminality is explained by the lack of socialization, the absence or failure of parental influence. The concept of sociopath extends to most criminals. "With DSM-III and the concept of APD...," Lykken says, "American psychiatry took a sharp turn toward conventional criminology. In their quest for diagnostic reliability through use of specific and noninferential criteria, they devised a category into which most common criminals will comfortably fit."[33]

Sociopath is understood as the product of poor upbringing. The chief cause of criminal sociopathy is single-parent households. The absence of a father, combined with poor parenting skills on the mother's part, produces a child with antisocial tendencies. John J. DiIulio, a political scientist, advanced the idea of the sociopath in presenting his idea of *superpredator*. The superpredators who commit homicidal violence are "very bad boys from very bad homes." They are children who have witnessed violence or have been victimized by violent crime. "These juveniles are not criminally depraved because they are economically deprived; they are totally depraved because they are completely unsocialized."[34] Superpredators develop, DiIulio said, in conditions of *moral poverty*—"the poverty of growing up in the virtual absence of people who teach morality by their own everyday example and insist you follow suit...the poverty of growing up surrounded by deviant, delinquent, and criminal adults in abusive, violence-ridden, fatherless, Godless, and jobless settings."[35] DiIulio described the superpredator personality as "radically-present oriented" and "radically self-regarding;" they live entirely for the moment, they never think about the future; they regret none of their depredations, only getting caught. DiIulio's prediction of a sharp increase in juvenile crime, based on the demographics of sociopathic juvenile delinquents, drew fire from juvenile justice officials, including Shay Bilchik, Administrator of the Office of Juvenile Justice and Delinquency Prevention, and J. Dean Lewis, president of the National Council of Juvenile and Family Court Judges.[36]

The concept of sociopathy coexists with another extension of psychopathic personality, one that associates the psychopath with more clinically-serious forms of mental illness. *Borderline personality disorder* made its first appearance in the *DSM III* (1980). Borderline personality disorder refers to an individual on the borderline between neurosis and psychosis. The *DSM IV* (1994) describes the markers of borderline personality as instability of mood, relationships and self-concept; impulsivity, intense anger, and perennial feelings of boredom. There is a profound sense of abandonment and rejection, leading to becoming manipulative of other people. In response to a stressful situation, borderline types become psychotic, or lose contact with reality, for brief periods. Unlike the sociopath, the borderline personality is capable of feeling remorse after hurting other people.[37]

Within psychoanalysis, the term "borderline" is related to the concept of narcissism. Freud gave several meanings to the word "narcissism;" since Freud it has found a place in normal and abnormal psychology. Contemporary psychiatrists define narcissism as an exaggeration of attitudes concerning self-regard that would otherwise be normal. Persons with narcissistic personality disorder display an all-consuming self-centeredness and indifference to the needs of family, friends, and others.[38] The term "borderline patient" has also been used to refer to individuals who, as a part of a range of symptoms, become very disturbed and angry when asked to do psychoanalytic work during therapy, a condition that has been called "negative theraputic reaction." Freud used the phrase "negative theraputic reaction" to describe those patients who appeared to have become worse after a successful phase of treatment. Freud attributed their negative response to therapy to an unconscious sense of guilt which punished them for taking advantage of something that made them feel better.[39]

Borderline personality has been used to explain the behavior of those who commit crimes which appear to be out-of-character, inconsistent with their personalities and life histories. These crimes have bizarre, violent and often sexual features, such as serial murder. Criminologists James Alan Fox and Jack Levin discuss borderline personality disorder as an explanation for the mental state of serial murderers. The major explanation of serial murder is that of sociopathy; serial murderers lack a conscience, feel no remorse, care solely for their own pleasure. Borderline personality may help explain the impulsive attacks of serial murders who kill in a state of frenzy without making much effort to plan or conceal their activities. They kill in a state of confusion and anger, and when not killing, demonstrate capacity for empathy and compassion. Because of their modus operandi, they are typically discovered before killing many victims.[40]

Fox and Levin believe, however, that the most important explanation for serial murder, and other atrocities, is compartmentalization. *Compartmentalization* allows serial killers to divide people into two categories—those they care about (family members, friends), those they victimize (strangers, prostitutes). Compartmentalization explains how serial criminals can live "normal lives" while carrying out their depredations—many serial murderers maintain jobs, live with families, and have normal interests. Compartmentalization is an extension of an ordinary mental technique used by normal people who manage multiple roles of work and family. A tough, demanding boss may be a warm and loving mother at home. Compartmentalization allows serial murderers to dehumanize their victims, to kill without feeling guilty. Serial murderers slaughter innocent people because they view them as worthless and expendable.[41]

DEVELOPMENTAL PATHWAYS. Extension of the concept of psychopathy in the direction of sociopathy paved the road to a developmental approach to psychopathology. What makes some people raised in unfavorable family situations become antisocial while others adhere to social conventions? Why do some sociopaths become criminals and other sociopaths do not? These are difficult questions for the psychiatric perspective. The short answer begins with a combination of internal predisposition and interactive situations. A little psychopathy goes a long way in altering personality and determining the direction of the life-course. Even a mild case of APD during the formative years could lead to a life a crime. This sort of explanation, however, requires a different research method than clinical case study, the traditional basis for psychiatry.

The developmental strategy explores the life-course of persons with antisocial personalities and examines which become criminal, at what age, and so on. Using this strategy, and DSM III criteria for APD, psychiatrist Lee Robins concluded that the disorder begins around age eight and peaks during the twenties and thirties. What begins with behavior problems at home and school later manifests itself as job and marital problems. Few of those with signs of antisocial personality have serious difficulties with the law. Antisocial personality disorder affects men primarily. There is a strong correlation between APD and substance abuse. Robins and associates also found that persons with APD tend not to seek treatment, that effective treatment was seldom available to those who did, but that remission is high, especially after age forty.[42]

Developmental criminology looks at the life-course of groups of individuals with a focus on changes within individuals rather than across individuals. The theory developed out of longitudinal cohort studies in which researchers track a group of people who have something in common (they were born the same year, graduated from high school the same year, were arrested the same year) over a decade or longer. Using a combination of police records and self-report surveys, researchers chronicle criminal careers and investigate the life course or pathway leading to crime. In the Pittsburgh Youth Study, a longitudinal study of 1,517 boys from inner-city Pittsburgh, researchers have followed three samples of boys for more than a decade to figure out how and why some become delinquent.[43]

Developmental criminologists focus on two areas: how patterns of delinquency and crime change with age, and what factors can be said to be associated with the activation of delinquency. Rolf Loeber, a psychiatrist a the University of Pittsburgh and Marc LeBlanc, a professor of Psycho-education at the University of Montreal, describe three concepts important to the developmental perspective. "Activation" refers to the way criminal activities begin, along with their frequency and diversification. "Aggravation" refers to the escalation of criminal activities, increased seriousness over time. "Desistence" refers to decreasing frequency, reduction in variety and seriousness, and cessation of activities. Together these processes can be described in terms of a developmental trajectory or pathway.[44]

A *developmental pathway* exists when a group of individuals display a behavioral development different from the behavioral development of other groups of individuals. Loeber, David P. Farrington, professor of criminal psychology at Cambridge University, and their colleagues have identified three pathways: "authority conflict" (defiance and running away), "covert actions" (lying and stealing), and "overt actions" (aggression, violent behavior). Pathway theorists distinguish "persisters," who enter pathways at the first stage, from "experimenters," who enter pathways at third and final stages. Persisters are more likely to display disruptive behavior.[45]

The primary idea is that just as normal behavior progresses through developmental stages, delinquent behavior takes place in a developmental manner as well, with less serious problem behaviors preceding more serious behaviors. "One of the main tenets of developmental criminology," Loeber and Le Blanc explain, "is that conduct problems often predate and predict involvement in delinquency."[46] By "conduct problems" they mean aggression, lying, stealing, and drug abuse along with other troublesome behaviors. Or, to put it simply, those children diagnosed as sociopaths as adults had been antisocial as children. One of the major conduct problems is attention deficit/hyperactivity disorder (ADHD) defined in the DSM III (1985). In the Pittsburgh Youth Study, all of the youngest boys displayed ADHD, although researchers found the highest rates among the youngest boys in the covert or overt pathway. ADHD, Loeber and Le Blanc conclude, puts some at risk of becoming experimenters, and even more to becoming persisters. While ADHD does not necessarily signal a delinquent career, it is a warning sign of the early development of disruptive behavior. Unless intervention is made, ADHD can lead to delinquency through pathway development.[47]

Psychotropic Drugs and Criminal Behavior

Along with mental disorders, psychiatric criminologists have also formulated explanations of drugs and crime. The manufacture, distribution, and use of certain drugs are criminal activities in themselves, of course, and some crimes are likely committed by persons to obtain drugs (prostitution) or money to buy drugs (burglary, robbery). This might be called the social or economic aspects of drug crime. Rather, the psychiatric approach deals with the psychotropic or "mind altering" effect of drugs and the role of addiction in commission of crimes.

DRUGS AND CRIMINAL LAW. While the criminal law distinguishes between "good" drugs, those approved for medical use, and "bad" drugs, those prohibited from recreational use, the labels of "good" and "bad" do not refer to the physiological effect of the drug. Pharmacologically speaking, drugs are categorized based on the effect on the mind. There are stimulants, such as cocaine and caffeine; depressants, alcohol and sedatives, for example; and hallucinogens, such as LSD. Deciding which drugs ought to be illegal, and how drugs are related to crime, remains a difficult business. It is difficult to clarify how the physiological or psychological effect of a drug leads to the behavioral effect.[48]

The effects of alcohol intoxication have been known for centuries. The writer of the Psalms warned readers about the effects: "Wine is a mocker, strong drink is raging." Constables in colonial North Carolina contended with boisterous behavior at taverns, and more than one patron who "behaved themselves very insolently."[49] William Blackstone in 1769 compared alcohol intoxication to "voluntary contracted madness" which "depriving men of their reason, puts them in a temporary frenzy." Throughout the nineteenth century, numerous legal authorities believed that most homicides were caused by intoxication.[50] Reviewing Judicial Statistics for London available in 1898, the chaplain at Clerkenwell Prison found that "more than a quarter of the offenders were drunk." He concluded that anyone who explored the other cases would find that "half of the cases of common assaults, three-quarters of assaults on the police, and half the aggravated assaults, were committed by drunken persons."[51]

The physiological effect of alcohol is well known and the physiological state of intoxication can be measured by blood alcohol concentration.[52] As a physiological process, alcohol enters the blood stream where it quickly travels to the brain and suppresses thought control and muscle coordination. Low amounts of alcohol inhibit mental processes of judgment, memory and concentration. Extremely large amounts result in loss of consciousness and fatal suppression of circulatory and respiratory functions. The behavioral patterns of alcohol intoxication, however, vary by social setting and the expectation of the person drinking alcohol. Alcohol intoxication does not cause the same reaction in persons under similar circumstances; while some become cheerful, others depressed, and still others display aggressive behavior.[53] Aside from a time in the early twentieth century, alcohol consumption has remained lawful in the United States but subject to government regulation.

The effects of other drugs, such as cocaine, have been recognized only during the past century. The drug that led to the "crack wars" of the 1980s first came to the attention of medical doctors as a "new and valuable anesthetic" a hundred years earlier. It had been introduced by an American physician returning from an Austrian medical conference.[54] Freud discovered cocaine while working at the Vienna General Hospital. After reading a report about how the substance had revived exhausted German soldiers, he began administering the drug to himself, his friends and his patients. He published a scientific paper, "Über Coca," in 1884 in which he explored the drug's effects on muscle performance. Although he concluded that the substance should be reserved for use as an anesthetic, he continued to take the drug himself, perhaps into the 1890s.[55] Many Americans heard about the substance in newspaper reports of Ulysses S. Grant, whose death from throat cancer in 1884 was widely reported. Grant's physicians prescribed cocaine to ease the pain, both as a topical analgesic applied directly to the throat and taken internally. The man who supplied it, Angelo Mariani, was a Parisian based chemist and entrepreneur who marketed cocaine throughout Europe and North America. In addition to Grant's doctors, Mariani supplied John S. Pemberton, an Atlanta pharmacist who experimented with patent medicines. In 1886, Pemberton mixed coca leaves with caffeine, sugar, lime juice, phosphoric acid, vanilla, and other ingredients including the extract from the African kola nut, to produce Coca Cola.[56] Cocaine did not become illegal for recreational use until the twentieth century.

DRUGS AND CRIMINALITY. Psychiatric explanations for drug-induced crime can be divided into two basic approaches: one physiological, the other psychological. The *classic disinhibition hypothesis* emphasizes the physiological effects of drugs on brain function and views criminal behavior as the result of the pharmacological effect of the drug. The substance interrupts neurological activity within

the brain leading to aggressive behavior. Alcohol, opiates, and cocaine are all drugs with pharmacological properties that may increase the probability of violent behavior. Such drugs effect brain
activity through various neurological mechanisms involved in the
provocation of antisocial and aggressive behavior. Psychological,
psychiatric, and behavioral conditions may be antecedent.[57] "Addiction is a brain disease," contends Alan I. Leshner, who directs the
National Institute on Drug Abuse. Virtually all drugs of abuse have
common physiological effects, either directly or indirectly, on a single pathway to the brain, the mesolimbic reward system. All drugs
operate on this same circuit and activation of this system keeps drug
users taking drugs. Initially drug use is a voluntary behavior, Leshner explains, but after this "switch" is thrown, the individual moves
into a state of addiction.[58]

The psychological version of disinhibition recognizes there is no
simple explanation for how drug use leads to crime, even given a
sophisticated understanding of a drug's physiological effect. Pharmacologically speaking, alcohol is a depressant. But as an explanation for crime, alcohol is thought to have the opposite effect—intoxication leads to aggressive behavior. How can a drug that
depresses the nervous system increase aggression? From a psychological perspective, "disinhibition" refers to a psychological process
associated with the physiological process of intoxication. The *psychological disinhibition hypothesis* holds that intoxication affects
the mind's restraints on aggressive feelings. Alcohol and other
chemical substances neutralize the moral judgment, which in a
sober state, would otherwise control antisocial aggression. Alcohol
does not motivate aggression, because if there is no source of aggravation, then there is no difference in the tendency to be aggressive
between the sober and the intoxicated. When there is a source of
aggravation, alcohol intoxication increases aggression because an
intoxicated person pays less attention to the consequences of aggression. In other words, "Intoxication encourages people to sing in
public not because drunks sing well but because they become less
concerned about singing badly."[59]

From the psychological perspective, the toxic effect of alcohol
may be explained more by the drinker than the drink. The disin-
hibiting effect accelerates personality characteristics within the
drinker. Those with a depressive personality become depressed
when intoxicated, those with aggressive personalities behave more

aggressively. It may be that the type of person who is a chronic alcohol abuser is also the type of person more likely to engage in physical violence.[60] Cleckley theorized that psychopaths possessed low tolerance for alcohol; that intoxication led to aggression in primary psychopaths. Researchers at the Criminological Institute, Leiden University, explored the link between alcohol consumption and aggression among 82 university students. They found a statistical correlation between research subjects who behaved aggressively after drinking and those who had tested higher ratings on the psychopathology scale.[61] "In psychoanalytic terms," Rutgers criminologist Jeffrey Fagan explains, "intoxication defends the ego against the superego's efforts to resist the neutralization of values, authority, temporal perceptions, and control or delay gratification." This is why, Fagan concludes, Alcoholics Anonymous works. It provides a substitute conscience figure, similar to transference in psychotherapy that suppresses intoxication-aggression psychodynamics.[62]

Influence on Criminal Justice

Forensic psychiatry is a branch of psychiatry dealing with the legal aspects of mental disorders. Those psychiatrists who specialize in this area testify in courtrooms about the mental fitness of defendants, particularly in those cases where the defendant's understanding of the criminal act or of court procedures is at issue. Psychiatric criminology has also influenced criminal law, criminal investigation, and other aspects of criminal justice.

INSANITY AND THE COURTS. Since psychiatrists first entered courts, the psychiatric explanation for crime has raised questions about the moral responsibility of the accused. The most important case dealing with mental illness and criminal responsibility is that of M'-Naughten, decided at the Old Bailey of London, in 1843.

Daniel M'Naughten, a Glasgow shopkeeper, walked up behind a well-dressed man near Charing Cross, put the muzzle of a pistol into the man's back, and pulled the trigger. He was about to fire a second pistol when a policeman seized him. "I suppose you are aware who the gentleman is you shot at?" a police inspector inquired of M'Naughten the following morning. "It is Sir Robert

Peel, is it not?" came the reply. It was not. M'Naughten had shot Edward Drummond, private secretary to Sir Robert Peel, the Tory prime minister of England. When Drummond died a few days later, M'Naughten expressed no remorse. Rather than attempt to defend his mistake, he calmly stated that the "Tories...have compelled me to do this. They follow, persecute me wherever I go, and have entirely destroyed my peace of mind."[63]

M'Naughten's sanity became the major issue at trial. The prosecution showed that the accused had loitered around Whitehall (the prime minister's residence) for two weeks, waiting for the opportunity. He had invented stories to explain his presence there—that he was waiting for someone. His landlady testified that "he appeared to be a particularly mild and inoffensive person." M'Naughten's attorney countered with nine experts to testify to his client's insanity. He also introduced the concept of insanity formulated by Isaac Ray, a Maine physician who founded what became the American Psychiatric Association. In his book, *A Treatise on the Medical Jurisprudence of Insanity* (1838), Ray noted that not all persons suffering from insanity are irrational or out of their mind; a person may know what is morally right and wrong in the abstract. However, insanity may lead persons to break the law because they do not associate the moral principle with a particular act. This disassociation, or defect of reason, may mean that a person may break the law, but not be able to appreciate the wrongfulness of their conduct. The court agreed and found M'Naughten to be legally insane.[64]

The decision created an immense controversy. The London *Times*, and Queen Victoria herself, feared a rise of assassinations by persons claiming insanity as an excuse. The Queen wrote to Peel, who raised the issue in Parliament, and the House of Lords summoned fifteen judges to clarify the law. The judges determined that the successful defense of insanity required proof that the accused was, at the time of the act, laboring under "a defect of reason, a disease of the mind" so as not to know the wrongfulness of the act. The *M'Naughten rule*, or "right and wrong test," became the basis for a judgment of not guilty by reason of insanity in English courts throughout the world. By 1851, the rule was adopted in the federal and most state courts in the United States.

The judges who framed the rules never defined "disease of the mind." In England, the M'Naughten test was supplemented in 1952 for homicide defendants by the concept of "abnormality of mind."

This concept of mental illness has received a much wider interpretation than "disease of the mind" and has been defined as "a condition of arrested or retarded development of mind or any inherent causes or induced by disease or injury." It provides for jury decisions based on expert evidence introduced by psychiatrists. English courts have permitted psychiatric evidence of sexual psychopathy as a form of abnormality of mind, but have decided not to allow the effects of self-induced intoxication as a source of mental abnormality.[65] In the United States, later cases considered "a disease of the mind" to include sleep walking, somnabulism, fugue, amnesia, epilepsy and post-traumatic stress. Some courts supplemented this concept of "knowledge of wrongfulness" with an additional "irresistible-impulse" test.[66]

The M'Naughten rule remained the primary legal understanding of insanity until 1962, when the American Law Institute added the concept of "substantial capacity" to the knowledge-of-wrongfulness test. The ALI test prescribed that a defendant was to be excused from criminal responsibility if the defendant lacked "substantial capacity to appreciate the criminality of his conduct." By 1982, every federal court of appeals and about half of the states had adopted the ALI test. When the California Supreme Court adopted the ALI formulation in 1978, the court's opinion reflected an assumption that the step was nothing more than recognizing scientific reality. But distrust of psychiatric testimony and its consequences had begun. A campaign to protect the liberties of the mentally ill called into question the ability of psychiatrists to predict dangerous behavior, and led to a distrust of psychiatric testimony.[67]

During 1982, the American Psychiatric Association, the American Bar Association, and the American Medical Association officially renounced the ALI test. The occasion for this shift was the jury verdict in the case of John Hinckley, who wounded President Ronald Reagan and several others in an assassination attempt outside a Washington hotel. Hinckley had been motivated by his desire to impress a movie actress, and the jury surprised many by actually following the judge's instructions that, following the ALI test, they should acquit if there was a reasonable doubt about the defendant's sanity. The decision provoked a re-thinking of the ALI test. The AMA wanted to abolish the insanity defense altogether, while the ABA and APA wanted to retain the defense, but limit it drastically. The psychiatrists favored a rewording of the M'Naughten test that limited "mental disease" to conditions that "grossly and demonstrably impair a person's perception or understanding or reality," and explicitly excluded conditions such as "psychopathic personality disturbance."[68]

The case led to the Insanity Defense Reform Act of 1984, which retained the not guilty by reason of insanity defense in federal trials but made it more difficult for persons using the defense to be acquitted. The case also led to the concept of "guilty but mentally ill," first enacted by the Michigan legislature in 1982. By 1992, eleven more states had passed statutes providing for a GBMI verdict. Although state statutes differ in the standards and procedures used in this verdict, this strategy intends to hold down the number of insanity acquittals by providing a "middle ground" between guilty and sane and not guilty due to insanity.[69]

SEXUAL PSYCHOPATH LAWS. The legal career of the concept of psychopath began in the 1930s when American criminal law identified the sexual psychopath for special treatment. Michigan enacted the first sex psychopath statute in 1937, followed by Illinois, Minnesota, Ohio, and California by 1939. The *sexual psychopath* was a person, neither criminal nor insane, but who for the individual's and society's best interest, required special consideration. Sexual psychopaths had mental conditions that not only influenced their actions but reduced for them the criminal law's deterrent effect. Essentially, they identified a kind of personality that could only be discovered by professional psychiatrists and provided that those declared sexual psychopaths could be transferred to psychiatric wards of prisons for an indefinite period while the psychiatrists cured them.[70]

In addition to passing laws, elected officials in ten states appointed special commissions to investigate the problem of sex crimes, the nature of sexual psychopathy, and to devise legislation to prevent predations. The New York legislature called on psychiatrists to develop a means of preventing sexual crimes. Mayor Fiorello LaGuardia appointed psychiatrists, lawyers, and criminologists to his Committee for the Study of Sex Offenses, and instituted a program that provided for transfer of those arrested for sex crimes to Bellevue Hospital for observation. In 1937, J. Edgar Hoover brought the might of the Federal Bureau of Investigation and its G-men to combat the sexual psychopath menace. He declared a "War on the Sexual Criminal," and warned: "the sex fiend, most loathsome of all the vast army of crime, has become a sinister threat to the safety of American childhood and womanhood."[71]

Following the commission's recommendations, six states funded psychiatric studies of sex offenders. The New Jersey Sex Offender Acts of 1949 and 1950 established a diagnostic center for the study of adult and juvenile offenders. New York's Sex Delinquency Research Project funded studies at Sing Sing prison. Other states established specialized institutions. The Ohio legislature in 1949 allocated over a million dollars for a facility for mentally defective and psychopathic criminals at Lima. Maryland legislators authorized Patuxent Institution, which had opened in 1951, for the psychiatric treatment of habitual offenders, mental defectives, and sexual criminals. In 1954, California transferred men sentenced as psychopaths to the ten-million dollar Atascadero State Hospital, where they received treatment for their "uncontrolled desires." Treatments included metrazol, electro-shock therapy, hormonal injections, sterilization, group therapy, and for a few, frontal lobotomy.[72]

These laws continued until 1968 when Michigan abolished the legal category of "criminal sexual psychopath." In 1977, a major organization of psychiatrists, the Group for the Advancement of Psychiatry, challenged the validity of sex psychopath laws. "First and foremost, sex psychopath and sexual offender statutes can best be described as approaches that have failed... Sex psychopathy is a questionable category from a legal standpoint and a meaningless grouping from a diagnostic and treatment standpoint," their report concluded.[73] By January 1980, twenty states had mentally disordered sex offender statutes. Seven states had repealed their statutes between 1978 and 1980 with the trend continuing toward repeal.[74] California's sexual psychopath law had become subject to increasing constitutional concern, and as legal challenges based in equal protection and due process doctrines mounted, the legislature renamed sexual psychopaths "mentally disordered sex offenders" in 1963. In 1976, the California Supreme Court ruled that MDSOs could not be detained in state hospitals any longer than they could have been confined in prison for the offense of which they had been convicted.[75]

It appeared the special status given to perpetrators of sex crimes had ended, but new sexual psychopath laws appeared as "sexual predator laws." The first of these passed in 1990, and by the summer of 1997, nine states had passed similar laws. Washington's sexual predator law gave the state the authority to detain sexual offenders who had reached the end of their criminal sentence but represented a risk to the public. The law targeted that group of "sexually violent predators" who do not have a treatable mental disease but who nevertheless possess an uncontrollable urge to sexually assault children, revealed by repeated criminal history of child sexual abuse. The law became the model for legislation passed in Kansas, Arizona, California, Wisconsin, Illinois, and North Dakota. Other states enacted new civil commitment statutes, registration laws, and community notification requirements directed at sex crimes against strangers and recidivism.[76]

INVESTIGATIVE TECHNIQUES. Psychiatric concepts of crime extended outside courtrooms. If there was a criminal mind, and psychiatrists understood it, then they could help the police catch criminals. In the early decades of the twentieth century, the concept of psychopath encouraged the establishment of psychiatric laboratories in police departments, courts, and prisons. These laboratories received financial support from eugenic organizations, such as John D. Rockefeller's National Committee on Mental Hygiene. Between 1915 and 1917, New York City's police department operated a Psychopathic Laboratory to show how science, psychology, medicine and sociology could contribute to crime control. Financed through private donations, the Laboratory taught police to distinguish mental defectives from common crooks. By May 1917, the laboratory had processed 502 cases, identifying 82 as mentally defective and 43 as "psychopathic characters."[77]

Forensic psychiatrists offered other assistance as well. During the 1950s, the Los Angeles Police Department began training officers in hypnosis to jar witnesses' memories. They were called the "Svengali Squad" after a 1931 film in which the evil Svengali (played by John Barrymore) entranced a young woman into a life of crime.[78] The psychiatrist who examined the man arrested for shooting Governor George Wallace in 1972 suggested hypnosis as a solution to witnesses with psychological amnesia. Writing in the FBI Law Enforcement Bulletin in 1975, he offered hypnosis to aid witnesses in recalling important facts, such as license plate numbers and descriptions of perpetrators.[79] Hypnosis never made it into courts, however. The majority of courts that have heard cases regarding the use of hypnotically-refreshed testimony have prohibited its use. Over half of the states specifically prohibit hypnotically-refreshed testimony, based on a determination that hypnotically refreshed testimony is inherently unreliable, or has little support from the scientific community. In recent years, cases in which therapists "restored" memories of childhood sexual abuse using hypnosis have created legal controversy.[80]

Profiling has received a more favorable reception. The idea of creating a psychological profile of an unknown criminal gained currency among police as a result of New York City's "mad bomber" case during the 1950s. The mad bomber detonated 32 explosive devices over a fourteen year period and taunted the police with letters. Desperate for leads, the New York City Police Department consulted with James A. Brussel, a psychiatrist, to construct a personality profile of the type of person capable of this terror. After analyzing the letters, Brussel predicted that the man they were looking for was rather average, polite, and neatly-dressed. The mad bomber would be of Eastern European ancestry, between 40 and 50 years of age, and living in Connecticut with a sister or aunt. He loved his mother but had a poor relationship with his father. He was Catholic, fairly well educated, and a sexual deviate. As a paranoid personality type, he paid great attention to details—Brussel predicted that the mad bomber wore a double-breasted suit, with every button fastened.[81]

Brussel helped the police write the mad bomber a letter and it appeared in a New York newspaper. The mad bomber wrote a reply, telling of his need for revenge against a utility company. Police searched the records of Consolidated Edison and found George Metesky of Waterbury, Connecticut, a former employee. In 1956 the New York City Police charged Metesky with the bombings. Metesky was of Slavic descent, was in his early 50s, and lived in Connecticut with two sisters. When arrested, he was wearing a double-breasted suit—every button buttoned. In the *Casebook of a Crime Psychiatrist* (1968), Brussel explained how he created the Metesky profile. A paranoid personality would plant bombs and paranoia reaches its height after age forty. Bombs had been a common form of political violence in Europe and the syntax used in the letters suggested eastern or central Europe. Most central Europeans were Catholics, and most Catholics near New York City lived in southern Connecticut. He was sexually abnormal because the bombs were shaped like phallic symbols and he looped the Ws in his letters, like women's breasts, while he printed other letters in block fashion. He was meticulous and feminine, possibly homosexual; he wore the double-breasted suit because it represented the neatest, most proper male attire. He kept it buttoned as psychological protection—he knew the police were looking for him.[82]

Despite the fact that Brussel led the police astray in the Boston strangler case a few years later, profiling entered criminal investigation. Using the same combination of logic, Freudian psychoanalysis, and police information, Brussel predicted a very different character than the man who later confessed. Boston police wasted thousands of hours searching for a man Brussel had said was homosexual. But beginning in the 1960s, the Law Enforcement Assistance Administration funded social psychological research. The Drug Enforcement Administration developed the "drug courier profile." Police departments constructed profiles of arsonists and rapists. The FBI first used the psychological profile in 1971 and the Behavioral Sciences Unit has been a major force for profiling ever since. No organization has done more to advance profiling than the Behavioral Sciences Unit.

In 1980, the FBI published a study of thirty-six serial killers distinguishing between "organized social" and "disorganized asocial." In 1981, the FBI commissioned a cost-effectiveness a study of the Behavioral Science Unit's work, and claimed an accuracy rate of 80 percent.[83] The FBI's profiling method does not rely so much on psychological inference and psychoanalytic theory as statistical probabilities. By 1984, the FBI had started work on a computer-based profiling system, a system that has become known is VICAP. The Violent Criminal Apprehension Program (VICAP) established a computer database for collection and distribution of information about unsolved homicides and extraordinary crimes across the country. The program relies on a questionnaire, completed by local police investigators, and VICAP analysts who assess victim characteristics, method of operation, aspects of crime scenes, and available criminal offender information. The term VICAP is a misnomer, however, because the program assists primarily in the detection of serial crimes rather than the apprehension of serial criminals. The profiles have a very low rate of success in leading to the identity of a serial killer.[84]

Assessment of Psychiatric Concepts

Psychiatric concepts of crime have had a major influence on criminology and criminal justice. Psychopath and sociopath are familiar terms, accepted by the public as explanations for criminal behavior.

THE TAUTOLOGY OF PSYCHOPATH. Psychiatric criminologists always had difficulty defining what was meant by "psychopath." Replacement of psychopath with sociopath within the APA manual, and later antisocial personality disorder, suggests that psychiatrists have made scientific progress. Use of the term "antisocial personality disorder" suggests an improved understanding of the mental disorders that lead to criminal behavior. Changes in the diagnostic categories within the APA manual, however, do not follow psychiatric research. The criteria are derived by consensus of committees of clinicians rather than clinical studies.[85] As a source of labels to be used in clinical diagnosis, concepts such as borderline personality disorder and antisocial personality disorder provide for consistent use of terms. But as an explanation for criminal behavior, they are inherently tautological.

A *tautology* is a circular argument—a statement of definition mistaken for a statement of cause and effect. The tautology of psychiatric labels limits their ability to explain criminal behavior. Why do some people commit bizarre, horrible acts? Because they do not have a conscience; they are psychopaths. How does one know that there are psychopaths out there? Well, because some people commit bizarre, horrible crimes without motive. This is the problem of tautology. When a person wants to know why some people commit bizarre crimes it is not helpful to know that people who commit bizarre crimes for unknown reasons are called psychopaths.

The problem with tautology is that because of the circularity of the argument, no evidence to the contrary can be found. That some people come from good homes with active parents and still break the law might be taken as evidence that antisocial personality disorder is not the cause of crime. That many people who come from bad homes without caring parents do not break the law might be taken as further evidence that antisocial personality disorder is not the cause of crime. But the tautology of psychiatric labels makes it easy to explain both. If a person from a good home breaks the law, it is because that person is a psychopath—a primary psychopath, in fact. If a person from a bad home breaks the law, it is because that person is a sociopath—a person with antisocial personality disorder. If the person fits neither psychiatric category, then it is clearly a case of borderline personality. If the label does not fit, it is not because the whole enterprise of labeling mental conditions is not productive as an explanation for crime. It is simply a matter of mis-diagnosis. If the clinical diagnosis of one sort of personality disorder does not fit, then the person has another personality disorder. Maybe one that has not been thought of just yet.

The testimony of a psychiatrist at the Alger Hiss trial in 1950 provides a prime example. The psychiatrist, Carl Binger, testified that the prosecution's star witness, Whittaker Chambers, a journalist at *Time* magazine, was a psychopath. Chambers, a former Communist, accused Hiss, President of the Carnegie Endowment for Peace who had clerked for U.S. Supreme Court Justice Oliver Wendell Holmes, of having been a Communist spy. In an effort to discredit Chambers, the defense asked Binger a forty-five minute question relating to Chambers's biography; that he had joined the Communist party using an alias, that he had hid microfilm in a pumpkin; that he lacked stable emotional attachments; that he had bad teeth and dressed shabbily, that he had informed on Hiss despite saying that Hiss had been his best friend.[86]

"I think he has a mental disease known as a psychopathic personality," Binger testified. "The psychopath knows what he is doing but he does not always know why he does it. His acts are frequently impulsive and often bizarre, so they don't make much sense to ordinary people." Binger also pointed out that Chambers often stared at the ceiling during his testimony as if he were trying to remember what he had said before, a sign of his pathological lying. "Psychopaths are deceptive and often paranoid. They have abnormal sexuality and abnormal emotionality. They may be alcoholics or drug addicts. Their actions are often bizarre. They are untidy. They cannot form stable attachments. They constantly lie...psychopaths believe that their fantasies are true. They may be a hero at one moment and a gangster at the next. They claim friendships where none exist, just as they make accusations which have no basis in fact. Chambers has all the marks of the classic psychopath except alcoholism and drug addiction."[87]

Binger's characterization of Chambers as a pathological liar became the subject of a three-day cross-examination:

Question: Aren't you making this diagnosis without much information on his early childhood and adolescence?

Answer: My diagnosis is based on thirty years of his behavior.

Question: Would a psychopath hold a ten-year job at *Time*?

Answer: Working around the clock as Chambers did usually means an emotional disturbance.

Question: Isn't being married for nineteen years and being the father of two children evidence of stable attachments?

Answer: It depends on the kind of attachment.

Question: Is there any evidence that Chambers deliberately and vengefully hurt a friend?

Answer: I don't recall his mentioning any friends except Hiss.

Question: You said hiding the microfilm in the pumpkin was bizarre. What about the colonists hiding the Connecticut charter from the British in an oak tree?

Answer: That was not bizarre because it took place over two hundred years ago in a very primitive community. Hiding microfilm in a pumpkin is not how a modern person behaves.

Question: Albert Einstein and Thomas Edison didn't dress very well either. Was that pathological?

Answer: One must look at the whole picture of a person's personality.

Question: I noticed that you glanced at the ceiling fifty-nine times in fifty minutes. Is this a symptom of a psychopathic personality?

Answer: Not alone.[88]

The problem with psychopath, sociopath, personality disorder and so on is that the "abnormality" of the behavior remains subjective, to be decided by what psychiatrists say constitutes abnormality. This subjectivity of psychiatric diagnosis is what the APA manual hopes to avoid but it remains a problem, particularly for forensic psychiatry. In cases of insanity, attorneys on each side hire psychiatrists to testify, and the jury must sort out which side made the better argument.

THE PROBLEM OF REIFICATION. "Sociopath" replaced "psychopath" in clinical diagnosis. Sociopath sounds less subjective, less judgmental because it suggests that something is wrong with one's behavior as viewed by society whereas psychopath implies there is something seriously wrong with a person's mind as viewed by psychiatrists.[89] "Antisocial personality disorder" sounds even better, because it moves away from the claim that psychiatrists can determine personality types and toward more limited statements that while psychiatrists may not understand enough about the mind to define personality, some people exhibit an abnormal aspect of personality. But whether the claim is made on psychiatric understanding of the abnormal mind, or the psychiatric understanding of what is abnormal behavior in society, the diagnosis is still subjective. Concepts of sociopathy and antisocial personality disorder rest on the interpretation of the difference between a person's behavior and social conventions.

The issue is not whether psychiatric labels such as "sociopath" can be misused for political purposes, but whether "sociopath" is anything more than a psychiatric label to begin with. *Reification* means to mistake an idea for a thing. John Stuart Mill explained reification this way: "The tendency has always been strong to believe that whatever received a name must be an entity or being, have an independent existence of its own."[90] The whole idea of mental illness, of a mind that does not think the right thoughts, is an elusive concept. Severe mental retardation may be evidenced by birth defects. Other forms of mental illness may be traced to an observable source within the body; an autopsy reveals a brain lesion, tumor, or some damage to the brain. But the mind cannot be found within the body. A abnormal mind can only by inferred from behavior considered to be abnormal.

Consider M'Naughten's case. M'Naughten was diagnosed with "monomania," confined to a London hospital, and later transferred to Broadmoor Lunatic Asylum where he died in 1865. The term monomania came from a British psychiatrist, James C. Prichard who divided mental illness into four categories: moral insanity, monomania, mania, and dementia (incoherence). In his *Treatise on Insanity, and Other Disorders Affecting the Mind* (1835), Prichard drew upon the work of French psychiatrist Jean E.D. Esquirol to define the term. Esquirol believed that the decline of religiosity in the nineteenth century had led to a decline in some forms of madness and an increase in others. The weakening of religion as a force had left no recourse for maintenance of social order except for the government to establish a regular force of police. This had a negative effect on mental health. "It is the police which haunts weak imaginations," Prichard quoted Esquirol, "Asylums are filled with monomaniacs, who, fearing this authority, have gone mad upon the subject, and believe they are constantly pursued."[91] Monomania represented an irrational fear of legal authority, a mental state that would later be redefined as "paranoid schizophrenia".

Did M'Naughten really have monomania? The answer hinges on whether he was delusional, had an irrational fear. A person who claims that the prime minister is out to do him bodily harm certainly sounds irrational, delusional, even paranoid. But if the prime minister really was out to do M'Naughten bodily harm, he would not be delusional, his fear would not be irrational. Peel had put in place the newly-created Metropolitan Police Force, and the Tories had created a network of spies to ferret out the Chartists, a political group believed responsible for political violence in the city. The Tories also engaged in "cooping," intimidating people into voting Tory. One Tory agent, Robert Lamond, had sought to influence M'Naughten's vote through a variety of harassing tactics. M'Naughten may have meant exactly what he said, that he had intended to kill Peel as a political act. He may have been paid to do it—he had a receipt for deposit of £750 in his pocket when he was arrested. As for the prosecution, to prove political assassination would have meant bringing spies to the stand, acknowledging their existence, exposing their cover. The prosecution did not challenge the insanity claim, in fact, the court paid for nine psychiatric experts to establish M'Naughten's insanity. The judge even allowed two experts to testify to M'Naughten's mental condition who had never examined him.[92] M'Naughten may not really have had a mental illness at all.

The bigger question though is not whether M'Naughten really had monomania, but whether anyone has ever had monomania. Monomania may have been the product of Prichard's mind rather than M'Naughten's mind. Prichard himself voted Tory; he adhered to notions of paternalism that he considered to be under threat from political radicalism and economic utilitarianism.[93] Monomania may have represented a political device used by Tories as a means of diffusing criticism of their policies—those who disagreed were crazy, suffering from a disease of the mind. And if monomania never really existed, what about contemporary psychiatric concepts? In what sense are they real mental conditions?

Consider the recent disease of the mind called attention deficit/hyperactivity disorder or ADHD. The disorder did not exist in 1952 when the first *Diagnostic and Statistical Manual* appeared. It was called hyperactive reaction of childhood in the *DSM II* (1968), became Attention Deficit Disorder in the *DSM III* (1989), before becoming ADHD in the *DSM IV* (1994). These shifts did not follow medical or scientific discovery but the beliefs of psychiatrists. For that matter, as Richard DeGrandpre, a Vermont psychologist points out, it is hard to imagine what kind of research findings would lead to diagnosis of a problem as a kind of behavior (hyperactivity), to a mental condition (inattention), to a problem of misbehavior and inattention.[94]

Part of the problem with ADHD is tautology. The present definition confuses ADHD as the name for a collection of behaviors, the causes of which are unknown, with ADHD as the cause and explanation for these behaviors. But unlike monomania, psychiatrists claim that there is an organic basis for the disorder; hyperactivity is a brain disorder, not a mind disorder. Medical researchers had for three decades looked for a biological basis for ADHD without success. There have been efforts to explain ADHD as a chemical imbalance in the brain, as the result of abnormalities in brain structure, and as a disorder of the brain's frontal lobes, where glucose utilization is thought to be abnormally low. Then, in November 1998, biomedical researchers at Stanford University announced that they had finally found it. Using functional magnetic resonance imaging (fMRI), the researchers said that ADHD is characterized by atypical functioning in the striatal region below the brain's frontal cortex. The headline for one major news magazine read: "Brain Scans Give New Hope for Diagnosing ADHD."[95]

Actually, DeGrandpre notes, the Stanford researchers did not find proof that a brain disorder causes hyperactivity. In order to see evidence of brain disorder as the cause of hyperactivity, it is necessary to overlook a fundamental difference between correlation and causation. Because there may be a correlation between atypical functioning in the striatal region below the brain's frontal cortex and hyperactivity—that children diagnosed as hyperactive also have atypical functioning as measured by a brain scan—does not mean that the atypical functioning causes the hyperactivity. The correlation may be explained by a third variable: the physiological process that corresponds with hyperactivity may be the product of the same experiences that cause the hyperactivity itself. The Stanford researchers did not even claim that the fMRI scans provided a better method of diagnosis (despite the headlines); brain scan results conflicted with behavioral diagnoses for five of the boys in the study. When the brain scan failed to find evidence of hyperactivity for two subjects psychiatrists had diagnosed with ADHD (and three had ADHD according to the brain scan but had not been diagnosed as having it), the researchers concluded that the psychiatrists were right, not the brain scan.[96]

So how do psychiatrists know that a child has ADHD? Unlike monomania, there is a drug—Ritalin—for hyperactivity and it seems to work. Psychiatrists admit to using the drug as a diagnostic—if the child responds to Ritalin, the diagnosis is ADHD. Does the observation that a child benefits from Ritalin constitute evidence of ADHD? No, because the drug also "works" on people who are not hyperactive. Ritalin is the trade name of methyphenidate hydrochloride. Pharmacologically, methyphenidate hydrochloride is similar to cocaine. The drug works in the brain neurotransmitters to produce a "high" similar to the alkaloid in cocaine. Stimulant drugs enhance performance for most people—for a while.[97] The paradox of a stimulant drug reducing hyperactivity is explained by understanding that Ritalin, like cocaine, replaces a "natural high" with a "chemical high." A child accustomed to the fast-paced lifestyle full of electronic excitement will likely have trouble sitting still and concentrating on homework. The child can be satisfied with a chemical stimulant and appear to slow down.[98]

Is hyperactivity really a mental disorder? There are, of course, children who listen less and misbehave more often than others. But whether they are "hyperactive" because of permissive parents, a culture of speed, a mental disorder, or a brain abnormality cannot be answered. DeGrandpre suggests that since stimulant drugs appeared about two decades before the diagnosis of Attention Deficit Disorder, it appears that the treatment prompted the disorder. A decade after Ritalin, developed in the 1960s by a pharmaceutical company, appeared, prescriptions surged along with the number of children diagnosed with ADHD. From 1989 to 1996, the number of children diagnosed with ADHD and walking out of a doctor's office with a Ritalin prescription increased from 55 percent in 1989 to 75 percent in 1996. Production of Ritalin increased sevenfold from about three thousand kilograms in 1989 to more than twelve thousand in 1997, more than 90 percent of it consumed in the United States.[99] "More than anything else, ADD represents a growing prejudice in our culture—led in large part by the powerful influence of psychiatry professionals and pharmaceutical companies—which is that personality and behavioral traits are inborn and biological," he observes. If ADHD is a brain disorder, then parents are off the hook, psychiatrists have an effective tool parents need to consult them about, and pharmaceutical companies increase their revenue.[100]

THE MIND-BODY PROBLEM. Given the inability to observe the mind, either normal or abnormal, there is a tendency to discount the mind altogether. As technological advances have detailed the brain's connection to human thought, they have enabled biological psychiatrists and neuroscientists to claim that all psychopathology is biological pathology. Historically, dualists such as Freud struggled with the relationship between mind, brain, and behavior. How do these relate? How do bodily processes become mental? How do mental processes become physical?[101] The new scientific dualism contends that all mental processes can be reduced to physiological processes so that all mental problems represent biological problems. In this view, the relationship between brain and mind is one of cause and effect—the brain is the cause and the mind is the effect.[102]

Psychiatrists, psychologists (as well as the biological criminologists from the previous chapter) who accept the new scientific dualism argue that criminologists who do not accept that the brain is in charge are behind-the-times. The "mentalists," like Freud, have simply not kept up with the "knowledge explosion in the neuroscience of the past three decades." In a recent article, two physicalists suggest that although "biological brain-proneness" is widely accepted by neuroscientists, social scientists stubbornly resist such a view. They attribute this stubborness to a communication lag—social scientists simply do not know any better.[103]

Scientific dualism contends that brain physiology explains how mental processes such as consciousness, sleep, dreams, memory, and so on actually work. John Searle, a philosopher, insists that theories of the mind are a function of the lack of understanding about how the brain works. He says that all mental processes are caused by brain processes. "The mind and body interact," Searle says, "but they are not two different things, since mental phenomena are just features of the brain."[104] What seem to be mental processes—consciousness, intentionality, subjectivity, and causation are really brain processes. Searle offers a description of the biological process of pain, beginning with nerve endings, Delta A and C fibres, the spinal cord, hypothalamus, and ending in the somato-sensory cortex. The that there must be some *elan vital* in addition to biological material in order for life to exist, is no longer taken seriously, he claims. This is because scientists have come to better understand the biological character of living organisms, and given this science, life itself no longer seems a mysterious issue.[105]

While Searle and the physicalists are confident that scientists have done away with ancient ideas of mind and such like, the scientists themselves do not agree. He notes that when he has lectured to biologists and neurologists, he has found them very reluctant to speculate about the mind in general, and consciousness in particular, as the domain of scientific investigation.[106] He expressed disappointment with the confusion in text books about the brain; the scientists themselves suggest that less is known about how the brain actually works than what Searle hopes. It may be, that as brain science advances, scientists will actually come to the same conclusions as Searle—that the brain is all there is. Searle believes that as brain science advances from weight to tissue, to lobes and cells, to molecules and atoms, the processes of the brain will reveal the neurological basis for the mind.

More likely, the scientists recognize what Searle does not. That brain science will never answer questions about the mind, about consciousness, about the soul, because they are not scientific questions. Nobel physicist Richard P. Feynman studied brain anatomy in an effort to understand the physics of color perception but decided the mind was the level worth studying. He concluded that the mind was a dynamical pattern, not so much contained within neurological substrate, but independent of it, floating above it. "So what is this mind of ours? What are these atoms of consciousness?" Feynman mused, "Last week's potatoes! They can now *remember* what was going on in my mind a year ago—a mind which has long ago been replaced...These atoms come into my brain, dance a dance, and then go out—there are always new atoms, but always doing the same dance, remembering what the dance was yesterday."[107] Physics, it seems to one physicist, does not explain away the mind.

Conclusion

The shift in psychiatric criminology, from psychopath to sociopath to antisocial personality disorder, illustrates the difficulty of studying something scientifically that cannot be observed. Unlike the brain, the mind cannot be located within the human body. It remains something like the light that comes from a light bulb when electric current flows through the filament. Psychiatric criminology began with a concept of criminality as an aspect of an abnormal mind and moved on to understanding the abnormal mind as an aspect of an abnormal social situation. Freud himself made the same transition throughout his professional career. He began with Darwin's conception of the brain, moved on to the Greek view of mind, and then to anthropologists' and sociologists' view of the individual in society. The ideas Freud borrowed for his *Civilization and Its Discontents* (1930) would be developed more extensively by sociological criminologists.

Chapter 5

The Social Sources of Crime

The sociological view of crime asserts that crime results from one or more aspects of society and that the task of the criminologist is to dig up these root causes. Sociology began in France, early in the nineteenth century, when Auguste Comte came up with the word "sociology" while teaching mathematics at a French engineering school. He brought the positive method to the study of society, and others applied the sociological perspective to the study of suicide. Later generations of sociologists, particularly in the United States, brought the sociological perspective to the study of crime.

Sociologists disagree about which aspect of society influences crime the most. Some look for the causes of crime in economic inequality, some in community disorganization, and others in the dynamics of social situations. Some sociological theories expressly reject other sociological explanations. All sociological criminologists, however, share a belief in structural causality; that crime results from social structures beyond individual volition. From this perspective, individual behavior is determined or controlled by these social structures. Sociologists generally believe that the efforts of government to curb crime are not as important as social structures, particularly those that operate within local social networks—communities and neighborhoods. Social structures act like the colossal tectonic plates of the earth's surface; when they shift, people, their activities, and their beliefs about the world shift too.

Sociological criminology has dominated criminology in the United States, or as David Matza put it, "Modern criminology is the positive school of criminology."[1] Part One reviews the sociological perspective with a look at what Emile Durkheim and the first sociologists had to say about suicide. Part Two discusses three staples of sociological criminology: strain, control, and shaming. Part Three reviews theories linking crime to place, including region, city, neighborhood and street corner. Part Four reviews the social psychology of crime, including social learning, situated transaction, and victim-precipitation theory. Part Five looks at the application of sociological criminology during the Johnson years. Part Six explores the idea of structural causality in sociological criminology with a critique of the proposed "rotten social background" defense.

The Rise of the Sociological Imagination

The sociological perspective insists that individual actions can be understood only within their milieu, their surroundings or environment. "The sociological imagination..." C. Wright Mills wrote, "is the idea that the individual can understand his own experience and gauge his own fate only by locating himself within this period, that he can know his own chances in life only by becoming aware of all those individuals in his circumstances." For the sociologist, society represents more than the aggregate of individuals. What appear to be personal troubles are in fact public issues, and only by understanding how an individual act fits into the social milieu, can these troubles be overcome. Sociologists seek to discover the laws of social activity that shape individual action, those aspects of collective existence that determine individual choice.[2]

THE SOCIOLOGICAL IMAGINATION. The doctrine of structural causality began at L'Ecole Polytechnique, an engineering school established in France in 1794. The scientific and technical progress of the eighteenth century created widespread enthusiasm for technological studies, and the Revolutionary Convention created a school for engineers. The curriculum closed the books of Latin and Greek, turned instead to mathematics, physics and chemistry, and it became a model for schools throughout the world. It was here, during the first twenty years of its existence, that Auguste Comte set out to discover the "laws" of society, like those laws of gravity, motion, and energy within the natural world using the new science of sociology.[3]

Comte first studied at the polytechnic school in 1814, and later, he became a professor there. He learned to apply the methods of technical sciences to people from Claude Henri de Rouvay, Comte de Saint Simon. Science did not mean to Saint Simon and Comte what it meant to the scientists themselves. Saint Simon and Comte thought of science not as the accumulation of knowledge by systematic observation and logical deduction, but as a historical process unfolding throughout world history. Each science passed through progressive stages, beginning with the theological, then metaphysical, and culminating in the positive, based on the mechanical simplicity of the natural world. Mathematics, astronomy and physics arrived at the positive stage first because of the simplicity of natural phenomena. The science of society, what Comte called "sociology," arrived last due to the complexity of the social world.[4]

Comte claimed that his new science of social physics allowed him to discover natural and inevitable laws of the progress of civilization. Comte rejected what he called "the anarchy of individualism" for a planned society; perfect social order could be obtained only by "assign[ing] to every individual or nation that precise kind of activity for which they are respectively fitted."[5] He dreamed of a society organized along the lines of his positivist laws of science. "True liberty," Comte summed up as nothing other than "a rational submission to the preponderance of the laws of nature."[6] During the last years of his life, he founded a positivist religion. Built around a trinity of humanity, world-space, and earth, positivist religion established its own priesthood, sacraments, and calendar. The cult spread from Paris to England, to Sweden, and then to Brazil and Chile. Thomas Huxley referred to this last phase of Comte's thought as "Catholicism *minus* Christianity."[7]

The practitioners of Comte's "science of society" began with the study of suicide. In France and other European countries, suicide was a subject of debate in the early nineteenth century. The founder of French psychiatry, Jean Etienne Esquirol, wrote about suicide as an expression of mental disorder. Esquirol, who began his career at the Salpêtrière in 1811, was among the first to identify mental disorders in patients by their use of language rather than sensations or physiognomy. He taught that suicide was a symptom of mental illness and was careful to note the difference between hallucination and illusion.[8] The sociologists disagreed. In Germany, Italy, and France, various writers provided statistics to show that suicide rates tend to rise during periods of social unrest and economic depression; and that rates vary positively with economic position, highest in the professions, lowest among the poor. Many writers also showed that suicide rates were higher in urban areas compared to rural areas. They viewed suicide as an artifact of social change rather than a form of mental illness.[9]

One of the first to analyze the variation in suicide rates was a Belgian statistician, Lambert A. J. Quetelet. He earned his doctorate in science at the University of Ghent in 1819 and went on to make contributions in mathematics and astronomy (that led to his being memorialized on a French postage stamp). In 1823, the Belgian Royal Academy sent him to Paris for the purpose of constructing an observatory in Brussels, and while he was there, he learned of the potential of applying statistical principles to social issues. When he returned to Belgium, he began studying mortality tables for calculating insurance rates and submitted plans for a national census. In 1835, Quetelet performed a statistical analysis of suicide. He observed the constancy of suicide rates from year to year in Belgium in comparison with other demographic information. If suicide were purely a matter of individual volition, the rates of suicide would be random, not constant over time.[10]

Quetelet believed that the same law-like regularity observed in the world of nature also existed in the world of people and society. "In following attentively the regular march of nature in the development of plants and animals we are compelled," he wrote, "to believe in the analogue that the influence of laws should be extended to the human species."[11] The demonstration of these laws by means of statistical analysis Quetelet called *social mechanics*. Suicide followed laws, not unlike the celestial mechanics displayed in the night sky. He applied the law of error used in astronomy to human beings and began to write of the "average man" in society. The average man began as a simple way of representing the typical characteristic of interest within a population, but became a model of perfection and deviations from the typical value errors. Eventually, his theory took on a eugenicist character. The average man, who displayed typical physical characteristics, did not commit crimes, while the inferior classes of gypsies, vagabonds, and vagrants deviated from the average physical specimen as well as in low moral character.[12]

DURKHEIM AND SOCIAL ORDER. Durkheim also conducted a statistical analysis of suicide. But while Quetelet had applied an abstract concept from the probability theory to social statistics, Durkheim offered a theory of society that defined the academic discipline of sociology. Although he was born into a poor Jewish family, Durkheim attend a prestigious secondary school in Paris, and after graduation, spent a year studying psychology in Germany. He attained at professorship in social philosophy at the University of Bordeaux in 1887, where he created the first course in sociology. He later became a professor at the University of Paris. While at Bordeaux, Durkheim sketched his social theory in two influential works *The Division of Labor in Society* (1893) and *The Rules of the Sociological Method* (1894). In *Suicide* (1897), Durkheim took the methodology and principles of social mechanics and developed them within a coherent theory. His first task was to sever the relationship between suicide and mental disorder. Durkheim insisted that the analysis of suicide rates should be separated from those relating to the psychology of individual suicide. The factors governing distribution of suicide rates was "obviously quite distinct" from those determining which particular individuals kill themselves. Rejecting inherited insanity, psychological limitation as well as race and cosmic influences, Durkheim explained suicide in terms of social structure.[13]

Egoistic, anomic and altruistic are not types of suicide, but three forms of social structure that encourage suicide. Egoism and anomie are the predominant types in society. Egoism refers to a low level of integration with society; anomie to the absence of social rules. The explanation flowed from Durkheim's more fundamental thesis that social facts ought to be studied as "realities external to the individual." Suicide could not be understood in terms of motive or intent because intent was too subjective to be inferred by another. Rather, "the suicides committed in a given society during a given period of time...is itself a new fact, *sui generis*, with its own unity, individuality and consequently its own nature—a nature, furthermore, dominantly social."[14] He observed that individuals more closely integrated with their culture were less likely to commit suicide.

Durkheim wanted to distinguish sociology from other positivist sciences of political analysis, biology, and psychology. He began by rejecting individual volition, and insisted instead that aspects of a society influenced individual decision making. The chief object for study was the world of *social facts*, by which he meant those aspects of social structure that influence individual behavior.

Durkheim said that social facts should be considered "as things;" not that society is similar to nature, but that society is itself a natural thing, a part of nature, and subject to its natural laws.[15] It had an influence in society not because many people believe a certain idea, but that the aggregate of belief collectively held has a force all its own. These were ways of thinking and acting that existed outside individual consciousness. Durkheim insisted that people are under the illusion that they have acted out of their own choice because in reality, the action was imposed externally on people. "Social phenomena," Durkheim wrote, should "be considered in themselves, detached from the conscious beings who form their own mental representations of them."[16]

Durkheim's concept of the collective conscience extended from Comte's view of natural laws at work in human history. The *collective conscience* represented the collective mind of a society.[17] Comte taught that the interaction of human minds produced something superior to what any individual mind could achieve. The intellectual development of the human race followed from the natural sciences to the social sciences and from a less to a more highly organized mind ultimately capable of a self-directing society. Given the present stage of historical progress, Comte denied the possibility of introspection. "Individual minds, forming groups by mingling and fusing, give birth to a new being, psychological if you will, but constituting a psychic reality of a new sort." It was within the nature of the collective mind, not individual minds, in which sociologists should inquire about the social facts. "Every time a social phenomenon is directly explained by a psychological phenomenon," Durkheim wrote, "we may be sure that explanation is false."[18]

The collective mind expressed itself in a system of moral authority. *Social solidarity* has to do with social cohesion, the social glue that holds a society together. From his perspective, relationships of solidarity corresponded to the systems of social control in which the prevailing moral authority was enforced. Social solidarity was for Durkheim "a completely moral phenomenon," meaning that human society is above all else a system of moral authority. The origins of morality are found within society, not within conscience. The strategy for finding the essential features of morality is sociology. "In a word," Durkheim wrote, "we must discover the rational substitutes for those religious notions that for a long time have served as the vehicle for the most essential moral ideas."[19]

Durkheim wanted to create a "science of morality" by understanding moral facts as they really existed, just as physics and physiology dealt with the facts of the earth and body.[20]

Durkheim wrote of a major transition in civilization from "mechanical" to "organic" solidarity. Mechanical solidarity, a characteristic of primitive societies, is based on resemblances or the uniformity of its members. Members do identical work, so they have identical values and beliefs. These societies are isolated and self-sufficient. Organic solidarity is based on the division of labor and is characteristic of more advanced societies. Advanced societies display high population, a fusion of markets, and growing cities. Social cohesion is based on a complex division of labor which fosters an interdependence among its members. Although their work differs, members develop similar values and beliefs because they need each other.[21]

Ideally, there is a fit between occupational positions and individual aptitudes. Discontent arises within society when occupational arrangements are out of sync with individual aptitudes, and particularly, when those accustomed to a position of superiority under one social arrangement refuse to yield to those better suited for the new arrangement. Durkheim's concept of anomie has been understood as valuelessness or normlessness.[22] It originates in the imbalance between body and mind, or as Durkheim put it "in the disassociation of individuality from the collective conscience." *Anomie* occurs when the collective morality is unable to regulate individual desires and aspirations. It accompanies periods of transition or social change; during a war, or natural disaster when the rules seem not to apply. Anomie also occurs when individual idiosyncrasy is encouraged beyond the number of specialized roles in society. It may occur with the accumulation of wealth to the point where individual appetites are no longer limited by traditional rules or economic regulation.

Social rules provide consistency and regularity in social life. To conduct oneself morally is to abide by these pre-existing social rules that guide individual conduct and promote respect for authority. The most important element of morality is *attachment to social groups*. As social beings, people cannot cut themselves off from society, they are fused with it. Society instructs persons in morality in two ways. First, it promotes an image of the good. As social beings people must be devoted to something other than themselves and the social group provides an image of morality that attracts people. Second, the social group requires service or duty. The fact of social life exerts a pressure on people to do their duty. This pressure constitutes moral conscience; it is society speaking with the individual. "Moral goals, then, are those the object of which is society," Durkheim wrote, "To act morally is to act in terms of the collective interest." The moral life required self-sacrifice and commitment to the social good; society could not exist without this self-sacrifice.[23] Durkheim expressed his view in the following maxim: "The domain of the moral begins where the domain of the social begins."[24]

DURKHEIM ON LAW AND CRIME. Durkheim wrote a great deal about law, usually to illustrate some larger point he wanted to make about society. Law represents the most visible form of moral authority. Law is derivative from and expressive of social solidarity. Law originated in the collective sentiment or moral conscience, and the philosophy of law is inseparable from its socio-historical origins. It represents an act of human beings to establish "what all may require from each and what each may expect from all."

Durkheim said that in primitive society (mechanical solidarity), customs or rules could be tied to concrete circumstances. Since all members occupy similar social positions, the rules could be made to apply to specific situations common to all. The primary form of law was "repressive law" (criminal); it imposes suffering, or some disadvantage on the law breaker. An act can be defined as a violation of the law when it offends the collective conscience; the sanctions imposed by the law are diffused throughout society. In advanced society (organic solidarity), more codes became more generalized due to the complexity of social life. The primary form of law is "restitutive law" (civil). Rather than impose suffering, the sanction is designed to restore the state of affairs prior to the illegal act. The aim of the law is restoration of the status quo. Implementation of the restitutive law requires specialized social institutions.[25]

Durkheim is best remembered for his claim that crime is normal, not pathological. As a normal aspect of maintaining social order, crime occurs in all societies. No society can ever be entirely free of crime; absolute conformity is impossible given individual adaptation to social rules. This is not due to the "incorrigible wickedness of men." Crime, as a social fact, must be understood within a specific social and historical context, against the background of a specific level of social development. What may be abnormal from the biological or psychiatric perspective is not necessarily so from the perspective of sociology. Social facts are never pathological. At any moment, society will express an average incidence of marriages, suicides, and so on; only deviations from these averages can be considered abnormal.[26]

Rather, Durkheim wrote that crime is "a factor in public health." By this he meant that it serves a social function. Crime, or more precisely the specification of certain behaviors as crime, marks the boundaries of the collective morality. If there were a society of perfect individuals, crime would need to be invented because it is useful. At the same time, crime is essential to the evolution of a society's collective morality. It is a manifestation of individual conduct and prepares a society for transition to alternative forms of solidarity. Crime has a revolutionary character; it operates on the boundaries of social organization. It keeps the path open to necessary changes and in some situations, directly prepares a society for these changes.[27] "Yesterday's criminal is tomorrow's philosopher." Durkheim offers Socrates as an example. "According to Athenian law, Socrates was a criminal, and his condemnation more than just. However, his crime, namely, the independence of his thought, rendered a service not only to humanity but also to his country."[28]

Crime and Society

Contemporary sociological theories have borrowed one or more ideas from Durkheim. Several recent sociologies of crime begin with society, as Durkheim did, and explain how aspects of social relations generate crime. These explanations generally deal with aspects of social cohesion. They include strain produced by inequality, weak social bonds linking the individual and society, and the maintenance of social relations through shaming.

STRAIN THEORY. Sociologists have not discussed poverty so much as inequality: the difference between rich and poor in society. American sociologist Robert K. Merton conceived of inequality as a strain on the impoverished. Merton, who read Durkheim as a graduate student at Harvard, decided to find the cause of anomie.[29] In 1938, he introduced the concept in "Social Structure and Anomie," an article that became "possibly the most frequently quoted single paper in modern sociology."[30] Several years later, he became Director of the Bureau of Applied Social Research at Columbia University, and he remained there throughout a distinguished career in sociology. He popularized the ideas of self-fulfilling prophecy and role models in the study of deviant behavior.[31]

Merton offered a critique of American society that became an explanation for crime. He began by distinguishing culture from social structure. "Culture" establishes the goals and means; it specifies what things should be desired and the proper means of obtaining them. The American dream of owning a home with two cars in the driveway and two children in the backyard swimming pool can be obtained by completing a college education, pursuing a professional career, and investing money wisely. "Social structure" limits the availability of those means. For some groups in society, the dream is not obtainable. No matter how hard a single parent works, she can never save enough for a down payment on a home. In a well-integrated society, the cultural goals and the availability of means are consonant with one another; both are available to each member of the society. But too many of those in American society, Merton felt, experience dissonance between the goals and the means.

Strain occurs at the disjunction of cultural goals and social structure. It occurs when aspirations are inconsistent with expectations—when people are led to desire something they cannot acquire. Specifically, strain develops in the incongruence between culturally defined goals and means, or what Merton called "cultural imbalance." Cultural imbalance refers to overemphasis on the goals and a corresponding de-emphasis on the means. In American society, the accumulation of wealth has become an end in itself—a desire to make money no matter how it is done.

Merton devised five *adaptation styles* pursued by groups or classes of people as a response to strain: conformity, innovation, ritualism, retreatism, and rebellion. Conformists accept the goals and means; they follow the proper means to the proper goals. Innovators accept the goals, but not the means; they pursue the proper goals by illegitimate means. Innovation, the most important concept for explaining crime, occurs primarily among the working class. Ritualists reject the goals, but accept the means; they respect the rules of society even after abandoning hope of success. This is typically a middle class phenomenon. Retreatists, the least common type, reject the goals and means; they escape into psychosis, drugs, and vagrancy. Rebels reject both goals and means but replace them with substitutes. They create alternative subcultures, such as delinquent gangs and criminal organizations.

Richard Cloward and Lloyd Ohlin relied on Merton's concept of strain to explain delinquency among lower-class urban boys. Delinquency resulted from ordinary problems of adjustment complicated by disparity between what lower-class youth are led to want and what is realistically available to them. Street gangs, or what Cloward and Ohlin called *delinquent subcultures*, represent specialized modes of adaptation to strain or "problems of adjustment." They specified three kinds of delinquent subcultures: "criminal subculture" refers to a type of gang specializing in theft and property crime; "conflict subculture," a type of gang devoted to fighting and violence; and "retreatist subculture," a gang type organized around the use of illegal drugs. However, as Cloward and Ohlin pointed out, a lower-class boy who decided he could not make it by legitimate means could not simply choose among the array of illegitimate means, but only those available to him. The particular subcultural adaptation depended on the kind of social support for one or another illegitimate activity within the social structure.[32]

This aspect of Cloward and Ohlin's work has been called "the other side of strain." While Merton had said that strain resulted from limited legitimate opportunities, Cloward and Ohlin emphasized that delinquency resulted from limited illegitimate opportunities. They discussed "illegitimate opportunities and the social structure of the slum." The criminal subculture formed when there was an integration of offender at various age levels and interaction between those with conventional and delinquent values. The conflict subculture, on the other hand, arose in slums that were not integrated, in lower-class neighborhoods that lacked unity and cohesiveness. Massive housing projects, that destroyed social relationships and re-assembled strangers, along with transiency and instability, created conflict, not necessarily criminal, subcultures. The retreatist subculture came about when both legitimate and illegitimate opportunities were blocked. Young people who faced double-failure—failure to succeed in the conventional world and the criminal world—turned to drug addiction and other self-destructive behaviors.

Robert Agnew, a sociologist at Emory University, developed a *general strain theory*. In addition to the classic concept of strain by Merton and Cloward and Ohlin as the inability to achieve middle class standing through legitimate channels, Agnew suggested that strain occurs in the disjunction between expectations and actual achievements and represents the disjunction between just/fair outcomes and actual outcomes. Strain, more broadly perceived, represents the failure to achieve positively valued goals, culminating in frustration and anger. Agnew also conceptualized strain as the "removal of positively valued stimuli" and the presentation of "negative stimuli." Young persons experience strain over the "removal of positively valued stimuli" when they loose a boyfriend or girlfriend, experience the divorce of their parents, or face suspension from school. They experience strain over "negative stimuli," or more specifically, frustration over the inability to escape from stressful life events, through such life experiences as abuse and neglect, and adverse school experiences.[33]

What Merton referred to as adaptations to strain, Agnew talked about as "coping strategies." These include both delinquent and non-delinquent strategies because not all individuals who experience strain resort to illegal behavior. Whether strain leads an individual to delinquency depends on a several factors. These are the initial goals and values of the individual, individual coping resources, and conventional social support. The larger social environment also affects the probability of delinquent conduct by shaping the individual's concept of what is adverse and by making it difficult to engage in non-delinquent behavior. "Certain groups, such as adolescents and the urban underclass, may face special constraints that make non-delinquent coping more difficult."[34] The selection of delinquent coping strategies is a function of temporal variables, prior learning history of the individual, individual beliefs, and the individual's attributions regarding the source of adversity. "Adolescents who attribute their adversity to others are much more likely to become angry...and anger creates a strong predisposition to delinquency," Agnew concluded.[35]

CONTROL THEORY. The concept of strain over-predicts the amount of criminality among the poor. If American culture was as imbalanced as Merton suggested, it seems that more people should turn to innovation and crime. Or at least that was the reasoning behind the concept of the social bond. For Travis Hirschi, a sociologist at the University of Arizona, the key question is not "why do some people commit crime?" but rather "Why do most people not commit crime?" For the answer, Hirschi turned to Durkheim's idea of attachment to social groups.

Social bond theory, alternatively called *control theory*, looks at the controlling or restraining forces at work which prevent criminal behavior. Hirschi proposed that individuals bonded to social groups of family, school, and church would be less likely to engage in criminal behavior. "Delinquent acts result when the individual's bond to society is weak or broken," Hirschi said. In a sense, society must purchase conformity from its members. The social bond develops as the individual accumulates rewards from following social rules. Failing this reward structure, society would be forced to rely on coercion alone, a breakdown of society requiring marshal law.[36]

Hirschi specified four elements of the social bond. "Attachment" refers to affection for and sensitivity to parents, teachers, peers, and others. The person who lacks attachment, Hirschi says, can be described as an antisocial or sociopathic personality. It is not that the conscience is lost but the affection for the group that is lost. "Commitment" Hirschi described as the "rational component in conformity," with calculation of the amount one stands to lose by not conforming. Most people obey the law not because they fear punishment so much as they do not what to jeopardize what they have acquired through investment of time and energy in conventional activities. "Involvement" is the amount of time spent on conventional activities. Persons who focus on conventional behavior are too busy to engage in criminal behavior. Finally, there is "belief." Belief in social values of kinship, loyalty and so on strengthen the attachment to conventional behavior. Hirschi believes that some people do not respect the rules of society, that there is variation in the extent to which they believe they should obey the rules, and that the less persons believe they ought to comply, the more likely they are not to comply.[37]

One contemporary control approach is the *life course* approach. Robert J. Sampson and John H. Laub agreed that informal social control derives from the interdependency of social life surrounding social institutions of work, family, and school. They began by thinking about desistance—the end of a criminal career. This had been observed by Sheldon and Eleanor Glueck who completed their study in the 1940s. The Gluecks created an experimental sample of five hundred delinquent boys and a control group of five hundred nondelinquent boys living in poor neighborhoods of Boston. They followed the boys during the decades of the 1940s and 1950s. The Gluecks reported little change in these two groups over time; the majority of those in the law-abiding group remained law-abiding, the majority of those in the delinquent group continued to be involved in criminal activities. Sampson and Laub decided it was worth another look. While rummaging through the Glueck papers stored in the basement of a Harvard library, they came across the original computer cards used by the Gluecks. Using elaborate statistical models, they re-analyzed the Gluecks' data.[38]

They suggested that although these groups appeared similar in statistical aggregate, there had been change in individuals. The connection between age and crime is paradoxical: "adult criminality seems to be always preceded by childhood misconduct, but most conduct-disordered children do not become antisocial or criminal adults."[39] To explain why, they offer life-course perspective. Children are subjected to "social control processes" through attachment to school and parents. The effectiveness of these control mechanisms is determined by larger structural factors. Unemployed parents who move often will be less effective at social control than those with permanent residences and steady income. Sampson and Laub introduce the idea of "social capital" to refer to the resources that accumulate from conventional social relations. As social capital increases, as marriage brings additional income, and with extended social relations, and emotional attachment to spouse, the relationship becomes an important source of social control. The accumulation of social capital in adulthood redirects the initial path toward crime and delinquency. They concluded, after completing their re-analysis of the Gluecks' punch cards, that the data supported their "socio-genic developmental theory."

Shaming Theory. In 1989, John Braithwaite, at Australian National University, proposed an explanation for crime based on an elaboration of several Durkheimian ideas. What Durkheim had described as organic solidarity and anomie, Braithwaite talked about as "interdependence" and "communitarism." He used interdependence to talk about individuals, "the extent to which individuals participate in networks wherein they are dependent on others to achieve valued ends and others are dependent on them." He used communitarianism as a characteristic of societies, the kind of society in which "individuals are densely enmeshed in interdependencies which have the special qualities of mutual help and trust."[40]

Braithwaite also specified Durkheim's idea about how the punishment of crime is essential to the maintenance of social rules. It works through shaming. Braithwaite explained the place of shame in history. During the seventeenth and eighteenth centuries, persons were punished in Europe by a variety of public punishments which occurred on scaffolds constructed in public places. During the nineteenth century and until the mid-twentieth century, the system became less punitive and more integrative, and crime rates fell sharply. By the late twentieth century, reintegrative shaming weakened, and from the 1960s to the present, punishment became more punitive and crime rates increased. While Durkheim worried about the loss of community in the transition to industrial cities, Braithwaite insists that "There is no inexorable historical march with modernization towards a society where shaming works less well."[41]

The shaming produced by interdependence and communitarianism could be either of two types: reintegrating or stigmatizing. Braithwaite suggests that nations with low crime rates, and periods of history with low crime rates, are characterized by effective reintegrative shaming. *Reintegrative shaming* dispenses social disapproval within an on-going relationship with the offender based on respect, bringing shame on the wrong rather than on the wrongdoer. The ceremony of punishment in this case provides for forgiveness, apology and repentance as culturally important. This means of sanction is in contrast to *stigmatization*, where "criminal" becomes a master status of the offender and where the bond to society is broken. Stigmatization involves status degradation ceremonies to condemn the offender as an evil person.[42]

Reintegrative shaming works best within social groups where communitarianism and interdependence are strong. Shaming works best within families, when interdependency is strong so that family members care about approval and disapproval or as Braithwaite puts it "shaming affects us most when we are shamed by people who matter to us."[43] Braithwaite insists that the twentieth century city provides more opportunities for interdependence, it is just that they are no longer geographically concentrated within a community. The interdependency of modern life means that persons will be more affected by being shamed by people they work with and who live some distance away than by a next-door neighbor who they do not know very well. While "non-geographical communities of modernity" make it easier to escape disapproval than it used to be when confined to a village, the reverse is also true: one cannot escape from one's professional community simply by moving into another house.

The Geography of Crime

The development of American sociology also led to development of a geography of crime. This branch of sociological thinking has involved regional areas and cities, neighborhoods and areas within cities, and specific places within neighborhood areas such as street corners and vacant lots. In the United States, this work began at the University of Chicago and the social ecology of urban neighborhoods. Since then, it has been applied to microspaces, specific places within neighborhoods. But a hundred years before sociologists calculated the crime rate for the first census tract in Chicago, a lawyer in France had spotted a link between crime and place.

SOCIAL CARTOGRAPHY. French lawyer André-Michel Guerry produced the first systematic maps of criminal activity. In 1829, Guerry and a Venetian geographer calculated crime rates for France using crime statistics for the years 1825 to 1827 and the census of 1822 which they illustrated with three shaded maps. The maps displayed rates of crime against persons, crimes against property, and rates of illiteracy. They commented that areas of high property crime had lower personal crime rates, and vice versa; that areas of the lowest rates of education had the highest rates of property crime, and that urban areas had comparatively higher rates of property crime and crime against the person.[44]

Exactly what the maps displayed, Guerry conceded, was open to interpretation. He faced two methodological problems in constructing his maps. The first had to do with whether the total number of crimes is better represented by the number of indictments or the number of convictions. He decided to use indictments even though a person charged with a crime is not necessarily guilty. The second problem had to do with how much the geographical distribution of crime is confounded by the changing composition of residents and strangers in a given area. Crime statistics of 1828 showed that 72 percent of those accused of crimes were either born in the department where their crimes were committed or else lived there. Guerry did not claim that aspects of society such as poverty caused crime, but that social problems encouraged immorality, which led to crime.[45]

Guerry mapped crime rates for departments across France along with measures of economic development and education. Guerry's maps challenged some of the conventional thinking of the day. He found that those departments with highest population density did not necessarily have the highest rates of crime and that the poorest departments had the lowest rates of property crime. He found that areas with the highest educational levels had the highest rates of crimes against the person and those with the lowest levels of education had lower rates of personal crime. The statistical relationships led Guerry to conclude that relationships among wealth, poverty, and crime were complex, and he challenged the notion popular in France that the lack of education led to crime.[46]

SOCIAL ECOLOGY. American social cartography, or social ecology as it has become known, began in the early twentieth century. When Robert E. Park became a professor at the University of Chicago in 1913, the university was a small, private institution financed almost exclusively by John D. Rockefeller. The university became the first American institution to establish a program in sociology, however, and it remained the premiere sociology program in the nation for nearly four decades. Park, who had joined the faculty after a career as a city newspaper journalist, helped give the Chicago School of sociology a prominent place in criminology.

Park's sociology focused on the question of how people form communities and how these communities develop around natural boundaries. For his model of human ecology, Park borrowed concepts from botany and the German philosopher-biologist, Ernst Haeckel.[47] Park compared neighborhoods to plant communities; they emerged as natural, unplanned but organized groups of people. They did not necessarily share the same beliefs, but were united never-the-less by a "symbiotic relationship," an interdependency fostered by the need for diverse capabilities to meet the challenge of urban life. Just as a new species upsets the equilibrium of a plant community, new immigrant groups threatened the interdependent relationships within neighborhoods. As Park described it, neighborhoods represented social worlds, not merely geographical space. The similarity of cultural patterns in neighborhoods was not explained by resemblances among persons, but social processes beyond individual control. Cultural patterns were preserved by a process of natural selection Park termed "the struggle for space." The struggle for space, characterized by a pattern of invasion, dominance and succession, explained patterns of urban growth and particularly patterns of ethnic succession in neighborhoods.[48]

Park and a colleague, Ernest Burgess, mapped the struggle for space among ethnic groups in Chicago. They began with the central business district, then moved outward through expanding co-centric zones. The core contained major corporate offices, banks, insurance companies, and government offices. The second zone they called the "zone in transition" because it contained a factory zone that encroached on the dwellings of the city's poorest residents. The third zone was the "zone of workingmen's homes," and finally the homes of the more affluent middle class, the "commuters" and residents of "satellite cities." As the city expanded outward, each zone eventually claimed the territory of the adjacent zone. The cycle repeated itself in the form of ethnic succession. The newest arrivals resided in the zone in transition, and as each immigrant group acquired social standing, migrated to the zone of workingmen's home then to the commuter zone.

Clifford Shaw, working at the Institute for Juvenile Research, used the *social ecology* model to explore how youth become delinquent. He theorized that when relationships within natural areas become too competitive, and less cooperative, equilibrium breaks down and delinquency ensues. Together with Henry D. McKay, Shaw mapped rates of delinquency and income for census tracts throughout Chicago. These "spot maps" showed that the areas with the highest delinquency rates were those adjacent to industry and commerce, those of the lowest economic status, and those areas with the greatest portion of immigrants and Blacks. Delinquency rates were highest in the zone in transition, Shaw and McKay explained, because the stability of cultural patterns had been weakened by dis-equilibrium. Dis-equilibrium generated wide standards from the conventional to the deviant, each of which offered opportunities for advancement, legitimate and illegitimate.

In 1989, Robert J. Sampson, a University of Chicago sociologist, and W. Byron Groves, a criminologist at the University of Wisconsin at Green Bay, published a study using information obtained from the British Crime Survey. They calculated crime rates and other social indexes for 238 localities across England and Wales. Three of the social indexes had been specified by Shaw and McKay as structural dimensions of social disorganization: persistent poverty, ethnic diversity, and residential mobility. Sampson and Groves suggested two more, urbanization and family disruption. They also suggested several "intervening dimensions of social disorganization," based on the prevalence of social networks within communities. They decided that communities differ in the collective capacity of residents to control one another based on differences in their ability to control "teenage peer groups" such as street-corner congregating, "local friendship networks," or social ties among residents, and participation in "formal and voluntary organizations," such as committees, clubs and local institutions. They concluded that the same processes that had occurred in Chicago during the 1930s also occurred in England during the 1980s.[49]

THE CRIMINOLOGY OF PLACE. Emphasis on the social aspect explains how neighborhoods can remain the site of high crime despite a complete turnover in their populations. The University of Washington's Rodney Stark suggests that neighborhoods cannot be thought of in terms of the characteristics of the people. Rather, there must be something about the places as such that sustain crime. Stark specified five features of neighborhoods leading to crime. These are: density, poverty, mixed use, transience, and dilapidation. Invoking Guerry's notion of immorality, these features have been thought to have impacts on the moral order as people respond to them. Response includes moral cynicism among residents, increased opportunities for crime and deviance, increased motivation to deviate, and diminished social control. These responses amplify the volume of deviance by attracting high crime-prone people, and deviant activities to neighborhoods, by driving out the least deviant, and by further reductions in social control.[50]

The geography of crime acquired increasing importance beginning in the 1960s. Jane Jacobs's *Death and Life of Great American*

Cities (1961) described the problems of urban renewal. She suggested that old urban neighborhoods, even though impoverished, had low crime rates. They protected people from crime through informal controls that encouraged individuals to conform with conventional behavior. Multiple land uses along residential streets provided an interaction between the physical design of urban space and the users (residents, pedestrians) which promoted natural surveillance. When city officials razed these neighborhoods to make room for high-rise public housing projects, crime rates increased because they had become sterile environments free from controls. She suggested that the high-rise buildings had crime problems built into their design. Jacobs had initiated an understanding of how the built environment can encourage or discourage criminal activity.[51]

Ten years later, C. Ray Jeffrey, a criminologist at Florida State University, described how crime could be prevented through *environmental design*. While the Chicago School compared rates across neighborhoods, place research compares rates at locations within neighborhoods. Within the Chicago School theory, neighborhoods represented social worlds not necessarily attached to specific locations in the city. Henry McKay, however, observed that even within high-crime neighborhoods of Chicago, entire blocks were free of delinquents. Jeffrey suggested that the physical characteristics of a place shaped the opportunities to commit crime and that security-conscious design provided the key to informal social control and safer cities. Jeffrey insisted that one of the major defects of ecological research had been using census tract data as Shaw and McKay had done. This approach glossed over the physical features of the urban landscape conducive to certain forms of crime. "We must look at the physical environment in terms of each building, or each room of the building. Fine grain resolution is required in place of the usual large-scale photographs...."[52]

Investigating the "criminology of place" became possible with the development of 911 communications. In 1989, Larry Sherman, a University of Maryland criminologist, and associates used police call data provided by the emergency three-digit dispatch system in Minneapolis, Minnesota to map the microspatial patterns of crime and delinquency.[53] The researchers calculated the number of crimes occurring at places throughout the city-intersections, street addresses—and found *hot spots* for predatory crimes of robbery, rape and auto theft. These hot spots included the bus depot, downtown mall, hotels, bars, and intersections surrounded by various combinations of bars, liquor stores, parks, and pornography book stores. Hot spots are bunched together along major streets in some neighborhoods, and because more of such places are located in cities, cities report higher crime rates. Other researchers have reported that city blocks that contain taverns are significantly more likely to have burglaries and other property crimes.[54]

Marcus Felson, a Rutgers criminologist, insists that changes in cities in recent decades have meant that the natural community areas Park talked about no longer exist. The immediate proximity no longer serves as the basis for developing symbiosis because the "socio-circulatory system" made possible by automobile travel and interstate freeways extends too far. The urban neighborhoods of Chicago have been replaced by new urban structures such as the "metroreef." First, developers built shopping centers and stripmalls, then other developers linked additional businesses, office complexes, adjacent to public facilities. These facilities are changing the spatial distribution of crime and have led to the prospect that urban space can be purposefully designed to redirect the flow of routine activities. "Perhaps the flow of routine activities could be diverted ever so slightly to reduce crime, without sacrificing prosperity or freedom," Felson concudes.[55]

The idea of *defensible space* led to three design principles: control natural areas, provide natural surveillance, and foster territorial behavior. The idea is that social behavior can be controlled through strategies for "marking transitions," subtle indicators about where one person's space begins and another's ends. Hedges, walkways, gates, doors and the like mark public, semi-public and private space; controlled and uncontrolled space. Urban space can be designed to discourage crime by increasing "territoriality" and "natural surveillance." Natural strategies rely on the design and layout of urban space.[56]

The Social Psychology of Crime

While sociologists since Durkheim generally hold that psychologists mistake social behavior for individual behavior, there is a tradition within sociology that has attempted to explain how social forces translate into individual decision-making. The ideas important to sociological criminology include imitation, social learning, and situated transaction.

IMITATION. Jean-Gabriel Tarde, a magistrate at Sarlat in the 1890s, was the foremost criminologist in France. Durkheim's work has been remembered as founding of sociology, but at the time, Tarde was the preeminent.[57] Tarde introduced his concept of imitation into the debate among French criminologists about volition and determinism. He developed a social psychology of crime based on the concept of "imitation."

Tarde described *imitation* as an unconscious decision making process involving the interplay between tradition, social morality, and desire. It did not operate at the individual level, however, but the social level. He developed his laws of imitation. Tarde postulated that people imitate each other in proportion to how close of contact they have with one another, which explains why cities have higher homicide rates than the country. He theorized that inferior people imitate superior people. Cities brought peasants and poor workers in contact with French nobility. Tarde insisted that crime originated in the higher ranks and passed down to the lower ranks—drunkenness, moral offenses, political assassination, arson. Tarde also explored the methods of various crimes which led him to propose that newer fashions follow older ones. He used French crime statistics to show that murder by knife had decreased while murder by shooting had increased—using a gun to commit murder had started out as a fashion and had become a custom.[58]

While Tarde described imitation as a psychological state, Tarde's social psychology explored two social factors. Urbanism became the greatest arena for the spread of crime. Cities had higher rates of homicide motivated by greed and in cities the murderer and murder victim were more likely to be strangers. Urban life also encouraged the greatest retreat from French moral customs into decadence. Tarde also explored crowd behavior. Mobs encouraged people to act on the whims of a few because the participants were detached from family and tradition. It was the unpredictability of crowd behavior, the spark that ignited violence, that led Tarde to define imitation as a form of somnambulism, a trance-like psychological state bordering on sleep-walking.[59]

SOCIAL LEARNING THEORY. In the United States, Indiana University's Edwin Sutherland expanded Tarde's concept of imitation with the notion of differential association. In 1924, Sutherland wrote a textbook on criminology in which he expounded on the role of communication in a child's learning experience. In *The Professional Thief* (1939), he offered a theory of social learning to explain "systematic criminal behavior" or criminal careers, and later expanded it to explain white collar crime in *White Collar Crime* (1949). Sutherland wrote that people learn to be criminal essentially the same way they learn to abide by the law. Sutherland stated his theory of *differential association* in nine propositions, beginning with the proposition that "criminal behavior is learned." Criminal behavior is acquired in the same way as conventional behavior, through the process of interaction and communication with others. "A person becomes delinquent," Sutherland proposed, "because of an excess of definitions favorable to violation of law over definitions unfavorable to violation of law."[60] The chance that a person adopts a criminal lifestyle is increased by the frequency of contact with criminals. Learning of criminal behavior includes not only the techniques, but also the motives and drives of a criminal. Although Sutherland died in 1950, his theory was left intact by Donald Cressey in subsequent revisions of the criminology text.

Albert Bandura, a Stanford University psychologist, developed a theory of learning based on the idea that children learn simply by watching others, which he called *observational learning*. After attempting systematic observation of children at play in their homes, he developed a technique for studying aggressive modeling in the setting of the psychological laboratory. Bandura conducted a series of experiments in which groups of nursery-school children observed a live adult, an adult on film, and a cartoon cat attack an inflated clown "Bobo doll." One group watched the adult hit the doll with a rubber mallet, one group watched a non-aggressive adult, one group saw no adult at all. Later, when the children were observed at play with the Bobo doll, Bandura concluded that children who had observed the aggressive model engaged in more aggressive play with the doll than those that had not.[61]

Bandura concluded that much behavior (ultimately he concluded that all behavior) is learned initially by watching others—models. Models include not only parents, teachers, siblings and friends, but also fictional characters on television and film. Bandura focused on the learning of aggressive behavior. He noted that television and films provide abundant role models demonstrating violent behavior. But watching televised violence does not necessarily lead to violence. The observed behavior of the model is more likely to be imitated by the observer if the model receives a reward. Once a person acquires a new behavior, whether he or she maintains it depends on the expected gain. When a child's behavior is reinforced or rewarded by praise and encouragement from models, the frequency of behavior increases. At the initial stage of learning, observation is important, but in later stages, reinforcement is essential. Up until adolescence, parents can be powerful role models for children, but after early adolescence, peer models predominate. If the model receives a reprimand or punishment during or after an aggressive episode, this will inhibit the observer's behavior.[62]

Ronald Akers, a sociologist at the University of Florida, has developed a *social learning* theory of criminology.[63] He combined earlier ideas of Tarde, Sutherland, and Bandura into an explanation of crime. Akers's theory rests on four major concepts. "Differential association" refers to the process where one is exposed to normative definitions favorable or unfavorable to lawful or unlawful behavior. "Definitions" are the person's attitudes or meanings attached to given behavior. "Differential reinforcement" has to do with the balance of anticipated or actual rewards and punishments that follow or are consequences of behavior. "Imitation" refers to engaging in behavior after the observation of similar behavior in others. The balance of learned definitions, imitation of criminal models, and the anticipated balance of reinforcement produces the initial criminal act. Whether a criminal act will be committed in any given situation depends on that individual's "learning history." Akers points out that social structure does, however, shape individual behavior. "Differences in group rates of criminal behavior" are a function of how "class, race, gender, religion, and other structures in society, provide the learning contexts for individuals," and these "learning environments" provide "immediate situations conducive to conformity or deviance."[64]

CRIME AS A SITUATED TRANSACTION. Other sociologists have tried to develop a micro-social explanation for crime based on characteristics of the criminal event. This line of thought, implicit in Tarde's discussion of crowd behavior, looks at aspects of social situations and how they lead to crime. It includes concepts of victim precipitation and situated transaction.

Marvin Wolfgang, a sociologist at the University of Pennsylvania, studied 588 criminal homicides that occurred in Philadelphia between 1948 and 1952. He reported that the social characteristics of victims and offenders were similar, challenging the popular notion of brutal, aggressive predators and weak, passive victims. He also determined that about one fourth of these were victim precipitated. By *victim precipitation*, Wolfgang meant that the person killed had been the first to use force or brandish a weapon that initiated the violence. Wolfgang suggested that homicide resulted from the interaction between the murderer and murder victim, through an escalation leading to the victim's death.

The idea of victim precipitation led to thinking of crime less as individual behavior and more as a kind of social situation; to thinking about the outcome of a crime situation not solely in terms of the criminal's motivation and action, but in terms of the interaction between the criminal, victim, and witnesses. From the perspective of the criminal law, what a person intends or the criminal's motive must be inferred by their words and actions. From this perspective, what a person intends by their words and actions is less important than how they are perceived by others in the social situation. What represents a defensive reaction on the victim's part then, may be interpreted as an offensive or life-threatening gesture on the criminal's part. This understanding of crime as a social event has been developed as situated transaction theory.[65]

Luckenbill defines a *situated transaction* as the process of interaction between two or more individuals that lasts the time they are in one another's presence. He culled information from the FBI's Supplementary Homicide Reports for homicides in a California county that occurred between 1963 and 1974. He identified several features of the social situation in which these homicides occurred. Many had taken place during "non-working hours," before an "audience" of family, friends, and acquaintances, and represented "ambiguous social occasions" in the sense that there was no specific purpose for gathering. Luckenbill characterized the interaction that led to the victim's death as an "character contest" in which both the victim and murderer attempt to save face at the victim's expense. In 63 percent of the cases, the victim made what the murderer perceived as an offensive gesture or remark. The murderer retaliated, and the victim reacted, created a "working agreement" to end the conflict by violence. The battle resulted in the victim's death.[66]

Applied Sociology

The sociological view of crime came to prominence in the United States during the 1960s, when the federal government translated a number of sociological concepts into social policy. Lloyd Ohin, Robert Merton and other sociologists became influential advisors during the Kennedy-Johnson years. The system of delinquency prevention put in place during those years continues into the twenty-first century.

Prior to the Kennedy-Johnson years, the federal government took little interest in juvenile justice and delinquency prevention. In 1912, Congress charged the Children's Bureau, U.S. Department of Health and Human Services, with investigating the operation of juvenile courts. In 1948, President Harry Truman convened the Mid-Century Conference on Children and Youth to explore methods of improving juvenile courts, improve police services to juveniles, and examine the prevention aspects of social service providers. But even during Roosevelt's New Deal, Congress enacted no new legislation dealing with juvenile justice. Roosevelt held an attitude of limited government action in social affairs and the public viewed delinquency as a state and local problem.[67]

The 1960 Democratic platform contained a statement that the federal government ought to prevent and control delinquency. At the same time, the Kennedy family was interested in youth problems; Robert Kennedy took particular interest in delinquency issues as they related to race and poverty. Within a week of the election, President-elect John Kennedy and Robert Kennedy, his attorney general designate, asked a member of their campaign organization to launch a national attack on delinquency. That individual, David Hackett, pulled together a circle of advisors, including people from the Children's Bureau of Health, Education and Welfare; the National Institute of Mental Health, and the Ford Foundation. Lloyd Ohlin, who had been serving as a consultant to the Children's Bureau and NIMH, was well-connected as an advisor to Hackett. Robert Kennedy read *Delinquency and Opportunity* by Cloward and Ohlin, and the theory appealed to him.[68]

In March 1961, Hackett called the first of a series of confer-
ences on juvenile delinquency, and "enlarging the opportunity
structure for youths in the areas of large cities" became the focus
for federal initiatives. Kennedy used the theme in establishing the
President's Committee on Juvenile Delinquency and Youth Crime
and the legislative proposals to Congress. Robert Kennedy
chaired the committee, Hackett served as executive director, and
Ohlin, designated by Hackett as his special assistant. The committee received Congressional support for a federal-funding initiative that provided ten million dollars a year over a three-year
period for initiatives to make the federal government a partner
with state and local government to prevent and control delinquency. Congress enacted the Juvenile Delinquency and Youth
Offenses Control Act in 1961. This legislation directed the Department of Health, Education and Welfare (HEW) to provide
funds to state, local and non-profit agencies to develop demonstration projects on improved methods of preventing and controlling crime. The federally-funded programs sought to improve
social conditions within the nation's cities through community
action. Many of these projects, such as Neighborhood Youth
Corps, Legal Services Corporation, and Head Start served as
models for the programs President Lyndon Johnson would initiate after the assassination of President Kennedy. They brought
community resources to prevention through combating the
sources of delinquency.[69]

The way the bill was administered raised some opposition. One
congressional member, Edith Green, objected to the political basis of
selecting grantees, to emphasis on planning versus demonstration
projects, and some other aspects. She had sponsored the bill in the
House and explained that "I surely wasn't thinking of what they refer
to in the profession today as the thirty million dollar test of Ohlin's
opportunity theory."[70] Despite opposition, the Kennedy Administration succeeded in winning Congressional support for the program for
another two years. Delinquency prevention became a major theme of
Kennedy's domestic program and a key theme in his planned reelec-
tion campaign for 1964. Failure to defend a ten million dollar delinquency prevention program would have weakened the administration's case for a one billion dollar-a-year poverty relief initiative.

One of the programs fostered by the Kennedy administration,
Mobilization for Youth, followed from Merton's and Cloward and

Ohlin's strain theory. The program sought to remove obstacles to upward mobility for youth in a poor Manhattan neighborhood. Program staff offered a series of interventions and specialized services to youth from low-income families. Specifically, the program aimed to: increase the employment opportunities available, make job-training and skill-development programs accessible to these youth, aid youth in securing employment equal to their capabilities, and to help minority youngsters overcome workplace discrimination. The program "was a far-reaching program of theoretically based social experimentation, an attempt to systematically blend sociology and social reform."[71]

Delinquency prevention became even more important after Kennedy's death, as an element of Johnson's Great Society program. Johnson supported the idea of community action to improve the conditions of the city. In a sense, Johnson's anti-poverty programs extended Kennedy's delinquency prevention programs on a larger scale. A Democrat who had represented an impoverished district of Texas, Johnson urged Americans to build a great society. He used the power of the presidency to direct federal spending toward reducing poverty, malnutrition, and improving education and medical care. The Office of Economic Opportunity, set up by Johnson to administer the program, funded programs such as Head Start, VISTA, Job Corps, Upward Bound, and the Community Action Program. In February 1967, Johnson proposed enactment of the Safe Streets and Crime Control Act. Although the legislation that eventually passed, the Omnibus Crime Control and Safe Streets Act of 1968, did not reflect the Great Society spirit, Johnson reluctantly signed the bill. Later, the Juvenile Delinquency Prevention and Control Act passed, which provided $150 million over three years to implement the recommendations of the President's Commission in the area of juvenile delinquency.[72]

Johnson established the President's Commission on Law Enforcement and the Administration of Justice in 1966 to investigate the causes of crime and delinquency and formulate a national crime prevention strategy. Johnson's Commission produced an influential report, *The Challenge of Crime in a Free Society* (1967), which reflected the thinking of several sociologists about crime. Lloyd Ohlin, who served as an associate director of the commission's staff, testified to the influence of *Principles of Criminology*, by Sutherland and Cressey, to the commission's outlook. The seventh edition had appeared in 1966.[73] During this period of time "criminology" became synonymous with sociological criminology.

The legislative process culminating in the Juvenile Justice and Delinquency Prevention Act (JJDP Act) of 1974 began four years earlier, when the U.S. Senate Subcommittee to Investigate Juvenile Delinquency began to look at the nation's juvenile justice system. The Subcommittee, chaired by Senator Birch Bayh of Indiana, heard from dozens of witnesses, including juvenile court judges, professors, child advocates, prosecutors, public defenders, parents and children. The Subcommittee concluded that large numbers of juveniles confined in training schools, detention centers and county jails were status offenders and victims of parental neglect. They found overcrowded and understaffed juvenile courts, training schools, and social services unable to provide adequate treatment. "The juvenile justice system is a failure," Bayh's Subcommittee concluded, "not only from the child's point of view but also from the point of view of our society."[74]

Bayh's subcommittee discovered that while the federal government had numerous juvenile justice programs, lack of coordination hampered their impact. There were five federal departments involved in juvenile delinquency (Justice; Health, Education and Welfare; Labor, and Housing and Urban Development) and at least 116 federal programs, and the overall federal effort lacked focus. In hearings leading up to passage of the legislation, Milton Rector, president of the National Council on Crime and Delinquency, advised Bayh's subcommittee that "A major weakness [in the federal effort] is the lack of a structure present where Federal juvenile and criminal justice planning can be coordinated with other human service agencies."[75]

The Act that Congress passed in 1974 established two themes that guided subsequent federal delinquency legislation. First, that financial assistance alone was an insufficient federal response to delinquency. The federal government had to provide comprehensive planning and coordination of services as well. Second, some practices, such as confining juvenile offenders with adults, did more harm than good.[76] Even more important, the JJDP Act provided a focus for the federal response to delinquency, a federal focus on delinquency prevention. Senator Bayh urged Congress to provide a one-word description of the JJDP Act — "prevention."[77]

The goals of the JJDP Act were, however, more limited than the strategies identified by Johnson's Commission on Law Enforcement in 1966. Although the new law did not decriminalize status offenses, it did encourage the use of non-secure treatment alternatives. The act provided federal funds to divert juveniles from correctional settings into restitution and other community programs and discourage large, warehouse institutions. The act did require removal of status offenders from secure incarceration. Specifically, the law required states to remove status offenders from secure confinement and separate adult and juvenile offenders in order to receive federal funds. Further, the law required that states dedicate three-fourths of federal funds they received to community-based programs in order to encourage diversification of services and decentralization of control. When juveniles were placed in residential facilities, they had to be in the least restrictive alternative appropriate to needs of the child and be in the reasonable proximity to their families.[78]

In 1988, an interviewer asked Ohlin about the Kennedy Administration's accomplishments in the area of delinquency prevention. "Unfortunately," he concluded, "the whole effort was escalated too quickly from the experimental stage and swallowed up in the war on poverty, building model cities, etc." Ironically, the effort created a strain of its' own: the rhetoric of reform exceeded the resources available. The experience affected Richard Cloward, Ohlin's *Delinquency and Opportunity* co-author. Cloward adapted to the strain by leaving the study of delinquency for that of poor people's movements.[79] (Which raises the possibility of academic research as a sixth adaptation to strain.)

Criminal Responsibility and Casuistry

Sociology makes very dry reading. Or at least that is what Howard S. Becker, a sociologist at Northwestern University who wrote one of the best-selling sociology books of the 1960s claims. This dryness comes from sociologists' preference for abstract nouns and passive verbs. They fill their paragraphs with lifeless phrases such as "broad social transformations have led to" and "structural changes have transferred." Sociologists rely on this language to cover up the absence of human agency in their thinking. Nothing that happens has any apparent cause, or any cause that can be recognized within the scope of human personality. "Who did the things the sentence says happened?... Sociologists often prefer locutions that leave the answer to that question unclear," Becker observes, "largely because many of their theories don't tell them who is doing what."[80]

The passive voice of the sociological imagination reflects the concept of structural causality. The doctrine of *structural causality* asserts that crime occurs for reasons outside human action; crime rates rise and fall with large-scale forces of urbanization, income distribution, demographic shifts, cultural habits and so on. Comte and Durkheim emphasized the influence of social forces to distinguish what they did as sociologists from what the psychologists did. And when they removed crime from the realm of human action, they created a void in the realm of moral responsibility. In the sociological scheme of things, individual values reflect the values of society, and social values reflect those values in place at a particular period in history. The whole structure of morality rises and falls with the tide of social change. From this point of view, the very concept of criminal responsibility, as something that attaches to individuals, derives from colossal shifts in social structure.[81]

Exactly what this means in the day-to-day world of individuals and their treatment of one another is not clear. It may be that social facts have no direct connection to a criminal case; the statistics of crime in general have nothing to say to judges and juries about whether one person lied, cheated or stole from other, and if so, what ought to be done about it. James Q. Wilson, who in 1966 chaired the White House Task Force on Crime, has decided that although sociologists have turned up some interesting statistics about aspects of crime, they have nothing to say about what should be done about crime based on these interesting statistics. He observes that the sociological view of crime, which assumes that social processes determine behavior, makes it difficult, if not impossible, to propose policy alternatives. The analysis leads in the direction of the material desires of life but stops short of coming up with a strategy for how those material desires are realized.[82] On the other hand, sociologists complain that public officials choose to ignore the sociological evidence and instead pursue their own biases. Harsh crime control policies result from public officials' inattention to the research evidence.[83] Social facts ought to influence the day-to-day decisions in courts, and if judges only took the time to learn about the statistical findings generated by sociological criminology, they would recognize its value.[84]

How would things be different in criminal courts if judges pursued the sociological imagination instead of traditional legal principles? No judge has thought more about this than David Bazelon, who served on the United States Court of Appeals for the District of Columbia from 1949 to 1986. Bazelon read sociology, or at least enough to know about the correlation between delinquency and impoverished neighborhoods. And given that social disadvantage translates into criminal behavior, the simple refrain that "individuals are responsible for their actions" does not apply. Criminologists might not possess complete knowledge of criminal behavior, but they know enough to understand that crime is a matter of social responsibility. "What we know about street crime might require us to provide every family with the means to create the kind of home all human beings need...to afford job opportunities that pose some meaningful alternatives to violence... [to] demand for all children a constructive education, a decent place to live and proper pre- and postnatal nutrition." When society fails to meet its social responsibility to individuals, individuals ought not be held responsible for their actions, even when they are criminal. He proposed the "rotten social background defense."[85]

The phrase "rotten social background" first appeared in the case of *United States v. Alexander and Murdock* (1973).[86] The defendant in the case shot to death a marine in a tavern after the victim had impugned him with racist vulgarity. The defense attempted to show that the defendant had an irresistible impulse to shoot as a result of a childhood in Watts, California, in which he had lived in severe economic deprivation. His father had abandoned the family, and the boy grew up in an environment of severe economic deprivation. He had experienced racist mistreatment and learned to fear white persons. A psychiatrist for the defense testified that while the defendant was sane, he suffered from impaired behavioral controls due to his rotten social background. The jury found the defendant sane and sentenced him to prison, and the D.C. Circuit Court of Appeals affirmed the decision on appeal. Bazelon outlined the theory of the rotten social background defense in a dissenting opinion.[87]

Judge Bazelon refined his theory in an address to the Hoover Institution.[88] Bazelon argued that a conviction in a criminal case expresses moral condemnation and that moral condemnation is not just unless the person could be reasonably expected to conform his or her behavior with the demands of the law. He urged consideration of social adversity defense to take into account the psychological effects of severe economic deprivation. "A defendant is not responsible," Bazelon proposed, "if at the time of his unlawful conduct his mental or emotional processes or behavior controls were impaired to such an extent that he cannot justly be held responsible for his act." Bazelon believed that the introduction of such a test would result in relatively few acquittals because he had set the standard of "cannot justly be held responsible" so high that juries would not be likely to acquit. Still, he concluded that the rotten social background defense represented an important part of the criminal law. People must not abide by the law because they live in fear of retribution but because they recognize the fairness of the laws. "The law's aims must be achieved by a moral process cognizant of the realities of social injustice," Bazelon said.[89] The criminal law should adhere to "the reality principle," that street criminals turn to crime as a consequence of their circumstances.[90]

Bazelon's argument drew fire Stephen Morse, a law professor at the University of Pennsylvania. Morse argued that all social environments affect choice. Although some decisions are harder to make than others, no social environment completely erodes the ability to make choices. Morse pointed out that the majority of people in impoverished areas do not commit crime; the vast majority of persons in impoverished areas obey the law and most families do manage to convey to their children a sense of order, purpose and self-esteem. Not only would the government be unable to eliminate poverty by means of public spending, but economic improvements tended to lead to more crime, not less. Further, the creation of a social adversity defense amounted to arrogant paternalism. When a person breaks the law, punishment amounts to respect. The assumption that a person is not capable of obeying the law is to think of them as something less than a person.[91]

Michael Moore, another University of Pennsylvania law professor, agreed with Morse particularly about the last point. The sentiment Bazelon extended to lawbreakers falls short of noble. On the surface, making an allowance for rotten social background appears to be an act of kindness and compassion. It reveals, however, an elitism and condescension. Moore reviewed traditional legal defenses with the idea of sociological determinism in mind. If "hard determinism" is true and people lack the ability to choose, the defenses are all meaningless to begin with. If determinism is not true and people always have the ability to choose, then recognizing the individual as a free moral agent becomes the first principle of the criminal law. There is no place in traditional legal defense for a legal excuse derived from a defendant's rotten social background.[92]

In 1985, Richard Delgado, then a law professor at the University of California Los Angeles, came to Bazelon's defense. Delgado took issue with Moore's conclusions and argued that the RSB defense did fit within conventional legal excuses. The traditional legal doctrine of justification does not seek to excuse the behavior. It recognizes that the behavior is wrong but that blame does not attach because the defendant's action was justified under the circumstances. Delgado identified several interests that individuals in impoverished circumstances would be entitled to defend, including attacks on their dignity. Delgado went on to argue that society's rationale for punishing would be undermined without recognizing a rotten social background. "Essentially, society's right to punish requires that individuals have a realistic chance to act in a socially acceptable way, or, once an offender, the possibility of becoming the sort of person who can benefit from acting in accord with social and legal norms."[93]

In 1995, the University of Minnesota's Michael Tonry took up the issue once again. He disagreed with Morse and Moore. Poverty does cause crime, at least in a probabilistic way. He suggested that the defendant's social background does make a difference in circumstances in which a youth from one neighborhood has a much higher chance of getting in trouble with the law than another.[94] Nevertheless, he raised several "practical objections" to application of a social adversity defense. Would the defense be available in all cases or only some? If available in every case, courts would still not be likely to release individuals considered dangerous; they would be detained to protect the public. This would create a preventive detention situation and the spectacle of detaining persons who have not been found guilty of a crime. What message would the court send to those acquitted by reason of rotten social background? Tonry reasoned that an RSB acquittal amounted to a label and raised the possibility of self-fulfilling prophecy. The defendant, formally recognized as crime-prone, would be likely to commit more crimes, not fewer. The defense would create a perverse incentive to break the law.[95]

Tonry, Morse and Moore raise some thoughtful objections to the RSB defense. None of their objections, however, confront the larger issue of "social responsibility." The idea that judges and other public officials possess a social responsibility that if not fulfilled leads to diminished individual responsibility creates a serious ethical dilemma. It gives license to immoral conduct, not merely on the part of citizens as has been pointed out, but on the part of public officials. Judges, freed from the legal responsibility to do justice in individual cases, can prescribe any number of outcomes in their effort to meet some greater social responsibility. It leads to casuistry.

Historically, *casuistry* appeared as an attempt to think through social responsibility and use it to create a special ethics for those in power.[96] The idea began with John Calvin, became the province of the Counter-Reformation, and developed into political ethics by Jesuits of the seventeenth century. The casuistic-thinking political rulers reasoned that their behavior affected more persons than themselves and their families. They decided that the rules to decide moral behavior do not apply equally, if at all, to those with social responsibility. The rulers claimed special exemption from the demands of conventional morality because their behavior could confer benefits on people.[97]

Casuistry led to a great deal of injustice because casuistic thinking can justify almost any immoral practice. Dostoyevsky explored this theme in his great novel *Crime and Punishment*. Raskolnikov reasons that murder is a terrible thing for a common man, but not for a great man, a man destined to make a contribution to world history. Raskolnikov commits murder, not out of hatred for his victim, but out his feelings of magnanimity for humanity as a whole. What makes Dostoyevsky's novel so troubling is that Raskolnikov appears not as a delusional psychopath, but as a representative human being who dares to take social responsibility to its conclusion: individuals do not exist. Raskolnikov views the people he meets with disgust; he cuts himself off from everyone. He is destined for greatness, he is not an ordinary person to whom traditional morality applies. Raskolnikov's crime is rebellion, his refusal to see that he really is just like everyone else. He refuses to accept God's world and its fundamental condition, mortality.[98]

In their pursuit of the social sources of crime, sociological criminologists have divorced justice from ethics. Crime must be attacked as it exists as an aggregate phenomenon. The exact sources of crime, or the precise social process by which social facts translate into individual action, sociological criminologists do not know. What they do know is that crime is not an individual phenomenon. And when the sociological imagination goes to court, casuistry happens. To appreciate the causes of crime, one must avoid individual cases for an understanding of the social landscape. Crime rates are calculated, the outcomes of court decisions tabulated, the data aggregated for analysis. Once the data of crime has been aggregated, it can be correlated with other social data—income distribution, opinion surveys, educational statistics, employment numbers and so on. Public policy must be designed to alter the dynamic between the crime rate and these basic correlates. There are communities to re-build, neighborhoods to re-design, behavior patterns to redirect. What is one theft in the scope of such grand designs? One rape, an assault, even a murder or two?

Sociological criminologists cannot be distracted with the justice of individual cases, with whether one person actually beat, cheated, or stole from another. Criminology must transcend the conventional view of right and wrong. Ethics are for police officers, judges, and lawyers to deal with. And so long as the practitioners of justice understand that they should listen to the community, and do their best to keep their personal views out of the way, criminologists will let them talk about professional ethics. Criminologists must fulfill another destiny. They understand why criminals, and those who respond to them, think as they do. They understand the social sources of morality. It is they, the immoralists, who must shape the conscience of both criminal and prosecutor. Criminologists have a social responsibility to do what is right for society.

Conclusion

The reference to social responsibility is not an appeal to justice, but rather, a comment about power. The analysis of social reponsibility is not really about what it means to love one's neighbor but about who has power in society. It is about recognizing who has it and taking some of it away. Michel Foucault, a leading thinker in the constructionist version of criminology made it plain: "The proletariat doesn't wage war against the ruling class because it considers such as war to be just…the proletariat makes war with the ruling class because…it wants to take power."[99] The analysis of power is what Marx and the Frankfurt School of critical social theory is all about.

Chapter 6

The Social Construction of Crime

The constructionist view of crime asserts that criminologists, from the classicists, and biologists, to the psychiatrists and sociologists, have asked the wrong question. Rather than "what causes crime?" the question should be, "Why are some activities defined as crime?" From the constructionist perspective, criminology ought to be about uncovering the social processes of defining certain activities as crimes, rather than the origins of the activities themselves. Those who insist that reality is a social construction spend more time on law and social control than crime because they want to show how the law creates crime; crime is less important than the structures of society that create both law and criminality. The social construction of crime perspective is not so much a theory of crime as a critique of other theories of crime. Constructionists do not ask what is true, only how concepts of truth function in society. French existentialist André Malraux put it this way: "The great mystery is not that we should have been thrown down here at random between the profusion matter and that of the stars; it is that from our very prison we should draw, from our own selves, images powerful enough to deny our nothingness."

This chapter begins with a look at the Frankfurt School of critical social theory. Part One provides an introduction to the Frankfurt School and their theory of knowledge derived from Karl Marx. Part Two, the sociology of knowledge, reviews legal realism, labeling and moral panics. Part Three, bourgeois ideology, considers Soviet legal theory, American radical criminology, and British critical criminology. Part Four reviews the thought of Jürgen Habermas, Michel Foucault, and Critical Legal Studies. Part Five considers the extent to which constructionists have advocated socialist government. Part Six takes the constructionists to task on their theory of knowledge and use of history.

The Frankfurt School

Criminology began, in the Federal Republic of Germany, as "criminal law theory," a field dominated by law professors. Academic positions for criminologists opened first at law schools, which offered courses in criminology, juvenile court law, and the law of corrections. Only later did criminology develop as an interdisciplinary subject with a sociological dimension.[1] Sociologists have exerted a powerful influence over German criminology since the 1970s, and no twentieth-century German sociologist has had more influence than the professors associated with the Institute of Social Research, established at the University of Frankfurt, Frankfurt-am-Main, Germany.

The Institute was founded in 1923 when a German-Jewish merchant, who had made a fortune exporting grain from Argentina to Europe, financed the establishment of a center for the study of social philosophy. The Institute would study social research, such as the origins of anti-Semitism, a topic neglected at German universities. Max Horkheimer, the Institute's first director, became one of the leading figures of the school, along with Theodore Adorno, Herbert Marcuse, Erich Fromm, and later, Jürgen Habermas. The "critical social theory" they articulated dealt with the "eclipse of reason;" the attempt to construct a moral theory out of social inquiry rather than higher moral principles. What united the school was an appreciation for Marx. Originally, the founders planned to call their school the Institute for Marxism, but they decided that Institut für Sozialforschung—Institute of Social Research—would be less provocative.

THE DIALECTICAL IMAGINATION. Marx had written that ideas are meaningful to people only when they appear relevant to their real, material situation. He wrote that "the economic structure of society is the real foundation...it is not the consciousness of men that determines their existence, but on the contrary, their social existence determines consciousness."[2] Marx proposed a philosophy of *dialec-*

tical materialism. It included G.W.F. Hegel's notion of progressive or dialectical change through history, a constant interplay between ideas and material conditions. But it was the physical and social environment that generated the ideas. Production and the exchange of products served as the basis for social change. Marx rejected the possibility of universal principles of justice, such as "equal rights" and "equality." He replaced them with concepts of production, distribution, and scientific socialism.[3]

Marx expressed his dialectical materialist view through the concept of *social labor.* Thinking about civilizations throughout history, Marx noted that the kind of work was determined by the physical environment, whether agriculture (climate, soil conditions), mining (ore sites), or manufacturing (cities were located on rivers to generate steam power). But the organization of that labor was always social. The laborer is never isolated but linked to other people; each laborer is assigned to different positions within the social organization: worker, manager, and investor. The mobilization, deployment and allocation of labor within a civilization characterized the "mode of production." The mode of production refers to an epoch in human history characterized by the way a society is organized to ensure its material survival. Within the mode, there are the "means of production," the land, resources, and industry used by the members to produce needed goods and services. There are also the "social relations of production," the relationship of people to the means of production and to one another. Specifically, people are divided into classes based on those who own or control the means of production, and those who are assigned positions of labor by the owners.[4]

Marx referred to a number of modes in history—the original, primitive, communitarian, Germanic, Slavonic, and Asiatic. He concerned himself with only one mode, the mode he lived within, the capitalist mode. The capitalist mode divided members of society into classes based on ownership of the means of production. The *bourgeoisie* or "capitalists," a small number of people, owned the factories, mills, banks and commercial establishments. The *petit bourgeoisie* or "small capitalists," consisted of the salaried managers and supervisors. They did not own the means of production but helped the capitalists to control it. The *proletariat* were the wage workers, those who owned nothing except for the productivity of their labor. Capitalism also produced a class Marx referred to as the *lumpen-proletariat*. These persons had no meaningful relationship to the mode of production. Rather than working, they created a livelihood for themselves by living off the backs of the workers by various means.[5]

The point of making all these distinctions is that everything that happens, happens in society, and that to understand society, one must understand class interest. The way each class relates to the means of production determines the way each relates politically and socially. To understand the values and behaviors of people, or the foundations of society (government, law, politics), Marx said that they must be placed in the class context. The *base-superstructure model* illustrates Marx's concept of how social structure shapes individual thought and behavior. This refers to the idea that the economic base of civilization will be supported by a superstructure of ideological elements — politics, education, law and others. The model is that of a determining economic foundation (ownership, value, exchange) and a determined superstructure of forms of consciousness (politics, culture, ideas). Marx suggested that superstructural elements may change without changes in the economic base, but changes in the base necessarily produce changes in the superstructure. This is called *economic determinism*, the idea that economic shifts precede ways of thinking.[6]

The primary means of understanding why things happen as they do has to do with the superstructure ideology. *Ideology* refers to a set of beliefs, structured by the social relations of production within capitalism, which mask the nature of these relations. Legal concepts, along with political ideals, cultural values, religious symbols, and educational systems will all reproduce capitalist social arrangements. Religion, for example, Marx called the "opiate of the people." Moral ideals represented bourgeois morality, a ruse on the part of the capitalists to keep the workers working. This Marx called *false consciousness*. Marx wanted workers to concentrate on their present situation, to create a heaven on earth, not wait for the after-life. He rejected bourgeois notions of marriage and family as well. All religious ideals represented limitations of freedom and reason, the dogmatic subordination of the individual. He replaced "bourgeois morality" with scientific socialism.

The Frankfurt School theorists did not pursue Marxism in the sense of a political revolution. With the Nazi seizure of power in 1933, the faculty left Germany. Horkheimer had transferred the In-

stitute's endowment to a Dutch bank, so the members were finan-
cially secure, wherever they choose to reside. But there was the problem of the library; some 60,000 volumes of Marxist thought. Despite
the Institute's Marxist orientation, no one considered moving east to
Stalin's Russia. Rather, they accepted an offer from Columbia University in New York City, the center of world capitalism.[7]

THE FIRST GENERATION. What the Institute thinkers pursued was
the *immanent critique* of capitalist society. Reality had to be judged
by reason, but critical theory never defined reason. Reason was not
a transcendent ideal, existing outside history. Each period of time
had its own truth, Horkheimer insisted, and there was no truth
above historical time. Truth was not outside society but contained
within its own claims. The Critical theorists offered their "immanent critique of bourgeois society, which compared the pretensions
of bourgeois ideology with the reality of its social conditions."[8]

Horkheimer and the first generation relied on Marx's overall social theory to explain culture as the product of the economy. They
wrote about superstructure, mass culture, bourgeois consciousness,
and the commodification of social life. The principle of exchange
dominates all human relationships so that everything becomes an
exchangeable good, including the products of the "culture industry." Horkheimer and Adorno emphasized cultural ideals as the extension of capitalist market mechanisms, along with other superstructural elements that comprise public administration in capitalist
societies. The cultural dominance of the exchange principle and increasing administrative power resulted in an absolute supremacy of
society over the individual and a lessening of the autonomous self.
Adorno referred to law as the "prototype of irrational rationality,"
because, "the law enthrones a principle of equality that is of merely
formal nature and hence becomes the hiding place of substantive inequality, owing to the fact that essential differences are struck
down." The law served an ideological function in legitimating capitalist market arrangements because "this concept of equality turns
into a surviving myth in a world where the undoing of myths is only
apparent."[9]

Punishment and Social Structure (1939) became the first of the
Institute's works to appear in English after the move to New York.
George Rusche wrote most of the chapters but the book was com-
pleted by Otto Kirchheimer. Rusche had submitted the proposal to

the Institute in 1931, but left Germany for London after Hitler came to power. He was on his way to Canada when a German U-boat torpedoed his ship.[10] They proposed that "punishment must be understood as a social phenomenon freed from both its juristic concept and its social ends." Reviewing historic shifts in sanctions, imprisonment, fines, solitary confinement, deportation, and forced labor, they found a rough correlation between changes in the labor markets and the circulation of money. "Every system of production," they concluded, "tends to discover punishments which correspond to its productive relationships."[11] It represented one of the first challenges to "legal syllogism," the commonsensical idea, originating in the classical school of criminal law, that punishment is simply the consequence of crime, and that if there was a need for sociological explanation, the explanation had to do with criminal behavior and the the punishment of this behavior. The way Rusche and Kirchheimer framed it, social structure explains crime and legal sanctions. The book inspired a number of socio-historical accounts of shifts in legal sanctions within the United States and European countries.[12]

THE SECOND GENERATION. In 1950, the Frankfurt School returned to Germany and the Institute re-opened in the rooms of a bombed-out building next to its original location. During their stay in the United States, members of the school involved themselves in a variety of projects and some, Herbert Marcuse and Otto Kirchheimer, decided to stay for good. Max Horkheimer and Theodore W. Adorno returned, and together they revived the German Sociological Association. Founded in 1909 by Max Weber and Georg Simmel it had been "put on ice" since the National Socialist take-over in 1933. Horkheimer and Adorno introduced the empirical methods they had learned in the United States to the post-war generation of German sociologists while Jürgen Habermas produced the second generation of critical social theory.

Habermas took the criticism of the Frankfurt School further in his comments about law than the others and developed considerable caché among sociologists in the United States. Habermas broke with Marx's view of economic determinism observing that economic crises appear to have lost their revolutionary impact.[13] Market exchange is no longer the pre-eminent mechanism of social relations, rather government has converted economic crises into crises of the political system. Dominance of society over the individual is only true within the power relations characteristic of distorted communication. This is because as soon as individuals talk to each other, they claim to be unique subjects, but their individuality can only be explained in the general categories of language. All that remains is to specify the mechanics of "moral discourse" within a broader understanding of communicative ethics. Habermas's linguistic analysis derives from his concept of the *ideal speech situation*, a utopian ideal marked by undistorted, unconstrained speech: no form of social domination exists, every participant has equal opportunity to speak, and every participant can engage in the widest variety of communicative patterns.[14]

Habermas combined Hegelian philosophy with the research results of social psychology. He drew on the moral development of the child formulated by Jean Piaget and Lawrence Kohlberg to construct his theory of morals. Habermas interpreted the course of history as cumulative progress toward the free speech situation by extending Kohlberg's six steps in the formation of moral thinking. The six steps advanced consciousness toward universal ethical principles and resulted in the seventh step, the post-conventional stage of moral consciousness or realm of universal linguistic ethics or the ethics of discourse. There is no linear progression, but at every level of learning, new challenges are produced. As new problem-solving capacities are defined, new problems come to mind. Since bourgeois consciousness has grown cynical and traditional cultural ideals (of the sort Horkheimer and Adorno wrote about) have been discarded, reality can no longer be explained with Christian or liberal moral values. Further, Habermas maintains that it is impossible to deduce moral values from higher principles (as the classicists wanted to do), or from an empirical analysis of behavior (as the positivists hoped).[15]

Habermas, and his followers, have applied the concept of undistorted speech to courtroom interaction.[16] The language of courtroom interaction does not fulfill the standards of the ideal speech situation; Habermas does not even refer to courtroom speech as "moral discourse" but as a form of "strategic activity." The law provides rules for political institutions that apply, in turn, social rules. But Habermas excludes from his analysis the objective function of legal principles and institutions because he considers them only patterns of justification in the mind of the individual acting within social institutions. For Habermas, legal issues and moral issues are alike, to be considered only as a reflection of the individual's orientation.[17]

The Sociology of Knowledge

The constructionist theory of knowledge began with Karl Mannheim, who shared office space with Institute faculty while he taught sociology at the University of Frankfurt.[18] The members never really claimed him as one of their own and his major work, *Ideology and Utopia* (1929) drew criticism from Horkheimer and Marcuse.[19] Mannheim laid the foundation for the *sociology of knowledge*, the most essential aspect of the constructionist critique. From this view, thought does not occur in isolation from the social context in which particular people think about particular things. Not only does society control people's movement, it shapes their identity, their thought and emotion. Society supplies people's values, logic and the information that constitutes "knowledge."[20] Mannheim joined the London School of Economics in 1933, the academic home to a number of professors who had been dismissed from German universities by the Nazis.[21] Not only did Mannheim help found British sociology, his work found a wide audience within legal studies and sociology in the United States. Three versions of constructionist theory can be identified: legal realism, labeling, and moral panics.

LEGAL REALISM. In the United States, Harvard Law School Dean Roscoe Pound first applied the sociology of knowledge perspective to law. In a series of law review articles written between 1905 and 1923, Pound advanced the idea that "legal principles are not absolute, but are relative to time and place." He rejected the "mechanical jurisprudence" view of judicial decision-making, the idea that judges straightforwardly apply specific rules to the facts of the case. From the mechanical point of view, the constitution, statutes, and legal precedent dictate the decision making process and issues outside the rules, such as the personal feelings of the judge, do not influence the outcome. Pound denied that just decisions could be produced by logical deductions from axiomatic principles of economy and society and asserted that judicial decisions reflected individual biases rather than universal truths. He called for a "sociological jurisprudence," a perspective that acknowledges that the law does not represent an autonomous collection of rules. Rather, judges ought to seek information from disciplines outside the law: the social sciences.[22]

Pound's views led to *legal realism*, a movement among law professors that began at Yale in 1916 and Columbia several years later. The leading legal realists were Felix Cohen, Karl Llewellyn, and Jerome Frank. All acknowledged their intellectual debt to Roscoe Pound, but criticized him for neglecting to finish what he had started. Like Pound, Cohen rejected mechanical jurisprudence, but unlike Pound, Cohen doubted that the law represented an autonomous discipline that could be used to further social ends. The law could never become the "science of social engineering" that Pound envisioned. Cohen argued that the law represented only those rules a government would enforce. He insisted that the rule of law could not be distinguished from crude political power. Llewellyn shared Cohen's skepticism about the rule of law. He doubted that any legislature or court could create a legal rule capable of constraining the judiciary. Llewellyn encouraged judges to acknowledge their role in creating law, not merely applying or interpreting law, and to take seriously their role as policy makers. Llewellyn wrote in 1930 that Pound's "sociological jurisprudence remains bare of most that is significant in sociology."[23]

Frank in particular took Pound's sociology of law to its conceptual conclusion. Frank served as a federal appellate judge from 1941 until his death in 1957 and a visiting professor at Yale Law School from 1950 to 1956. At Yale, Frank gained a reputation as a "high grader" and an "innovator" who urged clinical training for law students.[24] He introduced "rule-skepticism" and "fact-skepticism" into the realist critique of law. Rule skepticism has to do with the difference between "paper" rules and "real" rules. The realists denied that judges decided cases based on the written rule of law. Rather, the outcome is based on personal beliefs and biases. Rather than applying legal rules to fact situations it actually worked the other way around. Judges make a decision, according to a hunch, feelings, instinct or some other personal feeling, then search for justification in the statute books and case volumes.[25] Fact skepticism criticized emphasis on appellate courts as rule makers. Essentially, trial judges made the law because trial courts supplied appellate courts with the facts at issue. And the facts determined by trial courts reflected the "peculiar traits, dispositions and habits" of judges more than objective reality. The subjectivity of the facts led him to criticize his colleagues who subscribed to the "upper court myth" that appellate courts make the rules for trial courts to follow; it was the myth of "a 2 percent tail wagging a 98 percent dog."[26]

LABELING. The sociologists of the labeling school did to sociology what the legal realists had done to law. They emphasized social rules and the social response to violations of these rules. They focused on the effect of being labeled as deviant by a social group, or agency of social control, and how this label could lead to a situation where even without an initial commitment to deviant conduct, it could lead to a deviant lifestyle. The labeling approach found expression in the culture conflict theory of Thorsten Sellin, and in the social theory of Edwin Lemert and Howard S. Becker.[27]

Thorsten Sellin, who taught sociology at the University of Pennsylvania, offered his culture conflict theory of crime in 1938. It was after talking with Edwin Sutherland, who had brought his family to Sellin's farm in New Hampshire for a week that summer, that "it suddenly dawned on me that the legal definition of crime was a very artificial definition of a behavioral symptom." He decided that the legal definition represented a "conduct norm...the norm of only one particular social group — you might say the political group that controls the definition of crimes and punishments."[28] In *Culture Conflict and Crime* (1938), Sellin wrote that cultural conflict occurred when an individual was caught between conflicting cultural rules. Drawing on examples supplied by anthropologists, Sellin said that *culture conflict* arises on the border of contiguous social groups, when the law of one society is extended over the territory of another, and when members of one group migrate into another. When the French extended the Code Pénal over Algeria, magistrates confronted a conspiracy of silence among Algerians when investigating such crimes as ritual murder. Algerian custom provided for the murder of an unfaithful wife by her brother or father, the woman having brought dishonor to the family.

Sellin also used examples of the experience of immigrants to the United States, but insisted that he was not writing about immigration and crime. Sellin suggested that criminologists ought to take particular interest in the "conflicts between legal and nonlegal conduct norms." The law represented a standard of behavior relative to a particular culture and for a large number of people in modern urban society, particularly immigrants, "certain life situations are governed by such conflicting norms that no matter what the response of the person in such a situation will be, it will violate the norms of some social group concerned."[29] "The notion of conduct norms is ever-present..." Sellin said of his work, "there will always be conflict between various codes of conduct norms." While he had written about immigrants, the experience of juvenile gangs, the drug culture, and youth culture all represented the conflict of norms between subcultural groups.[30]

But it was Edwin Lemert, who received a Ph.D. in sociology from Ohio State University, who helped found the labeling school of American sociology. In 1951, Lemert distinguished between primary and secondary deviance. "Primary deviance" occurs for a variety of reasons. Whatever the reasons for engaging in antisocial behavior, it is less important from a sociological perspective than the antisocial identity that results. When deviant behavior generates a social reaction that erodes an individual's self-image to the point that the individual accepts a deviant self-conception, "secondary deviance" occurs. There are any number of reasons, for example, why a person might consume alcohol to excess: the death of a family member, business failure, or perhaps participation in a social circle given to alcohol consumption. But drinking excessively is not interesting sociologically until this activity becomes organized into a social role and the excessive drinker acquires the status of "drunkard." It was the excessive drinking that followed from perception of one's self as a drunkard that interested Lemert.

"This is a turn away from older sociology which tended to rest heavily upon the idea that deviance leads to social control," Lemert points out, "I have come to believe that the reverse idea, i.e. social control leads to deviance, is equally tenable and the potentially richer premise for studying deviance in modern society."[31] For Lemert, criminality involved a "progressive reciprocal relationship" between the individual's behavior and the social reaction to that behavior. A single deviant act seldom produced a strong enough societal reaction to produce a deviant status. But when the deviant behavior generated a consistent label, such as "bad girl" or "troublemaker," the person began to choose activities consistent with the label. "At this point," Lemert said, "a stigmatizing of the deviant occurs in the form of name-calling, labeling, or stereotyping."[32]

Becker followed up Lemert's book with an academic best-seller. Howard S. Becker, who began his professional career playing jazz piano, became professor of sociology at Northwestern University in Chicago. He provided the clearest expression of labeling in his book about marijuana-smoking by jazz musicians in the 1950s. *Outsiders* (1963) became the top-selling book by a sociologist on crime, selling more than 100,000 copies.[33] It was also the first published sociology to include vulgar words written out; previously, editors replaced these words with the first letter and three dashes.[34] What Becker wrote in the book is that the central fact about deviance is that it was created by society. "Social groups create deviance by making the rules whose infraction constitutes deviance, and by applying those rules to particular people and labeling them outsiders. From this point of view, deviance is *not* a quality that lies in behavior itself, but in the interaction between the person who commits an act and those who respond to it." It was not that deviants became jazz musicians and smoked marijuana, because marijuana-smoking was not an inherently deviant act; what made it deviant was the social reaction to it, the presence of a social rule prohibiting it.

Becker clarified that just because a social rule could be found did not mean that it was enforced. The enforcement of social rules was an "enterprising act," behavior that required someone take the initiative, a *moral entrepreneur*. He identified two categories of moral entrepreneurs: "rule creators" and "rule enforcers." The rule creators represented the crusading reformers in the classic prohibitionist tradition; often, their ranks filled with those in the "upper levels of the social structure." Once these moral crusaders began to experience "success" and had developed a taste for crusading, they typically found other social problems that needed rules. With creation of a new social rules, new agencies of "rule enforcers" also appeared. Marijuana-smoking became deviant after Harry Ainslinger and the Federal Narcotics Bureau campaigned for legislation and Congress enacted the Harrison Narcotics Act. Becker concluded that once organized, rule enforcers went about their activity to justify their existence.[35]

MORAL PANICS. The British version of labeling theory began with Stanley Cohen, a South African who while working on a Ph.D. in sociology at the University of London in 1964, decided to write about society's reaction to rebellious youth.[36] Cohen turned Becker's idea of moral crusades into the sociology of moral panics. In *Folk Devils and Moral Panics* (1972), Cohen described the "mods" and "rockers," middle and working-class versions of 1960s British youth counter-culture. He felt that newspaper reports of "abusive behavior" by the youth at a dance hall in a seaside resort community on England's southern coast were "fundamentally inappropriate." A *moral panic* occurs when "a condition, episode, person or group of persons emerges to become defined as a threat to societal values and interests," is reported in "stylized and stereotypical fashion" by media, and enclosed by the "moral barricades" thrown up by "editors, bishops, politicians, and other right-thinking people." Cohen described "folk devils" as the personification of evil and "demonology" as the process of assigning new members to the "gallery of contemporary folk devils."[37] Some moral panics fade harmlessly into cultural folklore but others, Cohen argued, produce permanent changes in law and social policy.[38] Cohen suggested that moral panics grip societies everywhere. His analysis of the part the press, the public, law enforcement, legislators, and action groups play in creating them, led to a series of moral panic studies by "social scientists of a liberal, left-leaning, or radical persuasion."[39]

In the United States, sociologists have pursued the moral panics idea within writing about the "discovery" of social problems. Malcolm Spector and John Kitsuse proposed that social problems, such as crime, do not exist "out there." Rather, they are creations of the human mind, called into being by the definitional process within society. Social problems exist when a group of people recognize or consider something as wrong, when they are concerned about it and take steps to fix it. The "demand by one party to another that something be done about some putative condition" they defined as *claims-making*.[40] The point is not what is going on but what claims-makers believe is going on, or are able to convince others is going on. The central issue to be understood about any social problem is the social group's definition of reality and consequent activities. They proposed moving from sociological study of the conditions to the definitional activities and interpretations of those making the claims. The central questions for analysis are the ways in which those who create the problem establish the existence of the problem. Constructionists rely on three major themes: the interests particular groups have in promoting a problem, their ownership over the issue, and the degree to which their version of the problem becomes the accepted view.

Philip Jenkins wrote about how serial murder became a major crime problem in the United States from 1991 to 1993, when the Federal Bureau of Investigation, Reagan Republicans, and fundamentalist Christians sold the nation on the threat of dangerous outsiders beyond the bounds of normal crime: murderous child-abusers, drug-dealing terrorists, and serial murderers. In his analysis, he summarized the process of discovering a social problem. Social events must be identified and "contextualized." During this process, events are placed within a context familiar to the audience, a process that typically occurs through mass media. Contextualization occurs through the process of "framing," organization of patterns in social experience that can be readily understood by the audience.[41]

Framing, Jenkins goes on to explain, is achieved through a number of rhetorical techniques. "Typification," a common framing technique, suggests that an issue represents one sort of problem or another and therefore merits a particular response. "Convergence," another framing strategy, occurs when claims-makers place the issue within the framework of a previously established problem. In one version of convergence, claims-makers stigmatize the behavior of those involved in the issue by linking it with another social problem perceived as more dangerous. The serial murder claims-makers linked serial murder with pornography, racism, homosexuality and child abuse. This was part of a "signification spiral" in which the original event escalated into a more serious social problem. The higher the issue ranks in the hierarchy of important social problems, the more valuable it is in justifying "campaigns of control," the intrusion of governmental social control to suppress the perceived social evil. Characterizing serial murder as "gay serial murder" and "satanic serial murder" elevated it to the pinnacle of social problems.[42]

No sociologist has taken the moral panics idea further than Boston College sociologist Stephen Pfohl, president of the Society for the Study of Social Problems in 1992.[43] In a 1977 article, Pfohl described the invention of child abuse. While child beating had gone on for centuries, "child abuse" became a social problem in the 1960s leading to the criminalization of the abuse of children by parents. Pediatric radiologists, who felt less attached to professional ethics requiring confidentiality between doctors and patients, made child abuse a social problem for doctors and social workers within four years. As the discoverers of a medical condition, pediatric radiologists created a new medical specialty out of what had been a limited area for medical practice. Pfohl later claimed that both "child" and "beating" were as much social constructions as "child abuse." For Pfohl, there is no "real world," only a surreal social world where all things, even "common sense...fact-like things" are the "fictive elements of powerful structuring practices."[44] In his 1992 presidential address, Pfohl presented an "analytic collage" dealing with the "twilight of the parasites," the new world of social domination within capitalist society in which exploitation was based not simply on the exploitation of human labor as Marx had said, but "a story of dominant ritual forms involved in the reproduction of an advancing whitemale, heterosexist, and transnational mode of CAPITAList domination." Pfohl left SSSP members concerned with a question: "How might social scientists concerned with social justice—also reinscribe and, thereby, also partially avert the networks of liquid CAPITAList power that engulf us daily?"[45]

Bourgeois Ideology

Mannheim had referred to Marxism as an ideology and Horkheimer and Marcuse objected. They also objected to the relativism inherent in the sociology of knowledge, that what is deviant at one time and in one social context may not be deviant in another. Horkheimer and Marcuse did not want to give up the idea of "ancient truths" to which they made vague references.[46] They wanted to preserve a distinction between true and false consciousness and the possibility of arriving at the truth through critical self-reflection. What is true, Horkheimer claimed, advances social change in the direction of a more rational society. The Frankfurt School took their social theory from Marx. From the Marxist perspective, the point is not that crime is a label, but that within capitalism, this label is applied to the wrong people. In the United States and Britain, criminologists came to share their view, particularly during the 1960s.

MARX, CRIME AND THE LAW. Marx began to write his philosophy while a member of a student study group that became less philosophical and more political. "Philosophers have only interpreted the world in various ways," Marx wrote, "the point is to change it." He had learned revolutionary politics by 1851, when the Prussian government brought communist party members to trial in Cologne. They attempted to implicate the Communist League in a conspiracy to overthrow the government through falsification of documents. Marx's wife Jenny explained how "the 'Marx Party' is active day and night...all the allegations of the police are lies. They steal, they forge, they break open desks, swear false oaths...claiming they are privileged to do so against Communists, who are beyond the pale of society."[47] Marx had worked to expose the fraud of prosecution and developed an understanding of the government. "Crime" is defined by the State—governmental authority—and is detected and punished by a repressive apparatus. The State is an instrument of class power. Paul Q. Hirst summarizes Marx's view: "The State intervenes in the class struggle with its ideological and repressive apparatus to break the power of the political movement of the workers by means of legal and extra-legal sanctions. To stigmatize political opponents as 'common criminals' is to deny ideologically their political character, and aims to castigate them as bandits and adventurers."[48]

Marx's comments about crime can be read as explaining the way crime supports capitalist social relationships, in particular, the occupational structure of nineteenth century capitalist economies in Europe. The Marxist concept of crime makes a distinction between "professional crime" and "political crime," based on whether the criminality contributes the workers' struggle or detracts from it. *Professional crime* is perpetrated by the "lumpenproletariat, this scum of the depraved elements of all classes." The lumpen-proletariat, or criminal class "which establishes its headquarters in the big cities" lived off the productive labor of the workers by theft, extortion and beggary and by providing "services" of prostitution, gambling, and drunkenness.[49] Marx also suggested that crime is not only the business of professional criminals. *Political crime* is perpetrated by the proletariat; these illegal actions take on a more political character. Acts of machine-breaking and industrial sabotage, and the murder of landlords by peasants, represent the immediate response to capitalist exploitation. Marx viewed these activities as the immediate reaction to the harsh and grueling conditions of industrial work. Where they supported the political program of the workers they represented a form of social protest or primitive rebellion.[50]

In *Criminality and Economic Conditions* (1916), Willem Bonger, professor at the University of Amsterdam, provided an explanation of crime faithful to Marx's political agenda. Bonger began by asking "Whence does the criminal thought in man arise?" For Bonger, criminality represented a form of egoism, that is, placing one's own interests above those of other people. Bonger insisted that egoism was a result of the social environment, a product of the mode of production. Capitalism encouraged egoism because as an economic system, individuals pursued self-interest regardless of its consequences on others. In Bonger's view, capitalism created a self-centered human nature; in his analysis of crime he would "show the influence of the economic system and of these consequences upon the social instincts of man."[51]

Capitalism encouraged crime among both the bourgeoisie and the proletariat. The bourgeoisie, those who own the means of production, used unscrupulous means to protect their economic advantage. They felt free to exploit the proletariat, paying as little for their labor as possible, and felt no obligation to provide for the human needs. The proletariat allowed crime to flourish. Their exploitation by the capitalists dulled their sense of caring. Children who grew up in conditions of poverty did not receive the moral education necessary to develop the sentiment of altruism. Crime could only be reduced by replacing capitalism with socialism, by a society in which "the means of production are held in common." The socialist society would remove the cause of egoism and reawaken feelings of altruism. Within a socialist society, only the crimes of a few "pathological individuals would remain."[52]

Evgeny B. Pashukanis advanced Marx's version of law in Russia after the Bolshevik Revolution in 1917. Pashukanis had joined the Bolsheviks in 1918 and served as a judge in Moscow before working as a legal advisor to the Commissariat of Justice. In 1924, Pashukanis had become a leading philosopher of law with the publication of *The General Theory of Law and Marxism*, in which he proposed that the law corresponded to the basic form of commodities traded on the market within a historical period. Within capitalist economy, the market value (what anyone is will to pay for a product) of commodities replaced the actual value (the amount of human effort to produce the product). The market exchange masked the different amount of labor required to make products and allowed the capitalists to profit through extraction of surplus value (the difference between exchange value and subsistence wages.)[53]

In a similar way, Pashukanis theorized, law reduced individuals, social groups and even government to legal subjects, to individuals with formal legal equality. The law accomplished this by abstracting them from their social contexts, and by extending a formal legal equality that within societies divided by classes, amounted to concrete social inequality. The capitalists accumulated profit not merely through surplus value but because the law allowed them to control the means of production through the legal system that protected private property and allowed for the ownership of jobs. Pashukanis urged that the law and legal institutions disappear with the construction of socialism and that the law that remained conform to the Communist Party's political needs. He expressed hostility to the study of criminology, which had flourished in Tsarist Russia, and worked to expose the errors of positivist criminologists working at the dozen or so institutes, centers, laboratories and clinics studying crime and criminals.[54]

AMERICAN MARXIST CRIMINOLOGY. Marxist criminology emerged in the United States during the 1960s, and particularly at the School of Criminology, University of California at Berkeley. The School of Criminology began when August Vollmer, the city of Berkeley's police chief, teamed up with a law professor to offer a summer program to train police recruits. Fifty or so years later, under a new dean, the School revised its curriculum away from technical emphasis on law enforcement to social science, and began offering graduate degrees in criminology. By 1968 the politics of the criminologists — Anthony Platt, Paul Takagi, and Herman and Julia Schwendinger — had moved left of the administration. During those years at Berkeley, police clashed with student demonstrators and faculty cancelled classes to protest the war in Vietnam. While Ronald Reagan was governor of California, the administration abolished the School and the non-tenured faculty left Berkeley for other academic positions.[55] Several Berkeley faculty organized a non-profit to continue publication of the journal established at the School, now called *Social Justice*, which became an outlet for leftist scholarship on crime.[56]

Platt, who had been arrested during a student celebration at a nearby park, waged an unsuccessful fight for tenure at the School prior to its closing. His book *The Child Savers* originally appeared in 1969. It had been written from the labeling perspective, a perspective he apologized for in an extensive preface to the second edition in 1977. He explained that the juvenile court had not really first appeared during the Progressive Era, but that systematic juvenile delinquency first appeared in the seventeenth century "in the wake of economic and political conditions which were being established everywhere in nascent capitalist societies."[57] The child savers were not alone, they reproduced the same class outlook of earlier generations of reformers, and took their place in a movement led by the most class-conscious sectors of monopoly capital. They sought to oppose traditional lassiez-faire business practices, increase the role of the state in economic regulation, and develop a new political economy through bureaucratic rationality. What the businessmen who led the Progressive Movement did for political economy the child savers did for the criminal justice system — "that is, achieve order, stability, and control, while preserving the existing class system and distribution of wealth."[58] But child savers created new methods of social control because unlike earlier generations they did not seek to rely on brute force, but sought to prevent disorder and harmonize social conflicts. In describing the labeling process with reference to how the political-business cycle affects the variable degree of probability that a certain behavior will be defined as normal or deviant, Platt provided a *grounded labeling theory*.[59]

Herman Schwendinger, along with his spouse Julia Schwendinger, joined the sociology department at the State University of New York at New Paltz after leaving Berkeley. In a 1970 article, they argued that criminologists should not limit themselves to those behaviors defined as crime by the criminal law, but "historically determined rights of individuals." Any violation of those rights essential to life, such as good health, and those essential to human dignity, such as the freedom of movement, should be viewed as crimes, along with anything that causes social injury. Violations of human rights due to racism, sexism, and imperialism along with unsafe working conditions, inadequate child care, insufficient opportunities for employment and education, and substandard housing and medical care. Governments that do nothing to alleviate poverty should be considered criminal.[60] In a later book, they pursued a version of *Marxist feminism*. They contended that in non-capitalist societies an egalitarianism prevails and violence against women is rare. In capitalist society, the level of male violence is determined by class relations and the mode of production. Women, like men, are exploited in capitalist society, but are also exploited by men. The two-fold exploitation leads to both their criminality and their victimization. Men view women as competitive threats that must be contained to keep their own position of power. Men rape women, an act not found in non-capitalist societies, and women, feeling guilty, blame themselves. Because men have succeeded in confining women to the domestic sphere, women commit few crimes. The criminality of men in a patriarchal capitalist society leads to the relative lack of criminality among women.[61]

Other leading figures of Marxist criminology were not at Berkeley. Richard Quinney had taken all of Howard Becker's courses while working on his Ph.D. in sociology at the University of Wisconsin. About the time Platt left Berkeley, Quinney took a sabbatical leave from New York University and moved to Chapel Hill, North Carolina, where he wrote books and distributed a socialist newspaper.[62] In an interview that year, Quinney expressed his view of human nature. "I don't think we need a criminal law with punishment to make people good. I'm assuming, as opposed to the traditional theory, that man is basically good rather than being evil... Basically man is good and given his chance to build decent institutions so he can live his life with others, man does not need formal authority over him."[63] In *The Social Reality of Crime* (1970), Quinney fused Pound's sociological jurisprudence with Becker's labeling theory. "Crime," he wrote, "is a definition of human conduct that is created by authorized agents in a politically organized society." He went on to explain how some groups, through their exercise of political power, could make their definitions stick to others. And when the powerless groups began to behave in ways consistent with how they had been politically defined, the process was complete.

But by the time it was published, Quinney himself had rejected it. At the American Sociological Association meeting that year, he criticized his own book, and turned instead to "a critical Marxian philosophy."[64] In 1973, Quinney published *Critique of Legal Order*, the manifesto of radical criminology. Crime is a category of thought, created then imposed on some people by others. Criminologists should not presuppose, only critique. "The operation is one of demystification, the removal of myths—the false conscious-ness—created by official reality." Only by applying Marx's view of society could the theorist emerge from "merely looking for an ob-jective reality" and become "concerned with the negation of the es-tablished order."[65] The rule of law, Quinney decided, masked the rule of class. The dominant ruling class, composed of the wealthy industrialists and government officials, controlled the working classes through their manipulation of the machinery of criminal jus-tice. Or, as another Marxist criminologist summed it up: "the rich get richer and the poor get prison."[66]

In 1971, William Chambliss made a contribution to radical crim-inology with his notion of structural contradictions.[67] Chambliss, President of the American Society of Criminology in 1988, and Uni-versity of Wisconsin sociologist Robert B. Seidman, published *Law, Order and Power*. The capitalists controlled government, Chamb-liss and Seidman agreed, but not so overtly as Quinney had made it seem. Capitalism worked in favor of the capitalist class because of "contradictions"—irresolvable problems imbedded within the po-litical economy. These strains, such as the tension between profit maximization and capital accumulation, generated conflicts be-tween classes and within the capitalist class itself. Government, pre-occupied with resolving conflicts and promoting the long-term sta-bility of existing economic structures, never got around to addressing the underlying contradictions.[68]

In his presidential address to the American Society of Criminol-ogy, Chambliss explained how the structural contradictions pro-duced specific forms of crime. He identified *state crime*: "acts de-fined by law as criminal and committed by state officials in pursuit of their job as representatives of the state."[69] State crime does not include criminal acts that benefit public officials personally, such as bribery and embezzlement, but other illegal political activities, in-cluding spying on citizens, diverting funds, and supporting terrorist activities. He reviewed examples of piracy during the eighteenth century, narcotics trafficking during the Vietnam War, and arms smuggling during the Reagan presidency. He explained that public officials create dilemmas for themselves when they enact law to protect their interests and are forced to pursue political objectives that violate these laws. Contradictions within world capitalism gen-erated not only conflicts between branches of government, but be-tween capitalist nations.[70]

While Marxist criminology percolated in the United States, critical criminology began in Britain. When Dahrendorf published his book on Marx in 1959, only the most prestigious universities — Oxford, Cambridge and London — offered graduate education in criminology, and that was at the graduate level. British criminology followed the "orthodox tradition" established by professors at these universities until 1968, when several hundred sociologists convened the National Deviancy Conference at the University of York. A younger generation of teachers from the newer universities opened after the war, they made the annual conference of the British Sociological Association appear middle-aged.[71] Stanley Cohen, Laurie Taylor, Ian Taylor, Paul Walton and Jock Young wrote about drug-takers, soccer hooligans, industrial saboteurs, and vandals and initiated the "renaissance in sociological criminology in Britain."[72]

CRITICAL CRIMINOLOGY. In 1973, Taylor, Walton and Young published *The New Criminology*, a book eventually translated into twenty languages. The new criminology found in Durkheim and the labeling perspective the ideas for a critique of psychiatric explanations for crime and the early sociologies of crime. They called for criminology theory "able to bring politics back into the discussion" and one that dealt with "society as a totality." Consequently, they focused their critique on the sociology of rule-making, rather than rule-breaking, and on "the structures of power, domination and authority...and the initiative of the state, and its entrepreneurial representatives, in defining and sanctioning certain forms of behavior at certain points in time."[73] They concluded that "deviance is normal" in the sense that it represented people consciously involved in "asserting their human diversity."[74] They noted that Marx had grasped the problem with unusual clarity when he wrote that legal relations and the State had their roots in the material conditions of life.

Despite the title, Taylor, Walton and Young never really explained exactly what the "new criminology" had to say; the book only offered criticism of current sociological theories. In *Critical Criminology*, a collection of essays that appeared two years later, Taylor, Walton and Young provided more description of what the new criminology was all about. "If criminology is to advance as a science, it must be free to examine not only the causes of crime, but also of the norms which, in a primary sense, create crime —

that is legal norms," they argued, "They analysis of particular forms of crime, or particular types of criminal, outside their context in history and society has been shown, in our view, to be a meaningless activity...."[75] Critical criminology began where the new criminology had ended, with Marx. Now, Taylor and colleagues explained that "the processes involved in crime-creation are bound up in the final analysis with the material basis of contemporary capitalism and its structures of law." From this perspective, crime involved processes of rule-making and rule-breaking that were *"fully social* in nature ... conditioned by the facts of *material reality."* Biological and psychological explanations for criminal behavior amounted to an ideology of "analytic individualism" that distorted the social reality of crime and supported the prevailing social interest.[76]

Later, Jock Young and other colleagues at Middlesex University in North London, introduced left realism. They characterized criminology of the Marxist sort that had emerged among leftist sociologists in the United States as "idealism" because it started with abstract concepts rather than concrete social realities.[77] *Left idealism* had romanticized conventional criminals and crime among the poor in general as the vanguard of political revolution, ignoring the reality that conventional criminals victimize poor people.[78] Young's *left realism* urged sociological criminologists to concentrate their theorizing on conventional crime. Crime was not simply the product of poverty, not simply a matter of primitive rebellion against capitalist exploitation. Rather, conventional crime resulted from relative deprivation, from perceived want, from selfish and individualist desire. Rather than waiting for the revolution, the left realists urged criminologists to do something about the victimization of poor people. Rather than dismiss government as a tool of capitalist oppression, the realists should lobby for meaningful crime control policies.[79]

The Architecture of Meaning

Habermas represents the second generation of Frankfurt Marxism because he abandoned the strategy of immanent critique. Since bourgeois consciousness has lost hope and traditional ideals discarded, Habermas taught, it no longer makes sense to confront reality with the hollow shells of Christian or classical liberal values. Values can no longer be constructed from social process or market exchange, but only from analysis of language by means of specifying the structures of moral discourse.[80] The linguistic model views language as a system of signs—symbols, sounds, and utterances—that refer to things. Language is not subjective in the sense that signs reflect individual predispositions—no communication could be possible if that were true. Language is subjective in that there is no objective referent that exists outside of language, things exist only as words. Knowledge can only be understood as forms of discourse that correspond to the structures of language at a more fundamental level than the rules of grammar, or so those who apply the linguistic model to morality say.

FOUCAULT'S CRIMINOLOGY. The reduction of ideas to language has been called *postmodernism*, an outlook that spread from linguistics across the humanities and social sciences. The word began with a school of architecture dedicated to designing structures other than glass and steel boxes. It became a technique of literary criticism, and eventually, an epistemology. In the same way that architecture shapes human activity, postmodernists look at the way language shapes what is knowable. The postmodern outlook does not ask about what is true or real, only how notions of truth and being arise in society. Or as Jacques Derrida put it: *il n'y a pas de hors texte*, language refers only to itself. The movement in moral philosophy can be said to have shifted from the premodern concern for a just society based on the laws of God, to the modern attempt to use reason as a guide to the just society, to postmodern despair of any universal or knowable conception of justice.[81] Nobody rode the postmodernist bus further than Michel Foucault.

Michel Foucault wrote books about crime and punishment, but he never claimed to be anything close to a criminologist. (Although, as a young man, Foucault worked at an electroencephalographic laboratory at a hospital and a prison.) Foucault attained the position of "Professor of the History of Systems of Thought" at the Collège de France in Paris. His followers claimed that he invented a new method of understanding the present by looking at the past, by looking at how the structure, particularly of language, shapes thought during historical periods. The archaeology of knowledge refers to a "set of rules of formation that determine the conditions of possibility of all that can be said within the particular discourse." The rules of discourse express relations of power, and when Foucault spoke of power he was only marginally concerned with the power exercised by governments. This set of rules reflects the power of society over the body, it creates the subject (the mind, consciousness, personality).[82] In *Madness and Civilization* (1965), Foucault argued that rational thought itself represents only a portion of everything that could be known. Madness was not a "fact of nature" but a "fact of civilization;" in every society it represents only "an other behavior" and "an other language." The invention of the Salpêtrière asylum in 1656 made rationality possible; it silenced the "other" voices of unreason so the reason of modern rationalism could prevail. Scientific thought in particular, and rational thought in general, originated together in the lunatic asylum.[83]

Foucault zeroed in on the mental asylum, medical clinic, and the prison, the social institutions where society exercised visible power over individuals. The French version of *Discipline and Punish* (1977), appeared two years earlier, three years after riots broke out at several French prisons.[84] Foucault and a few other intellectuals founded the Group d'Information sur les Prisons, and with the help of former prisoners, distributed surveys aimed at allowing prisoners to speak for themselves. In the book, Foucault reviewed historical documents of the eighteenth century, particularly Jeremy Bentham's plan for the panopticon. The fact that the panopticon never appeared is not important, Foucault insists; what is important is the science of power Bentham's plans revealed, and the broader purpose of social control for which the prison was invented. The prison was not designed to control criminals, but the opposite, to create criminals. Specifically, to create a "delinquent class" of persons that could be confined. "Crime produced the prison; the prison the delinquent class; the existence of a delinquent class an excuse for the policing of the entire population."[85] This policing led to the creation of information about criminals, the formation of the human sciences, including criminology, and provided a justification for examining all the members of society.

Crime, to Foucault's way of thinking, represents the authentic acts of individuals challenging the artificial rules of society. Foucault produced *I, Pierre Rivière* shortly before his book on the birth of the prison, which contains the autobiographical account of a twenty-year old Norman peasant, convicted in 1836 of murdering his pregnant mother, his eighteen-year old sister and seventeen-year old brother. The murderer tells of his life with his family, why he murdered them, and his wandering around the Normandy countryside before his arrest. The account, written to explain his rationality in committing the crimes and justify the death sentence, appears alongside the statements of the doctors and psychiatrists, newspaper reports and legal proceedings in which Paris psychiatrists attempted to prove his "monomania" (he killed himself in prison five years after his sentence had been commuted to life in prison.) The moral of the story, from Foucault's perspective, is not an immoral act and its consequences, but the way in which the various forms of discourse—the murderer's account, the psychiatric testimony, the judicial proceedings—reveal relations of power, and the possibility that insane criminals possess a knowledge lost when society brands them "insane" and "criminal." In 1975, a film was made about Pierre Rivière, based on Foucault's book, in which Foucault himself appeared as one of the judges.[86]

As Foucault's influence spread through American sociology, two Harvard law professors took the same tact in their view of courts. Duncan Kennedy and Roberto M. Unger initiated what became known as *critical legal studies* or CLS. In 1977, a network of law professors at prestigious law schools in the northeastern United States organized the Conference on Critical Legal Studies to offer a leftist critique of both conservative legal work and values of liberal democracy. Within ten years of the first conference on Critical Legal Studies convened at the University of Wisconsin at Madison, the Crits had become an organized a network of more than a hundred openly leftist teachers, students, and lawyers committed to exposing the hypocrisy of centrist legal culture.[87]

Reminiscent of the Realist concept of "the law in action," the Crits denied that legal doctrine was systematic, offered a definitive solution for all circumstances, or that it was value-free or free from political interests. All legal decision making is designed to reinforce the status quo, which is to say, social inequality. The proponents of CLS suggest that the concept of citizens with rights provides a false picture of society and the legal order. Beneath the process of courts deciding cases according to "neutral" and "fair" principles is a social order which is not impartial. The conception of "society as a collection of rights-bearing citizens, as if rights had an independent existence 'out there' " is, as Duncan Kennedy puts it, a "hallucination." The true picture of law within the capitalist state is "the mask for formal equality and paper rights," in which the law is a tool of domination and hierarchy. The liberal concept of right as a legal right to be enforced in court does not protect the individual from the subordination of classes and roles. The "rights" protected by liberal theory really only reinforce illegitimate hierarchies. Rights-holding serves not only as "false consciousness" that siphons energy from the struggle to break free from a forced division of labor, but serves as a barrier to attempts at social change.[88]

CRITICAL LEGAL STUDIES. Where Marx and radical criminologists had supposed a relationship between law and social convention as a matter of base and superstructure, proponents of the CLS project referred to this as the relationship between discourse (law) and nondiscursive practices (social conventions, economic practices). Brazilian-born Roberto M. Unger, on the faculty at Harvard Law School, insisted that the law was relative to social practice. In *Law in Modern Society* (1976), Unger described the rise and fall of the rule of law based on his premise that "bureaucratic law and a legal order emerge as alternative responses to the crisis of order that a weakening of custom represents."[89] He identified three categories of law, custom, regulation, and the legal system, based on their autonomy. While custom persisted "in the patterns of interactional expectations and usages on which the legal order relies," and regulation continued "in the form of policy decisions or administrative commands," the legal system existed only as an autonomous "system of specialized legal institutions, a well-defined legal doctrine, and a legal profession with its own relatively unique outlook, interests and ideals." Because the legal system operated independent from any single "moral, political, and economic discourse" originating in society, the legal profession operated according to its own "profane rules."

In their own immanent critique, the CLS group challenged the values of classical liberal theory by undermining the interpretations of private property, individual rights, meritocracy, and governmental power that has sustained oppressive hierarchies of wealth and power. But instead of tying legal principles to economic and social practices, they employed the technique of deconstruction. *Deconstruction* assumes that all discourse, historical as well as legal, is essentially rhetoric. No text contains objective, that is to say, a single meaning but several, ambiguous meanings. Everything "in" a text is really the product of interpretation by the reader. There is no objective description of reality, there is only interpretations of text. Deconstruction views law as politics and legal texts as an instrument of the ruling class; legal doctrine helps perpetuate social injustice by providing justifications for it. Critical analysis consists of deciphering the ways the legal system responds to the needs of capitalism by transforming rights into commodities that can be traded through relationships of power. The purpose is to "demystify" the liberal jurisprudence of rationality and rights by showing how these legal ideals legitimate the political strategies of capitalism.[90]

While Unger, Kennedy and other law professors pursued Critical Legal Studies, several criminologists offered a parallel analysis. Dragan Milovanovic, a professor at Northeastern Illinois University in Chicago, summarizes what he refers to as the *critical semiotic* approach to law. Language is not value-neutral or objective, but reflects the subjectivity of meaning. Language structures thought, and can be understood as a "linguistic coordinate system," or major forms of discourse including dominant, juridic and oppositional. Rationality and meaning are unique to the particular discourse in use; "reality" is constructed by the form of language used. Language may be analyzed at two levels, the political process of linguistic production by which words are given meaning, and once they are given meaning, by the way they circulate within particular linguistic coordinate systems. Any linguistic coordinate system can be evaluated by the ease with which things can be communicated. Linguistic coordinate systems are "relatively automomous," meaning that there is equal opportunity in the use of language, although use of language reflects socio-economic class. "Authentic and open communication (non-alienating communication)," Milovanovic explains, "can take place only within a mode of production where hierarchy, exploitation and repression are eliminated."[91]

Milovanovic has written about jailhouse lawyers to illustrate the juridic linguistic coordinate system. What happens in a courtroom is reality construction in a general sense and oppression of defendants in a specific sense. Defendants contribute to their own oppression by uncritical acceptance of the juridical language form. Professionally-credentialed lawyers, "the sellers of juridic linguistic skills," have learned these skills in specialized institutions—law schools—which reflect and support the dominant political and economic system. This occurs when lawyers translate "what happened" into legal words; some meaning is lost. Not all the reasons why a person acts the way they do are "justiciable" or valid juridically-speaking, so that the dominant form of discourse prevails (dominant meaning hierarchical, exploitive and repressive). Jailhouse lawyers, those prison inmates who have taught themselves law and practice it against their keepers, initially adopt the "linguistic coordinate system of the streets" and its notions of identity, cause, and responsibility. In learning the law, they learn how to situate what happened in the juridic linguistic coordinate system, and in this way, insert meaning into the discourse that is justiciable.[92]

Constructionism and Socialism

In one sense, the impact of constructionist criminology on criminal justice is hard to assess because with few exceptions, the constructionists did not have much to say about criminal justice. Foucault's biographer described the philosopher's work this way: "To some it was fascinating, to others irritating, or both at once, but believing in the theses of the work did not imply any precise political option, or any project for practical change."[93] The same might be said about other constructionists. A New York judge who read what the "very respectable living American academics, situated in the great institutions throughout the country" who had produced CLS had to say about legal institutions, and concluded: "I say to myself, there just has to be something here for the rest of us. I just can't seem to find it."[94]

The Frankfurt School sociologists spent all their time on the immanent critique of capitalism. Marx had referred to this as *praxis*, self-creating action which differed from the socially-determined behavior produced by social forces beyond individual consciousness. Horkheimer wrote about correct praxis, of theory as a guide to action. Habermas referred to this as critical self-reflection, of dissolving structural barriers to communication. Critical social theory educates, while conventional sociology manipulates. The purpose of the theorist was not to provide knowledge of social structures to policy makers for the purpose of manipulation, but to enlighten the members of society, who perceiving themselves in a new way can decide to alter those conditions they find oppressive.[95] Above all else, critical theory is about social change.

But change to what? Marx had said that the "realm of freedom" could not be envisioned by minds not yet free. Horkheimer and the Frankfurt School followed suit. They refused to describe their utopian vision, their silence attributed to the traditional Jewish prohibition on referring to God by his right name. (Traditionally, Jews do not pronounce the divine name [Exodus 6.3]; observant Jews use Adonai—"the Lord.")[96] Of any of the critical theorists of the Frankfurt tradition, only Habermas has broken rank. He has provided an idea of the utopian society in his conception of the free speech situation.

Habermas has said that creating such a situation requires giving everyone a chance to speak, a chance to criticize others, the opportunity to question any or all rules, and to voice their feelings, attitudes, motivations and interests. To ensure free speech, there must be reciprocity in discussion and no limits placed on the content of speeches. Participants must recognize the individuality of others, engage in discourse that is truthful and sincere, and free themselves from ideological, neurotic, or strategic mystifications. This can be achieved only through the "human emancipation of the masses" as individuals engage in *critical self-reflection.* This involves bringing to consciousness the unconscious determinism of society, and through this theraputic process of recognizing that society is a human product, reorganize society through conscious planning and control.[97] Still, what "ideal speech" means for criminology is hard to say. "Should criminals band together and reflect on quasi-causal determinisms? Or should they join more general processes of organized reflection with noncriminals?" inquire W. Byron Groves and Robert J. Sampson; "We suspect that Habermas would favor the latter strategy, but in either case we are left with an utterly impractical scenario predicated on a bland and unimaginative plea for consciousness-raising."[98]

Some have accused the Frankfurt School sociologists of being communists. When Sir William Beveridge, Director of the London School of Economics, wanted to bring the school to London, some of the faculty objected. Locating the Institute at the School, they feared, would have made it a "communist institution." "It's the kind of Marxism which I dislike the most," said Friedrich Hayek in reference to Marcuse's work, "It's a combination of Marxism and Freudianism." Ralf Dahrendorf thought otherwise. "Horkheimer, Adorno, Marcuse and Fromm were hardly Communists," Dahrendorf concluded, "They were what was called in Weimar Germany *salonbolschewisten*, who were always prepared to give up their political beliefs than the good life."[99] The same could be said of Foucault who joined the Communist Party as a young man in 1950. He remained a member for three years but he did not attend the meetings or sell newspapers. In later life, he became a strident anti-communist.[100]

Other constructionists, particularly the critical criminologists, did express their affinity for socialism. The critical criminologists offered some "short term policy recommendation[s] consistent with humanitarian objectives which could be carried out under our current system."[101] Anthony Platt recommended equal justice in the bail system, abolition of mandatory sentences, prosecution of corporate crimes, and promotion of community alternatives to imprisonment.[102] John Lea and Jock Young suggested *demarginalization*, that is, alternatives to prison such as community service, victim restitution, and decarceration in general. Imprisonment ought to be reserved only for those who present an extreme danger to the community. Lea and Young favor community policing in which citizens cooperate with the police to secure their own neighborhoods. The police ought to become accountable to the public, representing a police service rather than a police force.[103]

But the constructionists real project is not tinkering with criminal justice. Creating a more humanitarian justice system is allowed so long as it does not compromise the overall design for social change. The suggestions do not represent the ultimate goal of critical persuasion only steps to be taken "while we wait for a revolutionary transformation of society."[104] "Crime is ever and always that behavior seen to be problematic within the framework of those social arrangements: for crime to be abolished, then, those social arrangements themselves must also be subject to fundamental social change," explained Taylor, Walton and Young, "The task is to create a society in which the facts of human diversity, whether personal, organic or social, are not subject to the power to criminalize."[105] Ian Taylor in Britain, and Richard Quinney in the United States, both called for abolishing the capitalist system of justice in favor of socialist justice.[106]

Several of the CLS writers agreed. Roberto Unger's vision of an alternative society turns out to be Chinese Communism. Unger suggests that the ideal society is organized into "organic groups" that will overcome "systems of domination." The society will contain an organization of many groups, each practicing collective non-meritocratic decision-making. To prevent one group from dominating another there would be a "world state" and this world government "must reflect the same preeminence of democratic over meritocratic power that prevails within the organic group."[107] The Unger society "built on the...transformative action [of] revolutionary reform," is aimed at "freeing our practical and passionate dealings from the constraints imposed on them by entrenched social roles and hierarchies." It is the "vision of society in which individuals are freer to deal with one another as individuals rather than as placeholders in the system of class, communal, role, or gender contrasts."[108] To accomplish this society, the separation of powers and "classical technique of checks and balances" will have to be abolished. This will come about through a "cultural revolution" — a revolution "to remake all direct personal connections — such as those between superiors and subordinates or between men and women — by emancipating them from...social division and hierarchy." The historical analogy is to the Chinese Cultural Revolution of 1949, which failed not because it was a moral and economic disaster, but because it did not go far enough. In Unger's view, Communist party bureaucrats, after a confused and half-hearted attempt, called the interesting experiment to a halt.[109]

Duncan Kennedy envisioned a society "with a shared vision of a social harmony so complete as to obviate the need for rules any rules at all." In Kennedy's Shangri La, "The state, and with it the judge, are destined to disappear as people come to feel their brotherhood."[110] Kennedy's suggestion matches that of Soviet legal theorist Evgeny Pashukanis who urged that law and legal institutions disappear and that the remaining law become elastic and responsive to political needs. N.V. Krylenko, Pashukanis's associate and a leading prosecutor for the Commissariat of Justice, proposed a draft criminal code that anticipated the "withering away of law and the state." Krylenko proposed a new code each year from 1929 to 1935; the codes eliminated specific crimes and punishments and empowered judges to apply only "general principles of law."[111] Scholars at the State Institute for the Study of Crime and the Criminal opposed the code and it was never enacted. Krylenko did succeed in a "re-organization" of the State Institute in 1931 leading to the abolition of criminological research. Crime disappeared in the Soviet Union for the next two decades because until the 1950s, the government kept no crime statistics.

Krylenko also succeeded in using the law for political ends. During the 1930s, the major "crime" problem in the Soviet became the "kulaks" and other "class enemies" who sabotaged the collectivization and industrialization drives. Stalin's new constitution in 1936, with its reference to a "withering away of the law," became a mask for terror. He dumped Krylenko and Pashukanis in order to put a new face of legality on his terror, but he continued the ideological approach to crime they had advanced. Only after Stalin's death in 1953 did his terror end. The "de-Stalinization" policy led to freedom for some political prisoners and reforms in criminal law and procedure. It was Khrushchev's denouncement of Stalin at the twentieth congress of the Communist Party in 1956 that led to revelation of "Stalin's crimes" and the consequences of the "cult of personality."

Critique of Constructionism

Marxism has lost its appeal for many constructionists; few advocate a political shift to socialist government. Designations in constructionist criminology have changed from the 1960s and 1970s labels of "Marxist," "Socialist," and "Radical," to the 1990s labels of "Postmodern," "Critical," and "Constitutive" criminology.[112] The constructionist project continues, not so much as a political program, but as a cultural attitude that has moved from the university to political institutions. In a 1992 decision, the United States Supreme Court included the following statement in a decision: "At the heart of liberty is the right to define one's own concept of existence, of meaning, of the universe, and of the mystery of human life."[113] Jefferson had found the rights of individuals to be self-evident truths, given to people by their Creator. Two hundred years later, the Supreme Court has given each person the right to create truth as a matter of personal taste.

The constructionists have built their approach on a false theory of knowledge, even though some thoughtful and intelligent people believe that it provides the best understanding of crime. The constructionist critique of law and crime begins by rejecting the principles of justice on which they are based. It is not the failure to write these principles into law, or the failure to apply the law properly, that makes the law a tool of oppression. Rather, it is the principles themselves. Constructionists deploy of variety of strategies to denounce the ideals of equal justice under law, private property, democratic government, and so on. The sociology of knowledge group views moral ideas as social conventions, the beliefs of some people who are able to push their beliefs on others. Those who advance Marx's idea of the law as ideology denounce the rule of law as "bourgeois morality," a ruse invented by the capitalists to trap workers into lives of toil and drudgery. Those who follow the linguistic model view language itself as words: "morality" and "justice" are mechanisms of social hierarchy, the exercise of power. Oppressed persons must suffer in silence because they cannot find the words to identify the source of their oppression. Concepts of morality and justice are tainted at the source, whether they originate in social convention, economic relationships, or language.

The first question to be asked of the constructionists is whether all beliefs are tainted, or only some? To answer that all beliefs are tainted would make the idea of the social construction of reality tainted as well, and the starting point of the whole theory absurd. They would have just sawn off the branch they were sitting on. "There is no objective reality," says the constructionist, "this is how it really is." Sensible use of language such as "false consciousness" and "demystification" requires a knowable real world, a world that can be both accurately and inaccurately described. If no real world can be found, there would be no true consciousness to find, nothing to demystify. Each person's, or each group's myth, becomes as rational as any other and the truth itself becomes only the pretentious claim of what one person, or one particular group, wishes.[114] There would be no point in making claims of any sort, in writing books or giving lectures because there would be no way to decide which idea was worth believing.

If only some beliefs are tainted, if that is the constructionists' answer, then they can save their branch. This allows the possibility of true consciousness as well as false consciousness, a cyclical process of give and take in which consciousness is both made by and makes history.[115] It allows for the possibility that while the law reflects a strategy of power, the language of poor people really does express the truth of their oppression. The problem with this answer from the constructionist perspective is that it happens to be what every non-constructionist believes. Some beliefs provide rationalizations for unjust activities, some do not. And if some beliefs are not tainted; then the ideas of natural rights, private property, equal justice under law—they might not be tainted either. Maybe the constructionists have it turned around. Maybe natural rights and equal justice under law belong to the category of true consciousness, and those of critical self-reflection and immanent critique belong in the ideology category. Perhaps the idea of constructionism amounts to ideology, a ruse to oppress people.

How can one know whether a belief amounts to true or false consciousness? The answer to this question cannot be found by pointing to the reason for a belief, that is, by pointing out how a particular belief justifies the prevailing political arrangements. The source of an idea—its social origin, class interest, party affiliation—does not constitute evidence of its validity. To know "who" expressed an idea and "why" they believe it to be true does not make the idea true or false.[116] The customer may have a very good reason to doubt the motivation of the used-car salesperson and to believe that the salesperson is interested in a quick sale because there is something wrong with the car. But whether something is wrong mechanically with the car can never be established by considering the salesperson's financial motive. The only way to find out is to check under the hood and make an inference about the mechanical condition of the car based on the appearance and operation of its various parts. Evil people can say true things, and good people can be mistaken.

Constructionist critique, or "trashing" as one CLS proponent referred to it, is "fun."[117] On the assumption that the traditional conception of justice is false, it is easy to see how the constructionist criminologists can believe that the rule of law is a cover for the rule of class, how those at the top of the social hierarchy benefit from preservation of the prevailing social system, how the whole language of law and moral theory represent nothing more than ideological distortions. At best, they represent the rationalizations of the powerful few, the means by which the power elite lulls individuals into meaningless lives. But trashing can be worked the other way around. On the assumption that legal justice is true, it is easy to see why a few dinosaurs from the 1960s would want to break out the phonograph records and sing along with the Woodstock songs. Perhaps they want to relive past glory, need to justify the excesses of the past, or need a rationalization for the indulgences of their present lives. Looking for the motive behind ideas can be fun, but it moves no one closer to knowing which ideas are true and which are false.

In their critique of modern society, the constructionists sound like nihilists. *Nihilism* expresses moral relativity; there is no right and wrong. Various commentators on constructionist views have raised this criticism. Horkheimer and the Frankfurt Marxists accused Mannheim and his sociology of knowledge as relativistic, just as the radical and critical criminologists criticized those of the labeling school. Foucault and the Crits have been accused of this as well. Some have responded, insisting that moral panic ideas are not nihilistic.[118] But no can be a nihilist, not really.

Any theory that truly expresses nihilism has no point to make. If right and wrong are only words, if nothing is truly right or wrong, then what would be the point of writing a book, giving a lecture, teaching a class? If public opinion stigmatized jazz musicians in Chicago as marijuana-smokers, so what? If people thought of young people as hooligans because they dressed in the modernist fashions of the 1960s, who cares? If high school dropouts go prison because they do not understand their legal rights, what could it possibly matter? If there is no right and wrong, there can be no fair and unfair treatment, no just and unjust punishment. The nihilist edge only cuts so far. It is one thing to say that fundamentalist Christians dreamed up serial murder or that religiosity leads to intolerance. But once God is out of the way, then what?

The fact is everyone who has ever offered a theory about crime, law, and justice has a point to make. There is a moral to every story. Constructionist criminologists do not really want to say that there are no good guys or bad guys; they really want to make a case of mistaken identity. The poor who file into criminal courtrooms are not really the bad guys, the *real* bad guys are the affluent who use power to control, dominate, exploit and so on. The point of the critical critique of law and government is to point the finger where it ought to be pointed—to the crimes of the powerful, not those desperate acts of the powerless. The idea behind radical criminology is that the crimes of the poor—rape, robbery, and assault—are not the worst crimes. The worst crimes are crimes of those with great social power, white collar crimes, crimes that violate human rights, crimes that inflict injury to large numbers of people. Even Habermas and Foucault have a point to make—that society ought to be different, that there ought to be social equality, that people should not be constrained by artificial rules and bourgeois morality. The point of trashing justice is to make a point about justice.

God always reappears. No philosophy can escape transcendent morality for the simple fact that it is impossible to notice a crooked line without a straight line in mind. Joseph Heller captured this truth in his novel *Catch-22*. Captain Yossarian editorializes to Lt. Scheisskopf's wife about the amount of cruelty in the world.

> "[God] is not working at all. He's playing. Or else he's forgotten all about us ... Good God, how much reverence can you have for a Supreme Being who finds it necessary to include such phenomena as phlegm and tooth decay in his system of creation?" he muses.

Lt. Scheisskopf's wife attempts several rebuttals, but unable to match the captain's cynicism, resorts to screaming and punching him in the head.

> "What the h___ are you getting so upset about?" He asked her bewilderedly in a tone of contrite amusement. "I thought you didn't believe in God."

> "I don't," she sobbed, bursting violently into tears. "But the God I don't believe in is a good God, a just God, a merciful God. He's not the mean and stupid God you make him out to be."

Not even Foucault himself, who viewed factories, schools, hospitals and prisons as a conspiracy to stifle the individual longing for self-expression, could hold out. He supported the revolution in Iran until it became clear how the Ayatollah Khomeini's cadres had systematically murdered their rivals. Then he winced.[119] The philosopher who had found in the writings of a murderer a world view more valid than that of the judges who convicted him, could not live with the conclusions of his own relativism.

The whole attempt to destroy traditional morality as something subjective and substitute some new system of values is a waste of time because it cannot be done. In the first place, it is impossible to create moral value outside traditional moral values; the human mind is incapable of inventing some new human value.[120] Social equality? Parents, generation after generation, have taught their children about the importance of sharing. Lying, cheating, taking what does not belong to you—it has been covered. Further, all attempts to create a new moral value consist in arbitrarily selecting some maxim of traditional morality, setting it aside from the others, and pronouncing it some ultimate principle.[121] Consider social equality. To insist that there must be absolute social equality interferes with another maxim, that of self-determination or personal liberty. Should each individual get the chance to get what can be had out of life? Who has the right to take from some and give to others?

Then there is the reference to history within constructionist approaches. Various theorists look back to find the origins of the present, to explain why things are as they are, and to suggest how things might be different. Many rely on history to argue for what is and what is not the destiny of humanity. Marx prophesied the end of capitalist mode of production and beginning of the socialist mode of production. The critical criminologists foretell the collapse of capitalism; it will collapse either by conscious struggle on the part of the workers, or through the internal contradictions of capitalist production itself. Habermas suggested that the progression of moral consciousness through self-reflection would culminate in the ideal speech situation.

Actually, none of these views are about history; they express a philosophy of history called historicism. *Historicism* refers to the belief that human beings can, by means of their mental power, discover the inner meaning of history. Historicists claim to have figured out the inner meaning of history based on their explanation of people, society and their relationships.[122] Historicists say things like all of humanity is moving in a particular direction, or that civilizations proceed through various stages. They make some claim about contemporary events based on the claim of some metaphysical or philosophical concept of destiny.

Finding the inner meaning of history is, however, not a game for mortals. Historians may infer unknown events from known. Historians may suggest the meaning of particular events, even predict future events, based on an understanding of causes. Historians may say almost anything about past events except what it all means. The historian may infer unknown events from known, much like the card player who understanding the rules of the game, anticipates the next card thrown at the table. To do this, the card player must know not only what cards have been thrown but also the total number of cards that can ever be thrown. This is precisely the information the historicist lacks. Any philosophy of history confronts the future and the possibility that the point of the story has yet to occur. It would surely be one of the luckiest things in the world if all the content of time up to the point the historicist began writing happened to contain all that was required to reach the significance of history. But in a world where a rabbit's foot does not assure success, there is no guarantee that what people have lived up to this point in human existence contains all that is necessary for summing up the metahistorical meaning of human existence. History is a game, so to speak, that can only be played without knowing the total number of cards in the pack.[123]

Conclusion

Modern thinking about justice, which began with the Enlightenment, pursued universal reason as a guide. Postmodern thought despairs any universal standard for justice; Enlightenment democracy becomes postmodern anarchy. Dostoyevsky could see it in 1880. In *The Brothers Karamazov*, Ivan observes that if God is dead, then everything is permitted. There can be no crime in postmodern society because there can be no justice. Justice is only one story among many. To find universal justice it is necessary to go back—to go back *before* the beginning—to the pre-modern understanding. Pre-modern thought expressed a concern for a just society based on a revelation of God.[124] But first, a look at race, racism and crime.

Chapter 7

Race, Racism and Crime

Although the understanding of race has shifted from the biological view to the social view, the significance of race as a topic of study in criminology remains. The early criminologists, who took a biological approach to crime, believed that people could be divided into one of several races or subspecies, and that cultural differences between ethnic populations reflected racial differences. While criminology has not completely escaped from the biologistic view, the rise of sociological criminology has meant abandoning the biological concept of race.[1] Sociologists emphasize that race is a social concept; racial differences are real to the extent that people believe they are real. This sociological view of race has led to explanations of crime based on racism within society and the broad politics of race-relations.

Much of what criminologists have written about race, racism, and crime has to do with African Americans. "Black crime" has been an issue in criminology at least since 1935, when the Federal Bureau of Investigation began publishing arrest statistics by race. In that first report, FBI statisticians emphasized that the percentage of Blacks arrested for violent crimes was higher than the percentage of Black Americans in the general population.[2] Whether disproportionate crime statistics for Black Americans reflect greater criminal activity among African Americans, or reflect racial prejudice directed at African Americans, has continued to present a significant question in criminology. Criminologists have filled thousands of pages in research journals with analyses of these statistics. During the past decade, Black criminology has emerged, partly in response to persistent concern with Black crime. *Black criminology* promotes what Black criminologists have to say about race, racism and crime.[3]

This chapter addresses the issues of race, racism, and crime by exploring the issues of Black crime and Black criminology; it features what Black criminologists have to say about crime among

African Americans. African Americans are not, of course, the only racial group in the United States, but the White-Black confrontation has occupied a place like no other. "Southern trees bear strange fruit," blues singer Billie Holiday used to sing in the Harlem jazz clubs of 1930s, "Blood on the leaves and blood at the root, Black bodies swinging in the southern breeze, Strange fruit hanging from the poplar trees." Nobody else in America can sing that song.[4] Part One reviews the analyses of W.E.B. Du Bois, the first African-American criminologist. Parts Two through Four explore several strands of contemporary Black criminology: the liberal approach, the radical critiques, and the conservative approach. Each section describes the ideas that drive the perspective, the solutions suggested by proponents, and the proponents' critique of the other perspectives.

The First Black Criminologist

Few Americans at the end of the nineteenth century, Black or White, could best the academic credentials of W.E.B. Du Bois. After graduating from Fisk University, Du Bois gained admission to Harvard where he studied with William James and George Santayana. In 1892, he received a grant allowing him to study sociology in Germany, and he heard lectures by Max Weber. Three years later, he became the first Black person to receive a Ph.D. from Harvard. In 1897, he accepted an appointment as professor of economics and history at Atlanta University, and later helped found the National Association for the Advancement of Colored People (NAACP). In 1904, Du Bois hosted a conference dealing with Negro crime, and later edited a publication based on the conference. His interest in the topic has earned him the title of the first Black criminologist.[5]

DU BOIS ON RACE. The idea of race consumed Du Bois's intellectual energy throughout his professional life. It was Du Bois who observed in his famous work, *The Souls of Black Folk* (1903) that "the problem of the twentieth century is the problem of the color line—the relation of the darker to the lighter races of men in Asia and Africa, in America and the islands of the sea."[6] Du Bois wrote prolifically, and in his books and articles, he outlined a set of issues that defined the topic of study for sociologists, law professors, and criminologists for the rest of the century. It is difficult to identify an issue about race and crime that Du Bois did not address. Many criminologists working on black crime during the past few decades have announced insights only to find that Du Bois had already been there and moved on.

In 1897, the American Negro Academy published a short work by Du Bois entitled "The Conservation of the Races," in which he claimed that "the history of the world is the history, not of individuals, but of groups, not of nations, but of races... the race idea [is]... the central thought of all history."[7] Du Bois denied that race could be defined by physical differences, such as skin color and hair texture. He noted variations in skin color and hair throughout the African peoples of the world. He acknowledged that races represented vast families of people, "generally of common blood," but emphasized that their common history and traditions transcended physical differences. He identified eight historic races of humankind: Slavs, Teutons, English, Romance nations, Negroes, Semitic people, Hindoos, and Mongolians. None existed as a pure racial type. The most common, the Negro race, was the most ethnically diverse. Du Bois's own family tree included mixture as well — his father, Alfred Du Bois, was of French-Haitian extraction.

The Negro race included various mixed groups of the Americas as well various groups on the African continent. The definition of race in cultural and historical terms created a dilemma, however, leading to the question of whether the Negroes of America were Negroes first, or Americans first and last. "Am I an American or am I Negro? Can I be both? Or is it my duty to cease to be a Negro as soon as possible and be an American? If I strive as a Negro, am I not perpetuating the very cleft that threatens and separates black and white America?...Does my black blood place upon me any more obligation to assert my nationality than German, or Irish, or Italian blood would?"[8] Du Bois answered by suggesting that American society was large enough to include several races, that several national ideals could co-exist and perhaps, each would make more progress toward that "one far off divine event" than by striving in isolation.[9] He introduced a theme of *double-consciousness* that appeared several years later in *The Souls of Black Folk*. Unlike the other races, the Negro could experience no true self-consciousness, could never be free from looking at themselves through the eyes of others. "One ever feels his two-ness — an American, a Negro; two souls, two thoughts, two unreconciled strivings; two warring ideals in one dark body, whose dogged strength alone keeps it from being torn asunder."[10]

Du Bois placed great faith in Black Americans who represented the "advance guard" of all African peoples. They needed to establish cultural leadership through sustaining their cultural identity. Similarly, a small portion of African Americans represented the advance guard among African Americans. In his essay "The Talented Tenth" (1903) Du Bois explained how the contributions of a race are not made by the whole, but through the talented few and its representatives. The community supports the talented few, and allows them to enjoy greater social power and recognition than others, because they elevated the communty as a whole to a new level. "The Negro race, like all races, is going to be saved by its exceptional men," Du Bois insisted. Human progress did not occur from the bottom upward, but top downward. "The Talented Tenth...rises and pulls all that are worth saving up to their vantage ground. This is the history of human progress...."[11]

The talented tenth had the power to overcome race prejudice. Du Bois defined race prejudice in a way that suggested that racial groups have a tendency toward conflict, however, he emphasized cooperation over conflict. Racial groups in the United States had enough in common so that conflict could be avoided and mutual benefit achieved through cooperation. Racism stemmed from ignorance and stupidity; it occurred when one community lacked awareness of the cultural and intellectual achievements of another. Racism represented the sort of ignorance that could be eliminated by knowledge of the talented tenth's activities. The early Du Bois championed integrationist ideas. Generally speaking, *integrationist thinking* identifies racism as the historical cause of the subordinate status of Black Americans, and views racism not as a permanent feature, but as a system that can be altered. Altering racism required not only solidarity and unity of purpose among Black Americans, but inter-racial cooperation also. Black leaders needed to build broader support for equality by building coalitions with Whites. For this reason, the strategy for racial reform, given the soundness of the American system (except for racism), ought to rely on the conventional political process rather than attempt to subvert the system.[12]

In 1910, Du Bois left Atlanta University for the NAACP. He founded *Crisis*, the NAACP's monthly magazine, which he edited until 1934 when he resigned from the organization. Although other Black leaders, Booker T. Washington for instance, generally shared Du Bois's integrationist philosophy, Du Bois used the magazine to criticize Washington's Tuskegee Institute. Du Bois had great faith in knowledge and higher education as the means by which Blacks overcame poverty. He felt that Washington's emphasis on industrial training could not sustain itself, and while it lasted, threatened Black business enterprise.[13] Du Bois scoffed at Washington's emphasis on industrial training for Blacks, observing that Tuskegee would have no professors if not for those the Black colleges produced.[14]

During the last decades of his life, Du Bois abandoned integrationist thinking for Pan-Africanism, and later, socialism. Du Bois concluded that race and racism are of relatively recent origin. While the Medieval European world made Africans the subject of legend and curiosity, it was only with the development of slavery that skin color became a mark of inferiority.[15] Reading Marx, he attributed the tenacity of racism to economic life and the legacy of slavery. Racism was deeply entrenched within an economic system in which Whites regarded Blacks as inferior as a means of maintaining economic advantage. But even after his conversion to socialism Du Bois did not regard racism as an artifact of class division. Racism persisted as an irrationality that could not be explained in terms of economic interest. In order to rationalize slavery, the slaveholders had to insist that it did not offend Christian morality; they had to reduce Blacks to the status of children who needed guidance, as heathen who needed civilizing. This formed a collective unconscious that survived long after the institution of slavery ended.[16]

By 1952, Du Bois's socialist opinions alienated him from the majority of Black Americans. He eulogized Joseph Stalin as "a great man" who had the courage to "advance toward a real socialism" and praised Soviet control of the Balkans as freeing workers and peasants from Western exploitation.[17] In 1958, he began a world tour. He met Nikita Khrushchev, received the International Lenin Peace Prize, and visited Ghana, where at the invitation of Prime Minister Kwame Nkrumah, he became a citizen before his death in 1963.

DU BOIS ON CRIME. It was the Du Bois who viewed race, not economics, as the motor of history that addressed the problem of Negro crime. Du Bois viewed the problem of crime among Black

Americans, along with immorality and laziness, as the residue of slavery. The "first and greatest step" toward a solution had to begin with "the Negroes themselves," and "only earnest and long continued efforts on our part can cure these social ills." The second step of "greater respect for personal liberty and worth, regardless of race" depended on the "earnest efforts on the part of the white people."[18]

In *The Philadelphia Negro* (1899), a study of Black life in Philadelphia's seventh ward, Du Bois contrasted the talented tenth with the *submerged tenth* of "criminals, prostitutes and loafers...." Du Bois looked down on this class the way that Marx and Engels viewed the lumpen-proletariat, although Du Bois pointed out that a high rate of crime among Negroes after emancipation was inevitable. Based on his analysis of public documents, he concluded that Black crime concerned the city only after 1780, after slavery ended and freed Blacks migrated to the city in larger numbers. Migration to unfamiliar cities in the North after emancipation led to crime because African Americans found "a new form of oppression and ridicule, which translated into discrimination" and limited opportunities for Blacks.[19] By 1809, Black churches had mobilized to suppress criminal activity, but the state legislature undermined their efforts with a series of repressive measures passed in reaction to Nat Turner's revolt. In *The Black North in 1901*, Du Bois reiterated this theme in his discussions of crime in New York, Boston, and Chicago. Explaining the increase in arrests of Blacks in New York from 1885 to 1895, Du Bois observed that "the increase in arrests is undoubtedly due to migration—the sudden contact of newcomers with unknown city life." He went on to say "that the Negro under normal conditions is law-abiding and good-natured cannot be disputed. We have but to change conditions, then, to reduce Negro crime."[20]

Du Bois viewed crime "as a phenomenon of organized social life," the product of "open rebellion of an individual against his environment." Crime rates increased in Northern cities after the migration of Blacks in 1880, but Black migrants did not bring crime to the city so much as migration to the city brought crime to them. "If men are suddenly transported from one environment to another; the result is lack of harmony with the new conditions," Du Bois explained, and "...lack of harmony with social surroundings leads to crime." The statistics suggested that crime increased, for the same reasons, among White migrants to the city during the same period. Both Whites and Blacks engaged in crime for the same reasons; when crime increased among Whites, it increased among Blacks except that "among Negroes the change is always exaggerated—the increase greater, the decrease more marked...."[21]

Du Bois extended these themes in 1904, during the Ninth Annual Conference for the study of Negro Problems, which he hosted at Atlanta University. The conference produced *Some Notes on Negro Crime*, a collective work Du Bois edited for publication. In his comments about crime, and his perception of racial issues, Du Bois introduced themes that have resounded throughout the literature on race and crime for nearly a century.[22] Specifically, Du Bois identified six causes of crime: (1) The transient stage between slavery and freedom, characterized by "physical strain, mental bewilderment and moral weakness." (2) Race prejudice which narrowed opportunities for Blacks, which led in turn, to a loss of self-respect. (3) Less legal protection for Negroes than others against violations of their rights, liberty and prosperity; "this is particularly true for Negro women." (4) Laws dealing with vagrancy, work contracts, and crop liens crafted to entrap "ignorant, unfortunate, and careless Negroes." (5) Two sorts of justice administered by courts, one for Whites, and one for Negroes, which made it difficult for Negroes to secure justice when the opposing legal party was White. (6) The method of punishing Negro criminals, such as lynching and convict leasing, "is calculated to breed crime rather than stop it."[23]

The report appealed to the White people of Georgia for just laws, abolition of convict leasing, and fair punishment of those convicted. Honest, hard-working, law-abiding Black men made better neighbors, he suggested, than an ignorant and unpaid class of serfs that only served to breed dangerous crime. But Du Bois and his colleagues also appealed to the Black people of the state, listing ten "faults" of the emancipated Negro: abuse of their new freedom; loose ideas of property and petty pilfering; unreliability, deception and lying; exaggerated ideas of personal rights; sexual looseness, weak family life, and poor parental training of children; lack of proper self-respect; poverty and low wages; lack of thrift combined with a gambling spirit; waywardness of the "second generation," and use of liquor and drugs. The submerged tenth stained the Negro's reputation in the White world, and until "large numbers of the freedmen's sons" learned to be law-abiding citizens "the progress of race, of the South, and of the nation will be retarded."[24]

The Liberal Mainstream

Many criminologists have engaged the idea of a submerged tenth, a strata of Black people pressed down by the weight of White indifference and hostility, as an explanation for crime among African Americans. The *Black underclass* of America's great cities languishes while other immigrants have come and gone from the old neighborhoods. To explain why Black citizens stay at the bottom for so much longer has been explained by low self-esteem, family disorganization, and poverty.

THE MYSTERY OF THE UNDERCLASS. In every industrial city of the northeastern United States, there are pockets of poverty and despair. Places where visitors, White and Black, worry about stumbling into and in which residents live in fear. These areas, where economic prosperity never trickles down far enough and government assistance never elevates high enough, remain in the shadows of economic prosperity. To explain how these areas came to be is, for liberal criminologists, to explain Black crime. There is disagreement about exactly *how* the Black underclass came together, but complete agreement about *where* it happened. The underclass of gangs, drugs, and crime that rules of rough neighborhoods of northern cities originated in the South.

In one view, the Black underclass originated with Jim Crow and the system that segregated public facilities from theatres to cemeteries. Beginning in the late 1930s, Kenneth and Mamie Clark conducted a series of studies about self-esteem and African-American children. Their testimony before the United States Supreme Court supported the decision in *Brown v. Board of Education* (1954), which led to school desegregation. When offered a Black or White doll to play with, the Clarks found that 67 percent of Black children chose White dolls. When asked why, the children typically said that the White doll was "prettier" or "nicer."[25] The Clarks' research provided evidence that segregation, permitted by the Court with the doctrine of "separate but equal," had devastating effects. The provision of third-rate public services to Blacks made Blacks second-class citizens, leading to egregious outcomes for Black and White Americans. However separate segregation had been, it had not been equal.

While psychologists have argued about the methodology and the meaning of the research subjects' preference ever since, most agree with the Clarks that the results provide evidence of *lower self-esteem*, even self-hatred, within Black children. Darlene Powell-Hopson and Derek S. Hopson, a husband-and-wife team of psychologists, replicated the Clarks' study in 1985 and came to similar conclusions. The Hopsons found that 65 percent of the Black children in their sample chose the White dolls. Additionally, 76 percent of these children said that the Black doll "looked bad" to them. Despite the civil rights movement, the percent of Black children indicating a preference for white dolls barely changed. Black children identified with White images over Black images. This means, the Hopsons pointed out, that too many Black children concluded that they are not as good as Whites; that they reject themselves in effect and desire to be White.[26] Darlene Powell-Hopson became a consultant to Mattel Toys and helped the company develop a line of Black dolls with browner tone, fuller lips, and less-protruding noses.[27]

Lower self-esteem among Black adolescents might explain higher involvement in delinquency. Beginning in 1957, social psychologists and sociologists began dividing groups of school children into groups based on their responses to survey items about self-esteem, then comparing them to detect differences in the frequency of delinquent conduct. Several studies found that those who reported lower levels of self-esteem also reported having been involved in a larger number of delinquent activities. One study of school children, the esteem enhancement model, found that more of those who reported low self-esteem at the beginning of the school year reported having committed more delinquent acts during the year than those who had reported higher self-esteem at the beginning.[28] In a review of these studies, Lee Ross of the University of Wisconsin at Parkside, points out that the link between self-esteem and race is not as simple as it appears. There is a difference between personal identity and group identity. Measuring self-esteem across races assumes that each race views self-esteem in the same way, which presents a conceptual problem if White culture is more individualistic and Black culture more community-oriented. At the same time, it is not clear whether low self-esteem causes crime or crime causes low self-esteem. Or, for that matter, whether crime increases self-esteem. The decision to sell drugs might initially reflect low self-esteem, but as profits accumulate and the seller acquires success symbols (BMW, gold chain), the seller may begin to feel higher self-esteem.[29]

In another view, the Black underclass began in the fields and slave cabins with the terror of life during slavery. Later, the victims of racial violence turned on themselves. The *subculture of violence* suggests that African Americans possess a culture of their own that differs from the mainstream culture, and that this subculture values, or does not disapprove of, the use of violence as a means of resolving conflict. The subculture of violence theory comes from a 1958 study of homicide in Philadelphia and from a subsequent book by Marvin Wolfgang and Franco Ferracuti.[30] Wolfgang and Ferracuti relied on "psychological and sociological constructs to aid in the explanation of the concentration of violence in specific socioeconomic groups and ecological areas."[31] Their conclusion, that certain segments in society place a positive value on violence, has become "one of the most cited, but one of the least tested, propositions in the sociological and criminological literature."[32]

Wolfgang and Ferracuti speculated about a distinct subculture of violence among Black Americans. "Our subculture-of-violence thesis," they wrote, "would therefore, expect to find a large spread to the learning of, resort to, and criminal display of the violence value among minority groups such as Negroes."[33] As elaborated by others, the frequency of criminal violence among Blacks in northern cities can be attributed to their Southern heritage. Southern Blacks carried the values related to violence that they had learned as long ago as the era of slavery. Slavery destroyed the cultures of western Africa, from which Africans had been taken, and slaves learned the values of their masters. Slavery was an extremely violent institution; slave owners used slave codes and brutal bodily punishments to maintain it. The slaves internalized these values as they participated in a violent Southern subculture, then exported them north. Unable to assimilate into American culture, Blacks formed ghettos in northern cities, turned to violence, and turned on each other.[34]

In another version, it was culture, but a culture that developed in the aftermath of slavery, after emancipation, in the sharecropper shacks on the edge of the farms. "Every aspect of the underclass culture in the ghettos, is directly traceable to roots in the South," explained journalist Nicholas Lemann, "and not the South of slavery but the South of a generation ago. In fact, there seems to be a strong correlation between underclass status in the North and a family background in the nascent underclass of the sharecropper South."[35] Lemann told how migration of Blacks from rural areas of southern states to northern cities between 1940 and 1970 imported intact the caste system of *southern sharecropping*, and this distinctive culture constitutes the greatest barrier to progress. Sharecroppers had no money, no education; they depended on the landowner to provide everything. The similarities between sharecropping and welfare are "eerie": dependency on the system; more money for additional children, little value on education and home ownership, lack of interest in marriage. Working on shares translated into living on welfare. The skills of "getting over" — of surviving on the meager rations allowed by landowners — became the "hustling" culture of the ghettos — prostitution, bootlegging, drugs, and theft. The ghettos flourished during the 1970s, when jobs disappeared, families disintegrated, and crime soared. Black southerners clung to traditional African cultural practices adapted to life in the rural South, which left them out-of-place in the industrialization of America.[36]

In still another view, it was the impact of the South on Black families that exiled them to the underclass of urban ghettos. While many criminologists have commented on families, few investigated the matter more thoroughly than E. Franklin Frazier, who wrote two books and ten articles on the topic between 1926 and 1933.[37] Frazier, who in 1948 became the first African-American president of the American Sociological Association, taught sociology at Morehouse College in Atlanta and studied with Robert Park at the University of Chicago in 1927. Frazier described "the waste of human life, the immorality, delinquency, desertions and broken homes" as symptoms of *family disorganization* within Black America. Frazier investigated the absence of family traditions, the lack of legal marriage, children born to teenagers, and none of which represented cause for alarm during slavery.

During slavery, families struggled to maintain despite laws prohibiting their legal existence; some slave families cultivated "a degree of organization and a deep sense of family responsibility." But after slavery, many families in the rural South remained disorganized, dependent on the dominant White community. After the migration to northern cities, the "widespread disorganization of family life among Negroes had affected practically every phase of community life," generating an instability resulting in a "casual, precarious, and fragmentary" life.[38] Slavery, and the Reconstruction period that followed, left mothers and grandmothers to preserve the family, leading to the prevalence of female-headed households. Frazier counted female-headed households to show the over-reliance on women as family leaders due to the absence of fathers. Family disorganization, combined with poverty and the lack of health services, represented the chief handicaps to Black Americans and the most important explanation for crime within Black communities.[39]

Frazier's work gained new attention in 1965 when Daniel P. Moynihan used it in his report to President Lyndon Johnson. Moynihan, who later became a U.S. Senator from New York, wrote *The Negro Family: The Case for National Action*. He served as assistant secretary of labor for policy planning research when he wrote "The Moynihan Report." The report described a "tangle of pathology" within Black families responsible for poverty, unemployment, and delinquency in urban communities, and revived Frazier's concept of *Black matriarchy* as the root of pathology. Due to instability within the family structure in general, and a complete breakdown within urban Black families, "the Negro community has been forced into a matriarchal structure... which seriously retards the progress of the group as a whole, and imposes a crushing burden on the Negro male...."[40] Moynihan contended that American society presumes male leadership in both public and private affairs, and that in Black families, where female-headed households prevailed, this was not the norm. The matriarchal system, symptomatic of disorganization, left young Black men at a distinct disadvantage when they had relocated to northern cities in search of jobs because they grown up in a social situation so out-of-line with the rest of society.[41]

In suggesting that Black family structure was responsible for poverty, and crime, the Moynihan Report came to be seen as an exercise in blaming the victim.[42] Johnson gave a speech from the paper at Howard University in June 1965, an enormous success, but soon rioting broke out in the Watts area of Los Angeles. In response to questions, Johnson's press secretary (Bill Moyers) distributed copies of the report, and as Moynihan later observed, "In short order I became hugely disliked and indeed in some quarters anathemized... I had left

Washington and lost a primary election in New York City." Moynihan appeared on "Meet the Press" that summer and explained his views. "At any given moment two-thirds of the Negro families are husband and wife families, but over their lifetime only a little more than a third of Negro children come of eighteen having lived all their lives in such a family. That hurts people, that deprives them of opportunities, not to have a father, not to have a mother...So we can't act is if the family were just a result; it is also an effect."[43]

THE COLOR OF INEQUALITY. For William J. Wilson, the most prominent African-American sociologist since Frazier, the Black underclass came about because of the second great migration, not the first. The first migration occurred across country; it brought rural Blacks to the North from the South. The second occurred across town; it took Blacks from the inner-city to the suburbs. The second migration divided middle-class African Americans from the lower class, and when they left, there was nothing left.

Wilson's first book, *The Declining Significance of Race,* appeared in 1978. In it, Wilson described changes in the economic fortunes of African Americans and the creation of a Black middle class. While the new arrivals faced various forms of racism, in schools and neighborhoods, the expanding industrial economy provided economic opportunities for African Americans that did not threaten Whites. This economic opportunity created a class structure within the Black community, allowed some Blacks to escape menial tasks into skilled blue-collar and white-collar professions, and created a class structure within the Black community. The book earned Wilson an award from the American Sociological Association. It also drew fire from other Black intellectuals who felt that Wilson had understated the impact of racism.

Wilson was not the first to pursue the idea that class differences transcend race differences, but Wilson was a Black sociologist whose "conservative" thesis challenged the liberal views of Black and White sociologists. "Race relations in America have undergone fundamental changes in recent years, so much so now that the life chances of individual blacks have more to do with their economic class position than with their day-to-day encounters with whites" wrote one critic.[44] In response, the Association of Black Sociologists convened in San Francisco in 1978 to "express their outrage" at the conservative trend in analyses of race relations. The association is-

sued a statement criticizing Wilson for "draw[ing] inferences...
contrary to the conclusions that other black and white scholars
have reached with reference to the salience of race as a critical variable in American society." One of the Black sociologists who had
attended the San Francisco conference published his response to
Wilson. "There are so many faulty (even naive) interpretations in
[Wilson's] short book that it is an amazing piece of work coming
from a black sociologist."[45]

Wilson responded with a second book in which he wrote about a
"semi-permanent underclass" in the urban ghettoes, the product of
the same social and economic forces that allowed the formation of
the middle class. As economic conditions of Black urban dwellers
improved, those who could afford to move out of the inner-city to
the suburbs, did move out, leaving behind an underclass. During
the 1970s and 1980s, de-industrialization and the loss of entry-level
positions in factory work led to further isolation of the truly disadvantaged, a submerged portion of "long-term welfare families and
street criminals," within the underclass. The departure of the Black
middle class led to a downward economic spiral, the loss of contact
with middle class values and aspirations, and a culture of despair.
The Black community lost its "social buffer," its' ties to middle-
class role models, to children who help socialize others into middle
class life, and its community leadership. The truly disadvantaged
acted in deviant ways that deepened their isolation; they do not
cling to their families, insist on orderly schools, pursue employment
or resist drugs, alcohol and other means of escape.[46]

Wilson teamed up with Robert J. Sampson, a University of
Chicago sociologist, and rejuvenated the Chicago School delinquency research of Shaw and McKay to develop a theory of race,
crime, and inequality. "The basic thesis," they wrote (in language
only a sociologist could love) "is that macrosocial patterns of residential inequality give rise to the social isolation and ecological concentration of the truly disadvantaged, which in turn leads to structural barriers and cultural adaptions that undermine social
organization and hence the control of crime."[47] These macrosocial
patterns of segregation—migration, housing discrimination, and
de-industrialization—interacted with community factors, such as
residential turnover, concentrated poverty, and family disruption, to
undermine social organization. These impoverished urban areas are
characterized by "cognitive landscapes," or "ecologically structured

norms" of appropriate behavior in which residents come not to condemn crime, disorder and drug use, but expect them as part of everyday life. Cognitive landscapes are further strengthened within urban areas by "social isolation," the lack of contact with individuals and institutions that represent mainstream society. The roots of violence among Black youth of the 1990s stem from childhood experiences during the late 1970s and early 1980s, a period of rapid change when poverty, racial segregation, joblessness, population turnover, and female-headed households increased dramatically.[48]

From the social disorganization perspective, Black crime has the same roots as White crime, it is just that the social origins of disorganization disproportionately impact African Americans. "When people live in neighborhoods of concentrated disadvantage," explains Christopher Stone, who directs the Vera Institute of Justice, "victimization and offending rates are high. When researchers compare similar neighborhoods of different races, the racial differences seem to disappear. The problem is that researchers cannot find white communities to compare to the most disadvantaged urban communities."[49] Black crime can be explained due to a combination of desperation and discrimination. The concentration of the poorest Blacks into pockets of poverty led to the proliferation of drug abuse, gangs, and crime. Without stable families and the hope of meaningful employment, gangs proliferated. Drug dealers became a major source of economic opportunity as whole neighborhoods gave way to drug dealing. Drug-trafficking led to gangs, to drive-by shootings and gang violence. Other youth secured firearms, to protect themselves from gangs and drug dealers, leading to further erosion of schools and other positive avenues. At the same time, street crime generated a reaction from suburban Whites who perceived them as threats to social order and favored repressive crime control measures. This led to vigorous law enforcement efforts, to police crackdowns, and distrust between police and Black youth. Crime itself, and control efforts, further erode community life.[50]

LIBERAL SOLUTIONS. The road from the grime of the inner-city to the shade of the suburbs has not been easy to travel. For the liberal mainstream, the problems of city life that contribute to crime are clear enough: joblessness, out-of-marriage births, failing schools, lack of economic opportunity. The solution is clear as well; it begins with addressing the social problems. The criminal justice system needs repair, but mainly, it is the social life of the city that needs fixing.

A great deal of liberal emphasis has to do with measures to create a fairer criminal justice process. Young African-American men commit more than their fair share of crime but the criminal justice response bears the stain of economic and racial bias. Fred L. Banks, Jr., Mississippi's first Black judge, puts it succinctly: "Blacks commit a disproportionate amount of crime, but the criminal justice system has a different and disproportionate response to crime committed by Blacks."[51]

In this effort, Black liberals have received support from White allies. Liberals seek new policies to deal with overt and covert discrimination.[52] *Overt discrimination* occurs when decision makers treat similarly-situated Black and White people differently. The main remedy is to limit discretion of the part of police and prosecutors through legislation. Legislative interest in racial profiling began in 1997, after Black motorists filed a series of lawsuits against state police. In 1993, Robert Wilkins, a Washington DC lawyer, and three other Black citizens filed suit against the Maryland State Police. Wilkins had been stopped with his family while returning home from a funeral because as a Black man he fit the profile of a drug courier. As a part of the settlement, the Maryland State Police agreed to maintain computer records of all motorist stops between 1995 and 1997. The Maryland statistics, along with similar analyses conducted in Ohio, Texas, North Carolina, and New Jersey, provided clear evidence of what had been obvious to Black motorists: people had been stopped by police for no reason other than the color of their skin. It had been common enough, in fact, to have received its own shorthand: "driving while black" or simply, "DWB." In 1997, Congressman John Conyers introduced the Traffic Stops Statistics Act. The bill directed the Attorney General to collect statistics on all routine traffic stops made by law enforcement, identify the race of persons stopped, the reason for the stop, and whether an arrest was made.[53]

Covert discrimination has to do with harsh crime policies that even though they have the appearance of being color-blind have a disparate effect on Black Americans. Michael Tonry, a law professor at the University of Minnesota, has explained how the administration of justice accounts for Black crime. Tonry insists that racial disparities in African-American arrests and imprisonment increased during the 1980s due to the politics of race and crime. The increases did not reflect a proportionate increase in the frequency of crime among Black Americans, but rather, the consequences of harsh crime control strategies deployed during the Reagan and Bush years. Conservative candidates appealed to the anti-Black sentiments of White voters during national elections, then promoted harsh crime control strategies once in public office.[54]

Drug control strategies, in particular, have backfired. Tonry reviews prison admission data from the federal system and several states to show how drug arrests for Blacks increased. Drug arrests are easier in inner-city communities than suburbs. Drug sales in the city take place in the streets, abandoned buildings and other public spaces while drug sales in suburbs occur indoors. Dealers in urban areas tend to sell to strangers and new acquaintances rather than suburban dealers who are less likely to sell to uncover buyers. At the same time, penalties for drug crimes became harsh. Under federal law, a drug conviction involving crack cocaine received a longer prison term than for powder cocaine. This law had a disparate effect on Black Americans because they are more likely to sell and use the crack form even though it is pharmacologically indistinguishable from the powder form preferred by White suburbanites.[55]

Memphis Judge Joseph B. Brown, Jr., who became well-known after newspapers carried stories of his "reverse theft" sentence, puts this view succinctly: "Judges can make an impact on the crime problem by attacking its roots, not just alleviating its symptoms by sticking folks in jail. Courts can be used to effect social change."[56] Brown has used a surfeit of community-based sentences including requiring defendants to register to vote, earn a GED, complete job training, take drug tests, or to do community service work. He regularly sentences Black defendants to read *The Autobiography of Malcolm X* and write an essay; he also sentences some to watch films such as *Boyz in the Hood*. "It does good," he explains, "when they see somebody they can identify with and see how what they have become fits into the overall scheme of things. Maybe by seeing things on a movie screen, they can put in their minds a picture of what they are and what they can be. That can be motivational."[57]

Liberals emphasize that crime reduction can be obtained by means of social policy rather than crime policy. William J. Wilson, who has supported Democrat candidates in elections, influenced President Clinton. More than once, Clinton remarked publicly how profoundly he was influenced by *The Truly Disadvantaged*. He invoked the name of "the famous African-American sociologist William Julius Wilson" whenever he had to explain how Black Americans stood to gain from his economic policies.[58] Wilson offered his support for the Clinton administration's efforts to create universal health care, a national childcare system, and national education standards. Wilson advocates as a general strategy reliance on the federal government to initiate community development projects.

To redirect ghettos, Wilson has recommended establishing a Works Progress Administration (WPA) similar to the one Roosevelt established during the Depression Era. These jobs would not be Depression-era jobs, but useful jobs such as: cleaning the streets twice a day instead of once a day, picking up trash twice a week rather than once a week, opening libraries during Saturday and evening hours, cleaning graffiti, and providing adult supervision at parks and playgrounds. The new WPA would operate job information centers to distribute job information and coordinate car pools to bring people to job locations. Not only would the new WPA provide for improving the quality of life in urban neighborhoods, the jobs would provide a conduit to permanent jobs by teaching the soft skills of employability. "Soft skills" include cultural aspects, such as making eye contact, something young people learn not to do, Wilson points out, to survive in the inner-city but something middle-class shoppers expect from sales clerks.[59]

The Radical Critiques

America's first great African-American criminologist, W.E.B. Du Bois has been remembered for his founding of liberal integration. Du Bois taught that although racism had caused the historical subordination of Black Americans, it was not a permanent feature of American society. Since then, the radical critique of conventional criminology has been expressed in several ways including conspiracy theory, colonialism, Afrocentricity, and critical race theory.

Conspiracy Theory. The resurgence of Black Nationalism from 1965 to 1973 provided the intellectual energy for a number of radical critiques. *Black nationalism* refers a set of beliefs emphasizing White oppression as the chief source of the African-American predicament, the distinctiveness of African-American identity owing to the experience of slavery, the striving for unity among Black peoples throughout the world, and the belief that racial advancement can occur only through unity and self-reliance. During the twentieth century, Black nationalism was expressed through Marcus Garvey's Universal Negro Improvement Association, Stokely Carmichael and the Black Panther Party, and Elijah Muhammad's National of Islam.[60] It was Elijah Muhammad's most articulate spokesperson who personified Black nationalism to many. He called himself Malcolm X.

Malcolm X was born Malcolm Little in 1925. His parents, Earl and Louise Little, had been a member of Garvey's organization. As Malcolm told it, they had been driven from Omaha to Lansing by the Ku Klux Klan. At age six, Malcolm lost his father—local white supremacists pushed his head under a moving streetcar. As Malcolm's family life slipped from meager to desperate, Malcolm dropped out of school after the eighth grade. He moved to Boston where he turned to crime and eventually spent eight years in prison for burglary. Within a year of his release in 1952, he became a minister with the National of Islam. With Malcolm X as its national spokesperson, the nation grew to some forty temples and a hundred thousand members. And while Dr. Martin Luther King, Jr., urged the faithful to take up non-violent civil disobedience, Malcolm X talked about the beauty in Black and fighting back. "I don't profess to be anybody's leader," Malcolm X said, "I'm one of 22 million Afro-Americans, all of whom have suffered the same things...I don't profess to have political, economic or social solution to a problem as complicated as the one which our people face in the States, but I am one of those willing to try *any means necessary* to bring an end to the injustices that our people suffer."[61]

Malcolm X taught that self-hatred was at the heart of Black-on-Black crime. "We hated our heads, we hated the shape of our nose..." he wrote, "...we hated the color of our skin, hated the blood of Africa that was in our veins. And in hating our features and our skin and our blood, why we had to end up hating ourselves." Malcolm X emphasized that the most tragic consequence of institutional racism was the self-hate it produced within its victims.[62] He also referenced *conspiracy theory*, an extension of the Black Nationalist belief that White racism is the cause of Black misery. He said it like this:

The real criminal is the white man who poses as a liberal — the political hypocrite. And it is these legal crooks, posing as our friends, [who are] forcing us into a life of crime and then using us to spread the white man's evil vices among our own people. Our people are scientifically maneuvered by the white man into a life of poverty. You are not poor accidentally. He maneuvered you into poverty... There is nothing about your condition here in America that is an accident.[63]

Political activist Angela Y. Davis, among others, developed conspiracy theory as an explanation for crime in Black neighborhoods. Davis taught philosophy at the University of California-Los Angeles before being dismissed in 1969 for her membership in the American Communist Party. Later, the FBI placed her name on its' "Ten Most Wanted" list for her involvement with the Soledad Brothers. Although she spent eighteen months in jail, she was acquitted of all charges, and she became professor of the history of consciousness at the University of California at Santa Cruz. She observed that by the year 2000, the number of people imprisoned in the United States reached 4 million, most of them Black. "This out-of-control punishment industry is an extremely effective criminalization industry, for the racial imbalance in incarcerated populations is not recognized as evidence of structural racism, but rather is invoked as a consequence of the assumed criminality of black people."[64] Fear of the Black criminal justifies the *criminalization industry*, the same way that fear of Communism justified the military-industrial-complex during the Cold War. Fear of crime leads to more prisons for Black people, more Black people in prison leads to greater threat of Black crime, and the process leads to more fear, and more prisons and jails. Crime policy is ultimately race policy, hidden racist arguments that deflect criticism because they appear race-neutral.[65]

Malcolm X died a mysterious death 1965. Betty Shabazz, his widow, suggested that he had been murdered by assassins sent by the Nation of Islam, who her husband had angered by forming his own Organization of Afro-America Unity. The young, angry, Malcolm X continues to exert his influence, memorialized in the lines of rappers and the articles of university professors. Conspiracy theory also lives on. In 1997, when the National Association of Blacks in Criminal Justice convened in Charlotte, North Carolina, a majority of those 321 members who returned a survey expressed their belief in conspiracy theory. A majority—61 percent—agreed that there is a conspiracy to systematically destroy African-American communities.[66]

AMERICAN COLONIALISM. In 1965, the year Malcolm X was murdered, many Americans heard "Black Power" for the first time. Stokely Carmichael, who crashed a civil rights demonstration organized by Dr. King, shouted the words into the homes of television viewers. Carmichael became the leader of the Black Power Movement that lasted until 1973 with the demise of the Black Panthers. Dr. King opposed introducing the black power theme because it failed to express a theory for improving race relations.[67] Carmichael had decided to go ahead anyway and made "black power" the mantra of a movement within the civil rights movement. While King had found inspiration in the life of Indian leader Ghandi, the Black Power group found their ideology in the writings of a psychiatrist and political agitator from Martinique.

Frantz Fanon's *The Wretched of the Earth* and *Black Skin, White Masks* became popular among Black radicals in the United States after English translations appeared in 1967.[68] Eldrige Cleaver wrote that Fanon enabled those within the movement to organize their feelings and thoughts into a coherent political organization. Fanon grew up on the island of Martinique, a colony in the French Antilles, before joining the French army during World War II and completing the requirements in France to practice psychiatric medicine. He practiced psychiatry in Algeria, a French colony in northern Africa, before he joined the Front de Libération Nationale, and became a professional revolutionary. Armed revolution against the French presence in Algeria began in 1954.[69]

The French colonial rulers had maintained the upper hand in their colonies by violence, Fanon wrote, but also by a kind of psychological violence. Fanon described the psychological consequences of colonialism within the "colonized man" as *alienation*, the political and social arrangements that prevented an individual from pursuing the freedom to find the true, authentic self. Fanon described various forms of alienation, including alienation from one's own race, from other races, own culture, and from purposeful social action. Colonized persons, estranged from their own language, history, and people, believe that they have no choice, no measure of control over what happens to them.[70] This dehumanizing aspect of colonization is its most pernicious aspect because it maintained that to be human, one must be White. This was the key to understanding violent behavior among Black people. "The Algerian's criminality," Fanon wrote, "his impulsivity and the violence of his murders are therefore not the consequence of the organization of his nervous system nor of a peculiar trait in his character, but the direct product of the colonial situation."[71]

Fanon wrote that colonized people may respond to alienation in several ways.[72] They may choose to imitate the oppressor and assimilate in the colonizers' culture. Fanon called this "identification with the aggressor," and suggested that one result would be for the colonized individual to elevate lightness of skin and express the racist stereotypes of darker-skinned kinsmen. Colonized individuals may defend themselves by turning their anger against themselves and their own people. This results in alcohol abuse, psychiatric disorders, and crime, particularly criminal violence. "This is the period when the niggers beat each other up, and the police do not know which way to turn when faced with astonishing waves of crime."[73] Or, colonized individuals may openly resist the colonizers through violent revolt. This is the response Fanon himself had selected and believed to be essential for psychological fulfillment. Revolutionary violence is the only path to freedom, Fanon taught, the means by which Black people attain not only political and social liberty, but liberty of consciousness, the freedom to think, act, and live in a way other than that of the White people.

Rather than view segregation as racial power and seek integration as a remedy, Black Nationalists described racism as a form of colonialism, and power relations between "nations" of people rather than as exclusionary practices within a single national society. They did not view "race consciousness" as inherently bad, but rather encouraged Black Americans to identify as a group for political purposes.[74] *Internal colonialism* explains the experience of African Americans using concepts Fanon described. In this view, African Americans have suffered greater political, economic and social repression than Whites and develop feelings of alienation as a result. This alienation leads to assimilation, crime, or protest. Where crime is the outcome, the victims of criminal violence are other African Americans. As in other parts of the colonized world, suicide, homicide, and drug abuse occurs more frequently among persons of darker skin. When basic human rights are denied to a colonized people, crime becomes a form of social protest. Riots take the form of urban rebellions, and urban youth represent guerilla fighters in the struggle to be free from colonial rule.[75]

AFROCENTRISM. In the 1980s, Afrocentricists joined the Black Nationalists of the 1960s and 1970s in their view of society and of Black crime. One of the most vocal proponents in the United States, Molefi Asante, published his *Afrocentricity* (1988), and founded the *Journal of Black Studies* at Temple University in Philadelphia.

Afrocentricity, Asante said, recognizes a need for African Americans to look at their culture and history from its own center rather than from the Eurocentric view. Africa is the center or homeland for disaporic Africans in more cultural, symbolic, and metaphoric terms than geographical terms. Afrocentricity advances themes of freedom, community, and spirituality for Black people. The Afrocentric definition of "freedom" suggests that Black people are able to realize their own cultural and historical center, in a way continuous with the larger experience of African people. Afrocentricity advances a "community," that individuals find their worth in relationship to the community, and historicity, based on the respect for tradition and the wisdom of elder community members. Afrocentricity also advances a view of a "spiritual being" or idea that transcends human existence.[76] Many of these ideas find expression in Kwanzaa, a holiday created to enable Black Americans to celebrate their African roots.[77]

The Afrocentric view of crime begins with poverty and racism and how these lead to *deracination*, the extent to which Blacks feel alienated from their African heritage and other Blacks. To examine Black crime without reference to slavery, racism and poverty "is similar to trying to explain how batter becomes cake without examining the role that flour, eggs, and milk play in the baking process," explains the University of Alabama's Anthony O. King.[78] Ignorance of one's own heritage within a White society leads to living out White stereotypes of Black identity. These "self-destructive attitudes" include lack of self-knowledge and purpose, the lack of skills needed to compete in a hostile environment, and the lack of "connectedness" to the African-American community which leaves them without a "culturally specific world view" to guide them. Social and economic marginality increases frustration and anger, turned back at the self. Ignorance of one's own culture also leads to loss of dignity, to a self-hatred. This loss of personhood grounded in African culture, and ignorance of one's own culture, also leads to a loss of respect for people, reduction of victims' worth, and criminal violence directed at other Blacks.[79]

CRITICAL RACE THEORY. What became known as critical race theory began with Derrick Bell. He became the first African-American law professor at Harvard Law School after a career as a litigator in the civil rights movement. When Bell left Harvard in 1980 to become dean at the University of Oregon Law School, student activists demanded that Harvard hire a "teacher of color" to teach his course in constitutional law and minority issues. The Harvard administration insisted that there were no legal scholars of Harvard quality that happened to be Black, and that the curriculum need not include a special course in racial issues anyway. Rather than hire another faculty member to teach Bell's course, they offered a short course on civil rights litigation. Students and law professors of color from other law schools organized "the alternative course" in response. The faculty who participated in the alternative course—Charles Lawrence, Linda Greene, Neil Gotanda and Richard Delgado—and the students—Kimberlé Crenshaw and Mari Matsuda—wrote a series of law review articles that collectively expressed critical race theory.[80]

In *Race, Racism and American Law* (1980), Bell pursued a *race conscious* perspective. He denied that law is color-blind; the law is a reflection of racial politics. The law did not represent an independent or neutral referee of social conflict, but rather, was a reflection of white supremacy. The law reinforced white supremacy through establishing the rules of the game, deciding the eligibility of players, and determining the field where the game would be played. Legal concepts, such as "color-blindness," "formal legal equality," and "integrationism" served only to reinforce white supremacy under the guise of neutrality.[81]

In 1984, Bell created a fictional character, Geneva Crenshaw, when asked to write the forward for the Supreme Court issue of the *Harvard Law Review*. The character became the pedagogic strategy in his book *And We Are Not Saved* published three years later.[82] In the "Chronicle of the Constitutional Contradiction," Bell sent Crenshaw, the embodiment of the abolitionist and civil rights lawyers, back in time to the Constitutional Convention of 1787 in

Philadelphia. Armed with the knowledge of slavery and its aftermath, the Civil War and the struggle for civil rights, Crenshaw attempts to convince the delegates not to preserve slavery in the document they produced. Bell's fictional encounter became the setting
for a discussion of the contradiction in American constitutional law
between granting the equality of White men and preserving the en-
slavement of Black people. It was also Bell's way of saying that
since the law itself had been rigged from the beginning, it could not
be used to bring about social equality. Legal equality did not save
Blacks in the United States.[83]

The law cannot be used as a means to undue racism because the
law itself is the product of racism. The law is a "constitutive element of race itself...Racial power, in our view [critical race the-
ory], was not simply—or even primarily—a product of biased decision-making on the part of judges, but instead, the sum total of
the pervasive ways in which law shapes and is shaped by 'race relations' across the social plane."[84] This view of law extends to theorizing about the law. Racism is far more pervasive than even the
"white friends" of Blacks are willing to admit. Richard Delgado, a
University of Colorado law professor, insists that Whites rarely notice subtle acts of racism while Black people see them. This feature
influences the way people live their lives and for law professors, affects their theorizing about the law.[85] The critical race theorists rejected the "conventional" civil rights scholarship as the offerings of
White male constitutional law professors, who Richard Delgado labeled "The Imperial Scholar."[86]

During the 1990s, critical race theorists turned their attention toward criminal law, "Black" crime, and White crime. "Criminal law
is an obvious topic for a critical analysis of racial power," wrote
Georgetown University law professor Gary Peller. Peller observed
that while the conventional civil rights scholarship had limited the
issue of race to criminal procedure, the substantive criminal law
was also a reflection of racism. Criminal law, along with criminal
procedure, ought to be properly understood as branches of race
law. Peller rejected the liberal interpretation of the due process revolution and its assumption that defendants in cases like *Terry v. Ohio*
"just happened to be black." Peller's race-conscious approach
"would understand that the issue raised in the stop-and-frisk context arose precisely *because* police were suspicious of blacks in particular"[87] The marginalization of the racial significance of the pro-

cedure cases advanced the norm of "color blindness" and marginalized the emerging Nationalist view of law. Black Nationalists saw the problem in terms of Whites administering the Black community as a colony, through "their" police force.[88]

Critical Race Theory views Black crime within the context of White racism; proponents contrasted Black crime against White crime. Regina Austin, a professor of law at the University of Pennsylvania (who was denied a position at Harvard Law School and led to Bell's protest resignation), explored the image of Black crime. Austin described how some within the "Black community" condemn Black crime as detracting from racial uplift, "the politics of distinction," others choose to identify with the community's lawbreakers as an act of political defiance, what she calls "the politics of identification." She rejected that view of "ordinary black criminals" as "race-war guerillas," and offers instead a view of the Black community as populated with "bridge people." Bridge people, whose life chances are bound up with the lawbreakers, "know when to obey the law and when to ignore it;" their activities on the margins of legality create informal economies with social and political aspects, and provide a potential link to the Black middle class overlooked by conventional liberal prescriptions for revitalizing the Black community.[89]

Richard Delgado used his fictional character, Rodrigo (the half-brother of Geneva Crenshaw), to explain that what is important about Black crime is "the way the whole issue tends to be framed."[90] In reality, the street crimes for which Black men are sent to prison are "less bad" than the white-collar crimes of White men. The dollars lost to robbery, burglary, larceny, and vandalism are far less than those lost to tax fraud, anti-trust violations, defense procurement fraud, consumer fraud and other corporate crimes. At the same time, white-collar criminals escape penalties because their activities are not defined as crimes, and not popularly understood as crimes by the popular media. Meanwhile, African-American men receive harsh penalties, and their disproportionate confinement justifies further repressive measures.

White Americans benefit, Bell and Delgado insist, from the illusion of Black crime. The image of "a group that is criminal, vicious, animal-like, with designs on white people's lives and pocketbooks" justifies repressive legal strategies aimed at Black Americans.[91] The stereotype of the Black criminal diverts attention from white-collar crimes and allows a wealthy few White Americans to become wealthier. Demonized by the stereotype of violent crime, White Americans do not see African Americans for what they are, "a population that contains many poor—and some desperate—people living lives of danger because of the legacy of slavery, racism, and separate-but-unequal treatment"[92] Perhaps if middle class Americans recognized the biggest and worst criminals for who they are, they would favor a crackdown on white collar crime which could lead to a redistribution of wealth from the wealthy few to both middle class Whites and Blacks. Contrary to Delgado, Bell argued that even if by some magical stones every Black criminal transformed into a crime-fighter, Whites would still deny economic opportunity to Blacks.[93]

So pervasive is the image of the Black criminal that it allows for the perpetration of racial hoaxes. Katheryn K. Russell, at the University of Maryland, explains that a *racial hoax* occurs when one person accuses another of a crime because of that person's race; when, for example, a White South Carolina woman reported that a Black man kidnapped her two young sons. Although the woman later confessed to the murder, a massive search began, coinciding with news coverage that perpetuated an image of the Blackness and crime. Some racial hoaxes cover actual crime, in others, no crime has occurred. In any event, they cause serious social harm and create public expense.[94] A. Leon Higginbotham, who joined Harvard's Kennedy School of Government in 1993 after a career as a federal appeals court judge, provided several examples of cases in which "a white person made false accusations that an African-American man had committed a terrible crime." These cases illustrate "a direct and tragic nexus between the false allegations and perceptions of today, as we approach the twentieth century, and some of the perceptions of black inferiority that have endured from the colonial period to the present."[95]

THE RADICAL ALTERNATIVES. Perhaps the primary purpose of the radical critique is to debunk the White stereotype of Black crime. Because the problem of "black crime" is not so much criminal violence within Black communities as the stereotype of the "black criminal" in the White mind, the solutions have to do with challenging the image of Black crime.

Radical consciousness-raising begins with challenging the language used to describe crime and African Americans. The phrase "black-on-black crime," for example, implies that members of Black communities are their own worst enemy when crime constitutes only one of the threats. The greatest threats to Black communities include police brutality, unsafe workplaces, and retail businesses that take advantage of place-bound consumers. It implies that "Negroes are 'naturally' violent" and that criminality does not occur within White communities. Radicals encourage Black political leaders and their White allies to re-educate the public about the relative threat of crime in Black neighborhoods by placing it within a larger context of more serious white-collar crimes directed at Black communities from the outside. The goal of consciousness-raising of this sort is "an increased demand within the masses for a new level of social justice in American society."[96]

Legal instrumentalism refers to a form of "self-help" which "includes selective lawbreaking." Richard Delgado advises that "minorities should invoke and follow the law when it benefits them and break or ignore it otherwise—when it gets in the way, is unresponsive or adverse to their interests."[97] Regina Austin advances a similar argument, calling for "a legal praxis...[that] would find its reference points in the 'folk law' of those black people who, as a matter of survival, concretely assess what laws must be obeyed and what laws may be justifiably ignored."[98] Paul Butler, a law professor at George Washington University law school, called on African-American jurors to use their power to free guilty Black defendants accused of drug crimes. "For pragmatic and political reasons," Butler argued, "the black community is better off when some nonviolent lawbreakers remain in the community rather than go to prison."[99] The Black community should make case-by-case decisions about whether the community would be harmed or benefitted by freeing Black defendants accused of stealing the property of White people.

Critical race theorists reject the traditional civil rights strategies, and the efforts of liberals, White and Black, to legislate racism out of the system. Laws drafted with an eye on the prize of a color-blind society fall short because the permanence of racism will reveal itself in White efforts legislate in their interests. Laws referencing the ethos of a color-blind society allow Whites to promote their interests in the name of looking out for Black interests. The legislative solution is law that explicitly takes race into account, what Russell has termed affirmative race law.

Efforts to criminalize racial hoaxes represent one example of *affirmative race law*. Currently, state statutes enable prosecution for filing a false police report, that is all. Affirmative race law would enable prosecution for the damage to race relations caused by publicity surrounding the event by invoking race. Racial hoaxes are possible only because they reinforce existing stereotypes; damage that cannot be undone by a quiet admission of lying.[100] Laws criminalizing racial slights or microaggressions represent another example. *Microgressions* have been defined as "subtle, stunning, often automatic and non-verbal exchanges which are 'put downs' of Blacks" by Whites. New York University law professor Patricia Williams insists that insults based on a person's race are deeper, more hurtful assaults on that person's humanity than non-racial insults. She described being denied entrance to a clothing store by a White clerk based on her "blackness," a form of treatment that reached the level of "spirit murdering." While racial slurs appear to Whites as trivial compared to robbery, they are the immoral equivalent because as Williams points out, "a prejudiced society is not preferable to a violent society."[101]

The Black Conservatives

The conservative element in Du Bois's outlook on crime, evidenced by the proceedings from the 1904 conference at Atlanta University, persists as well. The contemporary Black conservative movement began in 1980 when several African-American political leaders gathered for the "The Black Alternatives Conference" in San Francisco. Organized by Thomas Sowell, an economist at the Hoover Institution at Stanford University, the conferees discussed around the theme of "re-thinking the black agenda." The conference brought together newspaper columnist Walter Williams, television journalist Tony Brown, and Clarence Thomas, later appointed Associate Justice of the U.S. Supreme Court, among others. The conferees concluded that the civil rights era had come to an end and Black leaders, who had come to leadership positions during the civil rights era, no longer served the interest of Black Americans. The conference led to the formation of the Council for a Black Economic Agenda, chaired by Robert S. Woodson of the National Center for Neighborhood Enterprise. Several other Black intellectuals, including Glenn C. Loury and Randall Kennedy, joined Sowell and Williams in articulating the ideas.[102]

CONSERVATIVES AND LIBERALS. Not all of those dedicated to "rethinking the Black agenda" identify with the "C" word. Sowell and the Black Alternatives group have been called "crazy," "anti-Black," and worse by members of the African-American intelligensia.[103] *Emerge*, "Black America's News Magazine," ran a cover with Justice Thomas, pictured in red coat and white pants holding a lantern, next to the caption: "Uncle Thomas: Lawn Jockey for the Far Right." The art accompanying the feature article showed Thomas, with a broad, toothy smile, shining the shoes of Justice Antonin Scalia.[104] Yet a few Black thinkers are unhappy enough with the status quo in Black-White politics to risk the conservative label in advancing their views.[105] Essayist Stanley Crouch, who describes himself as a "radical pragmatist," defends his conservatism by insisting that it does not matter who comes up with a better strategy for dealing with the problems confronting Black Americans, so much as that it is a better strategy. Or as he puts it: "It doesn't matter to me if the cow comes from the left, middle, or the right side of the pasture; I'm concerned with whether or not the milk is sour."[106]

In the political arena, Black conservatives have advocated *deracialization*, that is, political strategies that avoid appeals to racial justice based solely on the need to redress past injustice. The goal is to appeal to a broader base of support for initiatives that benefit poor Blacks by framing them in terms of economic benefit to all members of society. Rather than lawsuits aimed at discrimination and race-based policies such as affirmative action, the conservatives suggest that Black leaders pursue issues that would benefit Black communities but that appeal to Whites and other minorities as well, such as full employment and national health insurance. This was the strategy Martin Luther King, Jr. advocated prior to his assassination, when he said that "newer stages of struggle" required a new set of issues around which to mobilize support. The strategy had to shift, he thought, from civil rights to economic empowerment.[107]

In a broader sense, deracialization suggests that Black leaders ought to align themselves with people and institutions that best serve their interests, whether labeled liberal or conservative. "It is no longer effective...to present our problems as exclusive and connected only to the condition of our color," observed Haskell G. Ward, a deputy mayor with the Koch administration in New York City; "By tending to define our problems as uniquely related to our blackness, we have made people who are not black feel as though those issues have nothing to do with them."[108] Politically, this has meant a departure from automatic support for the Democrats. The traditional civil rights leadership, the NAACP and Congressional Black Caucus, offered unfailing support for the Democrat Party. Black candidates for public office have selected Democratic party affiliation, a strategy pursued by Black mayors such as David Dinkins in New York City, Thomas Bradley in Los Angeles, W. Wilson Goode in Philadelphia, as well as Douglas Wilder, who became the first African-American state governor when he won election in Virginia in 1989. But a new generation of mavericks have identified with the Republican Party, including Joe Rogers, Colorado's lieutenant governor, and J.C. Watts, an Oklahoma Congressmember.[109]

What sets the Black conservatives apart from their liberal colleagues is a faith in the power of Black communities. Rather than rely on government assistance to open doors to political, economic, and social institutions, they advocate building their own. "What is the difference between liberal and conservative?" Henry Bramwell, Brooklyn's first Black judge, explains: "A liberal approach says the government is responsible to give things that you need and would like to have. A conservative approach says you have got to work for what you get."[110] Judge Bramwell points out that "most of what needs to be done to correct crime in the Black community...must be drawn from the strengths of the community." He faults Black community leaders for deflecting attention away from crime within Black communities and emphasizes the need to promote intact families and a work ethic in Black communities.[111]

The Reverend Floyd Flake, who served in Congress from 1986 to 1997, represents one example of the self-help approach. Flake pastors the Allen African Methodist Episcopal Church in Queens. In addition to a school, the church manages a shopping center and other real estate ventures. Flake preaches African-American self-help through education and commerce. Although he served in Congress as a Democrat, he supports the Republican proposal of school vouchers, which would allow poor parents to send their children to schools that work. "Every day that a child is in a system that does not educate them properly to compete in our society is putting them in a position where they will ultimately become part of the jail population or have to be supported within some other areas in the social fabric of America." He points to the academic and vocational model pioneered by Booker T. Washington at Tuskegee. "In spite of all the criticism that Booker T. Washington has received, time has proven that his model of self-help with a focus on both academic and vocational education is and was an appropriate model. The fact that thousands of students have graduated from Tuskegee University and are doing so today dismissed the notion that he did not have a great commitment, as did W.E.B. Du Bois. The difference is that Washington actually built an institution."[112]

Flake's economic proposals emphasize economic participation and public policy based on "market realties." Economic participation is primary in a capitalist economy, Flake explains, social and political objectives are secondary. While in Congress he supported legislation to encourage investment in de-stabilized communities within inner-cities. Rather than seeking jobs programs, he favors creation of Black-owned businesses and home ownership for inner-city residents. Flake points out that homeowners take pride in their neighborhoods and invest in their communities because they expect to live in them for a large portion of their lives. Flake has built residential areas on single-family homes; they are offered to church members and others for a 5 percent down payment. "I'm a businessman when you really get down to it," Flake says, "I start off preaching but I end up doing business."[113]

CONSERVATIVES ON CRIME. Randall Kennedy, professor of law at Harvard Law School, and Glenn C. Loury, an economist at Boston University, have written about crime, law and African-American communities. Kennedy denounced the legacy of under-enforcement of the law in Black communities. "Deliberately withholding protection against criminality (or conduct that should be deemed criminal)," Kennedy observed, "is one of the most destructive forms of oppression that has been visited upon African Americans."[114] Mistreatment of suspects, defendants and criminals has been an aspect of racial oppression, but gangs of violent criminals, typically Black, impose a greater burden on the day-to-day lives of African Americans. Kennedy surmises that those who deny the extent of crime are simply too embarrassed admit the large role that it has in many

Black communities.[115] For Kennedy, crime in African-American communities is a reality. Historic deprivation, the legacy of segregation, and the indifference of government to the disadvantaged combine to create "criminogenic conditions" in which too many African Americans reside.

Kennedy suggests a *politics of respectability*. He is careful to point out that he is not talking about the historic efforts on the part of some African Americans to distance themselves from "bad Negroes." Misguided efforts along these lines have led to undue efforts to appease Whites, rejection of various aspects of Black culture, toleration of racist attacks, and a defeatist position relative to those who choose to break the law. Kennedy's *new* politics of respectability acknowledges that crime really is a problem in African-American communities because of under-enforcement of the law, and that the efforts toward upward mobility within Black communities must attend to the morality of means. African Americans should follow the high road, protecting the reputation of the race, being mindful that derogatory accusations will follow from a hostile environment.[116]

Kennedy's concern with the morality of means and the need to maintain respect parallel those of Glenn C. Loury. Loury, who directs the Center on Race and Social Division at Boston University, observes that the residents of African-American communities unfairly shoulder the burden of the few, but frequently violent, criminals in their midst. Loury identifies two enemies, the "enemy without," that is, racism, which diminishes the victims of violent crime. He also acknowledges "the enemy within," those dysfunctional behaviors that perpetuate poverty and prevent youth from seizing opportunity. It was Booker T. Washington, Loury observes, who recognized both enemies prevented Blacks from enjoying their rightful status as citizens in American society: defects of character demonstrated by some elements within Black people and the racist attitudes of Whites. Washington encouraged Black people to address the character defects part of the equation because he believed it would help overcome the racist attitudes part.[117]

Loury describes the way out as pursuit of both the "outside game" and the "inside game." The outside game refers to the continued pursuit of civil rights by legal means. Booker T. Washington thought this could wait and it was a mistake; the civil rights movement claimed the promised-land he failed to seek. By inside game,

Loury urges African-American community leaders to work toward developing "a disciplined, respectable Black demeanor." The inside game expressed a philosophy of self-help, racial uplift that simply cannot be done by outsiders. The plea for outside intervention, Loury observes, has only led to "perverse exhibition of non-achievement." Rather, pursuing self-help while maintaining "a disciplined, respectable Black demeanor" will generate political support within the broader community. "Can we really expect whites to agree that black 'lewdness' or criminality is no more than the consequence of white depravity—that is, conditions for which whites, not blacks, are ultimately responsible?"[118]

The inside game cannot be pursued by means of government intervention. It is not a task for government because it requires setting and enforcing standards on an individual basis, a task that requires a high level of knowledge about each individual's capabilities and circumstances. The judgments enforced under law necessarily reflect a "thin conception of virtue." Rather, the inside game is to be played by churches. Churches can exercise authority over their members because participation is voluntary and the social relations are close. Loury draws on the lesson of the prophet Nehemiah who worked to restore the physical environment while leading a spiritual renewal, the model for reclaiming impoverished African-American communities "one by one from the inside out."[119] Like Washington, Loury observes that the attainment of "true equality" does not depend on government intervention, no matter how benevolent, but rather on the drive from within to elevate to a position worthy of respect. "It is a mistake," writes Loury, quoting Washington, "to assume that one man can, in any true sense, give freedom to another. Freedom, in the larger and higher sense, every man must gain for himself."[120]

Black conservatives disagree with the view that crime in Black communities is solely the product of White indifference to Black poverty, or that it is an illusion perpetrated by the White captains of consciousness. Judge Bramwell agrees with Justice Thomas's approach to law and order. "Justice Thomas believes in a stricter enforcement of legal procedures against criminals. I believe stricter enforcement of criminal laws is needed to balance out the Black community." Bramwell, who confronted openly African-American leaders critical of Thomas's appointment, believes that this response is necessary because "In the Black community today there are serious, serious problems when it comes to crime."[121] Crouch adds that young people should be taught to respect law-abiding behavior. Lawbreakers should not be celebrated as cultural heroes. It must be reinforced constantly that "the hoodlum element that is so often celebrated in rap recordings is a bane on the black community."[122]

Others, most notably Reuben M. Greenberg, have taken a conservative approach and have become legends in the process. Greenberg serves as Chief of Police in Charleston, South Carolina; he has served for nearly two decades when most city chiefs last three or four years. (He is so beloved that the lunch menu at a local restaurant features the "Reuben Greenberg" sandwich.) Greenberg took what he calls a "market-oriented approach" to law enforcement. Greenberg avoided the traditional debate between federal support for drug treatment or mandatory sentences, and looked at drug dealing as a business enterprise. The police department identified thirty-one locations for drug dealing in the city then set about disrupting business-as-usual with uniformed officers armed with Polaroid cameras. Contrary to expectation, dealers did not simply move to another corner. Re-locating is difficult because customers do not automatically know the new location; it is also dangerous because other corners represent rival turf other drug-dealers will kill to protect. Greenberg brought back dealers in jail garb who had been arrested to pick up trash near their former corners. The return of those who had expensive clothes and cars to the scene in humiliated circumstances sent a message that drug dealing is not the road to success.[123]

One of Greenberg's most daring efforts was to curtail criminal violence within public housing projects in the city. Rather than process applications for Section Eight housing on a first-come, first-served basis, the police screened out convicted felons. While other landlords in the city kept them out, public housing represented the one place to live while living a life of crime. The police department also sought to evict those convicted of felonies while living in public housing using civil court. Greenberg reasoned that residents of public housing ought to enjoy the same level of safety as those who could afford to live in gated communities, so he took a "country club" approach to neighborhood safety. The police department set up roadblocks at the entrance to public housing on weekends. Anyone wishing to enter showed proof that they were residents or had to give the name of the resident they planned to visit. Using a cell phone, the officer called the tenant to ask if the visitor was wanted. Most residents, the police learned, had never heard of the visitor or did not want to admit that they knew them. Many of those who sought to enter public housing did not live there and many were wanted by the police on outstanding warrants. "Criminals," Greenberg concludes, "just like every one else, respond to market forces. We just needed to show them that, literally, crime does not pay."[124]

The Black conservative approach to law and order, however, does not neatly overlap that of "the crime war hawks"—to use Randall Kennedy's phrase. Political scientist John J. DiIulio emerged as the top-flying crime war hawk in the 1980s in a series of articles dealing with Black crime in *The Public Interest*. DiIulio advocated greater emphasis on the apprehension, conviction and incapacitation of the "truly deviant," the small percentage of Black Americans who have made predatory crime a way of life. Relying on government statistics, DiIulio argued that crime occurs most frequently in impoverished urban neighborhoods where Black Americans reside. "Badly stated, my hypothesis is that this victimization causes and perpetuates the other ills of our underclass neighborhoods," summarized DiIulio.[125] Black Americans within the inner-city suffer greater victimization from the violent few because they lack the resources to provide safe and secure neighborhoods for themselves. They cannot afford security systems and they cannot afford to move. They must rely, unlike affluent suburbanites, on the criminal justice system for protection, and the criminal justice system, DiIulio argued, has failed. Local governments have put too few police officers on inner-city streets and courts have failed to lock up violent and repeat criminals. Black crime is a matter of too few locks, police officers, and prisons. At the same time, social policies have failed to remove children from abusive homes but have allowed crime to spread from one generation to the next. Rather than returning abused and neglected children to these criminogenic environments, the government ought to provide safe, secure places for abused and neglected children, boarding houses located away from urban areas.[126]

Loury admonished DiIulio to listen to the Black community. He pointed out that Black liberal legislators oppose longer sentences, less plea bargaining, and tougher parole standards, not because they place political ideology above the safety of their constituents, but because those young men wreaking havoc in the city are still "our youngsters." Tougher penalties require writing off too many young people as beyond redemption; it may be the solution but the price is too high.[127] Kennedy agrees with Loury that sending more police into Black communities to bring more Black youth to prison does not represent the obvious answer. More members of the African-American community would associate themselves with the cry for law and order if they did not fear racially-prejudiced conduct by law enforcement officials in their neighborhoods. "History reinforced by persistent contemporary abuses gives credence and force to this fear," Kennedy observes, recalling gross injustice during slavery and segregation, J. Edgar Hoover's effort to suppress Black political activities from Marcus Garvey to Martin Luther King, Jr., and the contemporary practice of using skin color as a proxy for dangerousness.[128]

CONSERVATIVES AND RADICALS. The Black conservatives emerge in sharpest relief, as a group, when compared to the radicals. Conservatives do not accept the premise that those African Americans who flounder do so because they lack role models who look like them. "Nothing in my own experience or in the experience of Afro-Americans I have met or read about corroborates the idea that, to any significant extent, people of color are capable of being inspired only by people of their own race or sex," remarks essayist Stanley Crouch.[129] If that were the case, no Black achievement of any sort would have occurred unless it replicated some practice brought over from Africa; there would have been no Frederick Douglass or Harriet Tubman. Crouch recalled being taught that achieving great significance was not the franchise of any single group and learning models of exemplary achievement from across the globe. There was Jackie Robinson, Duke Ellington, and Marian Anderson along with Shakespeare and Dickens. Teachers knew that expectations were the route to achievement; they were tough and supportive. "If we had come up with some so-called cultural difference excuse, we would have been laughed at, if not whacked on the boody, for disrespecting the intelligence of the teacher."[130]

Crouch notes that the Afrocentric argument has been derived from nationalism, pluralism, and cultural relativity, none of which originated on the content of Africa. Afrocentrism is a western idea, or more specifically, a German-derived idea that attempts to fuse genetics and cultural vision to declare that race transcends place.

Crouch denies Black Americans are but one segment of an international Black world, and scoffs at the notion that all Black people are essentially the same (unless their identities have been distorted by Eurocentric influence). "African kingdoms, real or invented, make no impression on how I see myself, primarily because Africa had nothing to do with the conception of ideas that eventually led to the end of slavery."[131]

The public debate over the meaning of slavery and the war that ended it in the United States occurred in the United States, not the continent of Africa; African Americans, not Africans, waged it. At the very moment slaves were brought from Africa to America there were those who debated the practice as a violation of the Christian ethos. At the same time, there was no great African debate over the moral meaning of slavery. There is no historical record of an African people not being enslaved opposing the practice of slavery; there are no accounts of African William Lloyd Garrisons. Nor are there histories of African abolitionist movements, of African underground railroads, or of an African civil war in which slavery was at issue.[132] "Yet the central failure of Afrocentrism," Crouch concludes, "is that is doesn't recognize what Afro-Americans have done, which is realize over and over and often against imposing obstacles, the truest meaning of democratic possibility."[133] Black achievement in Africa is astonishing given the point of social origin; Black Americans have risen to the top in every area of society — scientists, educators, aviators, politicians, military leaders and so on, despite their arrival as slaves.

The conservatives also counter the critical race theorists. Randall Kennedy has taken them to task on their claim to a distinctive "voice of color" based on race. Kennedy views meritocracy as independent of the distinctive racial experience of the scholar, and denies that the "voice of color" is a specific consideration in evaluating the strength of an argument.[134] Kennedy has identified in critical race theory what has been called "essentializing," the argument that there is something essential about being Black and that all Blacks, as victims of racial oppression, share a similar perspective. Kennedy points out that the experience of racial oppression provides no special inoculation against complacency in racial justice. Neither the NAACP nor any other Black organization, Kennedy notes, submitted a brief to the U.S. Supreme Court opposing the internment of Japanese Americans in the case of Fred Korematsu. At the same time, the idea that all Blacks speak with the same voice reinforces the false notion of a monolithic population of Black Americans. It also stereotypes Black scholars in a way not unlike the remark White bigots have expressed about Black citizens, "they all look alike to me." It denies the possibility that Black scholars may have different perspectives based on their own life experiences shaped by economic status as well as racial division. "Delgado completely overlooks the contributions of black conservative intellectuals who vigorously oppose race-based preferential treatment."[135]

In "Dumb Bell Blues," Crouch challenged Derrick Bell's thesis that there had never been a time when anything that happened in the interest of Black Americans that was not the result of White people's acting in their interest. Crouch referenced the history of African Americans and how their intellectual and political engagement redefined every element of the social contract. African-American challenges to the founders' vision of democracy expanded outward what had been a restricted, limited vision of democracy. "There it is," Crouch summarized his opposition to critical race theory, "I accuse Bell and his ilk of being, fundamentally, defeatists, people who accept high positions of success, then tell those below them that they don't have chance."[136]

Conclusion

Black criminology represents the intellectual efforts of African-American thinkers to address crime within Black communities. Although it is a criminology by, and about, Black people, it raises fundamental questions about race, racism and crime. W.E.B. Du Bois, the first African-American criminologist, investigated crime among Black Americans. His work set the agenda for scholars working on Black crime throughout the next century. There are the elements in his work of three traditions of African-American scholarship dealing with crime: the liberal mainstream, conspiracy theory and the radical critiques, and Black conservatism.

Chapter 8

The Heart of Crime

Professional criminologists, whether classical, biologistic, psychiatric, sociological or constructionist, share at least one belief in common: they all express naturalism. Naturalists believe, or at least for purposes of thinking about crime believe, that nature is all there is. They view people as part of nature and seek to explain human behavior as it relates to other parts of nature. From the spiritual perspective, people cannot be reduced in this way. Human beings are part of nature, but the only "part" that can determine what their relationship to nature will be. There is something more to a person than body and mind. There is a source for consciousness, personality and intellect within; a source for creativity, insight, and innovation; for music, art, and poetry; for fear, bitterness, and hate; for integrity, sincerity, and loyalty; and for kindness, affection, and love. Something referred to in Jewish scripture as the heart.

The idea of the heart, as the source of moral consciousness, came to western civilization from the early Jewish people. The prophets of old used the word *lêb*, or heart, to refer to the feelings, will, and intellect. Heart means the center of a person. The prophet Jeremiah writes of the heart as the source of moral consciousness: "I will put My Teaching into their inmost being and inscribe it upon their hearts."[1] Early Christian writers used the Greek word *sunĕidēsis* meaning conscience. In neither understanding does it have a definitive place in human action. In Jewish thought, the heart reports; it does not originate. It does not make moral law but only tells an individual whether or not a violation has occurred. Christian writers, from the Apostle Paul to St. Augustine, agree; they recognized the conscience to be fallible. It can be overcome by the intellect, which can supply good reasons for doing wrong.[2]

Modern criminology attempts to explain away the heart. Biologistic criminologists insist that what the early Jews described as the heart really comes down to neurological substrate or DNA segments. The psychiatric criminologists say that the heart is a matter of personality and mind (and mental processes originate in the body anyway). The sociological criminologists view the heart as the product of socialization, the receptacle for internalized social rules. And the constructionists ask why societies, beginning with the early Jews and continuing to the present day, found it necessary to invent such a concept. This chapter pursues a criminology of the heart. It does not attempt to explain away moral consciousness as the product of biology, psychology, society, or something else. Rather, it attempts to explain crime, and what should be done about it, from the perspective of moral consciousness. "It is only with the heart," wrote pioneer French aviator Antoine de Saint-Exupéry, "that one can see rightly; what is essential is invisible to the eye."

Specifically, this chapter describes a Judaic-Christian outlook.[3] Part One looks at the Christian perspective through the writing of C.S. Lewis. Part Two discusses Judaism, particularly Jewish teaching on law, crime, and justice. Part Three explores restorative justice and victim-offender mediation as an expression of what a Judaic-Christian criminal justice would look like. Part Four discusses the threat to Jewish and Christian faith posed by empiricism and syncretism.

C.S. Lewis and Christianity

Millions throughout the world know of a place called Narnia, the imaginary world of C.S. Lewis. He wrote children's fiction, histories of sixteenth-century English literature, essays and literary criticism, and books about the Christian life. By 1947, *Time* magazine proclaimed him the "best selling author and one of the most influential spokesmen for Christianity in the English-speaking world." Every year since then, his books have sold more than a million copies. His fiction and his life have been dramatized in television programs, plays, and films.[4] Far fewer know that the man who became Christianity's most influential spokesperson began his professional life as a committed atheist.

THE UNIVERSE NEXT DOOR. Clive Staples Lewis was born in Northern Ireland in 1898, the son of a police court solicitor. In 1905, the

Lewis family moved into a large home, known as Little Lea, on the outskirts of Belfast. For three years, they enjoyed a happy life together. Lewis and his brother spent many hours in their father's library, reading and inventing stories. But after Lewis's mother died in 1908, his father sent him to boarding school in England, and by the age of seventeen, he abandoned his childhood faith.

"All religions," Lewis wrote in a letter to a friend in 1916, "that is all mythologies, to give them their proper name, are merely man's own invention."[5] That same year, Lewis won a scholarship to University College, Oxford. He began his university career, interrupted by military service during the First World War. During the Battle of Arras, he caught shrapnel in his chest, and returned to England. He recovered, completed his commitment, and returned to his studies. In 1925, he was elected a fellow of Magdalen College, Oxford, where he tutored English language and literature for nearly thirty years.

Lewis became a Christian after talking with J.R.R. Tolkien one blustery September evening. It was an unlikely friendship—Lewis, an Ulster protestant and Tolkien, a devout Catholic—but the two enjoyed a common interest in writing fiction. (Tolkien went on to write his fantasy trilogy *The Lord of the Rings,* a worldwide bestseller.) Tolkien joined Lewis for dinner at Magdalen College. Lewis confessed that he had during the summer of 1929 become a deist, acknowledging a simple faith in God.[6] But, Lewis protested, "how [could] the life and death of Someone Else (whoever he was) two thousand years ago could help us here and now—except in so far as his example could help us." Tolkien replied that the idea of sacrifice, of a dying and reviving deity, inspired so much of the mythology Lewis admired because it actually happened. Mythology represented a retelling, using various characters and settings, of an eternal truth. "You mean" asked Lewis, "that the story of Christ is simply a true myth, a myth that works on us the same way as the others, but a myth that *really happened?* In that case, I begin to understand." Three days later, Lewis told a friend that he "passed on from believing in God to definitely believing in Christ—in Christianity."[7]

Within a decade, Lewis had become more widely-known that Tolkien as a Christian author. Lewis enjoyed engaging skeptics, whether in the formal setting of the debate society at Oxford (the Oxford Socratic Club), or over a pint at a local pub (Lewis was a regular at the Eagle and the Child). The "foundation of twentieth century thought," Lewis observed, rested on a technique of explaining away ideas as artifacts of something else. Modern thinking placed religion in a category of belief that existed as a matter of social organization or psychological need. "But you cannot go on 'explaining away' forever..." Lewis pointed out, or "you will find that you have explained explanation away. You cannot go on 'seeing through' things forever. The whole point of seeing through something is to see something through it."[8] He referred to modern thinking about religion as *Bulverism:*

> ...I see my religion dismissed on the grounds that 'the comfortable parson had every reason for assuring the nineteenth century worker that poverty would be rewarded in another world.' Well, no doubt he had. On the assumption that Christianity is an error, I can see easily enough that some people would still have a motive for inculcating it. I see it so easily that I can, of course, play the game the other way around, by saying that 'the modern man has every reason for trying to convince himself that there are no eternal sanctions behind the morality he is rejecting.' For Bulverism is truly a democratic game in the sense that all can play it all day long... but of course it gets us not one inch nearer to deciding whether, as a matter of fact, the Christian religion is true or false."[9]

To arrive at truth, Lewis said, "you must show that a man is wrong before you start explaining why he is wrong. The modern method is to assume without discussion that he is wrong and then distract his attention from this (the only real issue) by busily explaining how he became so silly."[10]

No other aspect of modern thought struck Lewis as nonsensical as the idea of Jesus as great moral teacher. No moral teacher in history said the kind of things Jesus claimed for himself. Moral teachers said: "This is the truth about the universe." Jesus said: "I am truth." Some claimed to be prophets who spoke for God. Jesus said: "I and my Father are one." Some teachers said: "This is the way to heaven." Jesus said: "I am the way...no one comes except by me." Lord, liar, or lunatic, but not a great moral teacher. In fact, Jesus said nothing in the way of moral teaching that had not already been said; he was not a moral genius that offered some innovative philosophy. "Jesus uttered no command which had not been anticipated by the Rabbis—few, indeed, which cannot be paralleled in classical, ancient Egyptian, Ninevite, Babylonian, or Chinese texts," Lewis observed.[11] So either a person accepted Jesus's invitation to a universe next door or did not. If the door conceals nothing, then Jesus perpetrated the greatest fraud in history.[12]

THE CHRISTIAN OUTLOOK. During war years, Lewis did a series of talks for British and American radio that became *Mere Christianity* (1945). He began with recognition of traditional morality; the simple rules of fairness people expect others to know about. Christian morality reflected traditional morality, Lewis said, but traditional morality was not a particularly Christian idea. Common standards of right and wrong are also found in the moral codes of ancient civilizations — "pagan" civilizations of Egyptians, Romans, Greeks, Chinese, and Hindus. In later work, he referred to this common moral standard as "the Tao." The concept of the Chinese *Tao Te Ching* can be described in English as "the flow," "the life," and "the source;" it teaches that one must humbly accept what is.[13] In Hebrew, the word is *emeth* or "truth," something that does not deceive or change. In other words, the rules that people expect each other to know about are not particular to British culture of the twentieth century, but expressions of transcendent truth. The essence of world religions is that right-living corresponds with knowing the truth. The moral law cannot be avoided; it is the source from which all moral judgments must come.

Accepting that there is a good to be pursued and evil to be avoided is not, Lewis told his radio listeners, sufficient to become a Christian. From this first principle, that there is a basic right and wrong, flow two more: that human beings are incapable of living the moral law and that there is a Person or Mind behind the law. Traditional morality operates as the law of human nature, in the sense that gravity operates as a law of nature, but with an important difference: humans can choose to break the natural law whereas objects within nature cannot. Lewis distinguished Christianity as having a personal God at the center; God does not exist as part of nature (the materialist view), as a cultural ideal (the religious view), nor as an impersonal life-force (the spiritualist view). The Christian life could not be found by believing in a set of propositions or trying to follow a set of rules. God does not want simple-minded obedience to a set of rules but rather, He wants people of a particular sort.[14] God does not want, Lewis wrote, a person's time, or money, work or good intentions. "Give me all..." is what God says, "Hand over the whole natural self, all the desires which you think innocent as well as the ones you think wicked—the whole outfit. I will give you a new self instead. In fact, I will give you Myself: My own will shall become yours."[15]

Nor could Christianity be adopted by believing in a "good God in heaven...and leaving out all the difficult and terrible doctrines about sin and hell and the devil, and the redemption."[16] Sin and hell and the devil are essential to Christianity, Lewis concluded, because above all else, Christianity promised joy. The best non-believers can imagine is happiness. People came about as the accidental result of blind working of matter: they started as mere animals and have generally improved. They will live seventy years more or less, and they can attain happiness through good social services and political organization. Everything else is to be judged as good and bad insofar as it promotes this idea of happiness. Christians, on the other hand, believe that people started out with a purpose and that they will live forever. People will find true and lasting happiness only by being united with God in a life very different from earthly life.[17]

Now for anyone to taste that eternal joy there had to come a day when all those who rejected the invitation could not longer detract from it. A day when all the "the makers of misery" could no longer destroy for others the happiness they had rejected for themselves. If there was no hell, those who denied Christ could blackmail the universe by never allowing those who did to realize the joy that had been promised. Pain and suffering in the world existed to shatter the illusion that happiness is all there is, that what people have is enough for them. "God wants to give us joy, but how can He if our hands are full of happiness?" If people really had a choice in the matter, hell had to exist as well as heaven. Lewis explored the realm of sin and hell and the devil in his *The Screwtape Letters* (1941). In the book, Screwtape, who has retired from the Infernal Service, advises his nephew Wormwood, a junior devil still on earth, in the diabolical methods of corrupting a young man. Lewis dedicated the book to Tolkien.

During the 1950s, Lewis wrote his series of children's books that began with *The Lion, the Witch and the Wardrobe*. Lewis never set out to preach a Christian message, rather, he began with images he had found entertaining since childhood (a fawn carrying an umbrella, a majestic lion, a witch driving horses from a sleigh), and his Christian outlook simply came out as he wrote them. The four British schoolchildren Lewis sends to Narnia enter a strange land of fabulous animals, and yet, it is a place strangely familiar.

In the first book, Lucy's older brothers and sisters—Peter, Susan and Edmund—follow her through the wardrobe. They meet a friendly fawn and helpful beavers, Narnia's citizens. They also encounter evil, the White Witch who keeps Narnia in perpetual winter. All of the children, except for Edmund, join the animals in their struggle against the witch. They are empowered by the rumor that Aslan, the noble lion who created Narnia, is "on the move." Edmund, who climbs aboard the witch's sleigh for a taste of Turkish Delight, winds up prisoner in her castle. When Susan meets Aslan, she asks him to save Edmund. He listens but advises her: "It is not as easy as you think." Not only does the witch turn many animals into stone, she captures Aslan and puts him to death. When Aslan comes back to life, spring returns to Narnia, and Edmund breaks free. Aslan explains to Susan that the witch did have a claim to Edmund's life based on her knowledge of Narnia's "deep magic." Rather than abolish this deep magic and Narnia with it, Aslan gave himself as a sacrifice in Edmund's place, knowing that by "deeper magic before the dawn of time," his substitution would cause life and death to work backwards.

After Lewis's *English Literature in the Sixteenth Century* appeared in 1954, Cambridge University offered him the chair of Medieval and Renaissance English Literature, and he accepted. He finished *The Last Battle*, the final book in the Narnia series two years later, and in 1963, died of a heart attack. After his death, the wardrobe from his childhood home at Little Lea came to rest in a museum at Wheaton College in Illinois.[18]

LEWIS AND POLITICS. Exactly what Lewis thought about crime and punishment cannot be had with certainty because Lewis generally avoided writing about contemporary political questions. Generally speaking, he believed that the primary cause for evil and suffering in the world could not be found within the structures of society, or with a particular set of laws, but was rooted in the fallen nature of human beings. The wrong law and social institutions may aggravate the human condition and give license to a great deal more evil than might otherwise occur, but no amount of political or social re-structuring could eliminate selfishness, cruelty, or greed. He viewed legal and economic equality as essential remedies for the Fall, a hedge against injustice and cruelty.[19]

Lewis rejected any form of government which sought to replace the exercise of individual reason, conscience, and volition. He particularly disliked "theocracy" in which a elite claimed a special monopoly on God's will.[20] "I am a democrat because I believe that no man or group of men is good enough to be trusted with uncontrolled power over others. And the higher the pretensions of such power, the more dangerous I think it both to the rulers and to the subjects. Hence theocracy is the worst of all governments...it gives a seemingly high, super-personal sanction to the very ordinary human passions by which, like other men, the rulers will be frequently actuated."[21] He rejected, for this reason, the idea of forming a Christian political party in Britain.[22]

"The practical problem of Christian politics," he wrote, "is not that of drawing up schemes for a Christian society, but that of living as innocently as we can with unbelieving fellow-subjects under unbelieving rulers who will never be perfectly wise and good and who will sometimes be very wicked and very foolish."[23] Lewis denied that there was an alternative to traditional morality; but he did not claim that the Bible, or Christian ethics, expressed the solution to every problem. The moral law provides general principles that may be applied to particular issues; it does not eliminate the activities of fact-finding and determining causality.[24] When he did comment on public issues, including obscenity, crime, and capital punishment, he did so, not so much to argue that public policy ought to be based on Christian beliefs, but to point out that alternative philosophies did not really provide an alternative to traditional morality. His critique of contemporary public policy prescriptions represented an effort to elevate public discourse, to draw out the moral implications of particular policies. Politicians who claimed to legislate on an amoral basis deluded themselves. When they implied that all moralities are equally plausible, they engaged in a sham.

In "The Humanitarian Theory of Punishment," Lewis exposed the injustice of punishment delivered under the guise of treatment. He rejected the notion that it is wrong to punish lawbreakers because they deserve it, because this amounts to revenge, and that revenge is cruel and barbaric. The humanitarian view held that punishment should be regarded as a means of protecting society and as a means of reforming the criminal. Lewis's central objection to this view is that it destroys the concept of justice and leads to tyranny. Retribution, Lewis insisted, is the essence of justice because it involves desert. It is morally right that the punishment fit the crime. Further, the very idea of punishment affirms the dignity of the individual because it recognizes that a person is capable of choosing good or evil. The humanitarian approach abandoned justice as a guide to legal sanctions and regarded individuals as no more than domesticated animals.[25]

Giving the power of punishment to a collection of specialists, whose techniques could not be criticized within the conventional realm of law and justice, was a formula for tyranny. Regarding crime as a disease confuses the distinction between an immoral act and an amoral condition, and allowed the "doctors" to use the pretense of amoral therapy to carry out immoral schemes. Lewis prophesied about the use of psychiatric methods to quash dissidents within Soviet dictatorship.[26] "We know," Lewis wrote in 1949, "that one school of psychology already regards religion as a neurosis. When this particular neurosis becomes inconvenient to government, what is to hinder government from proceeding to 'cure' it? Such 'cure' will, of course, be compulsory; but under the Humanitarian theory it will not be called by the shocking name of Persecution."

Perhaps Lewis should have used the word "Torah" rather than "Tao" to refer to traditional morality. His allusion to Chinese Taoism illustrated the universality of traditional morality, but he did not mean to suggest that each civilization had discovered independently the same rules. Rather, traditional morality represented something more like the baton in a relay. "Every civilization...," he wrote, "has been derived from another civilization, and in the last resort, from a single centre...."[27] The ancient civilizations of Greece and Rome provided modern culture; the English words and concepts used for science, philosophy, criticism, government, and grammar are all Graeco-Roman. But the early Jews "turn out to be our brothers in a sense in which no Greek or Roman ever was," by supplying the moral law. Traditional morality within the ancient and modern world, originated in the ancient law of Jewish civilization. And any effort to discover a Christian view of crime and punishment begins in the same place. The Torah of Israel.

The Jewish Outlook on Crime and Justice

God first revealed the Torah at Mount Sinai. When Moses descended the mountain, he held the tablets containing the law of God.

The people of Israel put them in the Ark of the Covenant, and placed the ark in the most holy place of the tabernacle, the center of worship. Even after the destruction of Jerusalem and the dispersal of Jews throughout the world, the Torah remained. Torah scrolls, in hand-written Hebrew calligraphy on parchment, are read aloud every Sabbath, in synagogues throughout the world at the beginning of the twenty-first century, just have they have been for centuries.

The Torah remains the most sacred writing within Judaism. In the specific sense, it refers to the Pentateuch, the books of Moses. The Torah expresses the *mitzvot* or commandments, and provides the basis for the *halakhah*, rabbinical teaching concerning the law in Jewish life. The word Torah also refers to the entire Jewish Bible, the *Tanakh* (the Old Testament within the Christian Bible), or in its broadest sense, to the whole body of Jewish law and teachings. The literal meaning of "halakhah" is "the path one walks." A Roman once told Hillel, the great rabbi born a generation or two before the common era, that he would convert if the rabbi could tell him all there was to know about Judaism while he stood on one foot. "Certainly!" Hillel told him, "What is hateful to thee, do not unto thy neighbor. That is all there is in the Torah. All the rest is mere commentary. I suggest you study the commentary."[28]

The "commentary" can be found in the *Talmud*, the primary text of rabbinic Judaism since the Middle Ages. The Talmud represents written commentary on the *Mishnah*, the oral law, or chain of tradition in Jewish life. Until the Roman occupation of Israel, there had been no need to write it down because it had been preserved through personal relationships between rabbi and student. But the Roman army, who had called the area "Philistia" or "Palestine" after its former inhabitants as an insult to the Jews, represented a serious threat to the *mesorah* or chain of tradition. Rabbi Judah Ha-Nasi, "Judah the Prince," compiled the Mishnah during the first century of the common era, and Jewish scholars in Jerusalem and Babylon added additional commentary over the next centuries. The Babylonian Talmud consists of sixty-three books of legal discussion, folklore, and proverbs. It contains philosophical speculation, recipes, anecdotes on prophets, and astronomical observations.[29]

The Torah specifies criminal laws as part of the *mishpatim*, Jewish law providing instruction for everything from rituals of worship to the smallest details of one's personal life.[30] The crimes and punishments specified in the Torah do not, however, derive from the modern conception of crime as an offense against the government. The Mosaic law does not rank the severity of crime against the amount of harm to society. For example, the Torah states that a burglar who steals in secret must pay a fine, while a robber who steals openly only has to return the property.[31] The different consequences, as explained in the Talmud, do not derive from the value of the item stolen, but with what the crime implied about the heart of the criminal. The robber committed a lesser offense against the halakah because his attitude toward people equaled his attitude toward God; he stole openly without fear and shame. The burglar, on the other hand, who hid himself from people but not from God, demonstrated that he feared people more than God, and therefore deserved to be fined.[32]

Understanding the Judaic conception of crime requires a look at the concept of sin. Rabbinic Judaism teaches that God created people with two impulses: an impulse for good, the *yetzer tov*, and an impulse for evil, the *yetzer ra*. The impulse for good is the conscience, the inner voice that reminds a person of God's law when contemplating something wrong. Some rabbis taught that the impulse for good, or moral conscience, does not enter a person until the thirteenth birthday; the day a Jewish young man celebrates *bar mitzvah* and he becomes responsible for following the commandments. The words "bar mitzvah" mean "one who is obligated to fulfill the commandments." The impulse for evil does not necessarily lead to evil. God created the yetzer ra to give people the desire to satisfy personal needs; to build a house, to marry, to parent children, and work to provide for them. But it can lead to evil when not controlled by the conscience. There is nothing evil about sexual desire, but it can lead to rape, adultery, incest and sexual perversion.[33]

Rabbi Morris Kertzer distinguishes between two kinds of sin: offenses against God and offenses against people. Offenses against God occur by being "alienated from our faith." The prayers recited during the ceremony of Yom Kippur, the Day of Atonement observed each year, use "we" and not "I." There are individual sins, but also there are the collective shortcomings of humankind. The meaning of Hebrew word *chayt*, translated as "sin," means missing the target, or falling short of living by the commandments. Offenses committed against another person, on the other hand, cannot be forgiven through prayer alone. The individual who sins against a neighbor can be forgiven only by winning the forgiveness of the person wronged. The wrongdoer must seek out the person wronged, make a sincere admission of guilt, and ask that person for forgiveness. The person wronged must, according to Jewish tradition, grant that forgiveness. God does not intervene to relieve a person's duties to another person. In addition to the prayers on Yom Kippur, family members ask forgiveness of each other for the wrongs the have committed.

Ultimately, the remedy for sin is authentic repentance or *t'shuvah*. The word means "return," that is, return to the straight path. There are three aspects of t'shuvah within Jewish tradition. First, the wrongdoer must acknowledge violation of the commandments. Second, the wrongdoer must express remorse for the wrongful act. Third, the wrongdoer must resolve to correct the situation and take active steps to walk the correct path. Remorse for the past wrong and resolutions for the future are required.[34] King David retains his place among the greatest leaders of Israel because he acknowledged his sins before God.

The concept of justice found in the mishpatim concerning crime and punishment derives from the covenant of love between God and His people. In that sense, it is very different from the Graeco-Roman concept of rights possessed by individuals. In the Judaic concept, God did not make his covenant with individuals, but with a people already constituted as a community. The Hebrew root word for *t'sedakah*, often translated as "justice," is *tsedek*, or "rightness." The word can be translated as "righteousness," the standard of behavior between God and His people as well as between each other. This is what King David has in mind when he wrote: "The LORD is my shepherd...He guides me in right paths [tsedek] as befits His name."[35] The justice done among the Jewish people flows from a transcendent justice established by God; it is not an agreement between people subject to the political arena. The first time the word appears in the Torah, Abraham asks God to spare the wicked cities of Sodom and Gommorah because of the presence of ten tsedek individuals within them. In other words, it would not be just to treat the righteous and the unrighteous alike.

The concept of rights based on citizenship was the most other nations of the Near East could imagine, but it was for Israel the bare minimum the covenant guaranteed.[36] T'sedakah, within the Jewish tradition, also refers to "good deeds" or acts of charity. For Jews, giving to the poor is not an act of generosity but an obligation.

Rabbi Kertzer writes that the Talmud speaks of three central principles in life: learning, service, and charity. Charity refers to genuine charity that comes from the heart, that in many ways, has taken the place of animal sacrifice in ancient times. The Jewish emphasis on giving to the poor requires the faithful to give to Jewish as well as non-Jewish poor. It also goes so far as to require the poor who are receiving charity to give to those who are poorer.[37] But even during the time of the patriarchs, Jewish law prescribed the form of charity to the poor. As depicted in the account of Ruth, Jewish farmers had to leave a corner of their fields for the poor. If, during the harvest, a bundle fell or was forgotten, the farmer could not return for it. As well, farmers had to allow poor people to glean in their fields.

Tsedek provides the foundation for mishpatim. *Mishpat*, the root word for mishpatim, means "verdict" or "judgment." The decisions made by judges had to meet the standard of tsedek. The early Jews had courts, just as the nation of Israel has courts today, but even then the purpose of these courts differed from the Graeco-Roman version. The Torah directs that courts be held at *sh'arecha*, the city gates.[38] Following the Greek and Roman custom, courthouses are built in central locations. Each person is entitled to equal justice and has equal access to them. But Jewish law provides that courts be established at the entrance to the city. This location makes the court a signpost that defines the community. Visitors and passersby know that it is a safe city, a city governed by justice.[39] This placement of courts reaffirms God's commandment concerning the justice practiced in courts. "You shall have one standard [mishpat] for stranger and citizen alike: for I the LORD am your God."[40] The Torah holds judges to a high standard of fairness because the law of the land represents a means of justice.

The practice of t'shuvah in pursuit of tsedek is essential for *shalom* or "peace."[41] The word shalom derives from *shalem* which means "completeness." The Jewish person who greets another with the salutation "shalom" extends the hope that everything is complete; that the person has suffered no injury, that no family member lies ill. In the larger sense, completeness within the community is maintained whenever persons have taken steps to correct wrongs. *Shillin*, the word for restitution, is derivative of shalem. Things will not be complete unless restitution has been made as a part of repentance. Martin Luther King, Jr., in his "Letter From Birmingham Jail," quoted the prophet Amos in this regard: "But let justice [mishpat] well up as water, Righteousness [tsedek] like an unfailing stream."[42]

Having explained the Judaic concepts of sin, repentance, and justice, it is now possible to consider that well-known portion of the Mosaic law that instructs the courts to impose the sanction of *ayen tachat ayen*, an "eye for an eye." The law of Moses required that a murderer must not suffer greater harm than had been caused by the act. The law further required the courts to distinguish between deliberate acts and accidents. In the case of murder, the literal meaning is intended: a life must be repaid with a life except in cases of accidental death. Maimonides interpreted this portion of the Torah to mean that the perpetrator of the crime must be punished symmetrically: the one who causes a person's limb to be lost must lose that limb in return.[43] The Talmud states that a person guilty of a capital crime should be put to death, even if they have repented. T'shuvah changes divine judgment; persons who repair their relationship with God will be forgiven of their sin. In human courts, however, judgment is based solely on past actions. No amount of repentance can change what has been done.[44]

But from ancient times to the present, the practice of capital punishment seldom occurred among Jewish people. The law also provided several safeguards to prevent wrongful convictions and carrying out vengeance. For conviction and execution in a homicide, the Torah required the eyewitness testimony of two persons. Not only must two persons witness the crime, the law required them to warn the perpetrator before the crime occurred. The criminal had to evidence knowledge of the wrongfulness of the act and of the punishment that would follow. The teaching related to the Torah also provided measures for questioning the witnesses to discover false testimony along with other measures to reduce the possibility of executing the wrong person.[45] The Talmud refers to a Sanhedrin that issued an execution order once in seven years as a "murderous court."[46] Moses established three cities of refuge prior to the Jews entry into the Holy Land, and Joshua established three more after settlement in Israel. These cities provided protective custody, a place for those accused of murder to escape the vengeance of the victim's surviving family members. The court at a city of refuge could prescribe work for the accused as a means of atonement, and could order the family of the accused to reside within the city as well.[47]

Over time, the law of an "eye for an eye" ceased to exist. The rabbis contributing to the Talmud interpreted the law as requiring compensation for loss of income, medical damages, damage for shame, and for physical or emotional pain and suffering. The Talmud interprets an "eye for an eye" to mean the *cost* of an eye for the *cost* of an eye. As clarified by the Mishnah, the Jew who steals and is unable to make financial restitution may be declared an *eved ivri*, that is, placed into servant-hood. The court could make a person a servant to the victim as a means of compensation for the stolen property. The eved was not a slave, but a servant entitled to be treated as a person. The law required that the person be maintained within the community in much the same way as an unruly child brought under the influence of a family. Under the arrangement, the master incurred several obligations to the servant. The master provided food, clothing, and shelter not only for the servant, but also for the servant's spouse and children. The servant had to be maintained at the level of the master's family; the Talmud goes so far as to say that if the master has one pillow, the servant is entitled to it. And, unlike slavery, servant-hood is only temporary. The servant would be free during the sabbatical year when debts were forgiven, or the servant could remain a servant until the Jubilee year when all debts were forgiven.[48]

The Judaic-Christian Response to Crime

Restorative justice represents one contemporary example of what a criminal justice system founded on Judaic-Christian principles might look like. *Restorative justice* emphasizes that when a person commits a crime, the wrongdoer injures another person and the community suffers along with the victim. Consequently, the person incurs an obligation to repair the harm done and "restore" the victim and the community—to the extent possible—to the state of being that existed before the criminal act. Restorative justice insists on core principles of accountability, restitution, and community-based sentences intended to bring about reconciliation, between the offender and the victim, and between the offender, victim and community.[49]

The term "restorative justice," invented by a psychologist,[50] remains vague. By no means do all programs referring to restorative justice pursue Christian or Jewish values. A number of groups have adopted the restorative justice banner, including some secular programs that derive their philosophy from the community, in the humanist sense, or from spiritual ideas outside the Judaic-Christian tradition.[51] Restorative justice includes a variety of practices: sentencing circles, family conferencing, police conferencing, and victim-offender mediation. In Canada and the United States, restorative justice began with victim-offender mediation. Since the first victim-offender mediation (VOM) program began two-and-a-half decades ago, more than 300 VOM programs have appeared in the United States and about 700 in Europe.[52]

What became victim-offender mediation began in Kitchener, Ontario, in 1974. Two young men, under the influence of alcohol, spent a Saturday night breaking windows and slashing tires in Elmira, a small town near Kitchener. The boys' arrest made headlines. Eventually, they plead guilty to twenty-two counts of willful damage. The judge in the Elmira case instructed the boys to return in June to be sentenced and sent them home. The probation officer assigned to prepare their presentence reports, Mark Yantzi, began thinking about a better response. Yantzi had been working for the Ontario probation service for five years; he had started as a volunteer through a program of the Mennonite Central Committee. The MCC of Ontario had been looking for an alternative to brick-and-mortar approaches to criminal justice since 1968. "Wouldn't it be neat for these offenders to meet their victims?" he asked the committee.[53]

As a Mennonite, Yantzi liked the peace-making aspect of offenders reconciling with their victims. The Mennonite movement began in Germany, during the sixteenth century, when a small group of believers insisted that Martin Luther's reform had not gone far enough. Known as the Anabaptists, they set themselves apart from the official church and the practice of infant baptism by declaring their faith in Jesus Christ and re-baptizing one another. The Mennonites became known for their pacifism, taken from Christ's way of peace. Many choose not to participate in military service; some object to government spending for military purposes. The church had traditionally maintained a separation from government, particularly, from the criminal justice system and its use of coercive power, and Yantzi wondered if the church would approve. He also wondered whether the judge would be willing to authorize a disposition that had no basis in Canadian law.

David Worth, another MCC member, encouraged Yantzi to give it a try. When he submitted the presentence reports, he enclosed a letter suggesting that "there could be some theraputic value in these two young men having to personally face up to the victims of their numerous offenses." At the sentencing hearing, the judge remarked about the lack of precedent for such an order, but agreed to a one-month remand to allow time for the two boys to meet with victims and assess losses. Accompanied by Yantzi and Worth, the two young men retraced their steps on that Saturday night. They visited each place where they had damaged property: homes, two churches, and a liquor store. They spoke to twenty-one victims in all and figured the total damage at $2,189.04. When they returned to court, the judge ordered a fine and a probation sentence, contingent on payment of restitution. Three months later, the youths had visited each of the victims and handed them a certified check for their losses.[54]

The Elmira case led to the establishment of the Victim/Offender Reconciliation Project in 1975. By 1980s, there were more than twenty VORPs in Ontario and projects in the United States and England. The first victim-offender mediation program in the United States began at Elkhart, Indiana in 1978. Yantzi spent part of 1976 in Elkart attending the Mennonite seminary, and the seminary approached the probation department with the idea. The probation department set up the program. Howard Zehr, a college professor who arrived that year to direct a local half-way house, took an interest in the project and helped organize a non-profit agency to direct the program called PACT (Prisoner and Community Together). He became director of the Mennonite Central Committee U.S. Office of Criminal Justice the following year.[55]

VORP went to England with Burt Galaway, a professor of social work at the University of Minnesota. Galaway organized the first international symposium on restitution in 1975, and in 1981, took a teaching assignment at the University of Birmingham in England. Galaway had learned of the program after completing a study of restitution programs throughout the country for the National Institute of Justice. He introduced audiences to the Mennonite Victim/Offender Reconciliation Program in Canada and the United States with a slide presentation. The following year, the BBC filmed program participants in Elkhart, Indiana, and the program provided a model for many English viewers.[56] Galaway helped organize a victim-offender mediation program in Minneapolis-St. Paul in 1985.

In 1982, the PACT Institute of Justice created the National Victim Offender Reconciliation Resource and Training Center. The Institute organized in 1984 the first VORP gathering in Valparaiso, Indiana. Annual meetings occurred thereafter leading to organization of the United States Association for Victim-Offender Mediation. Zehr, who had an interest in photography, helped write a training manual. Victim-offender reconciliation, or *victim-offender mediation* as the programs became known, involved a face-to-face meeting between the victim and the offender facilitated by a trained mediator. The program offered victims an opportunity to hear the facts, express their feelings, and receive restitution. For the offender, VOM offered an opportunity to learn first-hand about the harm caused, to acknowledge responsibility for wrongdoing, and to make amends.

The approach in the Elmira case had been fairly simple. "We were pretty brutal," Yantzi recalled, "We walked up to the door. They knocked. We stood back with our note pads."[57] The training materials PACT developed divided the mediation process into four components. In step one, the program coordinator completes the intake process and assigns the case to a mediator, typically a community volunteer, who represents the community's interest. In step two, the mediator holds preliminary meetings with the offender and victim separately, to find out about the facts of the case, explain the process, explore restitution possibilities and learn about their willingness to meet. The mediation session, step three, begins with "story-telling;" the victim relates his or her account of the crime and the offender responds. The mediator explores facts and feelings, and moves the victim and offender toward a restitution agreement. The offender agrees to a contract which typically involves paying restitution, although victims may request other conditions such as the offender repairs property damage, donates community service hours, or agrees to attend counseling for alcohol abuse or other life problems. In step four, program staff monitor the offender's progress and report to the court.

In the original Elkhart version, the program operated outside the criminal justice system. Program staff worked for a church-based or non-profit organization and the mediators came from the community. Referrals came from courts, and the agreement became part of the sentencing process. The program dealt with property crimes mostly, and most often burglary.[58] As other programs appeared, the structure changed along with the types of cases handled. The program in Genesee County, New York, became a model for handling violence cases. Since the program began in 1982, Genesee has taken more than 400 cases involving serious or violent crime including a sniper shooting and a vehicular manslaughter case. Sheriff Doug Call founded the program after winning his 1980 election on a promise to come up with a better solution than building another jail. The program operates out of the Sheriff's office, with more than 120 agencies that employ offenders in community-based work programs. The sheriff's office also dispatches patrol officers to ensure that offenders meet their agreements.[59]

Victim-offender mediation expresses Judaic and Christian beliefs. It began with the goal of *reconciliation*, of recognizing the importance to both victim and offender, and ultimately the community, of offenders taking responsibility for their actions and taking steps to repair the damage. The process provides for a change of heart through confession, repentance, and forgiveness. Judaism emphasizes repentance and reconciliation as part of the process, that wrongdoing against another can only be forgiven by the victim, and that the wrongdoer must face the victim, admit the wrong, and ask forgiveness. This expresses t'shuvah, of admitting wrongdoing, accepting responsibility, and resolving not to re-offend. Emphasizing reform of the criminal justice system along the lines of restorative justice also presents an issue of *tikkun olam* or "reparing hurt" within the world. This Jewish tradition teaches that the faithful ought to work toward doing good within the world. Working toward a compassionate meaningful response to crime is also consistent with the mission of t'sedekah or charity.[60]

Howard Zehr outlined the Christian theology of restorative justice in his book *Changing Lenses* (1990). He begins with the Bible word "peace," *shalom* in the Hebrew, *eirene* in Greek. Peace means more than the absence of war, it means a state of "all rightness": personal peace with God, peace in human relationships, peace among nations, and peace within God's creation. The absence of oppression is prerequisite for peace. Zehr's concept of justice is holistic; injustice of any kind, whether exploitation of the poor or mistreatment of lawbreakers, threatens peace. Zehr's concept of Christian justice draws on the covenant, an agreement between God and His people, and rights and responsibilities in the law it expressed. While "an eye for an eye" expresses retributive justice, Christ called on His followers to do more. "You have heard it said 'an eye for an eye' but I tell you, do good to those who harm you."

The model of justice Christ established for lawbreakers, Zehr writes, is grounded in restitution, not retribution. No matter how many times God's people failed to fulfill their responsibilities under the covenant, He never gave up on them. Christians ought to imitate God's forgiveness and mercy.[61]

The Mennonite Church found an ally in the restorative justice effort in Justice Fellowship, an organization founded by Charles Colson. From 1969 to 1972, Colson served as Special Counsel to President Nixon. In 1974, he entered federal prison at Maxwell, Alabama, the first member of the Nixon administration to be imprisoned for crimes related to the Watergate scandal. While in prison, Colson rekindled his Catholic faith and vowed to do something about the pain and injustice of crime. Colson founded Prison Fellowship Ministries after leaving federal prison, the world's largest outreach program to prisoners, crime victims, and their families.

In 1983, Colson founded Justice Fellowship, a church-based criminal justice reform organization. Led by Daniel W. Van Ness, Justice Fellowship developed a plan to reform the criminal justice system along the lines of restorative justice principles. Colson and Van Ness offer three principles of restorative justice: crime causes injury that should be repaired, all of those injured should be included in the process, and government and communities ought to work together.[62] Together, they have emphasized the needs of victims. They emphasize individual responsibility, making things right. Crime results in injuries to victims, communities and offenders, and the criminal justice system ought to be repairing those injuries. Victims, offenders and citizens ought to be actively involved in the criminal justice process: doing justice should be the sole province of government. Justice Fellowship helped establish a Victim-Offender Reconciliation Program in Columbia, South Carolina.

"In promoting justice," Van Ness concludes, "the government is responsible for preserving order, and the community is responsible establishing peace." The government's function is to establish order through enforcement of laws and carrying out of sanctions for violations of those laws. Offenders have an interest in due process. But the criminal justice process is bigger than that, or it should be. It should seek reconciliation between victim, offender and community by seeing to it that the process aims to restore the victim to a sense of wholeness.[63]

The Faith Factor

Criminologists have discovered religion. Throughout the twentieth century, as the social-scientific perspective dominated criminology, criminologists avoided reference to religious ideals. But as twenty-first century commences, criminologists have taken an interest in "the faith factor."[64]

Research articles dealing with the link between religiosity and crime have appeared in major journals of *Criminology* and *Justice Quarterly*.[65] Major funding organizations, such as the Pew Charitable Trust, Lily Endowment, and the Robert Wood Johnson Foundation have expressed a willingness to fund research. John J. DiIulio, who left Princeton University to head a center for the study of religion and social policy at the University of Pennsylvania, helped found the Jeremiah Project at the Manhattan Institute. The Project researches the impact of inner-city churches in reducing poverty and crime.[66] President George W. Bush named DiIulio to direct the White House Office of Faith-Based Community Initiatives. Byron Johnson, a Vanderbilt University criminologist affiliated with DiIulio's Center, has looked at the impact of religiosity, measured by church attendance, on delinquency and drug abuse. He has also looked at the impact of participation in Prison Fellowship programs on institutional infractions and success after release.[67]

The growth of victim-offender mediation programs led to evaluation research. Researchers have conducted numerous studies to find out the impact of participation in victim-offender mediation. Researchers have explored the impact on the offender's behavior, and other aspects program operations, including victims' level of satisfaction with the outcome, mediator styles, and program administration. Research directed at discovering the impact of mediation on the offender's behavior has assessed the amount of restitution paid, frequency of sentence completion, and the portion of offenders rearrested.[68] In 1993, the Office of Juvenile Justice and Delinquency Prevention funded restorative justice centers at Florida Atlantic University and at the University of Minnesota.

It may well be, all else being equal, that religious people are less likely to engage in criminal behavior. The faithful may behave better than the faithless for any number of reasons. Adherence to a religious ethos might promote self-discipline and enhance self-control.

The faithful might fear judgment in the afterlife for sins committed in this life, or perhaps the feeling of connectedness to a social group—a religious institution—promotes a sense of well-being that is simply good for the soul. Professor DiIulio hopes his center will investigate why these programs work. What is it about the faith factor that makes religious programs effective? Even scholars interested in the faith factor concede that there is still scant evidence on the effectiveness of such programs.[69]

Now it is one thing to document the range of social services inner-city churches provide, to look at the type of programs that take referrals from police and courts, or to find out how many offenders who participate in victim-mediation make restitution as agreed. And, if the programs work, society might profit by them, even if none of the experts can pinpoint *why* they work. One observer of Japan explains that the Japanese enjoy one of the lowest crime rates in the world because they pursue an informal process within their criminal justice system that incorporates key elements of victim-offender mediation (confession, repentance, absolution).[70] But the notion that there needs to be social-science research into the faith factor raises a troubling question.

Who needs empirical proof of the faith factor? Certainly God does not need social-scientists to confirm His existence.[71] The young people and prisoners who participate in church-based programs do not do so because they are skeptical about the role of faith in people's lives. Nor do those who attend weekly services at the churches and synagogues that sponsor these programs—they do not need to see the research findings before they decide to give of their time and money. The skeptics, it appears, are the criminologists who want social-scientific evidence for use in convincing government sponsors. If criminology needs social-scientific evidence to make religion palatable, it is not worth the effort.

Criminologists who pursue a social-scientific understanding of faith will never find the answer, no matter how much research they conduct. The question of faith can never be answered by social science because science studies the *natural world* and the question has to do with the *supernatural world*, something outside of nature. Social science, limited as it is to the natural world, can never prove or disprove what happens in the spiritual realm. The attempt to look for social-scientific proof of the faith factor necessarily distorts the meaning the faith. Criminology says: "Believe in faith-based programs, not because what the faithful believe is really true, but for some other reason—faithful people make better citizens." To make faith a subject of social-scientific study it is necessary to see faith as something it could never be.

To make faith palatable to government sponsors it must pass from the spiritual realm to the social realm. As explained by OJJDP Director Shay Bilchik, the "venerable concept of restorative justice" holds that when a crime occurs the criminal incurs an obligation to repair the harm to the victim and the community. In dealing with juvenile criminals, the concept of balance insists that juvenile courts should give equal weight to ensuring community safety, holding offenders accountable to their victims, and teaching young lawbreakers skills needed for participation in their community.[72] In this way, government pursuit of restorative justice has led to *syncretism*, the blending of religious beliefs. The concept that emerges no longer expresses Judaic-Christian beliefs but a mixture of beliefs, including elements within Muslim, American Indian, and Pacific Rim societies. It draws on the beliefs of Maori peoples of New Zealand as well as native peoples of Canada.[73]

The process transforms the restorative approach of confession, forgiveness, and restitution, as something God requires, to a social ethos emphasizing ideals of strengthening social ties, reconciling order with autonomy, and voluntary social control. Reconciliation, the purpose identified by the Mennonite founders, gave way to *community justice*, defined as "an ethic that transforms the aim of the justice system into enhancing community life or sustaining community."[74] The desire for egalitarianism replaces obedience to God as the foundation. "Egalitarianism in this context..." an article in the *National Institute of Justice Journal* explains, "[means that] community members treat each other fairly (equality), tolerate the attitudes and behaviors of others (inclusion), balance self-interest with concern for the collective good (mutuality), and are willing to put the common good above their own wants and needs (stewardship)."[75]

Peter Drucker could see the futility of such thinking fifty years ago. The author of thirty books on management, business, economics, politics and other topics, Drucker has been consultant to corporations throughout the world. Before becoming a business consultant, he taught religion and philosophy.[76] In 1949, he published an essay entitled "The Unfashionable Kierkegaard" to explain why a social ethos is not enough—not even for society.[77] The essay, written during the years of despair after witnessing the holocaust, deals with solemn philosophical issues. In the essay, Drucker explains why recognizing the social utility of religion could never replace individual faith.

Drucker observed that all philosophical attempts to answer the question "How is society possible?" arrive at a negative concept of human existence. Individual freedom can be understood as what does not disturb society. Existence in society requires that an individual accept as real the spheres of social values and beliefs. To exist in society is to exist in time; in time individuals eat and drink, work and vacation, marry, raise children, retire, succeed and fail. But in eternity, the realm of the spirit, or as Kierkegaard phrased it— "in the sight of God"—society does not exist. In eternity, each individual stands alone. No family stands near, no friends, or co-workers; nothing any other has experienced can help the individual. Existence in the spirit realm requires that an individual regard all social values as deception, invalid, unreal.[78] Rather than "How is society possible?" the question should be "How is human existence possible?"

The idea of the individual in society, Drucker acknowledges, makes it all sound so gloomy. The belief that people can, through the accumulation of social-scientific knowledge, make steady progress, appears so much more optimistic. But where does this optimism lead? The belief in progress holds that eternity can be reached in time: that truth can be reached by majority vote, equality can be experienced through fair distribution, that personal fulfillment can be achieved by striving for the common good. All attempts to avoid eternity fail because of one stubborn fact of human existence that progress cannot suppress: death.[79] The nineteenth century, Drucker wrote, made every effort to deny death its' individualism. It made death a datum in vital statistics, a quantity measurable in statistical analysis, an incident predictable through actuarial laws. The nineteenth century tried to get around death by planning for its social consequences. The insurance company, designed to "spread the risks," represents the nineteenth century's most significant institution.[80] The twentieth century brought its own institution, it might be said, the institute of criminology to calculate the likelihood of violent death in an average year. Both institutions attempt to make death an incident in human life rather than the end of one's life.

An "optimism" that reduces human existence to existence in society leads to despair. "Society must make it possible for man to die without despair if it wants him to be able to live exclusively in society," Drucker wrote, "And it can do so in only one way: by making individual life meaningless."[81] This is because all attempts to reduce ethics to social values could not provide meaning for individual existence. The concept of social value, while it might lead to sacrifice and benevolence, could not give a purpose for the years of a person's life. Because as soon as ethics becomes a community ideal, it degenerates into solipsism. "For if virtue is to be found in man, everything that is accepted by man must be virtue," as Drucker puts it. Every attempt to find a permanent community ideal ends in the denial of permanence, with no escape from despair. Nowhere was this more true, Drucker wrote, than the efforts of the various Christian political parties and the movement for social Christianity.

Conclusion

The philosophy of social Christianity could give a person something to die for. In times of crisis, fear and soulful want, it is a great thing to be able to die. But only through faith can a person find something to live for. Faith, reduced to the faith factor, offers only a clumsy imitation. No community ethos, not even one dressed up in religious symbolism, can really provide a satisfying reason to think more about others than about oneself. Individual existence becomes the only basis for the individual in society. Only in faith does permanent social value emerge to make existence in society meaningful and to express genuine charity. The individual becomes the irreducible starting point in any moral philosophy of crime. Kierkegaard, in the nineteenth century, explored the meaning of this; Michael Oakeshott, in the twentieth century, has as well. Together they suggest a framework for thinking about crime, law, government and morality.

Chapter 9

The Death and Rebirth of Criminology

In 1995, the *New York Times* announced that criminology had arrived as an academic discipline. An article noted the popularity of
criminology and criminal justice programs at universities. The difference between the two, that was hard to explain. Larry Sherman, who
chaired the Department of Criminology and Criminal Justice at the
University of Maryland, told the journalist that the older criminology
had been pioneered by sociologists at the University of Chicago in the
1890s. The criminologists faithful to this tradition studied the causes
of crime; issues like poverty, families, neighborhoods, gangs and increasingly, biology. The newer brand of applied criminology specialized in studying police, courts, and corrections. Applied criminologists, Sherman assured the journalist, relied on the scientific method
just as the sociological criminologists had. The newer criminology
"combine[d] sociology, psychology, history, economics, politics and
statistics" in its approach to the institutions of criminal justice.[1]
   Philosophy did not even make the list. Criminologists debate the
preeminence of psychological, sociological, biological, and other
factors in explaining criminal behavior. They are also undecided
about whether "real" criminologists study police and courts rather
than the roots of crime. But explaining crime has nothing to do
with moral philosophy, at least they can all agree about that. Criminologists keep their values from interfering in their research, and
students should keep their values out of the criminology classroom.
If students really want to discuss values, maybe they could do so in
a separate course on professional ethics. But credible criminologists
leave ethics for the professions themselves—the police academy, judicial college, corrections training center. Ethics in criminology
serves about the same purpose as the designated driver: it is useful

for the advertising campaign, and maybe even useful to have around at the party, so long as the person tries not to spoil the fun by interjecting meaningful conversation.

This chapter explains how justice became separate from ethics, and why it is important for criminology to unite the two. Part One considers the legacy of natural law thinking. Part Two describes the criminological view of social control. Part Three explains the hazards of reducing the understanding of moral conduct in criminology to social justice. Part Four sketches a moral philosophy of crime derived from British philosopher Michael Oakeshott and the Danish philosopher Søren Kierkegaard.

The Legacy of Natural Law

The ancient philosophers understood justice as a virtue, as a quality an individual can have. Justice occurs when individuals treat others fairly; injustice results when people treat others unfairly. The ancient definition of justice, found in Plato and Aristotle, and written into Roman law, is expressed in Latin as *suum cuique*, or "to each his own." As it appears in Justinian's *Corpus Juris Civilis* it reads: "Justice is a habit whereby a man renders to each one his due with constant and perpetual will."[2] This understanding of justice explained the relationship of the individual to society as well as citizen to government. It was a matter of what they read in the natural law.

As a term of jurisprudence, *natural law* may be defined as a loosely-knit body of rules prescribed by an authority superior to government. Depending on the version, these rules derive from divine commandment, from human nature, from abstract reason, or from the long experience of people living in community.[3] The idea first appeared among the Greek Stoics. Plato relates a dialogue between the heretic Socrates and the Athenian, Euthyphro. Socrates tells Euthyphro that he can no longer believe the Greek myths because the gods behaved so immorally; he mentions Zeus's murder of his father, the titan Cronos. Socrates questions his religion based on an appeal to a common-sense understanding of moral conduct.[4]

The Romans, influenced by Stoic philosophy, enshrined this common-sense view of justice within their law. They recognized the law of nature, *jus naturale*, as distinct from the law of nations, *jus gen-*

tium. The most important early definition of natural law can be found in Cicero's *De Re Publica*, in which human laws are imperfect copies of eternal laws, laws that existed before any written law existed or any government had been established. Marcus Tullius Cicero, a Roman orator and statesman (murdered by emissaries of Mark Anthony), wrote that "law is the highest reason, implanted by nature, which commands what ought be done and forbids the opposite."[5] To the extent that human laws follow eternal laws, he said, they will either promote the public welfare or bring about confusion and disaster.

In the thirteenth century, St. Thomas Aquinas produced an important formulation of natural law in his "Treatise on Law." It appeared as part of his *Summa Theologiae*, an attempt to systematize all of the church doctrine known to him. Aquinas's understanding of law begins with *eternal law*; this emanated from God and constituted the source of all other laws. Eternal law included scientific laws that governed the cosmos, revolution of the planets, and so on. *Natural law* represented a society's participation in the eternal law; a form of law that could be discerned by means of the intellect. People could grasp the natural law through practical reason corresponding to the conscience. The natural law could not be altered because it was part of human nature; the natural law included prohibition of sexual desire, responsibility to children, and other matters. *Human law*, Aquinas said, emanated from people. Government made laws to regulate the interaction of people including civil and criminal laws. Aquinas insisted that natural law was the standard for human law because unjust laws in principle did not bind the conscience.[6]

The ideas of the Enlightenment, so important to classical criminology, included reference to natural law. Thomas Hobbes and John Locke used the terms "natural law" and "law of nature" but in a new sense. They introduced the idea that there was a time when people lived without being organized into societies and had founded civilization after experiencing the struggle of individual existence. The source of natural law could be found in a desire for self-preservation. With this starting point, they concluded that obligation to the authority of government arises from the consent of individuals. They emphasized the role of natural rights in order to limit government use of coercive power. Thomas Jefferson, in the Declaration of Independence, refers to "the Creator" as the source of natural rights, but he too meant natural in a secular sense. He did not believe they had actually been handed down to Moses by God at Mount Sinai. Histories, and not Bibles, should be put into the hands of children he taught, so that "their memories may be stored with the most useful facts" from ancient and modern times. He found no place for metaphysics or theology in the curriculum he planned for the University of Virginia.[7]

Beccaria and the classical criminologists made a distinct separation between crime and sin, and the church did not protest. Christianity recognizes a difference between crime and sin. A *crime* is an act or omission which the law punishes on behalf of the state, whether because the act is prohibited by statute, or is so injurious to the public as to require punishment on the ground of public policy. A *sin* is a transgression against the moral law, with the law's divine sanctions. It is God, not government, who punishes and forgives sin. So government is unconcerned with sins unless they threaten the rule of law and the church accepts the rule of law provided it does not compel them to do acts contrary to the Christian faith.[8]

The classical criminologists sustained this distinction by investing in the rule of law. Two-and-a-half centuries ago, in fact, the study of law was not limited to professional law schools. William Blackstone offered a series of lectures to students at Oxford in 1753 that became his *Commentaries on the Laws of England.* In 1795, Edmund Burke commented that Blackstone's Commentaries sold better in the American colonies than in England.[9] At Yale, Harvard, Columbia, Pennsylvania, and William and Mary, professors gave lectures about the law to students who had no intention of becoming lawyers. Yale University established the Kent Professorship of Law and Legal History in 1801, about forty years before Yale Law School opened its doors. James Wilson, in his lectures at the University of Pennsylvania in 1790–91, advised that the "science of law should, in some measure, and in some degree, be the study of every free citizen... The knowledge of those rational principles on which the law is founded ought, especially in a free government, to be diffused over the whole community."[10]

Jeremy Bentham, who attended Blackstone's lectures as a student, graduated to become one of his harshest critics. Blackstone the lecturer, Bentham said, was about "what you would expect from the character of his writings: cold, reserved and wary." Bentham concerned himself with finding the inner meaning of the law.

"To know the true good of the community is what constitutes the science of legislation," he wrote, "the art consists in finding the means to realize that good."[11] Blackstone did not attempt a philosophy, but rather, had set out to systematize British law as a guide to the practice of the law for lawyers at the bar and those who would sit as justices of the peace. In his volume on *Public Wrongs*, he provided the classic legal definition of crime. "A crime, or misdemeanor," he wrote, "is an act committed, or omitted, in violation of public law, either forbidding or commanding it."[12] Blackstone goes on to explain how crimes, as public wrongs, differ from civil injuries or private wrongs. Private wrongs infringe on the civil rights of individuals while public wrongs violate the rights and duties due to the whole community. Refusing to surrender a parcel of land to its rightful owner constitutes a civil injury because it involves individuals, Blackstone explains, while treason, murder, and robbery are crimes because they "strike at the very being of society; which cannot possibly subsist, where actions of this sort are suffered to escape with impunity."[13] The fact that Blackstone could provide a practical guide in 1769, and define crime as an offense against the public rather than against God, meant that classical criminology had already achieved hegemony.

Natural law thinking, however, has never disappeared altogether. Joseph Story, an Associate Justice of the United States Supreme Court, pursued natural law early in the nineteenth century. In Story's view of government, the judiciary fortified itself with jurisprudence to protect the constitution from interest groups acting through the legislature. Story desired to put public law beyond the reach of those who would manipulate it by embedding it in an objective legal science of natural law, common law, and comparative law. The status of slavery created a dilemma for Story; he opposed it on moral grounds but recognized that the constitution sanctioned it. He resolved the dilemma by deciding for freedom when the law gave him room, and upholding the constitution when the law gave him no choice. In *Le Jeune Eugenie* (1822) he relied on a natural law interpretation of international law to outlaw the international slave trade (a decision reversed three years later by John Marshall); in *The Amistad* (1841), he freed Africans sold into slavery by a narrow reading of the treaty with Spain.[14]

More than a hundred years later, Martin Luther King, Jr., relied on natural law in his attack on the evil of segregation. In his "Letter

From Birmingham Jail," written in 1963 while confined in Alabama, King explained the difference between criminal disobedience and civil disobedience. The White clergy of the city had criticized King as a troublemaking outsider and praised the police for enforcing public order. King read their views while sitting in jail for leading the march and sketched his response on the margins of the newspaper where the article appeared.[15] In the letter, King charged that the city officials been more interested in maintaining civic order than promoting justice. He rebuked the ministers for praising police efforts aimed at "keeping order" and "preventing violence." What about the violence directed at Black people by means of the segregation laws they enforced?[16]

Christians, King told the clergymen, are justified in breaking the law by means of direct action because there are two types of law. "A just law is a man-made code the squares with the moral law of God. An unjust law is a code out of harmony with the moral law."[17] Segregation laws in Birmingham were unjust because they had been enacted by a power majority group that had made them to apply to others and denied those to whom they applied a say in their formulation. The group under authority of the law had no part in writing the law. King defined *civil disobedience* as "individuals who break a law conscience tells them is unjust, who willingly accept the punishment of imprisonment in order to arouse the conscience of the community." The pursuit of civil disobedience expresses the highest respect for law.[18]

Although King relied on a Christian view of natural law it is not necessary to share in the Christian faith to recognize its legacy. The whole point of natural law can be summarized with the recognition that law is a part of ethics. It does not really operate as a body of ethical rules to be held up against laws applied by courts. Rather, it operates quietly, unnoticed, as a habit of conduct that governs the life of individuals. The tension between law and morality becomes visible in emergency situations when moralists turn to natural law when they try to express why it is important to do what is right. The tension also appears, to use Oakeshott's example, "when a man preaches 'social justice'...and at the same time is obviously without a habit of ordinary decent behavior." The fact that people notice this, he observes, means that justice is not merely an abstract ideal.[19] But it is an observation that criminology has completely ignored.

The Age of Social Control

From its inception, professional criminology had no use for natural law. Social-scientific criminology cannot fathom the moral conduct of individuals as a category of thought. Criminologists replaced the legal understanding of crime the classicists had established by making it an analog for social convention. The shift in thinking began with the Italian positivists, who needed crime to be something that could be understood by means of science. The criminal anthropologists advanced their biological determinism with the view that criminal behavior resulted from multiple causes, causes that could be identified by application of the scientific method. Baron Raffaele Garofalo knew immediately that no science of criminal behavior could be built on a legal definition; the science of criminality required a definition of crime uncluttered by the practices of police and judges.

In his book *Criminology*, Garofalo attempted to formulate a universal scientific definition of crime. He proposed the "natural crime" as an objective social-scientific definition; behavior which offends social convention. Specifically, the natural crime offended the moral sentiments of pity, revulsion against the voluntary affliction of suffering on others, and probity, respect for the property rights of others. These sentiments, Garofalo insisted, appear in all civilized societies. Collectively they expressed the average moral sense of the community; some individuals may be above or below the average. In some persons, these altruistic sensibilities failed to develop sufficiently, Garofalo theorized, and it was up to criminology to find out why.

Edwin Sutherland, the American sociologist, helped institutionalize this understanding of crime among criminologists. It was Sutherland who added the term "white-collar crime" to the English language with his study of the unlawful activities of respectable persons. He conducted a twenty-year study of illegal business practices within the nation's seventy largest corporations. Before his *White Collar Crime* appeared in 1949, his publisher insisted that he use fake corporate names to forestall litigation. Sutherland's research challenged the legal definition of crime used by the academic lawyers. They believed they were writing about crime when they wrote about persons convicted of crime. Sutherland pointed out that many of the corporate illegalities he uncovered had never been prosecuted. Criminology ought to be about all criminal activity, whether it comes to the attention of police and courts or does not.

Since Sutherland, sociological-criminologists have preferred the term "deviance" to "crime" as their topic of study. *Deviance* refers to acts that deviate from social convention, and it sounds more objective. Crime is not the opinion of criminologists, they are only reporting the opinions of others. In this view, criminologists ought to concern themselves with the spectrum of human activity that differs from the normal or conventional social activity, whether or not such acts are the subject of the court process or legally prohibited in the first place. A criminal act is not criminal because it violates the law but because it violates the social conventions on which the law is based. Generally speaking, criminal laws reflect social conventions, either that of society as a whole, or those in a position to impose their view on others.

Associate Justice Oliver Wendell Holmes, who had championed legal positivism even before his tenure on the Supreme Court, advanced this view. Holmes dismissed the natural law theorists for their simple-minded notion that what they thought is what everybody thought. Holmes insisted the law merely reflected those rules that a sovereign power in society would enforce. He stated, "Truth (is) the majority vote of that nation that could lick all others" and "When it comes to the development of a *corpus juris* (body of law), the ultimate question is what do the dominant forces of the community want and do they want it hard enough to disregard whatever inhibitions may stand in their way?" Holmes's view prevailed in the form of pragmatism, as represented in the work of Harvard law professor Roscoe Pound, who emphasized adaptation of law through social change. Together, they removed natural law as a lodestar for public law.

Law, from the deviance perspective, operates as a means of social control. The social control view of law basically holds that social harmony proceeds not from voluntary association but from some external means of compulsion. It can mean something as straightforward as arrest or something as intangible as peer pressure. Barrington Moore, a social historian, expressed it this way: "To maintain and transmit a value system human beings are punched, bullied, sent to jail, thrown into concentration camps, cajoled, bribed, made into heroes, encouraged to read newspapers, stood up against a wall and shot, and sometimes even taught sociology."[20] Edward Ross, a sociologist, introduced the concept in his 1901 book entitled *Social Control: The Foundations of Order.* Ross served up the idea as an alternative to the assumption that social order rested on the coercive power of government or the narrow self-interest of individuals competing in the marketplace (as the classical criminologists assumed). Ross wanted to understand how the members of a society could "live closely together and associate their efforts with that degree of harmony we see about us," and to show how voluntaristic cooperation led people to perform common endeavors.[21] At the beginning of the book, Ross defined social control as the purposeful attempts to compel deviants within a society to conform to pre-existing patterns of social order.[22]

For criminologists, who had wrested law from the grasp of moral philosophy, it was a concept that made perfect sense. One could not speak of moral conduct, only what a majority of people thought about moral conduct. Their opinions functioned to limit the range of conduct, and when written into law, gained an undeniable legitimacy. They came to view the penitentiary, juvenile court, and the reformatory as institutions of social control and their founders as agents of social control. Eventually, they came to see that social control operated not only through institutions, but social structures such as the market, family relations, and politics. Ross himself had found this more expansive version of the term "social control;" by the middle of the book he referred to all those means, unconscious as well as conscious, by which society tries to order the individuals that make it up.[23] When criminologists thought of social control in general form, they saw something more sinister. Social control represented not the outcome of shared values, but the subject of manipulation.

Criminologists decided that the formal machinery of the criminal law did not merely function to harmonize a few dissonant voices, but to make sure there was only one tune to sing. The agents of social control, and the institutions they created, controlled more than deviants. They policed middle-class values, gender roles, worker discipline, and a wide range of other things.[24] "Is it surprising," French social philosopher Michel Foucault asked in his influential *Discipline and Punish* (1977) "that prisons resemble factories, schools, barracks, hospitals, which all resemble prisons?" When Foucault wrote about the birth of the prison, he concerned himself with power, but not with the kind of power exercised by government. He made Bentham's architectural plans for his panopticon prison into a design for the whole of social existence. He wrote about how "panoptisme" diffused throughout society; no aspect of social existence did not represent social control.[25] In Foucault, social control crossed over from an external influence on individuals into the realm of the unconscious. Foucault saw moral consciousness itself as a fabrication of society, the product of efforts to restrict individual expression. Foucault wanted people to understand that social control can be maintained precisely because the members of a society carry it with them in their minds, and that they are ignorant of their complicity in this pernicious scheme.[26]

Foucault made criminologists feel self-conscious, and in the process, transformed the very idea of moral conduct within criminology. "Responsibility," "sensitivity," "justice," "truth," and "law" — all tokens of ideology, circuits of power in the grand wiring harness of social life. The criminologist, like the doctor, teacher, and lawyer, became a "specific" type of intellectual, engaged in the specific production of knowledge for social control. Criminology as a "learned" discipline failed to explain crime, yet each failure became the rationale for a newer, more insidious means of social control. The real function was to provide a rationalization for the ever-wider grasp of social control through welfare and justice.[27] Criminologists had to realize that they, like the public officials who administered justice, were controllers too. In 1994, when MIT's Gary T. Marx addressed the American Society of Criminology, he described the "maximum-security society."[28] He advised criminologists about their fate with an opening joke:

> There came a time, in the not-too-distant-future, when the guillotine returned to use. As it happened, a priest, a politician, and a criminologist became the first three to be executed.
>
> The priest went first. The executioner positioned him in the device and pulled the cord. But the blade did not fall. The priest stood to his feet, said "It is the will of God," and walked away.
>
> The politician went second. The executioner positioned him in the device and pulled the cord. But the blade did not fall. The politician stood to his feet, said "It is the will of the people," and walked away.
>
> Then it was time for the criminologist. The executioner positioned him in the device and pulled the cord. But the blade did not fall. The criminologist looked up and confidently said, "Hey! I think I can fix that!"

Ethical criminologists redeemed themselves by enlightening controllers, by helping public officials understand how in arresting, prosecuting, and locking up deviants they had deprived society of the self-expression each troubled soul brought to the great mosaic of social life.

Then, John Braithwaite, James Q. Wilson, Marcus Felson and others helped criminologists feel good about themselves again. They distinguished "bad" social control from "good" social control. Bad social control relied on the formal machinery of government—on police, courts, and prisons. Good social control relied on informal sources within communities. The criminal justice system should acknowledge the limitations of official intervention and divert public resources into informal community controls, which were more effective at controlling social behavior. Better that communities control their members than the formal agents of social control step in and impose their values.[29]

When social control became good, criminology became a noble profession once again. The more communities could do for themselves, and the more government could do in the name of community, the better. Public officials rescued lawbreakers from government control by keeping them in the community. They helped organize neighborhood watch programs, citizen patrols, and other forms of friendly control. The agencies of government re-invented themselves; they emphasized community policing, community corrections, and even community courts.[30] Criminologists helped as well. They wrote the grants, did the research, and supplied the facts and figures for public officials charged with complying with community wishes.[31]

Frances T. Cullen, president of the Academy of Criminal Justice Sciences in 1994, anticipated where criminology was going. He offered *social support*, an idea implicit in mainstream sociologies of crime, as an organizing concept for criminology. The idea, reminiscent of Ross's original formulation of social control, pointed out that people avoid crime to the extent that the community, social networks, and neighborhoods meet their material and psychological needs. "An important key to solving the crime problem," Cullen wrote, "is the construction of a supportive social order."[32] If enough common resources flow to areas of need, people will commit fewer crimes, and there will be much less need for harsher measures of government crime control. At the same time, government should prevent crime by means of social policy rather than crime control policy. Social justice expresses criminology's highest ambition. Or as he put it, "good criminology" pursues the "good society."

The Ideal of Social Justice

The ideal of social justice certainly has allure. Some people, by accident of birth, must endure difficult and adverse circumstances. Society should recognize this and take active steps to make things more equal. Yet criminology will not find salvation in social justice.

The trouble with using the concept of social justice as a solution to hurt and pain in the world begins with trying to figure out exactly what it means. Articles and books have been written about social justice without ever defining it. The closest the author of *Social Justice* comes to a definition is to say that it "concerns the distribution of benefits and burdens throughout a society, as it results from major social institutions—property systems, public organizations, etc."[33] But throughout the book, social justice remains an ethereal concept, floating above the pages but never finding expression in the text. This is because, as philosopher Michael Novak points out, attempting to define social justice creates serious intellectual difficulties. The advocates of social justice give it the status of a moral virtue, but most descriptions attach to it impersonal aspects of society such as "inequality of incomes" and "lack of a living wage." Either social justice is a virtue or it is not. If it is, it can be described as the deliberate acts of persons in a society. But most references to social justice are not to the acts of individuals, but aspects of society itself—social structures.[34]

The term "social justice" first appeared in 1840 in the writings of a Sicilian priest, Luigi Taparelli d'Azeglio, but it was the British philosopher John Stuart Mill who gave it its contemporary anthropomorphic appeal. "Society should treat all equally well who have deserved equally well of it... This is the highest abstract standard of social and distributive justice towards which all institutions, and the efforts of virtuous citizens, should be made to the utmost degree to converge."[35] Mill imagined that societies could be virtuous in the same way that individual citizens could be. This may have been possible, Novak observes, in ancient societies ruled by kings who had personal control of their kingdoms. But the demand for social justice did not appear until the age of social science, and the attempt to create a just social order without reference to moral philosophy. In the modern era, persuasion of this sort takes the form of "scientific proof." The leader purports to have correct political proposals, derived from indisputable scientific laws of which the proposals are said to be specific instances.[36] Or, in the case of criminology, empirical data verified by statistical analysis.

"'Social justice' is empty and meaningless," F.A. Hayek observed, because incomes are "partly dependent on accident." Economic rewards are obtained as part of a vast, unplanned system. No person or entity distributes the awards, and no one can prevent their fortunes from being affected by others, including the actions of people in remote corners of the globe. Success or failure in the market depends not only on skill, knowledge and effort, but serendipity, luck, and unforeseen circumstances.[37] The "system of perfect liberty," otherwise known as commercial capitalism, recognizes that sometimes, the well-intentioned, and those who back them, go broke. The government that protects personal liberty cannot pick winners and losers. The economic system that provides for trial-and-error cannot guarantee outcomes in advance; just as people have the right to succeed, they have the right to fail—to purchase lottery tickets, to ignore location when starting a small business, to put their money under a mattress for safe-keeping.[38]

Social justice intimates a "command economy," as Novak puts it, in which individuals are told what to do so that laws can be made to guide what they are told. This notion presupposes social control, the idea that people are led by external directions from social institutions more than government, and by social institutions and government more than an internalized sense of what constitutes just conduct.[39] It cannot tolerate what Oakeshott termed the *morality of individuality*. The morality of individuality recognizes a society of free moral agents, individuals with diverse talents and interests. It recognizes the disposition to make choices for oneself to the maximum possible extent concerning activities, occupations, beliefs, opinions, duties, and responsibilities. It regards self-determined conduct as the conduct appropriate to a human being, and to deprive the individual of the capacity for choice diminishes that moral stature.[40] Social justice requires the *morality of collectivism*, a counterfeit form of an ancient morality based on community ties. Collectivism requires anti-individuals who look to government to make choices they are unwilling to make for themselves. It champions not "liberty" or "self-determination," but "solidarity," "equality," and "the common good." It makes every individual a debtor to society and imposes a debt that can never be repaid.[41]

Social justice exists as an expression of collectivist political ideology. It implies that individuals ought not be held responsible for their relative position. No individual should be thought to have, in any significant way, some responsibility for their position in the lower half of the social hierarchy. To imply such is to engage in victim-blaming. To imply that lawbreakers from impoverished backgrounds retain responsibility for their acts is to express indifference and vengeance. Collectivism seeks a public not accustomed to making moral choices, but who have feelings and impulses rather than thoughts and passions. It seeks citizens who prefer to surrender their rights to a government founded on "the common good" with its managerial activities expressed in the "rule of law."[42] It transforms moral agents into reasoning animals who merit, not fairness, or sanction, or mercy as human beings, but a perverse pity. "Do you see anyone here who could plan a murder, a robbery, can plan—can plan—can plan anything?" Jefferson's public defender asks the jury in Ernest J. Gaines's *A Lesson Before Dying*, "No, gentlemen, this skull here holds no plans...Justice, gentlemen? Why, I would just as soon put a hog in the electric chair as this."[43]

The problem with social justice is that it makes justice an abstraction. It binds everyone but no one in particular. It indulges people in a life without personal responsibility. "It may even be easier and more convenient, and more cowardly to hide oneself among the crowd," Søren Kirkegaard wrote, "in the hope that God should not be able to recognize one from the other."[44]

Moral Philosophy and Crime

Traditional criminology begins by recognizing individual conduct as the basis for moral behavior. *Justice* as an ideal cannot be divorced from *just acts* of individuals. It means that all moral judgments must be made by individuals and judged by individuals, not as part of wholes.[45] Professional criminology cannot sustain its distinction between explanations of criminal behavior and thinking about ethical behavior. Criminologists ought to pursue a unified understanding of morality; criminal conduct on the one side and moral conduct on the other. Or at least Oakeshott and Kierkegaard think so.

MORAL CONDUCT. Michael Oakeshott became the chair of political science at the London School of Economics in 1951. He devoted his professional life to writing two accounts of the moral life, one historical and one philosophical. He attacked the whole post-Enlightenment habit of thought and its attempt to subsume all political activity within a single plan by which the planners claimed the power to re-make the world according to their scheme. He cultivated a respect for custom or tradition as the spring of moral behavior.[46] In outlook, he shared much with Danish philosopher Søren Kirkegaard, the son of a Copenhagen merchant. Although Kirkegaard has been regarded as "the first existentialist," he produced a political philosophy that became quite clear, especially after his death in 1855.[47]

Neither pursued criminology in any deliberate way; Kierkegaard would have deplored what Lombroso and the professional criminologists were up to, if he had known ("Materialistic physiology is comic.")[48] And Oakeshott refused to corrupt his thinking with contemporary political questions. If asked what he thought about Cambridge's Institute for Criminology, he would likely have answered the same way he replied when asked for his thoughts about British entry into the European Community: "I do not find it necessary to hold opinions on such matters."[49] Never-the-less, they provide a moral philosophy of crime that transcends natural law thinking, that avoids the trap of social control, and that brings the airy ideal of social justice down to the realm of human conduct. In their understanding of moral conduct, they provide an understanding of crime, ethics, law, and government.

It begins with an understanding the moral way of life. Oakeshott has written that moral behavior does not come about in society through self-conscious pursuit of an abstract ideal such as "the common good" or "the public good." "Moral ideals are not, in the first place, the products of reflective thought...they are the products of human behavior, of human practical activity, to which reflective thought gives subsequent, partial and abstract expression in words."[50] He described moral behavior as "poetry in the conversation of mankind," by which he meant that moral action does not spring from the deliberate effort to translate reality into some idealized conception of what it ought to be.[51] Moral ideals arise out of habitual behavior: they are what philosophers find "intimated" or implicit in people's perceptions.[52]

Nothing is inherently right or wrong about the differences assigned to individuals by birth into earthly life. To deny that such differences are acceptable is to impose some grand blueprint for humanity, or in the words of Kierkegaard, some concept of "pure humanity." *Pure humanity* represents an attempt to create heaven on earth in the form of a perfect society; an attempt made possible only by destroying each individual's claim to self-determination. Oakeshott denies that fair arrangements in society can begin with a premeditated ideology, with independently acquired ideas about what ends individuals should assume. Moral conduct requires free moral agents, that is, individuals who are accustomed to the responsibility of making moral choices for themselves.[53] This is the problem, he points out, with the concept of natural law when taken to represent a guide to political action rather than as an explanation of political activity.[54]

The moral mode of existence cannot be reduced to human experience, nor can it be adequately expressed in ideas about human experience. A balanced moral tradition is one in which the intellect acts as a critic of the moral tradition. It does not attempt to supplant learned behavior as the originator or spring of conduct because moral behavior rests on the concreteness of individual action. The moral life requires that everyone who shares it understands what they are doing and why, which protects moral tradition from superstition and prejudice. Oakeshott refers to this as a "reflective morality" that engenders a "stable and flexible moral tradition."[55]

Moral eccentrics, those individuals who pursue activities outside the moral tradition, present no threat to this reflective morality. They are understood in the sense that no person can achieve perfection in living the moral life. The threat to reflective morality comes from the profusion of abstract ideals that combine to have a "disintegrating effect upon habit of behavior."[56] Political ideologies, such as "freedom," "equality," "maximum productivity," and "racial purity," lead to a decline in moral conduct. Moral behavior becomes problematic; when action is called for, speculation or criticism will intervene. Moral agents surrender their autonomy to self-appointed moral teachers—philosophers, political leaders, even criminologists—who offer a coherent ideology. Possessing a coherent ideology becomes more important than a ready habit of behavior. "In a world dizzy with moral ideals we know less about how to behave in public and private than ever before..." Oakeshott observes, "The truth is that morality in this form, regardless of the quality of ideals, breeds nothing but distraction and moral instability."[57]

Oakeshott, the philosopher, is content to discuss the form of moral life without discussion of its content. In defining morality, Oakeshott goes no further than his suggestion that conscious moral reflection plays a secondary role. Oakeshott makes no attempt to unravel the springs of human conduct, but is content to "let mystery be."[58] In the simplest terms, moral behavior can be understood as the habits and beliefs that have long persisted within family and community.[59]

Oakeshott the historian, however, does refer to "early Christianity" as the origin of the moral tradition of modern Europe. "In the earliest days, to be a Christian was to be a member of a community animated by a faith and sustained by a hope—faith in a person and hope for a coming event. The morality of these communities was a custom of behavior appropriate to the character of the faith and to the nature of the expectation"[60] While the moral life originating in early Christianity persists, it lost preeminence because it ceased as a habit of conduct and has become an abstract ideal. Oakeshott writes that "A Christian habit of moral behavior was swamped by a Christian moral ideology, and the perception of the poetic character of human conduct was lost."[61] Kierkegaard saw the same thing in the nineteenth century and labored to re-introduce Christianity to Christendom. He railed against the established church in Denmark for its formalism and indifferentism. Christianity as expressed by the Danish church lacked passion, that quality of earnest and sincere faith that characterized early Christianity. In "the present age..." Kierkegaard lamented, "If anyone desires to be a Christian with infinite passion he is judged to be a fool."[62]

LAW AND GOVERNMENT. Both Oakeshott and Kierkergaard preferred limited government to managerial government. Both rejected teleocracratic government in which public officials lay down plans or schemes. The government's function is to lay down neutral rules for citizens to observe while pursuing whatever ends or purposes they choose for themselves. Social order amounts to an unending series of adjustments, in which no overall objective operates, other than fostering the quality of individual lives to the greatest extent possible.[63] Or as Kierkegaard put it, "If everyone is to share in the governing, the state must be very small."

In *On Human Conduct*, Oakeshott distinguished between civil and enterprise association. *Civil association* describes a compulsory association. The rules are not authoritative in themselves, nor do they attempt to bring about some ulterior purpose. Persons within civil association cannot remove themselves from the association, nor can they exempt themselves from the rules. Because civil association seeks no common purpose, persons remain free to choose their own conduct in pursuit of whatever goals they set for themselves. *Enterprise association* is a voluntary association in which the rules are acknowledged in order to achieve some common purpose. Persons may disassociate themselves from enterprise association, but if they choose to participate, they surrender their choice to pursue their own purpose (to the extent that their purpose does not coincide with the common purpose).[64]

Oakeshott preferred civil association as a form of government because he regarded human beings as free moral agents. Since most people acquire their citizenship by birth, civil obligation is not a matter of choice.[65] If the distinguishing feature of living under government is its compulsory character, then it approximates civil association. Misunderstanding government as enterprise authority compromises the choice of moral agents. It denies the only freedom government can guarantee—the freedom to pursue self-determined ends.[66]

Civil association then, is the product of neither a contract (as the classical criminologists supposed) nor shared purpose (as mainstream sociological criminologists think), but can be thought of as a model of conversation. The assent to civil authority approximates a willingness to speak French while in France, as distinguished from approving of the French language or the commitment to speak only certain sentences in French.[67] Because individuals assent to this and nothing more, there is no place for social justice, as understood as governmental scheme, within the rule of law. Social justice requires an overall purpose and rules constructed to attain it; these features are unknown to civil association. Because individuals' assent to civil authority embodies no common purpose, the law cannot be used to bring about a collective result. There can be no scheme, embodied in law, which limits the sentences to be spoken or provides the purpose for public speech.[68]

For Oakeshott, the *rule of law* is a moral practice in which citizens interact in their common acknowledgement of authority, and which the laws articulate obligations without assignment of specific obligations. Oakeshott describes the rule of law in civil association in terms of "non-instrumental rules." In civil association, the rule of law is purposeless or "adverbial" on self-chosen actions. A moral system of law does not prescribe to individuals what they should do, but rather tells them how to do whatever they wish to do.[69] Although a particular law may have the appearance of forbidding or requiring particular purposive activities, Oakeshott insists this is not so. Even "a criminal law, which may be thought to come nearest to forbidding actions, does not forbid killing or lighting a fire, it forbids killing 'murderously' or lighting a fire 'arsonically'."[70]

Kierkegaard pursues a similar understanding of the rule of law. He rejects all attempts at the political leveling of society because they substitute a false sense of equality—the abstract ideal of pure humanity—for the concreteness of individual action. However, since all persons deserve respect regardless of their political or economic status, and regardless of their physical capacities, they are entitled to redress when the interests of other persons, or the group, impinge disrespectfully on their interests. Differences between people become unjust when they lead to disrespect for persons, or when political decisions create differences across classes or groups of individuals. Unjust differences are those that come about from social interaction in which undeserved overcapacities are used to gain advantage over or exploit those with undercapacities, or when political, economic, and cultural structures create differences more broadly. The inequities that ensure from unequal treatment create injustices that ought not survive. The purpose of government is to "watch over the differences," that is, to ensure that individual inequality does not become injustice.[71]

If excessive individualism in the United States "degenerates into a politics justifying either the crass pursuit of rights or materialistic self-aggrandizement,"[72] it did not for Kierkegaard. For Kierkegaard, the individual existed in anxiety. Only a leap of faith could rescue the individual from deep moments of anguish and despair. Nice people, for whom virtue is easy, had best beware. Much is expected from those to whom much is given. The person who mistakes what God gives as the product of his or her own merits has much to answer for. People born into difficult circumstances, saddled with family and personal problems, need not despair. God knows about it, and offers a redemption in which the last will become first.[73]

Not every person, Oakeshott acknowledges, will approve of every law. Those who assent to authority may express their disagreement with one or more rules by means of "politics." Politics in civil association "is concerned with the approval or disapproval of the rules."[74] Persons who express disagreement with the rules by other than political means commit criminal acts when they do not comply with the law. They have not forfeited their citizenship, however, because there is no self-imposed exile in compulsory association. The criminal act does not remove an obligation to comply, it makes the rule-breaker liable to be punished.[75] Legal justice, then, ought not be confused with social justice. Legal justice stipulates the conditions for which punishment must be inflicted ("no penalty without specific offense"), and the procedures for applying the law ("rules not arbitrary, secret, retroactive or awards to interests"). For the administration of justice to maintain an "inner morality," as Oakeshott phrases it, there can be no other purpose for justice in individual cases than justice.[76]

Politics provides a forum in which rules can be removed or introduced while maintaining the civil association. Both Oakeshott and Kierkegaard favored the creation of "new points of departure"—to use Kiekegaard's phrase—under government. Kierkegaard imposed two requirements on political leadership. First, it must be done "religiously." By this he meant that self-appointed leaders ought never use force in an attempt to bring about political change. Leaders should endure suffering, witnessing to the truth, until the other party can no longer hold up in doing wrong and gives up. Second, Kierkegaard insisted that leaders become "unrecognizable," by claiming no authority to lead. The religious individual, Kierkegaard wrote, learns "to be content with himself, and learns instead of dominating others, to dominate himself, content as priest to be his own audience, and as author his own reader," because this expressed a contentment that recognized equality before God. "In antiquity...the outstanding individual was what others *could not be*; the inspiration of modern times will be that any man who finds himself, religiously speaking, has only achieved what *every one can achieve.*"[77]

Conclusion

Second things cannot be obtained by putting them first; second things can only be obtained by putting first things first. Modern criminology has made economic equality, public health, and so on, the primary concerns. But these are second things, not first things. Moral conduct, justice, faith—these are first things. Peace in society cannot be obtained by pursuing social or government schemes for peace; peace in society can be obtained by putting individual moral conduct first.[78]

Notes

Notes for Preface

1. Albert Camus, "On Jean Paul Sartre's *La Nausée*" in *Albert Camus: Lyrical and Critical Essays* (Philip Thody, ed.) New York: Vintage Books, 1970, p. 199.
2. Michael Oakeshott, *Experience and Its Modes*. Cambridge: Cambridge University Press, 1933. See also Josiah Lee Auspitz, "Michal Joseph Oakeshott (1901–1990)" in *The Achievement of Michael Oakeshott* (Jesse Norman, ed.) London: Duckworth, 1993.
3. W. Byron Groves, *Discovering Criminology* (Graeme R. Newman, Michael J. Lynch, David H. Galaty, eds.). New York: Harrow and Heston, 1993.

Notes for Chapter 1

1. Lucy N. Freidman, Susan B. Tucker, Peter Neville, *From Pain to Power: Crime Victims Take Action*. Washington, DC: Office for Victims of Crime, 1998, pp. 9–10; Daniel Van Ness, *Crime and Its Victims*. Downer's Grove, IL: InterVaristy Press, 1986, pp. 32–35; Aurthur J. Lurigio and Patricia A. Resick, "Healing the Psychological Wounds of Criminal Victimization: Predicting Postcrime Distress and Recovery," in *Victims of Crime* (Arthur J. Lurigio, *et al.*, eds.) Newbury Park, CA: Sage, 1990, pp. 58–61.
2. The quote appears in Edward Hallett Carr, *What is History?* New York: Vintage Books, 1961, p. 5.
3. Larry Siegel, *Criminology*. 7d. Belmont, CA: West/Wadsworth, 1998, p. 5.
4. Piers Beirne, *Inventing Criminology: Essays on the Rise of "Homo Criminalis"* Albany: The State University of New York Press, 1993, pp. 233–238.
5. Beirne, *Inventing Criminology*, pp. 233–238.
6. Stephen Jay Gould, *The Mismeasure of Man*, New York: WW Norton, 1981, pp. 135–136.
7. William R. Roalfe, *John Henry Wigmore: Scholar and Reformer*. Evanston: Northwestern University Press, 1977, p. 85.
8. Roalfe, *John Henry Wigmore*, p. 85.
9. Roalfe, *John Henry Wigmore*, p. 85.

10. Nathan Douthit, "August Vollmer, Berkeley's First Chief of Police, and the Emergence of Police Professionalism," *California Historical Quarterly*, 54 (1975), 101–124.

11. Albert Morris, "The American Society of Criminology: A History, 1941–1974," *Criminology* (1975) 123–167.

12. Douthit, "August Vollmer," p. 110.

13. Leon Radzinowicz, "Hermann Mannheim (1889–1974)" in *A History of British Criminology* (Paul Rock, ed.) Oxford: Clarendon Press, 1988, p. 18.

14. Lord Butler, "The Foundation of the Institute of Criminology in Cambridge," in *Crime, Criminology and Public Policy* (Roger Hood, ed.). New York: Free Press, 1974, pp. 1–3.

15. Günther Kaiser, "Criminological Research in the Federal Republic of Germany," *Crime and Justice: An Annual Review*, 5 (1983), 297–310

16. Annika Snare and Ulla Bondeson, "Criminological Research in Scandinavia," *Crime and Justice: An Annual Review* 6 (1985), 237–259.

17. David Biles, "Criminological Research in Australia," *Crime and Justice: An Annual Review* 5 (1983), 235–252.

18. Richard A. Wright. "Sutherland, Edwin H." *Encyclopedia of Criminology*. Sutherland became chair of the sociology department at Indiana University, and in 1935, he joined with Jerome Hall, a law professor, to establish the Institute of Criminal Law and Criminology. In 1939, Sutherland became president of the American Sociological Association (ASA), and four years later, members organized the ASA's criminology section.

19. Edwin Sutherland and Donald R. Cressey, *Principles of Criminology*. (6d) New York: Lippencott, p. 3.

20. Wright, "Sutherland, Edwin A.," p. 2.

21. Jonathan R. Sorensen, Alan G. Widmayer, and Frank R. Scarpitti, "Examining the Criminal Justice and Criminological Paradigms: An Analysis of ACJS and ASC Members," *Journal of Criminal Justice Education*, 5 (1994), pp. 156–158. In 1963, after a series of sociologists presided over the Society, some members of the Society broke away and formed another organization. The new organization, which later became the Academy of Criminal Justice Sciences, returned to Vollmer's emphasis on an eclectic mix of theoretical perspectives. Current statistics for ACJS members reveal the impact of sociology on this organization as well. Membership information for 1999 showed that 34% of members had completed graduate degrees in sociology, 25% in criminal justice, and 11% in criminology. Todd Clear, "President's Message," *ACJS Today* [Academy of Criminal Justice Sciences] 23 (2001), pp. 2–3.

22. John Croft, "Criminological Research in Great Britain, with a Note on the Council of Europe," *Crime and Justice: An Annual Review* 5 (1983), p. 269.

23. Kaiser, "Criminological Research," p. 302.

24. Snare and Bondeson, "Criminological Research in Scandinavia," p. 247.

25. Jonathan H. Turner, "Sociology in the United States: It's Growth and Contemporary Profile,"in *National Traditions in Sociology* (Nikolai Genov, ed.) Newbury Park, CA: Sage, 1989, pp. 223–224. The route to academic respectability had been mapped out as early as 1926 when John L. Gillin used his presidential address to the American Sociological Society to pronounce that "the application of the scientific method and the increasing emphasis on objective data have been acting as selective agents in consigning these enemies of sociology to a deserved innocuous desuetude."

26. Turner, "Sociology in the United States," p. 235.

27. See the opening chapter in Michael Gottfredson and Travis Hirschi, eds., *Positive Criminology*. Newbury Park, CA: Sage, 1987.

28. "...criminologists believe that using the scientific method is more likely to lead to answers to theoretical questions than hunches, guesses or groundless speculations." John H. Laub, "Data for Positive Criminology," in Gottfredson and Hirschi *Positive Criminology,* p. 56.

29. George B. Vold, Thomas J. Bernard, Jeffrey B. Snipes, *Theoretical Criminology*, New York: Oxford University Press, 1998, pp. ix–x.

30. Michael R. Gottfredson and Travis Hirschi, *A General Theory of Crime*. Stanford: Stanford University Press, 1990, pp. 48–49.

31. Gottfredson and Hirschi, *A General Theory*, p. 70.

32. Ronald L. Akers, *Criminological Theories: Introduction and Evaluation*. Los Angeles, CA: Roxbury, 1997, p. 205.

33. Akers, *Criminological Theories*, pp. 207–208.

34. Travis Hirschi, "Exploring Alternatives to Integrated Theory," in *Theoretical Integration in the Study of Deviance and Crime* (Steven F. Messner, Marvin Krohn, and Allen Liska, eds.) Albany: State University of New York Press, 1989, pp. 44–45.

35. Akers, *Criminological Theories*, pp. 219–220.

36. Karl Popper, *Conjectures and Refutations: The Growth of Scientific Knowledge*. Routledge: London, 1963.

37. Pierre Manent, "The Return of Political Philosophy," *First Things*, 103 (May 2000), pp. 15–16.

38. Ralf Dahrendorf, "Max Weber and Modern Social Science," *Max Weber and His Contemporaries* (Wolfgang J. Mommsen and Jürgen Osterhammel, eds). London: Allen and Unwin, 1987, p. 577. "We want to remember," three prominent criminologists assert, "that the search for explanations of criminal behavior is not easy because we must constantly guard against our biases, mistaken perceptions, and prejudices," J. Robert Lilly, Francis T. Cullen, and Richard A. Ball, *Criminological Theory*. Newbury Park, CA: Sage, 1989, p. 17.

39. The University of Florida's Ronald Akers explains that scientific theories about crime represent "statements about relationships between actual events; about *what is* and *what will be*. They are not answers to questions of *what ought to be*, nor are they philosophical, religious, or metaphysical systems of beliefs and values about crime and society." Akers, *Criminological Theories*, p. 2, 9, 12.

40. And maybe not even for scientists. Hayek began his critique with the observation that scientism derived from what social scientists mistook for science; he later came to conclude that what social scientists derived from naturalism could characterize science as well. Fritz Machlup, "Friedrich von Hayek's Contribution to Economics," *Swedish Journal of Economics*, 76 (1974), p. 521.

41. F.A. Hayek, *The Counter-Revolution of Science*. Indianapolis: Liberty-Press, 1979, pp. 47–50.

42. Hayek, *The Counter-Revolution*, p. 255.

43. Hayek, *The Counter-Revolution*, p. 255.

44. Carr, *What is History?* p. 16.

45. Hayek, *The Counter-Revolution*, p. 24.

46. Machlup, "Friedrich von Hayek's," pp. 521–522.

47. For an example of how observing children at play leads to an epistemology, see Albert Bandura. *Social Learning Theory*. Englewood Cliffs, NJ: Prentice-Hall, 1977, pp. 11–12.

48. Marcus Felson, a criminologist at the Rutgers School of Criminal Justice,

wrote a fascinating book about crime. *Crime and Everyday Life* "challenges the conventional 'wisdom' of crime control by demonstrating how often simple and inexpensive changes in the physical environment and patterns of everyday activity can produce substantial decreases in crime rates." Felson advises "those who really want to learn about crime" to "focus on crime itself" and not the "distractions" of "social, political and moral agendas." He advises his readers to "learn everything about crime for its own sake rather than to satisfy ulterior motives, such as gaining political power or religious converts" and "set your agenda aside while you are learning about crime. If your political and religious ideas are worthwhile, they should stand on their own merits." These are not unusual statements. In making them, Felson carries on the fact/value distinction in social science. But he appears to be saying that criminology can really proceed quite nicely without politics or religion. If so, why should anyone bother? The answer cannot be that crime is "wrong" because that would mean that it has something to do with politics, or even religion. Nor can the answer be that a deeper understanding of crime might lead to a better response, because what would "better" mean? Better implies a judgment of value, not a statement about what is. And who, with all due respect, gave Marcus Felson or any criminologist, the right to rearrange people's everyday lives? People might expect that they should have a say in changes that would impact their everyday lives, but bringing up the idea of "rights" has to do with politics and morals and the serious criminologist will have none of it. Social-scientific criminologists have set aside their political agenda for purposes of describing the truth about crime, so their critics should be reasonable enough to set theirs aside as well. They should limit their objections to technical issues and not the "distractions" of "social, political and moral agendas." Marcus Felson. *Crime and Everyday Life*. Thousand Oaks: Pine Forge Press, 1998, back cover, p. 20; Lilly *et al., Criminological Theory*, p. 10.

49. Butler, "The Foundation of the Institute," p. 8.

50. See for example,Lilly *et al.* On p. 10 they say: "Academic criminologists and government officials who formulate crime policy have a professional obligation to set aside their personal biases, read the existing research, and endorse the theory which the evidence most supports." Several pages later, they explain that one must not "decontextualize criminological theory: the very changes in theory that undergird changes in policy are themselves a product of transformations in society," and therefore, advise their readers that "thought be given to how your own context may have shaped your thinking." In other words, you must not object to public policy based on social science evidence; social scientists are decent enough to set their religious and political values aside, you should too. But social scientists have not kept their values out; they use their social science to explain religious and political values by claiming that they are the product of social forces.

51. Vold *et al., Theoretical Criminology*, p. 4.

52. Vold *et al., Theoretical Criminology*, pp. 5–6. The distinction is made by Lilly *et al., Criminological Theory*, pp. 19–22.

53. Phillip E. Johnson, *Darwin on Trial* Downer's Grove, IL: Inter Varsity, 1993, pp. 161–162.

54. Ralph Lerner, "Moses Maimonides 1135–1204" in *History of Political Philosophy* (Leo Strauss and Joseph Cropsey, eds.) Chicago: University of Chicago Press, 1987, pp. 228–247.

55. Frank J. Leavitt, "Commentary on Salvi," *Eubious Journal of Asian and International Bioethics*, 5 (1995), 153–154.

56. Charles E. Hummel, *The Galileo Connection*. Downers Grove, IL: InterVarsity Press, 1986.

57. Simon Sing, *Fermat's Enigma*. New York: Anchor Books, 1997, pp. 20–26. See also, Leonhard Euler, "The Seven Bridges of Konisberg," in *The World of Mathematics* (James R. Newman, ed.). Redmond, WA: Tempest Books, 1998, pp. 565–572.

58. Simon Singh, *Fermat's Enigma*. New York: Anchor Books, 1997, pp. 20–26.

59. This account is taken from Singh, *Fermat's Enigma*, pp. 76–79.

60. Singh, *Fermat's Enigma*, pp. 76–79.

61. Singh, *Fermat's Enigma*, pp. 76–79.

62. Michael Oakeshott, *On History and Other Essays*. Totowa, NJ: Barnes and Noble, 1983.

63. See chapter 6.

64. This summary is taken from Josiah L. Auspitz, "On History and Other Essays," *National Review*, 36 (Feb. 10, 1974), 42–48; see also Nathan Rotenstriech, *Philosophy, History and Politics*. The Hague [Netherlands]: Martinius Nijhoff, 1976, pp. 132–151.

65. Michael Oakeshott, *Rationalism in Politics and Other Essays*. New York: Basic Books, 1962, pp. 72–73.

66. Akers, *Criminological Theories*, p. 11.

Notes for Chapter 2

1. The quotes from Vold's book have been lifted from Bob Roshier, *Controlling Crime: The Classical Perspective in Criminology*. Chicago: Lyceum, 1989, p. 3.

2. Ronald V. Clarke, "Situational Crime Prevention—Everybody's Business," Canberra: Australian Crime Prevention Council, 1995, p. 1. Bertus R. Ferreira, "Situational Crime Prevention and Displacement: The Implications for Business, Industrial, and Private Security Management," *Security Journal*, 6 (1995), 155–162.

3. Piers Beirne, *Inventing Criminology*, Albany: State University of New York Press, 1993, p. 13.

4. See Jefferson's Autobiography in *Thomas Jefferson: Writings* (Merrell D. Peterson, ed.) New York, 1984, p. 39; Paul M. Spurlin, "Beccaria's Essay on Crimes and Punishments in Eighteen Century America," *Studies on Voltaire in the Eighteenth Century*, 27 (1961), pp. 1495, 1501–1502. James Madison, on the other hand, found the book unconvincing and criticized Jefferson for his "Beccarian illusions." Madison, a colleague of Jefferson in the Virginia House of Delegates who later introduced Jefferson's bill, explained to Jefferson that the legislators' believed the elimination of the death penalty for horse thieves to be contrary to the will of the people.

5. See "Enlighted Despotism" in *The Eighteenth Century 1715–1815* (George Rudé, ed.). New York: The Free Press, 1965, pp. 141–149.

6. Beirne, *Inventing Criminology*, p. 19.

7. See the introduction by Henry Paolucci to Cesare Beccaria, *On Crimes and Punishments*. Englewood Cliffs, NJ: Prentice Hall, 1963, p. xv.

8. Douglas Hay, "The Meanings of the Criminal Law in Quebec, 1764–1774," in *Crime and Criminal Justice in Europe and Canada* (Louis A. Knafla, ed.). Waterloo, Ontario: Wilfred Laurier University Press, 1981, p. 96.

9. The account comes from Michel Foucault, *Discipline and Punish.* New York: Vintage Books, 1978, p. 3.

10. Robert Darnton, *The Great Cat Massacre and Other Episodes in French Cultural History.* New York: Vintage Books, 1984, pp. 145–189.

11. Francis Shaeffer, *How Then Should We Live?* Old Tappan, NJ: Fleming H. Revell, 1976, p. 122.

12. Quoted in Michael Oakeshott, *Rationalism in Politics and Other Essays.* New York: Basic Books, 1962, p. 5.

13. Schaeffer, *How Then Should We*, p. 156.

14. Robert L. Heilbronner, *The Worldly Philosophers.* New York: Simon and Schuster, 1980, pp. 40–71.

15. Dennis E. Curtis and Judith Resnick, "Images of Justice," *Yale Law Journal,* 96 (1987) 1727–1772.

16. Beccaria, *On Crimes and Punishments,* p. 93.

17. Jeremy Bentham, "An Introduction to the Principles of Morals and Legislation," in *Classics of Criminology* (Joseph E. Jacoby, ed.) Prospect Heights, IL: Waveland Press, 1979, p. 61.

18. Michael Oakeshott, *Morality and Politics in Modern Europe.* New Haven: Yale University Press, 1993, pp. 73–78.

19. Michael A. Rustigan, "A Reinterpretation of Criminal Law Reform in Nineteenth Century England," *Journal of Criminal Justice,* 8 (1980), p. 207.

20. Job 41.

21. Oakeshott, *Morality and Politics,* pp. 53–54.

22. Ben Rogers, "Portrait: John Rawls," *Prospect* (June 1999). Rawls's second book *Political Liberalism,* contains fifteen articles in which Rawls responds to criticisms of his theory.

23. John Rawls, *A Theory of Justice.* Cambridge: Belknap Press, 1971, pp. 60–64. John Braithwaite and Phillip Petit devised a "Republican" theory of justice reminiscent of Rawls's. "Dominion" expresses the republican ideal of liberty. A person enjoys full dominion if (1) she enjoys no less a prospect of liberty than is available to other citizens, (2) It is common knowledge among citizens that this condition obtains, and (3) she enjoys no less a prospect for liberty than the best that is compatible with the same prospect for others. See John Braithwaite and Phillip Petit, *Not Just Deserts: A Republican Theory of Criminal Justice.* New York: Oxford University Press, 1990.

24. Oakeshott, *Morality and Politics,* pp.56–57.

25. Beccaria, *On Crimes,* pp. 13–15.

26. Cesare Beccaria, "On Crimes and Punishments," in Jacoby, *Classics of Criminology,* p. 212.

27. Rawls, *A Theory of Justice,* pp. 240–241.

28. Rawls, *A Theory of Justice,* pp. 240–241.

29. Roshier, *Controlling Crime,* pp. 10–11.

30. Ira J. Silverman and Manuel Vega, *Corrections: A Comprehensive View.* Minneapolis: West, 1996, p. 501.

31. Alfred H. Holt, *Phrase and Word Origins.* New York: Dover, 1960, p. 100.

32. Douglas Hay, "Property, Authority, and the Criminal Law," in *Albion's Fatal Tree* (Douglas Hay et al. eds.) New York: Pantheon Books, 1975, pp. 17–20.

33. Henry C. Black, *Black's Law Dictionary,* 4d. St. Paul, MN: West, 1968, pp. 200–201.

34. Hay, "Property, Authority," p. 112. By the Act of Congress of April 30,

1790, it was provided, that the benefit of clergy shall not be allowed, upon conviction of any crime, for which, by any statute of the United States, the punishment is, or shall be declared to be, death.

35. Jeremy Bentham, "Panopticon Papers," in *A Bentham Reader* (Peter Mack, ed.) New York: Pegasus, 1969, pp. 189–208. A few Panopticons did appear; the penitentiary at Stateville, Illinois, operated out of four in 1977.

36. Oakeshott, *Morality and Politics*, p. 74.

37. Howard C. Rice, "A French Source of Jefferson's Plan for the Prison at Richmond," *Journal of the Society of Architectural Historians*, 12 (1953) 28–30; John M. Bryan, "Robert Mills, Benjamin Latrobe, Thomas Jefferson, and the South Carolina Penitentiary Project, 1806–1808," *South Carolina Historical Magazine* 85 (1984) 1–21.

38. Agnes A. Gilchrist, "John Haviland Before 1816," *Journal of the Society of Architectural Historians*, 3 (1961) 136–137; Norman B. Johnston, "John Haviland, Jailor to the World," *Journal of the Society of Architectural Historians*, 7 (1965) 101–105.

39. Hay, "Property, Authority," p. 103.

40. Donna J. Spindel, *Crime and Society in North Carolina, 1663–1776*. Baton Rouge: Louisiana State University Press, 1989, p. 35.

41. David A. Jones, *History of Criminology* Westport, CT: Greenwood, 1986, pp. 64–65.

42. Jones, *History of Criminology*, pp. 66–67.

43. David R. Johnson, *American Law Enforcement: A History*. St. Louis: Forum Press, 1981, p. 28.

44. Piers Beirne and James Messerschmidt, *Criminology*, 3d. Boulder, CO: Westview Press, 2000, p. 68.

45. James Q. Wilson, *Thinking About Crime*. New York: Basic Books, 1975.

46. John J. DiIulio, "Help Wanted: Economists, Crime and Public Policy," *Journal of Economic Perspectives*, 10 (1996), p. 16.

47. James Q. Wilson, *Thinking About Crime*. New York: Vintage Books, 1985, p. 121.

48. Wilson, *Thinking About Crime*, p. 260.

49. Gary S. Becker, "Crime and Punishment: An Economic Approach," *Journal of Political Economy*, 76 (1968), 169–217.

50. Gary S. Becker, "The Economics of Crime," *Cross Sections* [Federal Reserve Bank of Richmond] 1995.

51. Gary S. Becker, "Book 'Em," *Hoover Digest* [Hoover Institution] 2 (1999) 1–3.

52. Becker, "The Economics of Crime."

53. James Q. Wilson, "Culture, Incentives, and the Underclass," in *Values in Public Policy* (Henry J. Aaron, Thomas E. Mann, and Timothy Taylor, eds.) Washington, DC: Brookings Institution, 1994, p.56.

54. Derek Cornish and Ronald V. Clarke, *The Reasoning Criminal*. New York: Springer-Verlag, 1986, p. 1.

55. Derek B. Cornish and Ronald V. Clarke, "Understanding Crime Displacement: An Application of Rational Choice Theory," *Criminology* 25 (1987), p. 935.

56. Marcus Felson, *Crime and Everyday Life*. Thousand Oaks, CA: Pine Forge Press, 1998, pp. 179–181.

57. Felson, *Crime and Everyday Life*, p. 181.

58. James R. Lasley and Leslie Rosenbaum, "Routine Activities and Multiple Personal Victimization," *Sociology and Social Research* 73 (1988) 47–50.

59. Ichiro Tanioka, "Evidence Links Smoking to Violent Crime Victimization," *Sociology and Social Research*, 71 (1986), p. 58.

60. Marcus Felson, "Routine Activities and Crime Prevention in the Developing Metropolis," *Criminology* 25 (1987) p. 914.

61. Lawrence Cohen and Marcus Felson, "Social Change and Crime Rate Trends: A Routine Activity Approach," *American Sociological Review* 44 (1979) 588–608.

62. Lee Ellis and Anthony Walsh, "Criminologists' Opinions About Causes and Theories of Crime and Delinquency," *The Criminologist* [American Society of Criminology] 24 (July/Aug. 1999), p. 5.

63. Travis Hirschi and Michael Gottfredson, "Commentary: Testing the General Theory of Crime," *Journal of Research in Crime and Delinquency*, 30 (1993), p. 49.

64. Michael Oakeshott, *Rationalism in Politics*, pp. 1–36.

65. Quoted in Russell Kirk, "Renewing a Shaken Culture," Lecture # 434. Washington, DC: The Heritage Foundation, 1992.

66. Quoted in Oakeshott, *Rationalism in Politics*, p. 28.

67. George M. Fredrickson, *White Supremacy: A Comparative Study in American and South African History.* New York: Oxford University Press, 1981, pp. xi–xii.

68. Bill Lawson, "African-Americans, Crime Victimization, and Political Obligation," in *To be a Victim: Encounters with Crime and Justice* (Diane Sank and David I. Caplan, eds.) New York: Plenum Press, 1991, pp. 141–158.

69. Lawson, "African-Americans," p. 145.

70. Derrick Bell concludes that it would have made no difference — things would have went just as bad for Black people even if they had participated in the original position. In the "Parable of the Constitutional Contradiction," he imagines a scenario in which Geneva Crenshaw, the personification of the great civil rights lawyers, journeys back in time. She returns to Independence Hall to convince the founders that they are about to make a big mistake by agreeing to the three-fifths compromise. They should abolish slavery and avoid the Civil War. Bell thinks that they would have decided to preserve slavery anyway: it had generated the wealth that made independence possible and was necessary to secure ratification by the southern states. After arguing with her about the need to preserve slavery as a political expedient, they would have kicked her out because as a Black woman she was out of her place. Derrick Bell, *And We Are Not Saved.* New York: Basic Books, 1987.

71. Rawls defines civil disobedience as "the public, nonviolent, conscientious yet political act contrary to law usually done with the aim of bringing about a change in the law or policies of the government." Rawls, *A Theory of Justice*, p. 264.

72. Quoted in Mary Beth Rogers, *Barbara Jordan: American Hero.* New York: Bantam Books, 1998, p. 214.

73. Alan Keyes, "The Declaration of Independence and the Spirit of the Law," President's Day Lecture. Santa Paula, CA: Thomas Aquinas College, February 21, 1997.

74. Wendell John Coats, *Oakeshott and His Contemporaries.* Selinsgrove: Susquehanna University Press, 2000, pp. 89–102.

75. Michael Oakeshott, *On History and Other Essays.* Totowa, NJ: Barnes and Noble, 1983, pp. 165–194.

76. Auspitz, "On History and Other Essays," p. 44.
77. J.H. Ahn, "Michael Oakeshott, R.I.P." *National Review*, 43 (Jan. 28, 1991), p. 19.
78. Quoted in Russell Kirk, "The Meaning of 'Justice'" Heritage Lecture 457. Washington, DC: Heritage Foundation, 1993.

Notes for Chapter 3

1. Stephen J. Gould, *The Mismeasure of Man*. New York: W.W. Norton, 1981, p. 123.
2. Nicole H. Rafter, *Creating Born Criminals*. Urbana: University of Illinois Press, 1997, p. 111.
3. Nicole H. Rafter, "Criminal Anthropology in the United States," *Criminology*, 30 (1992), pp. 525–546.
4. Randy Martin, Robert J. Mutchnick, and W. Timothy Austin, *Criminological Thought: Pioneers Past and Present*. New York: Macmillan Publishing, 1990, p. 23.
5. Martin *et al.*, *Criminological Thought*, pp. 22–23.
6. Quoted in Ian Taylor, Paul Walton and Jock Young, *The New Criminology*. New York: Harper and Row, 1973, p. 41.
7. Gould, *The Mismeasure of Man*, pp. 114–115.
8. Martin *et al.*, *Criminological Thought*, pp. 29–31.
9. Lee Ellis, "Introduction: The Nature of the Biosocial Perspective," in *Crime in Biological, Social, and Moral Contexts* (Lee Ellis and Harry Hoffman, eds). New York: Praeger, 1990, pp. 3–17; Pauline S. Yaralian and Adrian Raine, "Biological Approaches to Crime: Psychophysiology and Brain Dysfunction," in *Explaining Criminals and Crime* (Raymond Paternoster and Ronet Rachman, eds.) Los Angeles: Roxbury, 2001; James Q. Wilson and Richard J. Herrnstein, *Crime and Human Nature*. New York: Simon and Schuster, 1985, esp. pp. 69–103.
10. Kenneth Moyer, "What is the potential for biological violence control?" in *Biology and Crime* (C.R. Jeffrey, ed.) Beverly Hills, Calif.: Sage, 1979, p. 23.
11. Ferri's concept of social responsibility later found expression in the concept of *social defence*. Social defence, which became a section of the United Nations Organization in 1948, expresses the goal of criminal law not as sanctioning a conscious violation of a rule, but at protecting society against criminal acts. It advocated prevention and treatment of criminals through social institutions outside the legal system, based on the "scientific understanding of the phenomenon of crime and the offender's personality." In the words of Marc Ancel, who wrote *Social Defence* in 1954, "social defence recalls the positivist revolt against the traditional criminal law." Marc Ancel, "Social Defence," in *Classics of Criminology* (Joseph E. Jacoby, ed). Prospect Heights, IL: Waveland Press, 1979, pp. 215–216.
12. Martin *et al.*, *Criminological Thought*, pp. 29–31, 38–39.
13. Martin *et al.*, *Criminological Thought*, pp. 32–40.
14. Quoted in Stuart M. Persell, "Jean de Lanessan and the French Positivist School of Criminal Reform, 1880–1914," *Criminal Justice Review* 12 (1987), p. 4.
15. David A. Jones, *History of Criminology*. New York: Greenwood Press, 1986, pp. 98, 101, 103, 105.

16. Diana Fishbein, "Biological Perspectives in Criminology," *Criminology* 28 (1990), pp. 30–31.

17. James Q. Wilson, *Moral Judgement: Does the Abuse Excuse Threaten Our Legal System?* New York: Basic Books, 1997, pp. 24–28.

18. Quetelet, the Belgian astronomer and mathematician, pursued a similar view from a statistical perspective. After calculating the average height and weight by age and sex, Quetelet invoked the normal curve. The "average man" deviated only slightly from the mean, but that suggested those with unsual deviation. Using the same normal curve, he concluded that the "average man" possessed a certain inclination to break the laws, but that there were statistical deviates predisposed to crime, the vagabonds, vagrants, gypsies: those "inferior classes" of "inferior moral stock." He concluded that these represented biological defects transferred by heredity. He began to make anthropometric measurements of the body, particularly the head; measurements that were popularized five years later by Lombroso. Piers Beirne, *Inventing Criminology*. Ablany: State University of New York Press, 1993, pp. 89–90.

19. Jones, *History of Criminology*, p. 107.

20. Martin *et al.*, *Criminological Thought*, pp. 126–127; Jones, *History of Criminology*, pp. 108–109.

21. Martin *et al.*, *Criminological Thought*, pp. 119–135.

22. David T. Lykken, *A Tremor in the Blood.* New York: McGraw Hill, 1981.

23. S. Stansfield Sargent and Kenneth R. Stafford. *Basic Teachings of the Great Psychologists.* Garden City, NY: Dilphin Books, 1965, p. 200.

24. Patricia A. Brennan, Sarnoff A. Mednick, and Jan Volavka, "Biomedical Factors in Crime," in *Crime* (James Q. Wilson and Joan Petersilia, eds). San Francisco, Calif,: ICS Press, 1995, pp. 83–84.

25. Leonard Savitz, Stanley H. Turner, and Toby Dickman, "The Origin of Scientific Criminology: Franz Joseph Gall as the First Criminologist," in *Theory in Criminology: Contemporary Views* (Robert F. Meier, ed.). Beverly Hills, Calif.: Sage, 1977, p. 43.

26. Savitz *et al.,* "The Origin of Scientific," p. 46.

27. Jones, *History of Criminology*, p. 137.

28. Sargent and Stafford, *Basic Teachings*, p. 86.

29. Gould, *The Mismeasure of Man*, pp. 86–87.

30. Gould, *The Mismeasure of Man*, p. 83.

31. Martin *et al.*, *Criminological Thought*, p. 23.

32. Gould, *The Mismeasure of Man*, pp. 94–95.

33. James Gleick, *Genius: The Life and Science of Richard Feynman.* New York: Pantheon Books, 1992, p. 311–312.

34. Sargent and Stafford, *Basic Teachings*, pp. 201–202.

35. Victor Milstein and Larue D. Carter, "EEG Topography in Patients with Aggressive Violent Behavior," in *Biological Contributions to Crime Causation* (T.E. Moffitt and S.A. Mednick, eds). Boston: Martinus Nijhoff Publishers, 1988, pp. 40–52.

36. Sargent and Stafford, *Basic Teachings*, pp. 93–94.

37. Del Thiessen, "Hormonal Correlates of Sexual Aggression," in *Crime in Biological, Social*, pp. 154–155.

38. Thiessen, "Hormonal Correlates," p. 157. Although there are side effects, such as fatigue, depression, and headaches, they are considered less unpleasant than large doses of female hormone, estrogen. Estrogen, when administered to men, results in loss of body hair and growing of breasts. Jon

Zonderman, *Beyond the Crime Lab: The New Science of Investigation*. New York: John Wiley, 1990, pp. 180–182.

39. Julie Horney, "Menstrual Cycles and Criminal Responsibility," in *Biology, Crime and Ethics* (Frank H. Marsh and Janet Katz, eds.). Cincinnati, OH: Anderson, 1985, pp. 159–175.

40. Robert Prentky, "The Neurochemistry and Neuroendocrinology of Sexual Aggression," in *Aggression and Dangerousness* (David P. Farrington and John Gunn, eds.) New York: John Wiley and Sons, 1985, pp. 7–56.

41. Rafter, *Creating Born Criminals*, p. 155.

42. Persell, "Jean De Lanessan," pp. 1–6. To restore a healthy society, Lanessan prescribed the government provide a regimented environment for youth, compulsory school attendance, lessons in civic virtue and quasi-military training. He advocated that judges examine the individual circumstances in dealing with young criminals. Judges must examine each case carefully before finding for transportation to prison colonies of Guyana and New Caledonia.

43. Rafter, *Creating Born Criminals*, pp. 36, 59, 85.

44. Nicole H. Rafter, *White Trash: The Eugenic Family Studies 1877–1919*. Boston: Northeastern University Press, 1988, pp. 1–4.

45. Rafter, *Creating Born Criminals*, p. 38; Rafter, *White Trash*, 1988, 33–34.

46. Since the man had produced both good and bad lines, Goddard combined the Greek words for "beauty" (kallos) and "bad" (kakos), and gave him the psueodonym, Kallikak. Gould, *The Mismeasure of Man*, p. 168.

47. Rafter, *White Trash*, pp. 18–26.

48. Ratfer, *White Trash*, pp. 18–26; Gould, *The Mismeasure of Man*, pp. 168–169.

49. Lykken, *The Anti-Social Personalities*, p. 89.

50. Except in what became the Soviet Union. Lamarckism was advanced by Soviet biologist T.D. Lysenko, who denied the presence of genes and chromosomes in heredity. Lysenko insisted that all parts of an organism take part in heredity, that they are changed by their environment, and passed on in the form of a changed offspring.

51. Weismann's germ plasm theory rejected Larmarckism; Weismann taught that germ plasm was not affected by environmentally induced changes.

52. Fishbein, "Biological Perspectives," pp. 27–72.

53. Sargent and Stafford, *Basic Teachings*, pp. 49–50.

54. Wilson and Herrnstein, *Crime and Human Nature*, pp. 90–92.

55. Wilson and Herrnstein, *Crime and Human Nature*, pp. 95–98.

56. Thomas Regulus, "Race, Class, and Sociobiological Perspectives on Crime," in *Ethnicity, Race and Crime* (Darnell F. Hawkins, ed.). Albany: State University of New York Press, 1995, pp. 46–65. See also Glenn D. Walters and Thomas W. White, "Heredity and Crime: Bad Genes or Bad Research?" *Criminology* 27 (1989), pp. 455–486; Patricia A. Brennan and Sarnoff A. Mednick, "A Reply to Walters and White: 'Heredity and Crime'" *Criminology* 28 (1990), 657–662; Glenn D. Walters, "Heredity, Crime and the Killing-the-Bearer-of-Bad-News Syndrome: A Reply to Brennan and Mednick," 28 *Criminology* (1990), pp. 663–667.

57. Fishbein, "Biological Perspectives," p. 42; Adrian Raine, *The Psychopathology of Crime*. San Diego: Academic Press, 1993, p. 48.

58. Avery A. Sandberg et al., "XYY Genotype," *New England Journal of Medicine*, 268 (1963), p. 587.

59. Named after Langdon Down, who first described the syndrome, the effect used to be referred to as mongolism, because persons affected tend to have

almond-shaped eyes. The probability of Down's syndrome increases with the age of the parents at conception, the older the mother, the greater the risk, but is highest for teenage mothers.

60. Jones, *A History of Criminology*, p. 124.

61. Brennan, "Biomedical Factors," pp. 89–90.

62. Richard J. Herrnstein, "Criminogenic Traits," in *Crime* (James Q. Wilson and Joan Petersilia, eds). San Francisco, Calif.: ICS Press, 1995, p. 61.

63. Fishbein, "Biological Perspectives," p. 42.

64. See the exchange between Austin Hughes and Tom Bethell in *First Things* 112 (2001), 2–3.

65. James Gleick, *Chaos:Making a New Science*. New York: Penguin Books, 1987, prologue.

66. James R. Newman, "Commentary on Sir Francis Galton," in *The World of Mathematics*, Redmond, WA: Tempus, 1988, pp. 1142–1143.

67. Galton conducted the first systematic study of fingerprints and created a system for classifying them for filing. In *Finger Prints* (1892) Galton described the basic principles for identification and presented statistical proof supporting his idea that as unique, they could be used for identification Richard Saferstein, *Criminalistics: An Introduction to Forensic Science*. Englewood Cliffs, N.J.: Prentice Hall, 1987, p. 4.

68. Sargent and Stafford, *Basic Teachings*, pp. 13–14.

69. Gould, *The Mismeasure of Man*, pp. 148–149.

70. Gould, *The Mismeaure of Man*, pp. 155–157.

71. Rafter, *Creating Born Criminals*, p. 40. Edwin Sutherland recognized the flaws in Goddard's methods in 1931. Sutherland's criminology text refuted Goddard's findings and argued that the deficiency did not lie in those with low intelligence quotients, but in the testing procedure itself. Wilson and Herrnstein, *Crime and Human Nature*, p. 153.

72. Travis Hirschi and Michael Hindelang, "Intelligence and Delinquency: A Revisionist View," *American Sociological Review*, 42 (1977), pp. 571–587.

73. Gould, *The Mismeasure of Man*, pp. 151–152.

74. Richard J. Herrnstein and Charles Murray, *The Bell Curve*. New York: Free Press, 1994; Charles Murray and Richard J. Herrnstein, "Race, Genes and IQ—An Apologia," *The New Republic*, Oct. 31 (1994), pp. 35–37.

75. Stephen Jay Gould, "Curveball," in *The Bell Curve Wars* (Steven Fraser, ed.). New York: Basic Books, 1995, pp. 17, 22; Francis T. Cullen, *et al.* "Crime and the Bell Curve: Lessons From Intelligent Criminology," *Crime and Delinquency* 43 (1997) 387–411.

76. Mark Haller, *Eugenics: Hereditarian Attitudes in American Thought*. New Burnswick, NJ: Rutgers University Press, 1963.

77. Jenkins, "Eugenics, Crime and Ideology," p. 69.

78. Rafter, *Creating Born Criminals*, pp. 101–102.

79. Gould, *The Mismeasure of Man*, pp. 165–166.

80. Jon Beckwith, "Social and Political Uses of Genetics in the United States: Past and Present," in *Biology, Crime and Ethics* (Frank H. Marsh and Janet Katz, eds.) Cincinnati, OH: Anderson, 1985, p. 319.

81. Rafter, *Creating Born Criminals*, p. 126.

82. Rafter, *Creating Born Criminals*, p. 63.

83. Rafter, *Creating Born Criminals*, p. 126.

84. Philip Jenkins, "Eugenics, Crime and Ideology: The Case of Progressive Pennsylvania," *Pennsylvania History* 51 (1984), p. 71

85. Rafter, *Creating Born Criminals*, p. 155.

86. Nancy L. Gallagher, *Breeding Better Vermonters: The Eugenics Project in the Green Mountain State*. Hanover: University Press of New England, 1999.

87. Philip Jenkins, "Eugenics, Crime and Ideology," p. 68.

88. Rafter, *Creating Born Criminals*, p. 153.

89. Rafter, *Creating Born Criminals*, p. 228.

90. Beckwith, "Social and Politica," p. 318.

91. Fred D. Ragan, "Buck v. Bell," in *The Oxford Companion to the Supreme Court of the United States* (Kermit L. Hall, ed.) New York: Oxford University Press, pp. 98–99. See also, Paul A. Lombardo, "Three Generations, No Imbeciles: New Light on *Buck v. Bell*," *New York Law Review* 60 (April 1985), pp. 30–62.

92. Jeremy Noakes, "Social Outcasts in the Third Reich," in *Life in the Third Reich* (Richard Bessel, ed.) New York: Oxford University Press, 1987, p.94.

93. Richard Moran, "Biomedical Research and the Politics of Crime Control," in *Biology, Crime and Ethics* (Frank H. Marsh and Janet Katz, eds.). Cincinnati, OH: Anderson, 1985, p. 329.

94. Gina Lombroso-Ferrero, "Criminal Man," in *Classics of Criminology* (Joseph E. Jacoby, ed). Prospect Heights, IL: Waveland Press, 1979, p. 84.

95. James H. Jones, *Bad Blood: The Tuskegee Syphilis Experiment*. New York: Free Press, 1981, p. 23.

96. Rafter, *White Trash*, 1988, p. 8.

97. Jenkins, "Eugenics, Crime and Ideology," p. 74.

98. Hooton, *The American Criminal*, pp. 93, 309.

99. Frank Fitzpatrick, *And the Walls Came Tumbling Down: Kentucky, Texas Western, and the Game that Changed American Sports*. New York: Simon and Schuster, 1999, p. 58.

100. Although there are a few that do: J. Phillipe Rushton, *Race, Evolution and Behavior*. Somerset, NJ: Transaction Publishers, 1999. Herrnstein and Murray avoid any discussion of sterilization, but do suggest altering immigration policies and the establishment of internment camps for the "cognitive underclass." "In short, what we have in mind is a high-tech and more lavish version of the Indian reservation for some substantial minority of the nation's population while the rest of America tries to go about its business. Quoted in Gould, "Curve Ball," p. 21. Rushton recognizes the parallel between his race science and that of the Nazis but contends that they used their knowledge for bad purposes, and he wants to use it for good purposes. "Science...is objective," Rushton concludes, "It can't give us our goals...[but] knowing more about race differences may help us to give every child the best possible education and help us to understand some of our chronic social problems better." Rushton, *Race, Evolution and Behavior*, p. 105.

101. In 1992, the National Institute of Health withdrew funds for a conference to explore the relationship between genetics and crime to be held at the University of Maryland. The theme of the conference raised concern about the search for the crime gene in general, and the racial implications of the study in particular. NIMH researcher Frederick Goodwin, the spokesperson for the initiative, compared the inner city to a jungle and inner-city Black youth to rhesus monkeys who are predatory and excessively focused on sex. C. Ray Jeffrey, a Florida State University criminologist, decried the suppression of the conference noting that scientific research can always be misused for political purposes. He denied the racial implications of the research insisting that genetics determines individual behavior, not the behavior of a group as "genetically mixed" as African Americans. He then argued that genetic research would

benefit African Americans. "Over 90 percent of the violence in the black community is by blacks against blacks. If clues as to the causes of violence can be found in brain structure and neurotransmitter systems, then these studies would primarily benefit the black community." Katheryn K. Russell, "Development of a Black Criminology and the Role of the Black Criminologist," *Justice Quarterly* 9 (1992), p. 670, note 7; C. Ray Jeffrey, "Genetics, Crime and the Cancelled Conference," *The Criminologist*, 18 (Jan./Feb. 1993), pp. 1, 6–7.

102. Biologist Stephen Jay Gould refers to his description of the criminality of insects as "the most ludicrous excursion into anthropomorphism ever published." Gould, *The Mismeasure of Man*, p. 125.

103. Fishbein, "Biological Perspectives," p. 31.

104. James Q. Wilson, *The Moral Sense*, New York: Free Press, 1993, p. 24.

105. James Q. Wilson, "The Moral Sense," Presidential Address to the American Political Science Association, 1992. Printed in *American Political Science Review*, 87 (1993), p. 1–9.

106. Wilson, *The Moral Sense*, p. 24.

107. Wilson, "The Moral Sense," p. 2.

108. Wilson, *The Moral Sense*, p. 23.

109. Tom Bethell, "Against Sociobiology," *First Things*, 109 (2001), p. 19. I took the basic argument here from Bethell's article.

110. Wilson, *The Moral Sense*, p. 23.

111. Wilson, *The Moral Sense*, p. 123. Wilson appears to be aware of this problem, although he appears to be talking about how the evidence of moral behavior ought to be interpreted rather than the larger problem of trying to use human behavior as evidence of his explanation for human behavior. See his preface, p. xiv.

112. Bethell, "Against Sociobiology," p. 23.

113. The reference to Kipling's fiction in critique of evolutionary biology can be found in Bethell, "Against Sociobiology," p. 21.

114. Wilson, *The Moral Sense*, p. 251.

115. Wilson, *The Moral Sense*, p. xv.

116. Darwin made this statement in a letter to W. Graham quoted in *The Autobiography of Charles Darwin and Selected Letters* (1892; reprint New York: Dover, 1958). It is quoted here courtesy of James W. Sire, *The Universe Next Door*. Downer's Grove, IL: InterVarsity, 1997, p. 83; see also footnote 17 on p. 210.

117. Bethell, "Against Sociobiology," pp. 18–19. See also, Richard C. Lewontin, "The Fallacy of Biological Determinism," *The Sciences*, (March/April 1976), 6–10.

118. Bethell, "Against Sociobiology," pp. 19–20.

119. Mike Perry, "H.G. Wells, C.S. Lewis and the Evolutionary Myth," Seattle, WA: The Discovery Institute, 1998.

120. The point is made by C.S. Lewis, "On Living in an Atomic Age," in *Present Concerns* (Walter Hooper, ed.) San Diego: Harcourt Brace Jovanovich, 1986.

121. Thomas S. Kuhn, *The Structure of Scientific Revolutions*. 2d. Chicago: University of Chicago, 1970, p. 2.

Notes for Chapter 4

1. William F. Bynum, "Rationales for Therapy in British Psychiatry, 1780–1835," *Medical History* 18 (1964), pp. 322–323.

2. Lucille B. Ritvo, *Darwin's Influence on Freud.* New Haven: Yale University Press, 1990, p. 113.

3. Bynum, "Rationales for Therapy," p. 318.

4. J.N. Isbister, *Freud: An Introduction to His Life and Work.* Cambridge: Polity Press, 1985, p. 47.

5. Isbister, *Freud*, p. 54.

6. Isbister, *Freud*, p. 48.

7. Isbister, *Freud*, p. 53.

8. Isbister, *Freud*, p. 58.

9. "The theory of repression," Freud later wrote, "is the cornerstone on which the whole structure of pyscho-analysis rests." See Ritvo, *Darwin's Influence on Freud*, p. 187.

10. Robert W. Lundin, *Theories and Systems of Psychology*, Lexington, Mass.: D.C. Heath, 1979, p. 269.

11. Lundin, *Theories and Systems*, pp. 269–270.

12. Lundin, *Theories and Systems*, p. 272.

13. Lundin, *Theories and Systems*, pp. 275–277.

14. Lundin, *Theories and Systems*, pp. 277–278.

15. Lundin, *Theories and Systems*, p. 270. August Aichhorn, a prominent psychoanalyst, developed an explicitly psychoanalytic theory of delinquency in his *Wayward Youth* (1936). Aichorn explained delinquency as the expression of feelings youth could not express in some other socially-approved way. See Joseph E. Jacoby, *Classics of Criminology.* Prospect Heights, IL: Waveland Press, 1979, pp. 58, 120–124.

16. David A. Jones, *History of Criminology.* New York: Greenwood Press, 1986, p. 146.

17. Nicole H. Rafter, "Psychopathy and the evolution of criminological knowledge," *Theoretical Criminology*, 1 (1997), p. 236.

18. David T. Lykken. *The Antisocial Personalities.* Hillsdale, NJ: Lawrence Erlbaum Associates, 1995, p. 113.

19. Rafter, "Psychopathy and the evolution," p. 242.

20. Quoted in Nicole H. Rafter, *Creating Born Criminals.* Urbana: University of Illinois Press, 1997, p. 175.

21. Rafter, *Creating Born Criminals*, pp. 176–182.

22. Jones, *History of Criminology*, pp. 145–146.

23. Estelle B. Freedman, " 'Uncontrolled Desires': The Response to the Sexual Psychopath, 1920–1960," *Journal of American History* 74 (1987), p. 91.

24. Hervey Cleckley, *The Mask of Sanity* (Rev. Ed). St. Louis, C.V. Mosby, 1982, p. 204.

25. Robert D. Hare, "A Research Scale for Assessment of Psychopathy in Criminal Populations," *Personality and Individual Differences*, 1 (1980), pp. 111–119.

26. Quoted in Michael H. Stone, *Abnormalities of Personality.* New York: W.W. Norton, 1993, p. 282.

27. Robert Hare, *Psychopathy: Theory and Research.* New York: Wiley, 1970.

28. Gisli H. Gudjonsson and Joanna C. Roberts, "Psychological and Physiological Characteristics of Personality Disordered Patients," in *Aggression and Dangerousness* (David P. Farrington and John Gunn, eds). New York: John Wiley, 1985, pp. 81–102. Researchers have reported that the brain waves of psychopaths are abnormal, with "psychopath" and "abnormal" being defined in different ways. Hare has noticed a similarity between the brain wave activity of psychopaths and children. He offers the maturation lag hypothesis to explain this similarity, suggesting that brain functioning within the psychopath is childlike. See Hare, *Psychopathy*.

29. Lykken, *The Antisocial Personalities*, pp. 134, 116. Lykken "would classify Roy Cohn and Lyndon Johnson as primary psychopaths and yet they both followed life plans with great success," p. 143.

30. Lykken, *The Antisocial Personalities*, p. 113.

31. Stone, *Abnormalities of Personality*, p. 301.

32. Lykken, *The Antisocial Personalities*, pp. 3–4.

33. Lykken, *The Antisocial Personalities*, pp. 5–6.

34. John J. DiIulio, "White Lies About Black Crime," *The Public Interest* (1995) 30–44.

35. John J. DiIulio, "The Coming of the Superpredators," *The Weekly Standard* [Washington, DC], Nov. 27, 1995, p. 25.

36. Earl E. Appleby, "An Evolving Juvenile Court: On the Front Lines with Judge J. Dean Lewis," *Juvenile Justice* 6 (1999) p. 9; Howard N. Snyder and Melissa Sickmund, "Challenging the Myths," *1999 National Report Series*. Washington, DC: Office of Juvenile Justice and Delinquency Prevention, 2000, p. 1.

37. Stone, *Abnormalities of Personality*, p. 216.

38. Stone, *Abnormalities of Personality*, p. 258.

39. Patrick L.G. Gallwey, "The Psychodynamics of Borderline Personality," in Farrington and Gunn, *Aggression and Dangerousness*, pp. 130–131.

40. James Alan Fox and Jack Levin, "Multiple Homicide: Patterns of Serial and Mass Murder," *Crime and Justice: A Review of Research*, 23 (1998) pp. 420–421.

41. Fox and Levin, "Multiple Homicide," pp. 421–423.

42. Lee Robins, J. Tipp and T. Przybeck, "Antisocial personality" in *Psychiatric Disorders in America* (Lee Robins and D. Regier, eds.). New York: Macmillan, 1991.

43. Katharine Browning et al., "Causes and Correlates of Delinquency Program," *OJJDP Fact Sheet #100*. Washington, DC: Office of Juvenile Justice and Delinquency Prevention, 1999.

44. Rolf Loeber and Marc LeBlanc, "Toward a Developmental Criminology," *Crime and Justice: A Review of Research* 12 (1990), pp. 375–473 and Marc Le Blanc and Rolf Loeber, "Developmental Criminology Updated," *Crime and Justice: A Review of Research,* 23 (1998), pp. 115–198.

45. Barbara T. Kelley, Rolf Loeber, Kate Keenan, and Mary DeLamatre, "Developmental Pathways in Boys' Disruptive and Deliquent Behavior," *Juvenile Justice Bulletin*. Washington, DC: Office of Juvenile Justice and Delinquency Prevention, 1997; Katharine Browning and Rolf Loeber, "Highlights of Findings from the Pittsburgh Youth Study," *Fact Sheet*. Washington, DC: Office of Juvenile Justice and Delinquency Prevention, 1999.

46. Loeber and LeBlanc, "Toward a Developmental," p. 387.

47. Kelley *et al.*, "Developmental Pathways," pp. 10–13.

48. One of the major issues in whether intoxication should be a mitigating or aggravating factor is determining the culpability of a criminal defendant. See James Q. Wilson, *Moral Judgement: Does the Abuse Excuse Threaten Our Legal System?* New York: BasicBooks, 1997.

49. Alan D. Watson, "The Constable in Colonial North Carolina," *North Carolina Historical Review*, 68 (1991), p. 10.

50. Chester N. Mitchell, "The Intoxicated Offender-Refuting the Legal and Medical Myths," *International Journal of Law and Psychiatry*, 11 (1998), p. 80.

51. J.J. Tobias, *Nineteenth Century Crime in England: Prevention and Punishment*. New York: Barnes and Noble, 1972, p. 13.

52. Glenn E. Rohrer, Brian A. McMillen, and Joyce G. Reed, "Calculation of Blood Alcohol Concentration in Criminal Defendants," *American Journal of Trial Advocacy* 22 (1998) 177–190.

53. Mitchell, "The Intoxicated Offender," p. 84. This has led some criminologists to conclude that despite all the research, not enough is known to discount the possibility that the crime-alcohol connection is spurious. See James Q. Wilson and Richard Herrnstein, *Crime and Human Nature*, New York: Basic Books, 1985, p. 357. The crime-alcohol connection appears to be supported by statistics indicating the proportion of known criminal activities involving drug use. This may be as high as 50%. But to judge whether alcohol intoxication leads to crime requires the opposite statistic, the portion of drunken events that involve serious criminal activity. A large portion of Americans consume alcohol regularly, and millions become legally intoxicated without breaking the law. It is difficult to say that intoxication leads to crime because a large percentage of those who break the law were intoxicated when the largest percentage of those who become intoxicated do not break the law. See Mitchell, "The Intoxicated Offender," p. 89.

54. Henry O. Whiteside, "The Drug Habit in Nineteenth-century Colorado," *The Colorado Magazine* 55 (1978), p. 55.

55. Isbister, *Freud*, pp. 33–35.

56. Frederick Allen, *Secret Formula: How Brilliant Marketing and Relentless Salesmanship made Coca-Cola the Best-Known Product in the World*. New York: HarperBusiness, 1994, p. 23. Pemberton died (not long after perfecting Coca-Cola) of a stomach disorder complicated, perhaps, by a cocaine habit. He had suffered from gastroenteritis for some time, and cocaine available in liquid form on his pharmacy shelves would have provided relief. Whether Doc Pemberton was a "dope fiend" as two disgruntled employees claimed, his son, was an addict. Charley Pemberton died in 1894 of an overdose of opium. See the footnote on p. 29.

57. Diana H. Fishbein and Susan E. Pease, "Neurological Links Between Substance Abuse and Crime," in *Crime in Biological, Social and Moral Contexts* (Lee Ellis and Harry Hoffman, eds.). New York: Praeger, 1990, pp. 218–246.

58. Alan I. Leshner, "Addiction is a Brain Disease—and It Matters," *National Institute of Justice Journal*, 237 (1998), pp. 2–6.

59. Mitchell, "The Intoxicated Offender," p. 85.

60. Mitchell, "The Intoxicated Offender," p. 86.

61. Wouter Buikhuisen, Corry van der Plas-Korenhoff, and Elisabeth H.M. Bontekoe, "Alcohol and Violence," in *Biological Contributions to Crime Causation* (Terrie E. Moffitt and Sarnoff A. Mednick, eds.). Boston: Martinus Nijhoff Publishers, 1988, pp. 264, 273.

62. Jeffrey Fagan, "Intoxication and Aggression," *Crime and Justice: A Review of Research* 13 (1990), pp. 261, 291. Other psychoanalytic explanations

for addiction explain substance abuse as a substitute for sexual pleasure or as a fixation at the oral or other stage of psychosexual development. Addiction may be the expression of unmet needs for love, of ambivalent feelings toward parents, or self-destructive drives, p. 304.

63. Norman J. Finkel, *Insanity on Trial*. New York: Plenum Press, 1988, p. 17.

64. Finkel, *Insanity on Trial*, pp. 18–20. Ray corresponded with Associate Justice Charles Doe of the Supreme Court of New Hampshire. In 1869, Josiah Pike confessed to murdering Thomas Brown with an ax. Doe reasoned that if the action was the product "of mental disease in the defendant," Pike ought to be acquitted. Pike was hanged, but two years later, the justices affirmed Doe's (and Ray's principle) and the New Hampshire rule became law. Thomas Maeder, *Crime and Madness*. New York: Harper and Row, 1985, pp. 39–46.

65. R.D. Mackay, "The Abnormality of Mind Factor in Diminished Responsibility," *Criminal Law Review* (Feb., 1999), pp. 117–125.

66. Philip E. Johnson, 'The Turnabout in the Insanity Defense," *Crime and Justice: A Review of Research* 6 (1985), p. 222.

67. Johnson, "The Turnabout," pp. 223–224.

68. Johnson, "The Turnabout," pp. 225–226.

69. Curt R. Bartol, *Criminal Behavior: A Psychosocial Approach*. Upper Saddle River, NJ: Prentice Hall, 1999, p. 150.

70. Roxanne Lieb, Vernon Quinsey, and Lucy Berliner, "Sexual Predators and Social Policy," *Crime and Justice: A Review of Research*, 23 (1998), p. 55.

71. Freedman, "Uncontrolled Desires," p. 94.

72. Freedman, "Uncontrolled Desires," p. 99.

73. John Monahan and Sharon K. Davis, "Mentally Disordered Sex Offenders," in *Mentally Disordered Offenders* (John Monahan and Henry J. Steadman, eds.) New York: Plenum Press, 1983, pp. 191–192.

74. Monahan and Davis, "Mentally disordered" p. 192.

75. Lieb *et al.*, "Sexual Predators," pp. 64–65.

76. Lieb *et al.*, "Seuxal Predators," pp. 66–67.

77. Rafter, *Creating Born Criminals*, pp. 193–195.

78. Donald D. Jackson, "You Will Feel No Pain," *Smithsonian* 29 (1999), p. 139. The term hypnosis was coined by a British surgeon, James Braid, during his experiments with "nervous sleep." He had used hypnosis in his medical practice in the 1840s, reporting cures for deafness, rheumatism, and paralysis. Freud himself abandoned hypnosis for free association and dream analysis.

79. Jonas R. Rappeport, "The Forensic Psychiatrist," *FBI Law Enforcement Bulletin* 44 (1975), p. 8.

80. Gary M. Ernsdorff and Elizabeth F. Loftus, "Let Sleeping Memories Lie? Words of Caution about Tolling the Statute of Limitations in Cases of Memory Repression," *Journal of Criminal Law and Criminology*, 84 (1993), pp. 129–174.

81. Anthony J. Pinizzotto, "Forensic Psychology: Criminal Personality Profiling," *Journal of Police Science and Administration* 12 (1984), p. 32; Jon Zonderman, *Beyond the Crime Lab: The New Science of Investigation*. New York: Wiley Science, 1990, pp.125–126.

82. Zonderman, *Beyond the Crime Lab*, 125–126.

83. Pinizzotto, "Forensic Psychology," p. 37.

84. Fox and Levin, 427–428.

85. Lykken, *The Antisocial Personalities*, p. 5.

86. Doreen Rappaport, *The Alger Hiss Trial*. New York: HarperTrophy, 1993, p. 131.

87. Rappaport, *The Alger Hiss,* pp. 131–133.
88. Rappaport, *The Alger Hiss,* pp. 134–135.
89. Stone, *Abnormalities of Personality,* p. 239.
90. Quoted in Stephen Jay Gould, *The Mismeasure of Man.* New York: WW Norton, 1981, p. 320.
91. Hannah F. Augstein, "J.C. Prichard's Concept of Moral Insanity—A Medical Theory of the Corruption of Human Nature," *Medical History* 40 (1996) pp. 333–334.
92. Finkel, *Insanity on Trial,* pp. 17–19. The classic study of the political dimensions of the M'Naughten case was written by Richard Moran, *Knowing Right from Wrong: The Insanity defense of Daniel McNaughtan.* New York: Free Press, 1981.
93. Augstein, "J.C. Prichard's Concept," p. 315.
94. Richard DeGrandpre, *Ritalin Nation: Rapid-Fire Culture and the Transformation of Human Consciousness.* New York: W.W. Norton, 1999, p. 38.
95. Richard DeGrandpre, "Just Cause? Many Neuroscientists Are All Too Quick to Call a Blip on a Brain Scan the Reason for a Behavior," *The Sciences* 39 (1999), pp. 14–15.
96. DeGrandpre, "Just Cause?" p. 15.
97. DeGrandpre, "Just Cause?," p. 18. The drug was developed in the 1960s by Ciba pharmaceuticals (Novartis), and remains a Schedule II drug according to the Drug Enforcement Administration, along with morphine and cocaine.
98. DeGrandpre, *Ritalin Nation,* pp. 42–43.
99. Nancy Gibbs, "The Age of Ritalin," *Time* 152 (Nov. 30, 1998), pp. 86–96.
100. Pharmaceutical companies promote their drugs by asserting that anxiety and so on are biological illnesses in need of medical treatment. Eli Lilly marketed Prozac in 1997 and 1998 with the pitch "Depression is a real illness with real causes. It can be triggered by stressful life events…to help bring serotonin levels closer to normal, the medicine doctors now prescribe most often is Prozac." DeGrandpre, "Just Cause?"p. 17.
101. See Richard Warner and Tadeusz Szubka, eds., *The Mind-Body Problem.* Oxford, UK: Basil Blackwell, 1994.
102. DeGrandpre, "Just Cause?" p. 15.
103. Nathaniel J. Pallone and James J. Hennessy, "Brain Dysfunction and Criminal Violence," *Society* (Sept/Oct. 1998), p. 21. See also, Diana Fishbein, "Building Bridges," *ACJS Today* [Academy of Criminal Justice Sciences], 17 (Sept/Oct 1998), pp. 1, 3–5.
104. John Searle, *Minds, Brains and Science.* Cambridge, Mass: Harvard University Press, 1984, p. 26.
105. Searle, *Minds, Brains,* p. 23.
106. Searle, *Minds, Brains,* p. 10.
107. Quoted in James Gleick, *Genius: The Life and Science of Richard Feynman.* New York: Pantheon Books, 1992, p. 321.

Notes for Chapter 5

1. Quoted in Piers Beirne, *Inventing Criminology.* Albany: State University of New York Press, 1993, p. 225.

2. C. Wright Mills, *The Sociological Imagination*, London: Oxford University Press, 1959, pp. 5-19.

3. F.A. Hayek, *The Counter-Revolution of Science*. Indianapolis: Liberty-Press, 1952, pp. 186-211.

4. Mary Pickering, "A New Look at Auguste Comte," in *Reclaiming the Sociological Classics* (Charles Camic, ed). Malden, Mass.: Blackwell, 1997, pp. 20-21.

5. Hayek, *The Counter-Revolution*, p. 258.

6. Hayek, *The Counter-Revolution*, pp. 258, 353.

7. Hayek, *The Counter-Revolution*, p. 355.

8. Leonard Zusne, *Names in the History of Psychology*. New York: John Wiley and Sons, 1957, p. 80.

9. Anthony Giddens, "The Suicide Problem in French Sociology," *British Journal of Sociology* 16 (1965), pp. 4-5.

10. Beirne, *Inventing Criminology*, p. 75.

11. Beirne, *Inventing Criminology*, p. 75.

12. Beirne, *Inventing Criminology*, p. 89.

13. Giddens, "The Suicide Problem," pp. 4-5.

14. Emile Durkheim, *Suicide*. New York: Free Press, 1951, p. 46.

15. Robert A. Jones, "The *Other* Durkheim: History and Theory in the Treatment of Classical Sociological Thought," in Camic, *Reclaiming the Sociological*, p. 154.

16. Beirne, *Inventing Criminology*, p. 165.

17. Ian Taylor, Paul Walton and Jock Young. *The New Criminology*. New York: Harper and Row, 1973, p. 76.

18. Durkheim, quoted in Ian Taylor, *et al.*, *The New Criminology*, p. 72.

19. Emile Durkheim, *Moral Education*. New York: Free Press, 1973, p. 9.

20. Stjepan G. Mestrovic and Helene M. Brown, "Durkheim's Concept of Anomie as Dereglement," *Social Problems*, 33 (1985) p. 95.

21. Taylor *et al.*, *The New Criminology*, p. 77.

22. But see Mestrovic and Brown, "Durkheim's Concept of Anomie," pp. 81-99. The French word *anomie* meant something closer to "derangement" in a moral sense. Durkheim described anomie as a painful condition of confusion concerning moral choice.

23. Mestrovic and Brown, "Durkheim's Concept of Anomie," pp. 93-94. This is the point that Freud would make in *Civilization and its Discontents*.

24. Durkheim, *Moral Education*, pp. 59-60.

25. Steven Lukes and Andrew Scull, *Durkheim and the Law*. New York: St. Martin's Press, 1983, pp. 39-59, 146-157.

26. Lukes and Scull, *Durkheim and the Law*, pp. 59-101.

27. Beirne, *Inventing Criminology*, pp. 166-167.

28. Taylor *et al.*, *The New Criminology*, p. 80.

29. Morton Hunt, "A Biographical Profile of Robert K. Merton," *The New Yorker* 28 (1961) p. 58.

30. Marshall Clinard quoted in David A. Jones, *History of Criminology*. New York: Greenwood, 1986, p. 173.

31. Patricia Cohen, "An Eye for Patterns in the Social Fabric," *The New York Times*, Oct. 31, 1998.

32. Richard A. Cloward and Lloyd Ohlin, *Delinquency and Opportunity*, New York: Free Press, 1960. For a summary, see the excerpt of this work in *Criminological Theory* (Francis T. Cullen and Robert Agnew, eds.) Los Angeles: Roxbury, 1999, pp. 134-140.

33. Robert Agnew, "A General Strain Theory of Crime and Delinquency," in Cullen and Agnew, *Criminological Theory: Past to Present*, pp. 151–158. See also, Robert S. Agnew, "Foundation for a General Strain Theory," *Criminology* 30 (1992) 47–87.

34. Agnew, "A General Strain," p. 159.

35. Agnew, "A General Strain," p. 159.

36. Travis Hirschi, "A Control Theory of Delinquency," in *Classics of Criminology* (Joseph E. Jacoby, ed.) Prospect Heights, IL: Waveland Press, 1979, p. 185. See also Travis Hirschi, *Causes of Delinquency*. Berkeley: University of California Press, 1969.

37. Hirschi, "A Control Theory of Delinquency," pp. 185–190. For an attempt to reconcile the 1969 Hirschi of social bond theory with the 1990 Hirschi of the general theory of crime, see Marcus Felson, "Reconciling Hirschi's 1969 Control Theory with the General Theory of Crime," in *Crime Prevention at a Crossroads* (Steven P. Lab, ed.) Cincinnati, OH: Anderson, 1997.

38. Cullen and Agnew, *Criminological Theory*, p. 187.

39. Robert J. Sampsonb and John H. Laub, "Crime and the Life Course," in Cullen and Agnew, *Criminological Theories*, pp. 187–198. See also Robert J. Sampson and John H. Laub, *Crime in the Making: Pathways and Turning Points Through Life*. Cambridge, Mass.: Harvard University Press, 1993.

40. John Braithwaite, "Crime, Shame and Reintegration," in Cullen and Agnew, *Criminological Theory*, pp. 286–293. See also John Braithwaite, *Crime, Shame and Reintegration*. Cambridge: Cambridge University Press, 1989.

41. John Braithwaite, "Shame and Modernity," *British Journal of Criminology* 33 (1993), p. 15.

42. Braithwaite, *Crime, Shame and Reintegration*, 1989.

43. Braithwaite, "Shame and Modernity," p. 12.

44. Beirne, *Inventing Criminology*, pp. 114–115.

45. Beirne, *Inventing Criminology*, p. 124.

46. Beirne, *Inventing Criminology*, pp. 119–127. In Britain, Guerry's conclusions about the effect of education created a stir among public officials. In 1840, Richard W. Rawson, secretary to the Statistical Society of London, explained that Guerry's maps confused "mere instruction" in reading and writing with an education to teach moral principles. Beirne, *Inventing Criminology*, p. 131.

47. Taylor *et al.*, *The New Criminology*, p. 112.

48. Taylor *et al.*, *The New Criminology*, p. 115.

49. Robert J. Sampson and W. Byron Groves, "Community Structure and Crime: Testing Social-Disorganization Theory," *American Journal of Sociology* 94 (1989), pp. 774–802; see also Robert J. Sampson, Steven W. Raudenbush, and Felton Earls, "Neighborhood and Violent Crime: A Multilevel Study of Collective Efficacy," *Science* 277 (August 15), pp. 918–924.

50. Rodney Stark, "Deviant Places: A Theory of the Ecology of Crime," *Criminology* 25 (1987), pp. 893–909.

51. Marcus Felson, *Crime and Everyday Life*. Thousand Oaks, CA: Pine Forge, 1998, pp. 82–83.

52. C. Ray Jeffrey quoted in National Crime Prevention Institute, *Understanding Crime Prevention*. Boston: Butterworths, 1986, p. 120.

53. Lawrence W. Sherman, Patrick R. Gartin, and Michael Beurger, "Hot Spots of Predatory Crime: Routine Activities and the Criminology of Place," *Criminology* 27 (1989), pp. 27–55.

54. Dennis Roncek and Mitchell A. Pravatiner, "Additional Evidence that Taverns Enhance Nearby Crime," *Sociology and Social Research* 73 (1989), pp. 185–188; Dennis W. Roncek and Pamela Maier, "Bars, Blocks and Crimes Revisted: Linking the Theory of Routine Activities to 'Hot Spots.'" *Criminology* 29 (1991), pp. 725–754.

55. Marcus Felson, "Routine Activities and Crime Prevention in the Developing Metropolis," *Criminology* 25 (1987), p. 912.

56. Tim Crow and Diane Zahm, "Crime Prevention Through Environmental Design," *Land Management* 7 (1994), pp. 22–27.

57. Lukes and Scull, *Durkheim and the Law*, pp. 15–18.

58. Bierne, *Inventing Criminology*, pp. 159–163.

59. Bierne, *Inventing Criminology*, pp. 159–163.

60. Quoted in Mark Warr, "The Social Origins of Crime: Edwin Sutherland and the Theory of Differential Association," in *Explaining Criminals and Crime* (Raymond Paternoster and Ronet Bachman, eds.) Los Angeles: Roxbury, 2001, p. 183.

61. Albert Bandura, Dorthea Ross and Sheila Ross, "Imitation of Film-Mediated Aggressive Models," *Journal of Abnormal and Social Psychology* 67 (1963), pp. 601–607.

62. Bandura extended his modeling conception to virtually every aspect of human experience. Bandura made clear that "In the social learning view, people are neither driven by inner forces nor buffeted by environmental stimuli. Rather, psychological functioning is explained in terms of a continuous reciprocal interaction of personal and environmental determinants...In actuality, virtually all learning phenomena resulting from direct experience occur on a vicarious basis by observing other people's behavior and its consequences for them." Albert Bandura, *Social Learning Theory*. Englewood Cliffs, NJ: Prentice Hall, 1977, pp. 11–12.

63. Robert L. Burgess and Ronald L. Akers, "A Differential Association-Reinforcement Theory of Criminal Behavior," *Social Problems* 14 (1966) pp. 128–147; Ronald Akers, *Deviant Behavior: A Social Learning Approach*. Belmont, CA: Wadsworth, 1973.

64. Ronald Akers, *Criminological Theories*. Los Angeles: Roxbury, 1997, p. 68.

65. Vincent F. Sacco and Leslie W. Kennedy. *The Criminal Event*. Belmont, CA: Wadsworth, 1996, p. 146.

66. David D. Luckenbill, "Criminal Homicide as a Situated Transaction," *Social Problems* 25 (1977), pp. 176–186.

67. Arnold Binder and Susan L. Polan, "The Kennedy-Johnson Years, Social Theory, and Federal Policy in the Control of Juvenile Delinquency," *Crime and Delinquency* 37 (1991), pp. 243–244.

68. Binder and Polan, "The Kennedy-Johnson Years," p. 249.

69. Binder and Polan, "The Kennedy-Johnson Years," pp. 249–251.

70. Binder and Polan, "The Kennedy-Johnson Years," p. 250.

71. Stephen Pfol, *Images of Deviance and Social Control*. New York: McGraw-Hill, 1994, p. 277.

72. Binder and Polan, "The Kennedy-Johnson Years," p. 257.

73. James Q. Wilson, *Thinking About Crime*. New York: Vintage Books, 1983, p. 43.

74. Ira Schwartz, *(In)Justice for Juveniles*. Lanham, MD: Lexington Books, 1989, p. 110.

75. Michael Saucier, "Birth of Partnership," *Juvenile Justice* 2 (1995), pp. 19–21.

76. Gordon Raley, "The JJDP Act: A Second Look," *Juvenile Justice* 2 (1995), p. 13.

77. Saucier, "The Birth of a Partnership," p. 20.

78. Raley, "The JJDP Act," p. 14.

79. Randy Martin, Robert J. Mutchnick, W. Timothy Austin, *Criminological Thought: Pioneers Past and Present.* New York: Macmillan, 1990, p. 280. Congress established the Law Enforcement Assistance Administration (LEAA) in 1968 and in 1974 assigned to it responsibility for the JJDP Act. The LEAA provided funds to states (based on population), and directly to organizations, for various crime reduction strategies. As it turned out, the JJDP Act survived longer than the LEAA. LEAA funded programs ranging from juvenile diversion to computerized record-keeping, and critics charged that the agency threw money at the crime problem without sense or strategy. Congress abolished LEAA in 1984 and assigned its responsibilities for federal grants to a new Bureau of Justice Assistance within the U.S. Department of Justice. The JJDP Act would also survive a change in presidential leadership and garner more than two decades of congressional support.

80. Howard S. Becker, *Writing for Social Scientists.* Chicago: University of Chicago Press, 1986, p. 9.

81. J. Robert Lilly and Richard A. Ball, "A Critical Analysis of the Changing Concept of Criminal Responsibility," *Criminology* 20 (1982), 169–184.

82. Wilson, *Thinking About Crime*, p. 50.

83. Paul J. Lavrakas, "Politicians, Journalists, and the Rhetoric of the 'Crime Prevention' Public Policy Debate," in *Crime Prevention at a Crossroads* (Steven P. Lab, ed.) Cincinnati, OH: Anderson, 1997.

84. David L. Faigman, "To Have and Have Not: Assessing the Value of Social Science to the Law as Science and Policy," *Emory Law Journal* 38 (1989) 1005–1095.

85. David Bazelon, *Questioning Authority: Justice and Criminal Law.* New York: Alfred Knopf, 1988, pp. 91–100.

86. *United States v. Alexander and Murdock*, 471 F2d 923 (DC Circuit 1973). Richard Delgado, " 'Rotten Social Background' ": Should the Criminal Law Recognize a Defense of Severe Economic Deprivation?" *Law and Inequality*, 3 (1985), p. 11, footnote 11.

87. Bazelon, *Questioning Authority*, pp. 101–117; Delgado, "Rotten Social Background," p.p. 20–21.

88. David Bazelon, "The Morality of the Criminal Law," *Southern California Law Review* 49 (1976) 385–405; "The Morality of the Criminal Law: A Rejoinder to Professor Morse," *Southern California Law Review* 49 (1976) 1269–1274. The debate is summarized in Michael Tonry, *Malign Neglect: Race, Crime and Punishment in America.* New York: Oxford University Press, 1995, pp. 134–145.

89. Bazelon, "The Morality of the Criminal," p. 386.

90. Bazelon, *Questioning Authority*, pp. 16–17.

91. Stephen Morse, "The Twilight of Welfare Criminology: A Reply to Judge Bazelon," *Southern California Law Review* 49 (1976) 1247–1269; "The Twilight of Welfare Criminology: A Final Word," *Southern California Law Review* 49 (1976) 1275–1284.

92. Michael Moore, "Causation and the Excuses," *California Law Review*, 73 (1985) 1091–1149.

93. Delgado, "Rotten Social Background," p. 74.

94. Tonry, *Malign Neglect*, p. 139.

95. Tonry, *Malign Neglect*, pp. 145–147.

96. Peter Drucker, *The Ecological Vision*. New Brunswick, NJ: Transaction, 1993, p. 434.
97. Drucker, *The Ecological Vision*, p. 434.
98. Sidney Monas, "Afterword: The Dream of the Suffering Horse," in Fyodor Dostoyevsky, *Crime and Punishment* (Sydney Monas, tr.). New York: Signet, 1968.
99. Quoted in Roger Kimball, "The Perversions of Michel Foucault," 11 *New Criterion* (1993), p. 5.

Notes for Chapter 6

1. Günther Kaiser, "Criminological Research in the Federal Republic of Germany," *Crime and Justice: An Annual Review of Research* 5 (1983), pp. 297–298.
2. Marx quoted in Michael J. Lynch and W. Byron Groves, *A Primer in Radical Criminology*. New York: Harrow and Heston, p. 11.
3. Paul Q. Hirst, "Marx and Engels on Law, Crime and Morality," in *Critical Criminology* (Ian Taylor, Paul Walton and Jock Young, eds.) London: Routledge and Kegan Paul, 1975, p. 213.
4. Lynch and Groves, *A Primer*, pp. 9–10.
5. Lynch and Groves, *A Primer*, pp. 10–11.
6. Lynch and Groves, *A Primer*, pp. 11–13.
7. Martin Jay, *The Dialectical Imagination: A History of the Frankfurt School and the Institute of Social Research 1923–1950*. Boston: Little, Brown and Co., 1973.
8. Jay, *The Dialectical Imagination*, p. 63.
9. Hubert Rottleuthner, "The Contribution of the Critical Theory of the Frankfurt School of the Sociology of Law" in *Sociological Approaches to Law* (Adam Podgórecki and Christopher J. Whelan, eds.). New York: St. Martin's Press, 1981, p. 112.
10. Gerda Dinwiddie, "Labor Markets and Penal Sanction: Thoughts on the Sociology of Criminal Justice," *Crime and Social Justice* (1978), p. 2, see biographic note.
11. George Rusche and Otto Kirchheimer, *Punishment and Social Structure*, New York: Russell and Russell, 1968, p. 5.
12. Dario Melossi, "An Introduction: Fifty Years Later, *Punishment and Social Structure* in Comparative Analysis," *Contemporary Crises* 13 (1989), p. 311. See James Inverarity and Daniel McCarthy, "Punishment and Social Structure Revisited: Unemployment and Imprisonment in the United States, 1948–1984," *Sociological Quarterly* 29 (1988), pp. 263–279; Matthew Yeager, "Unemployment and Imprisonment," *Journal of Criminal Law and Criminology* 70 (1979), pp. 586–588.
13. Critics partial to Marx's view have suggested that Habermas has left Marx behind in an attempt "to step outside Marxism and create a new theoretical tradition." Henning Ottman, quoted in W. Byron Groves and Robert J. Sampson, "Critical Theory and Criminology," *Social Problems* 33 (1986) p. 75.
14. Rottleuthner, "The Contribution," p. 117.
15. Rottleuthner, "The Contribution," p. 119.
16. Dragan Milovanovic "Anarchism, Liberation Theology and the De-

commodification of the Juridic and Linguistic Form," *Humanity and Society* 9 (1985), pp. 182–196; "Juridico-Linguistic Communicative Markets: Towards a Semiotic Analysis," *Contemporary Crises* 10 (1986), pp.281–304; "The Political Economy of 'Liberty' and 'Property' Interests," *Legal Studies Forum* 11 (1987), pp. 147–172.

17. Rottleuthner, 'The Contribution," p. 125.

18. Max Scheler, a philosopher, proposed the term *wissenssoziologie*, translated into English as the "sociology of knowledge," in the 1920s. But it was Karl Mannheim, one of Scheler's students, who introduced British criminologists to the idea.

19. Jay, *The Dialectical Imagination*, pp. 63–64. As Marcuse wrote, critical social theory "is interested in the truth content of philosophical concepts and problems. The enterprise of the sociology of knowledge, to the contrary, is occupied only with the untruths, not the truths, of previous philosophies."

20. Peter L. Berger, *Invitation to Sociology*. New York: Anchor Books, 1963, pp. 117, 121. Also, Thomas Luckman and Peter L. Berger, *The Social Construction of Reality*. New York: Doubleday, 1966.

21. Ralf Dahrendorf, *LSE: A History of the London School of Economics and Politic Science*. New York: Oxford University Press, 1995, p. 295.

22. Laura Kalman, *Legal Realism at Yale 1927–1960*. Chapel Hill: University of North Carolina Press, 1986, pp. 45–46.

23. Quoted in Kalman, *Legal Realism*, pp. 44–45.

24. Kalman, *Legal Realism*, p. 167.

25. Bernard Schwartz, *Main Currents of Legal Thought*. Durham, N.C.: Carolina Academic Press, 1993, p. 483; Kalman, *Legal Realism*, pp. 165–166.

26. Kalman, *Legal Realism*, pp. 167–169.

27. The labeling theorists explained the production of crime statistics themselves. John I. Kitsuse and Aaron Cicourel, "A Note on the Uses of Official Statistics," *Social Problems* 11 (1963), pp. 131–139.

28. Sellin, quoted in John Laub, *Criminology in the Making*. Boston: Northeastern University Press, 1983, p. 174.

29. Thorsten Sellin, *Culture Conflict and Crime*. New York: Social Science Research Council, 1938, pp. 59–60.

30. Laub, *Criminology in the Making*, p. 175.

31. Taylor *et al.*, *The New Criminology*, p. 139.

32. Edwin Lemert, *Social Pathology*. New York: McGraw Hill, 1951, pp. 75–78.

33. Mark Lanier and Stuart Henry, *Essential Criminology*. Boulder: Westview Press, 1998, p. 169.

34. Howard S. Becker, *Writing for Social Scientists*. Chicago: University of Chicago Press, 1986, p. 100.

35. Howard S. Becker, "Outsiders" in *Classics of Criminology* (Joseph E. Jacoby, ed). Prospect Heights, Ill.: Waveland Press, 1979, pp. 196–202. The original work is Howard S. Becker, *Outsiders*. New York: Free Press, 1963.

36. Erich Goode and Nachman Ben-Yehuda, *Moral Panics: The Social Construction of Deviance*. Cambridge, Mass,: Blackwell Publishers, 1994, p. 23.

37. Stanley Cohen, *Folk Devils and Moral Panics*. London: MacGibbon and McKee, 1972, p. 44.

38. Cohen, *Folk Devils*, p. 9.

39. Goode and Ben-Yehuda, *Moral Panics*, p. 50.

326 · NOTES FOR PAGES 185–192

40. Malcolm Spector and John I. Kitsuse, *Constructing Social Problems.* Menlo Park, Calif.: Cummings, 1977, p. 78.
41. Philip Jenkins, *Using Murder: The Social Construction of Serial Homicide.* New York: Aldine de Gruyter, 1994, pp. 4–12.
42. Jenkins, *Using Murder*, pp. 4–7.
43. In 1961, Becker became editor of *Social Problems*, the journal of the Society of the Study for Social Problems. SSSP, "triple S P" as it is known among sociologists, formed when sociologists opposed the "establishment" the American Sociological Association had become. *Social Problems* featured articles without statistics and devoted to alternative theories in sociology (those that rejected the structural-functionalism of Talcott Parsons) and it became a major source for sociological constructionism.
44. Stephen Pfohl, "The 'Discovery' of Child Abuse," *Social Problems* 24 (1977), pp. 310–324.
45. Stephen Pfohl, "Twilight of the Parasites: Ultramodern Capital and the New World Order," *Social Problems* 40 (1993) pp. 125, 149.
46. Groves and Sampson, "Critical Theory," p. 60.
47. Hirst, "Marx and Engels," p. 221.
48. Hirst, "Marx and Engels," p. 220.
49. Marx speaks so harshly of this class and their crimes because he viewed them as a parasitic class who opposed the political interests of workers. They did not contribute to the worker's struggle, but siphoned off the energy of the workers. The criminal classes are the natural enemies of any principled and disciplined workers' movement. Hirst, "Marx and Engels," pp. 215–216.
50. Hirst, "Marx and Engels," pp. 218–219.
51. Willem Bonger, "Criminality and Economic Conditions," in *Criminological Theory: Past to Present* (Francis T. Cullen and Robert Agnew, eds.) Los Angeles: Roxbury, 1999, p. 303.
52. Bonger, "Criminality and Economic," p. 302.
53. Piers Beirne and Robert Sharlet, "Pashukanis and Socialist Legality," in *Marxism and Law* (Piers Beirne and Richard Quinney, eds.) New York: John Wiley and Sons, 1982, pp. 307–327.
54. Peter H. Solomon, "Soviet Criminology—Its Demise and Rebirth, 1928–1963," in *Crime, Criminology and Public Policy* (Roger Hood, ed.) New York: Free Press, 1974, p. 574.
55. Gilbert Geis, "The Limits of Academic Tolerance: The Discontinuance of the School of Criminology at Berkeley," in *Punishment and Social Control* (Thomas G. Blomberg and Stanley Cohen, eds.) New York: Aldine de Gruyter, 1995, pp. 277–304.
56. *Social Justice* began as *Issues in Criminology*, a publication of the Berkeley School of Criminology.
57. Anthony M. Platt, *The Child Savers: The Invention of Delinquency.* Chicago: University of Chicago Press, 1977, p. xviii.
58. Platt, *The Child Savers*, p. xxii.
59. Dario Melossi, "Overcoming the Crisis in Critical Criminology: Toward a Grounded Labeling Theory," *Criminology* 23 (1985), pp. 193–208.
60. Herman Schwendinger and Julia Schwendinger, "Defenders of Order or Guardians of Human Rights?" *Issues in Criminology* 5 (1970), pp. 123–157.
61. Julia Schwendinger and Herman Schwendinger, *Rape and Inequality.* Beverly Hills, Calif.: Sage, 1983.

62. Randy Martin, Robert J. Mutchnick, and W. Timothy Austin, *Criminological Thought: Pioneers Past and Present*. New York: Macmillan, 1990, p. 384.

63. Martin *et al.*, *Criminological Thought*, pp. 383, 387.

64. Martin *et al.*, *Criminological Thought*, p. 393.

65. Quoted in Martin *et al. Criminological Thought*, p. 394.

66. Jeffrey Reiman, *The Rich Get Richer and the Poor Get Prison*. Boston: Allyn and Bacon, 1974.

67. Both Quinney and Chambliss relied on Marx's theory of society, but their approaches came to characterize two different versions of radical criminology: Quinney, *instrumental Marxism*, Chambliss, *structural Marxism*. The structuralists tried to remove economic determinism from Marx's model. They claimed that Marx never meant to suggest a direct, causal relationship between the economic base and the ideological superstructure. The ideological elements, law, politics, and so on, had "relative autonomy" from the economy. The "ruling class" did not rule directly through control of government but rather, characteristics within the structural of capitalism ensure that their interests wound up being served in the end. They offered a kind of structural determinism in which the social relationships of capitalism constrained human behavior. While the instrumentalists foretold of the day when the proletariat would finally unite and overthrow the capitalists, the structuralists did not see the end coming that way. They talked about contradictions within the structure of capitalism itself, crises too large for the State to manage, and a collapse of its own weight.

68. William J. Chambliss and Robert J. Seidman, *Law, Order and Power*. Reading, Mass.: Addison Wesley, 1971.

69. William J. Chambliss, "State-Organized Crime," *Criminology* 27 (1989), p. 184.

70. Chambliss, "State-Organized Crime," p. 201.

71. Martin Albrow, "Sociology in the United Kingdom," in *National Traditions in Sociology* (Nikolai Genov, ed.) New Bury, CA: Sage, 1989, pp. 206, 210–211.

72. John Croft, "Criminological Research in Great Britian, with a Note on the Council of Europe," *Crime and Justice: An Annual Review of Research 5* (1983), p. 269.

73. Taylor *et al.*, *The New Criminology*, pp. 278–279.

74. Taylor *et al.*, *The New Criminology*, p. 282.

75. Taylor *et al.*, *Critical Criminology*, pp. 44–45.

76. Taylor *et al.*, *Critical Criminology*, p. 20.

77. Although Young named names, it was Quinney who had written that crimes among the working class as "crimes of resistance" that constituted "a struggle, however conscious or unconscious, against the exploitation of life and activity of the worker." Richard Quinney, *Class, State and Crime*. New York: David McKay, 1977, pp. 54–55.

78. Jock Young, "Left Idealism, Reformism and Beyond," in *Capitalism and the Rule of Law* (Bob Fine, Richard Kinsey, John Lea, Sol Picciotto, and Jock Young, eds.) London: Hutchinson, 1979.

79. John Lea and Jock Young, *What is to be Done About Law and Order?* New York: Penguin, 1984; John Lea and Jock Young, "A Realistic Approach to Law and Order," in *The Political Economy of Crime* (Brian McLean, ed.) Englewood Cliffs, N.J.: Prentice Hall, 1986; Jock Young, "The Failure of Criminology: The Need for a Radical Realism," in *Confronting Crime* (Roger Matthews and Jock Young, eds.) Beverly Hills, Calif.: Sage, 1986.

80. Rottleuthner, "The Contribution," pp. 115–116. See Martin D. Schwartz and David O. Friedrichs, "Postmodern Thought and Criminological Discontent: New Metaphors for Understanding Violence," *Criminology* 32 (1994), pp. 221–246; Bruce Arrigo, "The Peripheral Core of Law and Criminology: On Postmodern Social Theory and Conceptual Integration," *Justice Quarterly* 12 (1995), pp. 447–472; Dragan Milovanovic, "Postmodern Criminology: Mapping the Terrain," *Justice Quarterly* 13 (1996), pp. 567–610.

81. James W. Sire, *The Universe Next Door*. Downer's Grove, IL: Inter-Varsity, 1997, pp. 174–175. The story is told of a girl at a baseball game who asked about how the umpire could know whether the pitcher threw a ball or strike. "He calls them as they are," one fan replied. "He calls them as he sees them," another said. "Listen girl," said another, "the throw ain't nothin' till the umpire calls it." That expresses the last few centuries of moral philosophy.

82. W. Byron Groves and David H. Galaty, "Freud, Foucault and Social Control," *Humanity and Society* 10 (1986) pp. 297–318.

83. Alan Sheridan, *Michel Foucault: The Will to Truth*. New York: Tavistock Publications, 1980, p. 206.

84. Michel Foucault, *Discipline and Punish: The Birth of the Prison*. New York: Vintage Books, 1979.

85. Sheridan, *Michel Foucault*, p. 161.

86. Sheridan, *Michel Foucault*, pp. 131–134.

87. Schwartz, *Main Currents*, p. 604.

88. Schwartz, *Main Currents*, p. 608.

89. David A. Jones, *History of Criminology*. Westport, CT: Greenwood, 1986, p. 215.

90. Schwartz, *Main Currents*, p. 611.

91. Dragan Milovanovic, *A Primer in the Sociology of Law*. Albany, N.Y.: Harrow and Heston, 1988, pp. 127–128.

92. Milovanovic, *A Primer in the Sociology*, pp. 135–136.

93. Didier Eribon, *Michel Foucault* (Betsy Wing, tr.) Cambridge: Harvard University Press, 1991, p. 123.

94. Schwartz, *Main Currents*, 613. Duke University Law School Paul Carrington took a dimmer view; he suggested that Unger and the other Crits ought to resign. Any law professor who believed the law to be nothing but a cosmetic mask to shielding the dominant hierarchy ought not be teaching; some minimal belief in the law and the institutions of government necessary to enforce it ought not be teaching the profession of law. Paul Carrington, "Of Law and the River," *Journal of Legal Education* 34 (1984), pp. 222, 227.

95. Jay, *The Dialectical Imagination*, p. 4.

96. Jay, *The Dialectical Imagination*, pp. 56, 262.

97. Groves and Sampson, "Critical Social Theory," p. 73, footnote 14. Marcuse, who disagreed with Horkheimer privately but publicly supported the Institute, broke rank in the last chapter of his *Eros and Civilization*. He suggested that self-reflection could overcome time, even death. See Groves and Galaty, "Freud, Foucault," p. 314.

98. Groves and Sampson, "Critical Social Theory," pp. 74–75.

99. Dahrenforf, *LSE*, p. 291.

100. Eribon, *Michel Foucault*, pp. 36, 53, 136.

101. Lynch and Groves, *A Primer*, p. 107.

102. Anthony Platt, "Crime and Punishment in the United States: Immediate and Long-Term Reforms from a Marxist Perspective" *Crime and Social Justice* 18 (1982) pp. 26–34.

103. John Lea and Jock Young, "A Realistic Approach to Law and Order," in *The Political Economy of Crime* (Brian McLean, ed). Englewood Cliffs, NJ: Prentice-Hall, 1986, pp. 358–364.

104. Lynch and Groves, *A Primer*, p. 107.

105. Taylor *et al., The New Criminology*, p. 282.

106. Ian Taylor, *Crime, Capitalism and Community: Three Essays in Socialist Criminology*. Toronto: Butterworths, 1983; Richard Quinney,

107. Schwartz, *Main Currents*, p. 611.

108. Schwartz, *Main Currents*, p. 611.

109. Schwartz, *Main Currents*, p. 612.

110. Schwartz, *Main Currents*, p. 611.

111. Solomon, *Soviet Criminology*, p. 577.

112. See, for example, *Social Justice, Criminal Justice: The Maturation of Critical Theory in Law, Crime and Deviance*. Belmont, CA: West/Wadsworth, 1999.

113. *Planned Parenthood of Southeastern Pennsylvania v. Casey*, 112 S.Ct. 2807 (1992). See David F. Forte, "Eve Without Adam: What Genesis Has to Tell America About Natural Law," Heritage Lecture #570. Washington, DC: Heritage Foundation, 1996.

114. Gwynn Nettler, *Explaining Crime*, New York: McGraw-Hill, 1984, p. 193.

115. Jay, *The Dialectical Imagination*, p. 76.

116. This has been referred to as the genetic fallacy. Nettler, *Explaining Crime*, p. 194.

117. Schwartz, *Main Currents*, p. 610.

118. Among the sociological constructionists, Pfohl is labeled a "strict constructionist" while Philip Jenkins would be a "contextual constructionist." From the perspective of *strict constructionists*, who deny the presence of any objective reality, the contextual constructionists are only "partial constructions." Jenkins provides only a partial constructionist view because he refers to the reality of serial murder using crime statistics contrary to the claims made by those who elevated serial murder to the status of a social problem, "this type of violence [serial murder] accounts for only about 1 percent of American homicides, and possibly less" (p. 13). In the strict constructionist view, sociological analysis involves claims-making by sociologists who create their own social reality in the same way as those they study. See Stephen Pfol, "Toward a Sociological Deconstruction of Social Problems: A Response to Woolgar and Pawluch," *Social Problems* 32 (1985), pp. 228–29; Steve Woolgar and Dorothy Pawluch, "Ontological gerrymandering: The Anatomy of Social Problems Explanations," 32 *Social Problems* 32 (1985), pp. 214–227 and "How Shall We Move Beyond Constructivism?" *Social Problems* 33 (1985), pp. 159–162, along with Ronald J. Troyer, "Some Consequences of Contextual Constructionism," *Social Problems* 39 (1992) pp. 35–37 and Nicole H. Rafter, "Some Consequences of Strict Constructionism," *Social Problems* 39 (1992) pp. 38–39.

119. Eribon, *Michel Foucault*, p. 195.

120. C.S. Lewis, "The Poison of Subjectivism," in *The Seeing Eye* (Walter Hooper, ed.) New York: Ballantine Books, 1967, p. 103.

121. Lewis, "The Poison of Subjectivism," p. 103.

122. Lewis, "Historicism," in *The Seeing Eye*, p. 131.

123. Lewis, "Historicism," p. 145.

124. Sire, *The Universe*, pp. 102, 175.

Notes for Chapter 7

1. Scientific racism persists in criminology. For example, J. Philippe Rushton, at the University of Western Ontario, continues the views of the criminal anthropologists. For a discussion of Rushton's perspective, see chapter 3, especially the part about Nazi criminology.

2. Paul Knepper, "Race, Racism, and Crime Statistics," *Southern University Law Review*, 24 (1996). Pp. 86–87.

3. The call for a Black criminology came from Katheryn K. Russell in response to the observation by Vernetta Young and Anne Sulton about the exclusion of Black voices in criminology. Katheryn K. Russell "Development of a Black Criminology and the Role of the Black Criminologist," *Justice Quarterly* 9 (1992) 667–683; Vernetta Young and Anne Sulton, "Excluded: The Current Status of African-American Scholars in the Field of Criminology and Criminal Justice," *Journal of Research in Crime and Delinquency* 28 (1991) 101–116. See also Helen Taylor Greene and Shaun L. Gabbidon, *African American Criminological Thought*. Albany: State University of New York Press, 2000; Lee Ross, *African American Criminologists 1970–1996*. Westport, CT: Greenwood, 1998.

4. "The white-black confrontation..." as Harvard law professor Randall Kennedy points out, "is the conflict that has served as *the* great object lesson for American law." Black-white relations gave birth to much of the federal constitutional law of criminal procedure, and the conflict remains the most volatile in legislative efforts to formulate public policy concerning crime. Randall Kennedy, *Race, Crime and the Law*. New York: Vintage Books, 1997, p. xii.

5. David Levering Lewis, *W.E.B. Du Bois: Biography of a Race*. New York: Henry Holt, 1993.

6. W.E.B. Du Bois, *The Souls of Black Folk* (Arnold Rampersad, intr.) New York: Alfred A. Knopf, 1993, p. 16.

7. W.E.B. Du Bois, "The Conservation of Races," (1897), in *W.E.B. Du Bois: The Oxford Reader* (Eric J. Sundquist, ed.). New York: Oxford University Press, 1996, p. 40.

8. Du Bois, "The Conservation," p. 43.

9. Joseph P. DeMarco, *The Social Thought of W.E.B. Du Bois*, Lanham, NY: University Press of America, 1983, pp. 34–40.

10. Du Bois, *The Souls*, p. 9.

11. Du Bois, *The Souls*, p. 51.

12. Robert C. Smith, "Ideology as the Enduring Dilemma of Black Politics," in *Dilemmas of Black Politics* (Georgia A. Persons, ed.) New York: HarperCollins, 1993, p. 218.

13. Smith, "Ideology as the Enduring," p. 157.

14. Du Bois, *The Souls*, pp. 38–51.

15. Lewis, *W.E.B. Du Bois*, p. 42.

16. DeMarco, *The Social Thought*, p. 73.

17. Du Bois, "Joseph Stalin," in Sundquist, *W.E.B. Dubois*, pp. 287–289.

18. Du Bois, "The Conservation," in Sundquist, *W.E.B. Du Bois*, p. 47.

19. Quoted in Shaun L. Gabbidon, "An Argument for Including W.E.B. Du Bois in the Criminology/Criminal Justice Literature," *Journal of Criminal Justice Education* 7 (1996), p. 101.

20. Gabbidon, "An Argument," p. 103.

21. Quoted in Darnell F. Hawkins, "Ethnicity, Race and Crime: A Review

of Selected Studies," in *Ethnicity, Race and Crime* (Darnell F. Hawkins, ed). Albany: State University of New York Press, 1995, pp. 15–16.
22. Hawkins, " Ethnicity, Race and Crime," p. 16.
23. W.E.B. Du Bois, "Some Notes on Negro Crime Particularly in Georgia," in *The Atlanta University Publications* (William L. Katz, ed.) New York: Arno Press, 1968, p. 65.
24. Du Bois, "Some Notes," pp. 65–66.
25. Kenneth Clark and Mamie Clark, "Racial Identification and Preference in Negro Children," in *Readings in Social Psychology* (T. Newcomb and E. Hartley, eds.). New York: Holt, 1947.
26. Darlene Powell-Hopson and Derek S. Hopson, "Implications of Doll Color Preferences Among Black Preschool Children and White Preschool Children," *Journal of Black Psychology* 14 (1988) 57–63.
27. Kathy Russell, Midge Wilson and Ronald Hall, *The Color Complex*. New York: Anchor Books, 1992, pp. 63–64.
28. H. Kaplan, *Deviant Behavior in Defense of Self*. New York: Academic Press, 1978 and "Self-Attitudes and Deviant Response," *Social Forces* 54 (1980), pp. 788–801.
29. Lee Ross, "Blacks, Self-Esteem, and Delinquency: It's Time for a New Approach," in *African-American Perspectives on Crime Causation, Criminal Justice Administration and Crime Prevention* (Anne T. Sulton, ed.) Boston: Butterworth-Heineman, 1996, pp. 53–68.
30. Marvin E. Wolfgang, *Patterns of Criminal Homicide*. Philadelphia: University of Pennsylvania Press, 1958; Marvin Wolfgang and Franco Ferracuti, *The Subculture of Violence*. London: Social Science Paperbacks, 1967.
31. Wolfgang and Ferracuti, *The Subculture of Violence*, p. 167.
32. Liquin Cao, Anthony Adams, and Vickie Jensen, "A Test of the Black Subculture of Violence Thesis: A Research Note," *Criminology* 35 (1997), p. 367. See also, Jo Dixon and Alan Lizotte, "Gun Ownership and the Southern Subculture of Violence," *American Journal of Sociology* 93 (1987) pp. 383–405 and Christopher G. Ellison, "An Eye for an Eye? A Note on the Southern Subculture of Violence Thesis," *Social Forces* 69 (1991), pp. 1223–1229.
33. Wolfgang and Ferracuti, *The Subculture of Violence*, p. 264.
34. Lynn Curtis, *Violence, Race, and Culture*. Lexington, Mass.: Lexington Books, 1975; Thomas Pettigrew and Rosalind Spier, "The Ecological Structure of Negro Homicide," *American Journal of Sociology* 67 (1962), pp. 621–629; See also Marino A. Bruce, Vincent J. Roscigno, and Patricia L. McCall, "Structure, context, and agency in the Reproduction of Black-on-Black Violence," *Theoretical Criminology* 2 (1998) 29–55.
35. Nicholas Lemann, "The Origins of the Underclass," *Atlantic Monthly*, (June 1986), 31–55.
36. Lemann, "The Origins," pp. 35–40.
37. See, for example, E. Franklin Frazier, *The Negro Family in the United States*. Chicago: University of Chicago Press, 1939.
38. Tony Platt, *E. Franklin Frazier Reconsidered*. New Brunswick: Rutgers University Press, 1991, pp. 138.
39. Platt, *E. Franklin Frazier*, pp. 133–144.
40. Platt, *E. Franklin Frazier*, pp. 112–113. Platt points out that Moynihan quoted selectively from Frazier's work to legitimate Kennedy's welfare liberalism.
41. Platt, *E. Franklin Frazier*, pp. 112–113.
42. Critics charged that Moynihan had blamed the victim by shifting the

focus from social inequality to the victims of social inequality. Christopher Jencks wrote in 1965: "The guiding assumption [in Moynihan's analysis] is that social pathology is caused less by basic defects in the social system than by defects in particular individuals and groups which prevent their adjusting to the system," in "The Moynihan Report," in *The Moynihan Report and the Politics of Controversy* (Lee Rainwater and William L. Yancey, eds.). Cambridge: MIT Press, 1967, p. 443.

43. Quoted in Rick Ball, *Meet the Press: 50 Years of History in the Making.* New York: McGraw Hill, 1998, p. 84. Thirty years later, NBA star Charles Barkley made a similar observation on the same news show. "I think athletes are secondary role models. Your parents are your primary role models...I'm from a single-parent family. And my mother and my grandmother raised me and they were strong...They taught me great discipline and how to work hard...White people do not owe us anything but an opportunity. We have to sooner or later step up, get educated ourselves, stop having kids out-of-wedlock, stop gang-banging and things like that...There are a lot of strong black women out there, and there are a lot of strong black men out there raising their kids, seeing if they can handle it. But just not having one parent, that's a crutch" (p. 228).

44. William J. Wilson, *The Declining Significance of Race.* Chicago: University of Chicago Press, 1978, p. 1.

45. Alphonso Pinckney, *The Myth of Black Progress.* Cambridge: Cambridge University Press, 1984, pp. 14–15.

46. William J. Wilson, *The Truly Disadvantaged: The Inner City, the Underclass and Public Policy.* Chicago: University of Chicago Press, 1987.

47. Robert J. Sampson and William J. Wilson, "Toward a Theory of Race, Crime and Urban Equality," in *Crime and Inequality* (John Hagan and Ruth D. Peterson, eds.) Stanford, Calif.: Stanford University Press, 1995, pp. 37–54.

48. Sampson and Wilson, "Toward a Theory of Race," p. 53. For an interesting discussion of crime within Black and White suburban neighborhoods in Cleveland, and its implications for Wilson's concept of "the truly disadvantaged," see John R. Logan and Brian J. Stults, "Racial Differences in Exposure to Crime: The City and Suburbs of Cleveland in 1990," *Criminology* 37 (1999) 251–276.

49. Christopher Stone, "Race, Crime and the Administration of Justice," *National Institute of Justice Journal*, April (1999), p. 28.

50. Samuel Walker, Cassia Spohn, and Miriam DeLone, *The Color of Justice: Race, Ethnicity and Crime and America.* Belmont, Calif: Wadsworth, 1996, pp. 60–82; Darnell F. Hawkins, "Ethnicity, Race and Crime: A Review of Selected Studies," in *Ethnicity, Race and Crime* (Darnell F. Hawkins, ed.). Albany: State University of New York Press, 1995, pp. 11–41; Gary LaFree, *Losing Legitimacy: Street Crime and the Decline of Social Institutions in America.* Boulder, Colo.: Westview Press, 1998.

51. Quoted in Linn Washington, *Black Judges on Justice.* New York: New Press, 1994, p. 88.

52. Christopher E. Stone. " Crime and Justice in Black America." New York: National Urban League, 1999, pp. 8–9.

53. Katheryn K. Russell, *The Color of Crime.* New York: New York University Press, 1998, pp. 40–41.

54. Michael Tonry, *Malign Neglect-Race, Crime and Punishment in America.* New York: Oxford University Press, 1995.

55. Michael Tonry, "Racial Politics, Racial Disparities, and the War on

Crime," in *Examining the Justice Process* (James A. Inciardi, ed.). Fort Worth: Harcourt Brace, 1996, pp. 139–156.

56. Washington, *Black Judges*, pp. 55–56.

57. Washington, *Black Judges*, pp. 55–56.

58. Stephen Steinberg, "The Liberal Retreat From Race During the Post-Civil Rights Era," in *The House That Race Built* (Wahneema Lubiano, ed.). New York: Pantheon, 1997, p. 32.

59. "When Work Disappears," Interview of William Julius Wilson by David Gergen for the PBS Newshour, originally aired September 19, 1996.

60. Robert C. Smith, "Ideology as the Enduring Dilemma of Black Politics," in *Dilemmas of Black*, p. 214. See also Eugene F. Rivers, "Beyond the Nationalism of Fools: Toward an Agenda for Black Intellectuals," *Boston Review* 20 (1994/95) 1–6.

61. Quorted in Michael Eric Dyson, *Making Malcolm: The Myth and Meaning of Malcolm X*. New York: Oxford University Press, 1995, p. 3.

62. Dyson, *Making Malcolm*, p. 171.

63. Quoted in Dyson, *Making Malcolm*, p. 170.

64. Angela Y. Davis, "Race and Criminalization: Black Americans and the Punishment Industry," in Lubiano, *The House*, p. 268.

65. Davis, "Race and Criminalization," pp. 264–279 and "Prison Abolition" in *Black Genius* (Walter Mosley, Manthia Diawara, Clyde Taylor and Regina Austin, ed.) New York: W.W. Norton, 1999, pp. 196–214.

66. Research, History and Archives Committee, "A Report on the Perceptions of NABCJ Members of the Criminal Justice System," *Commitment* [National Association of Blacks in Criminal Justice] June 1999, p. 9.

67. Stephen B. Oates, *Let the Trumpet Sound: A Life of Martin Luther King, Jr.* New York: HarperPerennial, 1994, p. 400.

68. Frantz Fanon, *The Wretched of the Earth* (Haakon Chevalier, tr.). New York: Grove Press, 1967 and *Black Skins, White Masks* (Charles L. Markmann, tr.) New York: Grove Press, 1967.

69. Emmanuel Hansen, *Frantz Fanon: Social and Political Thought*. Columbus: Ohio State University Press, 1977, pp. 15–52.

70. Becky Tatum, "The Colonial Model as a Theoretical Explanation of Crime and Delinquency," in *African-American Perspectives on Crime Causation, Criminal Justice Administration and Crime Prevention* (Anne T. Sulton, ed.) Boston: Butterworth-Heineman, 1996, pp. 38–39.

71. Quoted in Hansen, *Frantz Fanon*, p. 91.

72. This summary belongs to Becky Tatum, who also provides a six-fold critique of internal colonial model. Tatum, "The Colonial Model," pp. 39–40.

73. Quoted in Tatum, "The Colonial Model," p. 40.

74. Gary Peller, "Criminal Law, Race, and the Ideology of Bias: Transcending the Critical Tools of the Sixties," *Tulane Law Review* 67 (1993) 2248–2252.

75. Robert Staples, "White Racism, Black Crime and American Justice: Application of the Colonial Model to Explain Race and Crime," *Phylon* 36 (1975) 14–22 and *The Urban Plantation*. Oakland, Ca'.`· Б' .ck Scholar Press, 1989.

76. Ayele Bekerie, "The Four Corners of a Circle: Afrocentricity as a Model of Synthesis," *Journal of Black Studies* 25 (1994), pp. 131–149; Normal Harris, "A Philosophical Basis for an Afrocentric Orientation," *Western Journal of Black Studies* 16 (1992), pp. 154–159. See also, Gordon D. Morgan, "Africentricity in Social Science," *Western Journal of Black Studies* 15 (1991) 197–206

and Perry D. Hall, "Beyond Afrocentrism: Alternatives for African American Studies," *Western Journal of Black Studies* 15 (1991), pp. 207–212.

77. Mary Jackson, "Afrocentric Treatment of African American Women and Their Children in a Residential Chemical Dependency Program," *Journal of Black Studies* 26 (1995) 17–30 and Amelia Roberts, Mary S. Jackson, and Iris Carlton-Laney, "Revisiting the Need for Feminism and Afrocentric Theory When Treating African-American Female Substance Abusers," *Journal of Drug Issues*, 30 (2000), 901–918.

78. Anthony O. King, "Understanding Violence Among Young African American Males," *Journal of Black Studies* 28 (1997), p. 80.

79. King, "Understanding Violence," pp. 79–96.

80. Kimberle Crenshaw, Neil Gotanda, Gary Peller, and Kendall Thomas, "Introduction," in *Critical Race Theory* (Kimberle Crenshaw *et al.*, eds.). New York: New Press, 1995, pp. xx–xxi.

81. Crenshaw *et al.*, "Introduction," *Critical Race Theory*, p. xiv.

82. Derrick Bell, *And We Are Not Saved: The Elusive Quest for Racial Justice*. New York: Basic Books, 1987.

83. Bell, *And We Are Not*, pp. 26–50.

84. Crenshaw *et al.*, "Introduction," p. xxv. Neil Gotanda, "A Critique of "Our Constitution is Color-Blind," and Cheryl I. Harris, "Whiteness as Property," both reprinted in the same volume.

85. Eleanor Marie Brown, "The Tower of Babel: Bridging the Divide Between Critical Race Theory and 'Mainstream' Civil Rights Scholarship," *Yale Law Journal* 105 (1995), p. 517.

86. Richard Delgado, "The Imperial Scholar: Reflections on a Review of Civil Rights Literature," *University of Pennsylvania Law Review* 132 (1984) 561–578.

87. Gary Peller, "Criminal Law, Race, and the Ideology of Bias: Transcending the Critical Tools of the Sixties," *Tulane Law Review* 67 (1993) p. 2224.

88. Peller, "Criminal Law," p. 2250.

89. Regina Austin, "'The Black Community,' Its Lawbreakers, and a Politics of Identification," *Southern California Law Review* 65 (1992) 1769–1817.

90. Richard Delgado, "Rodrigo's Eighth Chronicle: Black Crime, White Fears—On the Social Construction of Threat," *Virginia Law Review* 80 (1994) 503–448.

91. Delgado, "Rodrigo's Eighth," pp. 514–515.

92. Delgado, "Rodrigo's Eighth," p. 540.

93. Bell, *And We Are Not Saved*, pp. 245–247.

94. Russell, *The Color of Crime*, 1998.

95. A. Leon Higginbotham, *Shades of Freedom: Racial Politics and Presumptions of the American Legal Process*. New York: Oxford University Press, 1994.

96. Bernard Headley, "'Black on Black' Crime: The Myth and Reality," *Crime and Social Justice* 20 (1983) 50–62; Robert L. Bing, "Politicizing Black-on-Black Crime: A Critique of Technological Preference," in *Black-on-Black Crime: Facing Facts—Challenging Fictions* (P. Ray Kedia, ed.) Bristol, IN: Wyndham Hall Press, 1994, 245–257.

97. Jeffrey Rosen, "The Bloods and the Crits," *The New Republic*, Dec. 9, 1996, p. 33.

98. Rosen, "The Bloods," p. 33.

99. Paul Butler, "Racially Based Jury Nullification: Black Power in the Criminal Justice System," *Yale Law Journal*, 105 (1995), p. 679.

100. Katheryn K. Russell, "The Racial Hoax as Crime: The Law as Affirmation," *Indiana Law Journal* 71 (1996) 593–621.

101. Patricia Williams, "Spirit-Murdering the Messenger: The Discourse of Fingerpointing as the Law's Response to Racism," *University of Miami Law Review* 42 (1987), 127–157.

102. Georgia A. Persons, "The Election of Gary Franks and the Ascendancy of the New Black Conservatives," in *Dilemmas of Black Politics*, pp. 198–199.

103. Shelby Steele, "The Loneliness of the 'Black Conservative.'" *Hoover Digest* [Hoover Institution] 1 (1999). Excerpted from Shelby Steele, *A Dream Deferred: The Second Betrayal of Black Freedom in America*. New York: HarperCollins, 1999.

104. George E. Curry and Trevor W. Coleman, "Supreme Insult," *Emerge* 8 (1996) 38–48.

105. Tamar Jacoby, "A Whole Different Crop of Black Leaders," *City Journal* 5 (1995), p. 22.

106. Stanley Crouch, *The All-American Skin Game or, The Decoy of Race*. New York: Vintage Books, 1995, pp. ix–x.

107. Dr. King did not use the word "deracialization" to refer to this strategy. The word comes from an essay by Charles V. Hamilton, a political scientist who addressed a meeting organized by the National Urban League to discuss strategies after the closing of the "protest phase" of the civil rights movement. See Joseph P. McCormick II and Charles E. Jones, "The Conceptualization of Deracialization: Thinking Through the Dilemma," in Persons, *Dilemmas of Black Politics*, p. 70.

108. Quoted in Stanley Crouch, *Notes of a Hanging Judge*. New York: Oxford University Press, 1990, p. 105.

109. Jacoby, "A Whole Different Crop;" David C. Ruffin, "Rising Black Leaders," *Focus* [Joint Center for Political and Economic Studies], 28 (Jan. 2000), 5–6.

110. Bramwell in Washington, *Black Judges*, p. 174.

111. Bramwell in Washington, *Black Judges*, p. 177.

112. Deroy Murdock, "Faith-Based Social Services and Urban Development," Arlington, VA: Lexington Institute, 2000.

113. Quoted in Murdock, "Faith-Based Social."

114. Kennedy, *Race, Crime*, p. 24.

115. Kennedy, *Race, Crime*, p. 24.

116. Kennedy, *Race, Crime*, p 20.

117. Glenn C. Loury, "Two Paths to Black Power," *First Things* 26 (1992), p. 19.

118. Loury, "Two Paths," p. 20.

119. Glenn C. Loury and Linda Datcher Loury, "Not by Bread Alone: The Role of the African-American Church in Inner-City Development," *The Brookings Review*, Winter (1997), pp. 10–13.

120. Loury, "Two Paths," p. 21.

121. Bramwell in Washington, *Black Judges on Justice.*, p. 175. "I didn't think Leon Higginbotham's open letter to Justice Thomas was appropriate. I wrote him a letter a told him so. His letter smacked of Black racism, Black-on-Black racism. He only attacked Thomas because Thomas is Black. Who appointed Higginbotham a judge of the character and qualifications of other Black judges?" (p. 175).

122. Crouch, *The All-American Skin Game*, p. 31.

123. Reuben M. Greenberg, "Less Bang-Bang for the Buck: The Market Approach to Crime Control," in *Making America Safer* (Edwin Meese III and Robert E. Moffit, eds). Washington, DC: The Heritage Foundation, 1997.

124. Greenberg, "Less Bang-Bang," p. 51.

125. John J. DiIulio, "The Impact of Inner-City Crime," *The Public Interest* 96 (1989), p. 36.

126. DiIulio, "The Impact," pp. 28–47; "The Question of Black Crime," *The Public Interest* 117 (1994), pp. 3–32; "White Lies About Black Crime," *The Public Interest* 118 (1995), pp. 30–44.

127. Glenn C. Loury, "Listen to the black community," *The Public Interest* 117 (1994), pp. 33–37.

128. Kennedy, *Race, Crime*, p. 77.

129. Crouch, *The All-American Skin Game*, p. 23.

130. Crouch, *The All-American Skin Game*, p. 25.

131. Crouch, *The All-American Skin Game*, p. xiii.

132. Crouch, *The All-American Skin Game*, p. 55.

133. Crouch, *The All-American Skin Game*, p. 43.

134. Randall Kennedy, "Racial Critiques of Legal Academia," *Harvard Law Review* 102 (1989) 1745–1819.

135. Kennedy, "Racial Critiques," pp. 1784, 1787.

136. Crouch, *The All-American Skin Game*, p. 76.

Notes for Chapter 8

1. Jeremiah 31.33. All quotations from the Tanakh in this chapter come from *Tanakh: A New Translation of the Holy Scriptures*. Philadelphia: Jewish Publication Society, 1985.

2. Milton R. Konvitz, "Conscience and Civil Disobedience in Jewish, Christian, and Greek and Roman Thought," *Hastings Law Journal*, 29 (1978), pp. 1624, 1629.

3. The term "Judaic-Christian" appears throughout this chapter rather than the more familiar "Judeo-Christian" to emphasize that while Judaism and Christianity have much in common (both worship the same God), they differ in fundamental ways as well.

4. Sir Richard Attenborough directed *Shadowlands*, a film about Lewis's marriage, late in his life, to Joy Davidman.

5. Philip Vander Elst, *C.S. Lewis*. London: The Claridge Press, 1996, p. 5.

6. Lewis's confidence had been shaken by a committed atheist who grudgingly admitted that there was good evidence for the historicity of the Gospels and remarked "Rum thing. It almost looks as if it had really happened once." Vander Elst, *C.S. Lewis*, p. 7.

7. Humphrey Carpenter, *Tolkien: A Biography*. New York: Ballantine Books, 1997, pp. 163–164.

8. Quoted in Richard John Neuhaus, "C.S. Lewis in the Public Square," *First Things* 88 (1998), p. 33.

9. Lewis, "Bulverism," pp. 273–274.

10. C.S. Lewis, "'Bulverism' or, The Foundation of 20th Century Thought," in *God in the Dock* (Walter Hooper, ed.) Grand Rapids, MI: William B. Eerdmans, 1970, p. 273. Lewis made up the word "Bulverism," he said, after its imaginary founder, Ezekiel Bulver. Bulver realized the appeal of this kind of thought at the age of five years when he heard his parents

NOTES FOR PAGES 256–264 · 337

quarreling. His father claimed that two sides of a triangle, when taken together, amounted to more than the third side by itself and his mother dismissed this argument. "Oh you say that *because you are a man.*" It was at
this moment the young Bulver realized that "refutation is not a necessary part
of argument."
11. C. S. Lewis, "On Ethics,"in *The Seeing Eye* (Walter Hooper, ed.). New
York: Ballantine, 1967, p. 63.
12. C.S. Lewis, "Will Christianity Help Me?" in *C.S. Lewis: Readings for
Meditation* (Walter Hooper, ed.) Toronto: Thomas Allen, 1998, p. 10.
13. Kathryn Lindskoog and Gracia Fay Ellwood, "C.S. Lewis: The Natural Law in Literature and Life," in *The Taste of Pineapple* (Bruce L. Edwards,
ed.). Bowling Green, Ohio: Bowling Green State University Popular Press,
1988, pp. 197–198.
14. Lewis, *Mere Christianity*, p. 77.
15. C.S. Lewis, "The Cost of Discipleship," in *C.S. Lewis: Readings*, pp.
6–7.
16. Lewis, *Mere Christianity*, p. 47.
17. C.S. Lewis, "The Christian and the Materialist," in *C.S. Lewis:Read-
ings*, pp. 10–11.
18. A.N. Wilson, *C.S. Lewis: A Biography.* New York: WW Norton,
1990, p. xiii.
19. C.S. Lewis, "Equality," in *Present Concerns* (Walter Hooper, ed.). San
Diego: Harcourt Brace Jovanovich, 1986, pp. 17–18.
20. Vander Elst, *C.S. Lewis*, p. 83.
21. Quoted in Vander Elst, *C.S. Lewis*, p. 92.
22. C.S. Lewis, "Meditation on the Third Commandment," in Hooper,
God in the Dock, pp. 196–199.
23. Richard J. Neuhaus, "C.S. Lewis in the Public Square," *First Things*
88 (1988), p. 30.
24. Lewis, "On Ethics," p. 75.
25. C.S. Lewis, "The Humanitarian Theory of Punishment," in Hooper,
God in the Dock, pp. 290–294.
26. Vander Elst, *C.S. Lewis*, p. 88.
27. C.S. Lewis, *The Abolition of Man.* New York: Macmillan, 1955, p. 96.
28. Rabbi Morris Kertzer. *What is a Jew?* New York: Macmillan 1973, p. 8.
29. Eric M. Chevlen, "Discovering the Talmud," *First Things* 85 (1998)
pp. 40–44.
30. The civil law within the Torah concerns real property, social welfare, religious practices, torts, land ownership and money-lending. The criminal law
within the Torah identifies crimes against the public (bribery, contempt, perjury,
obstructing justice), crimes of immoral acts (adultery, rape, seduction, incest,
sodomy), crimes against persons (murder, manslaughter, assault, kidnapping, and
slander), and crimes against property (theft, arson, removing a landmark).
31. Shem MiShmuel, "When a Man Will Steal," *Torah Weekly* [Ohr So-
mayach, Jerusalem, Israel] Feb. 7–8, 1997, p. 2.
32. Chevlen, "Discovering the Talmud," p. 42.
33. This understanding of human nature comes from Tracey R. Rich who
while not a rabbi is an "observant Jew who has put in a lot of research."
34. Sholom D. Lipskar, "A Torah Perspective on Incarceration as a Modality of Punishment and Rehabilitation," 1996. Surfside, FL: Aleph Institute Center for Halacha and American Law, 1999.
35. Psalm 23.1 and 23.3.

36. Edward T. Oakes, "Nature as Law and Gift," *First Things* 93 (May 1999), p. 49.

37. Kertzer, *What is a Jew?* pp. 7–8.

38. Deuteronomy 21.19.

39. Barry Gelman, "Ideas in Jewish Philosophy and Practice: Signposts." Riverdale, Calf: Hebrew Institute, 1997.

40. Leviticus 24.22.

41. The Torah tells Jews to be loyal citizens of the lands to which they are dispersed. Jews are to abide by the law of land so that they may live in peace. The prophet Jeremiah instructed the people: "And seek the welfare (shalom) of the city to which I have exiled you and pray to the LORD in its behalf; for in its prosperity you shall prosper" (Jeremiah 29.7). Victimizing a non-Jew would be worse than victimizing a Jewish person. This is so because there would be no atonement for the Jewish criminal who robs, cheats, or assaults a non-Jewish person, and who dies without doing t'shuva (repenting), because of the *Chillul HaShem* involved. Chillul HaShem refers to the desecration of God's name, invoked because the crimes provoke non-Jews to say "There is no Torah is Israel."

42. Amos 5.24.

43. Shlomo Riskin, "Shabbat Parshat Mishpatim February 21, 1998." New York: Union of Orthodox Jewish Congregations of American, 2000.

44. Chaim Steinmetz, "Should Karla Have Been Executed?" Montreal, Quebec: Tifereth Beth David Jerusalem, 1997–98.

45. Yosef Edelstein, "Parshat Mishpatim February 4–5, 2000," New York: Union of Orthodox Jewish Congregations of American, 2000.

46. Riskin, "Shabbat Parshat Mishpatim," p. 2.

47. Lipskar, "A Torah Perspective," pp. 2–3.

48. Yosef Edelstein, "Mishpatim for February 21."

49. Joe Leconte, "Making Criminals Pay: A New York County's Bold Experiment in Biblical Justice," *Policy Review* [Heritage Foundation] 87 (1998) pp. 1–8.

50. Daniel Van Ness and Karen Heetderks Strong, *Restoring Justice.* Cincinnati, OH: Anderson, 1997, p. 24. In a 1977 article, Albert Eglash suggested that there were three types of justice: retributive justice based on punishment, distributive justice based on theraputic treatment, and restorative justice, based on restitution. As Eglash defined it, restorative justice focuses on the harmful effects of an offender's actions and actively involves victims and offenders in the process of reparation. Albert Eglash, "Beyond Restitution: Creative Restitution," in *Restitution in Criminal Justice* (Lexington, MA: DC Heath, 1977), pp. 91–92.

51. "Restorative Justice: An Interview With Visiting Fellow Thomas Quinn," *National Institute of Justice Journal,* 235 (1998), p. 14.

52. Mark S. Umbreit, "The Restorative Justice and Mediation Collection: Executive Summary," *OVC Bulletin.* Washington, DC: Office for Victims of Crime, 2000, p. 3.

53. Dean E. Peachey, "The Kitchener Experiment," in *Mediation in Criminal Justice: Victims, Offenders and Community* (Martin Wright and Burt Galaway, eds.). Newbury Park, CA: Sage, 1989, pp. 14–15.

54. Peachey, "The Kitchener Experiment," pp. 14–15.

55. Howard Zehr, *Changing Lenses: A New Focus for Crime and Justice.* Scottsdale, PA: Herald Press, 1990, pp. 126–157; John Bender, "Part II: Reconciliation Spreads to the U.S.," *Peace Section Newsletter* [Mennonite Central

Committee], 16 (Jan/Feb 1986), pp. 3–5.

56. John Harding, "Reconciling Mediation with Criminal Justice," in Wright and Galaway, *Mediation and Criminal Justice*, p. 31.

57. Zehr, *Changing Lenses*, p. 159.

58. Zehr, *Changing Lenses*, p. 163.

59. Leconte, "Making Criminals Pay," pp. 1–8.

60. Alma Norman, "*Tzedek Tzedek Tirdof*: Jewish Values and Criminal Justice." Ottawa: Correctional Service of Canada, 2000.

61. Zehr, *Changing Lenses*, pp. 126–157.

62. Charles Colson and Daniel Van Ness, *Convicted: New Hope for Ending America's Crime Crisis*. Westchester, IL: Crossway Books, 1989. See also Tucker Carlson, "Deliver Us From Evil: Prison Fellowship's Saving Grace," in *Making America Safer* (Edwin Meese III and Robert E. Moffit, eds.). Washington, DC: Heritage Foundation, 1997, p. 200.

63. Daniel W. Van Ness, "Pursuing a Restorative Vision of Justice," in *Justice: The Restorative Vision* (Howard Zehr, ed.) Elkhart, IN: Mennonite Central Committee U.S. Office of Criminal Justice, 1989.

64. D.W. Miller, "Measuring the Role of 'the Faith Factor' in Social Change," *Chronicle of Higher Education*, Nov. 26, 1999, pp. A21–22; Rodney Stark *et al.*, "Rediscovering Moral Communities: Church Membership and Crime," in *Understanding Crime* (Travis Hirschi and Michael Gottfredson, eds.) Beverly Hills, CA: Sage, 1980; Richard B. Freeman, "Who Escapes? The Relation of Church-Going and Other Background Factors to the Socio-Economic Performance of Black Male Youths From Inner-City Poverty Tracts," Working Paper, Number 1656, National Bureau of Economic Research, Cambridge, MA, 1985.

65. T. David Evans *et al.*, "Religion and Crime Reexamined: The Impact of Religion, Secular Controls, and Social Ecology on Adult Criminality," *Criminology* 33 (1995) 195–224.

66. See also Edmund McGarrell and Greg Brinker, "The Role of Faith-Based Organizations in Crime Prevention and Justice," Santa Barbara, CA: Hudson Institute, 1999.

67. Byron R. Johnson, David B. Larson, Timothy C. Pitts, "Religious Programs, Institutional Adjustment, and Recidivism Among Former Inmates in Prison Fellowship Programs," *Justice Quarterly*, 14 (1997) 145–166; Byron R. Johnson *et al.*, *Religion: The Forgotten Factor in Cutting Youth Crime and Saving At-Risk Urban Youth*. Jeremiah Project Report 98–2. Manhattan Institute, 1998; Byron R. Johnson, *A Better Kind of High: How Religious Commitment Reduces Drug Use Among Poor Urban Teens*. Philadelphia: Center for Research on Religion and Urban Civil Society, University of Pennsylvania, 2000; Byron R. Johnson *et al.*, "Escaping from the Crime of the Inner-Cities: Church Attendance and Religious Salience Among Disadvantaged Youth," *Justice Quarterly* 17 (2000), 377–391.

68. Robert B. Coates and John Gehm, "An Empirical Assessment," in Wright and Galaway, *Mediation and Criminal Justice*, pp. 251–263; Mark Umbreit, *Victim Meets Offender: The Impact of Restorative Justice and Mediation*. Monsey, NY: Willow Tree Press, 1994.

69. Miller, "Measuring the Role," p. A22. John J. DiIulio, "Supporting Black Churches: Faith, Outreach, and the Inner-City Poor." *Brookings Review* 17 (1999), p. 43; James Q. Wilson, "Religion and Public Life: Moving Private Funds To Faith-Based Social Service Providers," *Brookings Review* 17 (1999), p. 39.

70. John O. Haley, *Authority Without Power: Law and the Japanese Paradox*. New York: Oxford University Press, 1991, pp. 121–138.
71. Father Neuhaus comments that "Affirming religion because of its social utility is, to say the least, theologically problematic. It is, in fact, a kind of blasphemy." Richard John Neuhaus, "A Friendly But Dangerous Embrace," *First Things*, 62 (1996), p. 65.
72. Shay Bilchik, "Balanced and Restorative Justice," *Fact Sheet* #42. Washington, DC: Office of Juvenile Justice and Delinquency Prevention, 1996.
73. National Institute of Justice, "Restorative Justice: An Interview With Visiting Fellow Thomas Quinn," *National Institute of Justice Journal*, 235 (March 1998), p. 11; Todd R. Clear and David R. Karp, "Toward the Ideal of Community Justice," *National Institute of Justice Journal*, (Oct. 2000), p. 21.
74. Clear and Karp, "Toward the Ideal," p. 21.
75. Clear and Karp, "Toward the Ideal," p. 24.
76. Mike Johnson. "Drucker Speaks His Mind," *Management Review*, 84 (1995), p. 10.
77. The essay has been reprinted: Peter Drucker, *The Ecological Vision*. New Brunswick, NJ: Transaction, 1993.
78. Drucker, following Kierkegaard, quotes from Luke: "If any man come to me, and hate not his father, and his mother, and wife, and children, and my brethren, and sisters, yea, and his own life also, he cannot be my disciple." Luke 14.26.
79. Drucker, "The Unfashionable Kierkegaard," p. 434.
80. Drucker, "The Unfashionable Kierkegaard," p. 434.
81. Drucker, "The Unfashionable Kierkegaard," p. 435.

Notes for Chapter 9

1. Fox Butterfield, "A Newcomer Breaks Into the Liberal Arts: Criminal Justice" in *Criminology* (Steven H. Cooper. Ed.) Madison, WI: Coursewise, 1997, p. 187.
2. Russell Kirk, "The Meaning of 'Justice'" Lecture #457. Washington, DC: Heritage Foundation, 1993.
3. Russell Kirk, "The Case For and Against Natural Law," Lecture #469. Washington, DC: Heritage Foundation, 1993.
4. Edward T. Oakes, "Natural Law in Judaism by David Novak," 93 *First Things* (1999), p. 45.
5. Quoted in Kirk, "The Case For."
6. Sam S. Souryal, *Ethics in Criminal Justice*. Cincinnati, OH: Anderson, 1992, pp. 138–139.
7. George McKenna, "The 'Dualities' of Thomas Jefferson," *First Things* 104 (2000), p. 55.
8. Kirk, "The Meaning of 'Justice'"; Harold J. Berman, "The Influence of Christianity Upon the Development of Law," *Oklahoma Law Review*, 12 (1959), pp. 93–94.
9. Ethan Katsh, "Legal Studies Programs," in *The Bulwark of Freedom: Public Understanding of the Law* (Charles J. White and Norman Gross, eds.) Chicago: Public Education Division, American Bar Association, 1985, p. 62.
10. Quoted in Katsh, "Legal Studies," p. 62.

11. Quoted in Michael Oakeshott, *Rationalism in Politics and Other Essays*, New York: Basic Books, 1962, p. 116.

12. William Blackstone, *Commentaries on the Laws of England, Volume IV of Public Wrongs 1765–1769.* (Thomas Green, intr.) Chicago: University of Chicago Press, 1979, p. 5.

13. Blackstone's *Commentaries*, p. 5.

14. R. Kent Newmeyer. "Story, Joseph," in *The Oxford Companion to the Supreme Court* (Kermit L. Hall, ed.) New York: Oxford, 1992, pp. 841–844.

15. Stephen B. Oates, *Let the Trumpet Sound: A Life of Martin Luther King, Jr.* New York: Harper Perennial, 1994, p. 223.

16. King outlined four basic steps for collective action in such a situation: the collection of facts to determine if injustice exists; negotiation to bring about justice; self-purification (the willingness to endure hardship, even blows, without retaliating); and direct-action intended to bring injustice to the surface. The civil rights marchers were justified in their campaign of direct action because they had pursued each of the first three steps. Martin Luther King, Jr., *Why We Can't Wait.* New York: Signet Classic, 2000.

17. King, "Letter From Birmingham," p. 157.

18. Most recently, the United Nations Tribunal relied on natural law in the case of Dusko Tadic, the first individual to be tried for war crimes by an international tribunal (committed in the former Yugoslavia) since the trials of Nazis at Nuremberg. In denying an appeal from Tadic's lawyers challenging the jurisdiction of the Tribunal, the judges found that "State sovereignty must give way in cases where the nature of the offenses alleged does not affect the interests of one state alone but shocks the very conscience of mankind." Quoted in Michael P. Scharf, *Balkan Justice.* Durham, NC: Carolina Academic Press, 1997, p. 106.

19. Michael Oakeshott, *Rationalism in Politics.* New York: Basic Books, 1962, p. 75.

20. Quoted in Lawrence F. Kohl, "The Concept of Social Control and the History of Jacksonian America," *Journal of the Early Republic*, 5 (1985), p. 23.

21. Kohl, "The Concept of Social Control," pp. 21–22; David J. Rothman, "Social Control: The Uses and Abuses of the Concept in the History of Incarceration," *Rice University Studies*, 67 (1981), pp. 10–11.

22. Kohl, "The Concept of Social," pp. 21–22.

23. Kohl, "The Concept of Social," pp. 21–22.

24. Stanley Cohen, *Visions of Social Control.* Cambridge: Polity, 1985; David Garland, *Punishment and Welfare.* Aldershot: Gower, 1985; James W. Messerschmidt, *Masculinities and Crime.* Lanham, MD: Rowan and Littlefield, 1993.

25. John Lea, "Discipline and Capitalist Development," in *Capitalism and the Rule of Law* (Bob Fine *et al.*, eds.) London: Hutchinson, 1979, pp. 76–89; Dario Melossi, "Strategies of Social Control in Capitalism: A Comment on Recent Work," *Contemporary Crises*, 4 (1980), pp. 381–402.

26. W. Byron Groves and David H. Galaty, "Freud, Foucault, and Social Control," *Humanity and Society*, 10 (1986), p. 310.

27. Kevin Stenson, "Making Sense of Crime Control," in *The Politics of Crime Control* (Kevin Stenson and David Cowell, eds.) London: Sage, 1991, p. 13.

28. "We are far from being a maximum-security society, but the trend is toward—rather than away—from this. What Orwell did not anticipate or develop was the possibility that one could have a society where significant inroads were made on privacy, liberty, and autonomy, even in a relatively nonviolent environment with democratic forms and the presumed bulwarks

against totalitarianism in place. The velvet glove is replacing (or at least hiding) the iron fist." Gary T. Marx, *Undercover: Police Surveillance in America.* Berkely, CA: University of California Press, 1988, p. 232.

29. John Braithwaite, *Crime, Shame and Reintegration.* Cambridge: Cambridge University Press, 1989; George L. Kelling and Catherine M. Coles, *Fixing Broken Windows.* New York: Simon and Schuster, 1996; Marcus Felson, *Crime and Everyday Life.* Thousand Oaks, CA: Pine Forge, 1998.

30. Paul H. Hahn, *Emerging Criminal Justice.* Thousand Oaks, CA: Sage, 1998.

31. John Braithwaite, "Beyond Positivism: Learning from Contextual Integrated Strategies," *Journal of Research in Crime and Delinquency,* 30 (1993) 383–399.

32. Frances T. Cullen, "Social Support as an Organizing Concept for Criminology: Presidential Address to the Academy of Criminal Justice Sciences," *Justice Quarterly,* 11 (1994), p. 552.

33. David Miller, *Social Justice.* Oxford: Oxford University Press, 1976, p. 22.

34. Michael Novak, "Social Justice," *First Things* 108 (2000), p. 11. My analysis follows Novak's analysis, Novak's draws on that of F.A. Hayek.

35. Quoted in Novak, "Social Justice," p. 12.

36. David Boucher, "Politics in a Different Mode: An Appreciation of Michael Oakeshott 1901–1990." *History of Political Thought,* 12 (1991), pp. 727–728.

37. Quoted in Stephen Macedo, "Hayek's Liberal Legacy," *Cato Journal,* 19 (1999), pp. 292–293.

38. Novak, "Defining Social Justice," p. 12.

39. Novak, "Defining Social Justice,"p. 12.

40. Michael Oakeshott, *Morality and Politics in Modern Europe.* New Haven, CT: Yale University Press, 1993, pp. 20–21.

41. Oakeshott, *Morality and Politics,* pp. 25–27.

42. Boucher, "Politics in a Different," p. 726.

43. Ernest J. Gaines, *A Lesson Before Dying,* New York: Vintage, 1993, pp. 7–8. "The prosecutor's story was different. The prosecutor argued that Jefferson and the other two had gone there with the full intention of robbing the old man and then killing him so that he could not identify them. When the old man and the other two robbers were all dead, this one—it proved the kind of animal he really was—stuffed the money into his pockets and celebrated the event by drinking over their still-bleeding bodies," pp. 6–7.

44. Soren Kierkegaard, *Purity of Heart is to Will One Thing.* (Douglas V. Steere, tr.) New York: Harper Torchbooks, 1956, p. 185.

45. Wendell John Coats, "Michael Oakeshott as Liberal Theorist," *Canadian Journal of Political Science,* 18 (1985), p. 773–775.

46. Robert Grant, *Oakeshott.* London: Claridge Press, 1990.

47. Timothy Tian-Min Lin, *The Life and Thought of Soren Kierkegaard.* New Haven, CT: College and University Press, 1974.

48. "In the end all corruption will come from the natural sciences...a foolish, superstitious belief in the microscope." Søren Kierkegaard, "All Corruption Will Come From Science," *The Laughter is On My Side* (Roger Poole and Henrik Stangerup, eds.) Princeton, NJ: Princeton University Press, 1989, p. 185.

49. Quoted in Boucher, "Politics in a Different," p. 718.

50. Oakeshott, *Rationalism in Politics,* pp. 72–73.

51. Oakeshott, *Rationalism in Politics,* p. 72.

52. As Coates explains, Oakeshott's moral philosophy pursues a method a logical coherence. He begins from the premise that philosophy, as an investiga-

tion of conditions of intelligibility, has no direct bearing on practical experience, since philosophy and experience have no common subject-matter. In other words, theoretical conclusions have no immediate consequences for practical life because their authority rests not on understanding alone, but on assent. This means that Oakeshott can be fairly precise in his accounts of political matters without concern his suggestions will lead to undesired political consequences. At the same time, Oakeshott can maintain that the best guide to political action derives not from his particular political theory, but remains careful consideration of proposed policies and legislation in the light of the traditions or practices, with an eye toward what is "intimated" or tacitly acknowledged. Coats, "Michael Oakeshott," pp. 774–775.

53. Boucher, "Politics in a Different," p. 726.
54. Oakeshott, *Rationalism in Politics*, p. 118.
55. Oakeshott, *Rationalism in Politics*, p. 70.
56. Oakeshott, *Rationalism in Politics*, p. 71.
57. Oakeshott, *Rationalism in Politics*, p. 74. Kierkegaard makes a similar point: "Reflection is not evil; but a reflective condition and the deadlock which it involves, by transforming the capacity for action into a means of escape from action, is both corrupt and dangerous, and leads in the end to retrograde movement." Kierkegaard, *The Present Age*, p. 68.
58. Coates, *Oakeshott and His Contemporaries*, p. 101.
59. Kirk, "The Meaning of 'Justice.'"
60. Oakeshott, *Rationalism in Politics*, pp. 76–77.
61. Oakeshott, *Rationalism in Poltics*, p. 77.
62. Quoted in Tian-Min Lin, *The Life and Thought*, p. 29.
63. J.H. Ahn, "Michael Oakeshott R.I.P." *National Review* 43 (Jan. 28, 1991), pp. 19.
64. Glenn Worthington, "The Politics of Authority: Oakeshott and Radical Democracy," Cambridge, MA: Sabre Foundation [Michael Oakeshott Association], 2000.
65. Wendell J. Coats, "Michael Oakeshott as a Liberal Theorist," *Canadian Journal of Political Science* 4 (Dec 1985), p. 775.
66. Worthington, "The Politics of Authority,"
67. Coates, "Michael Oakeshott," p. 777.
68. Boucher, "Politics in a Different," p. 725.
69. Bocuher, "Politics in a Different," p. 725; Macedo, "Hayek's Liberal," p. 294.
70. Michael Oakeshott, *On Human Conduct*. Cambridge: Cambridge University Press, 1975, 58.
71. Alastair Hannay, *Kierkegaard*. London: Routledge and Kegan Paul, 1982, pp. 295–298.
72. Cullen, "Social Support," p. 551.
73. C.S. Lewis, "Nice People or New Men," in *C.S. Lewis: Readings, for Meditation* (Walter Hooper, ed.). Toronto: Thomas Allen, 1998, pp. 174–176.
74. Oakeshott, *On Human Conduct*, p. 174.
75. Worthington, "The Politics of Authority." Worthington observes that under such conditions, civil disobedience does not exist. Every failure to subscribe to a civil rule constitutes a case of criminal disobedience.
76. Oakeshott, *On Human Conduct*, p. 153.
77. Kirkegaard, *The Present Age*, p. 62.
78. C.S. Lewis, "First and Second Things," in *C.S. Lewis: Readings*, pp. 17–19.

Index

Bonger, Willem, 189
Borderline personality, 110
Bradley, Thomas, 243
Brain
  Addiction, 116
  ADHD, 130–131
  Alcohol intoxication, 114–115
  Biological determinism, 67,
    70–71, 132–133
  Craniometry, 72–73
  Einstein's, 72–73
  Freud and, 98, 101
  Localized function, 72–73
  Neurochemistry, 75–76
  Phrenology, 72
  Scientific racism, 91
  Waves, 74
Braithwaite, John, 148–150, 289
Bramwell, Henry, 243, 246–247
Breuer, Josef, 101–102
Broca, Paul, 73, 84
Brockway, Zebulon, 87
Brown, Joseph, 229
Brown, Tony, 241
Brücke, Ernst, 98
Brussel, James, 123
Buck, Carrie, 89–90
Bulverism, 256
Buridan, Jean, 48, 49
Burgess, Ernest, 152
Burke, Edmund, 60–61, 282
Bush, George W., 273
Butler, Paul, 240
Butterfly effect, 83
Call, Doug, 271
Calvin, John, 169
Camus, Albert, ix
Carmichael, Stokely, 231, 233
Carr, Edward, 15
Casuistry, 169–170
Catherine the Great, 28, 29
Clark, Kenneth, 220
Clark, Mamie, 220
Classical criminology.
  See criminologists.
Classic disinhibition hypothesis,
  115–116
Chambers, Wittaker, 126–127
Chambliss, William, 193

Charcot, Jean-Martin, 101–102
Choice structuring properties, 49
Choice theory, 45, 46–54
Churchill, Winston, 108
Cleaver, Eldrige, 233
Clinton, William, 229–230
Cicero, 281
Civil association, 296
Civil disobedience, 57, 283–284
Clarke, Ronald, 48–49
Cleckley, Hervey, 107, 117
Cloward, Richard, 46, 145, 160,
  161–162, 164
Coca cola, 115
Cohen, Felix, 181
Cohen, Lawrence, 51
Cohen, Stanley, 184–185, 194
Colquhoun, Patrick, 44
Colson, Charles, 272
Compartmentalization, 111
Comte, Auguste, 14–15, 16, 64,
  136–137, 140, 165
Conditional freewill, 68, 92
Conduct norm, 182–183
Conscience, 103, 105, 253, 259–260
Consciousness
  Body and, 95–96, 133
  Bourgeois, 179, 187
  Consciousness-raising, 202, 240
  False, 176, 199, 206–207
  Double-consciousness, 215
  Moral, 179, 253, 263, 210
  Race, 234, 236, 237
  Socially-created, 140, 156,
    174–175, 201, 202
  Unconsciousness and, 102,
    105–106
Conspiracy theory, 231–232
Control theory, 146–147
Conyers, John, 228
Constructionism, 185–186
Cooper, Anthony, 32
Cornish, Derek, 48–49
Craniometry, 72–74
Crenshaw, Kimberlé, 236
Cressey, Donald, 46, 157, 162
Crick, Francis, 82
Crime
  Abnormal mind and, 105, 127–128

Smith, Adam, 34
Snipes, Jeffrey, 17
Social cartography, 150–151
Social contract, 38–39, 54, 56, 59, 103
Social ecology, 151–153
Social labor, 175
Social learning, 157158
Social science, 4 273 274
  Criminal law and, 167
  Faith and, 274275 276
  Law and, 180–181
  Origins of, 136–137
  Progress, 11
  Reason in, 22–23
  Statistical analysis, 10
  Wilson's view, 46
Society
  Social change, 141, 202, 204, 204, 286
  Social control, 140, 148, 153, 154, 182, 186, 191, 285–290
  Social disorganization, 153, 226–227
  Social equality/inequality, 143–144, 198, 209–210, 246, 290, 298
  Social laws, 136–138, 141
  Social milieu/environment, 80, 81, 136, 146, 218–219
  Social order, 140, 148–149, 151–152
  Social problems, 185, 186–188, 227
  Social rules/conventions, 15, 149, 179, 184
Society for the Study of Social Problems, 186, 187
Sociobiology, 95–96
Sociology
  British, 180, 194
  Casuistic thinking in, 169–170
  Chicago school, 151
  Collective conscience, 140
  Epistemology and, 180
  Frankfurt School, 174, 176–180
  German, 174, 178
  Sociological imagination, 136
  Statistical method of, 10, 178

Structural causality, 164–165
Sutherland's influence, 8–9
Sociopath, 108–111, 125, 127–128, 147
Socrates, 143
Somatotyping, 70–71
Sowell, Thomas, 241
Spector, Malcolm, 185
Spiritual realm, 17–18, 19–20, 28, 235, 274
Spurzheim, Johann, 72
Stalin, Joseph, 177, 205, 217
Stark, Rodney, 153
State crime, 193
Sterilization, 89
Stoker, Bram, 63
Stone, Christopher, 227
Story, Joseph, 283
Stigmata, 69–70
Strain, 144–144, 146
Subculture of violence, 222
Supernatural. See Spiritual realm.
Superpredators, 109
Suicide, 137–138, 139
Sutherland, Edwin, 8–9, 46, 157, 158, 162, 182, 285–286
Syncretism, 275
Taft, William H., 6
Takagi, Paul, 190
Tarde, Jean-Gabriel, 156, 158
Tattoos, 45, 65
Tautology, 125–127
Taylor, Ian, 194, 203
Taylor, Laurie, 194
Taylor, Paul, 194–195
Theoretical integration, 12–13
Thomas, Clarence, 241, 242, 246
Tolkien, J.R.R., 255
Tonry, Michael, 168–169, 228–229
Topinard, Paul, 5
Torah, 262–263
Tower of Babel, 59–60
Tradition, 21–23, 37, 195–196, 207–208, 262, 264
Traditional morality, 209–210, 257, 260, 294
Truly disadvantaged, 226–227
Truman, Harry, 160
Tubman, Harriet, 249